Don Quixote

Don Quixote

The Re-accentuation of the World's Greatest Literary Hero

Edited by Slav N. Gratchev
and Howard Mancing

Lewisburg
BUCKNELL UNIVERSITY PRESS

Published by Bucknell University Press
Co-published with The Rowman & Littlefield Publishing Group, Inc.
4501 Forbes Boulevard, Suite 200, Lanham, Maryland 20706
www.rowmanlittlefield.com

6 Tinworth Street, London SE11 5AL, United Kingdom

British Library Cataloguing in Publication Information Available

Library of Congress Cataloging-in-Publication Data Available

Library of Congress Control Number: 2017957042

ISBN 978-1-61148-857-9 (cloth: alk. paper)
ISBN 978-1-61148-859-3 (paper : alk. paper)
ISBN 978-1-61148-858-6 (electronic)

Contents

List of Illustrations

CHAPTER 2: *DON QUIXOTE* RE-DEPICTED

CHAPTER 5: A HORSE OF A DIFFERENT COLOR:
SALVADOR DALÍ AND THE RE-IMAGINING OF CLAVILEÑO

Acknowledgments

We would like to express our thanks to West Virginia Humanities Council, which provided financial support for this important project. Also, we would like to thank the dean of the College of Liberal Arts of Marshall University, Dr. Robert Bookwalter, for his continued encouragement and sincere support of this initiative.

INTRODUCTION

Bakhtin, Cervantes, and Don Quixote

Howard Mancing and Slav N. Gratchev

In his great essay on "Discourse in the Novel," the final essay in *The Dialogic Imagination*, Mikhail Bakhtin divides prose fiction into two "Stylistic Lines." The First Stylistic Line has its origins in ancient fiction and is monologic, with a single voice shared between narrator and characters; basically, this is what we refer to today as "romance," as opposed to novel. But the Second Line is what we consider the novel, in the full modern sense of the term. In novels of the Second Line, "authentic double-voiced novelistic images fully ripen, now profoundly differentiated from poetic symbols, and become the unique thing they ultimately are."[1] In Bakhtin's terminology, "novelistic image" refers to the image the reader creates of the novelistic hero. Because of the novel's unfinalizability, these great novelistic images can be constantly re-accentuated: "Every age re-accentuates in its own way the works of its most immediate past. The historical life of classic works is in fact the uninterrupted process of their social and ideological re-accentuation."[2] The never-ending re-accentuation of the novelistic image has "great and seminal importance for the history of literature."[3] Bakhtin ends his essay by stressing this point, with reference to Don Quixote:

> In any objective stylistic study of novels from distant epochs it is necessary to take this process continually into consideration, and to rigorously coordinate the style under consideration with the background of heteroglossia, appropriate to the era, that dialogizes it. When this is done, the list of all subsequent re-accentuations of images in a given novel—say, the image of Don Quixote—takes on an enormous heuristic significance, deepening and broadening our artistic and ideological understanding of them. For, we repeat, great novelistic images continue to grow and develop even after the moment of their creation; they are capable of being creatively transformed in different eras, far distant from the day and hour of their original birth.[4]

1

Late in life, after his "rediscovery" by a younger generation of scholars and in response to an inquiry by a reporter from the prestigious monthly journal *Novy Mir* about the state of literary scholarship, Bakhtin criticized the tendency to evaluate a work of literature only in terms of its contemporary significance and understanding: "Everything that belongs only to the present dies along with the present."[5] Thus, Bakhtin effectively criticizes also our own contemporary tendency to over-value recent works and reject those of the past, a tendency we sometimes call "presentism." In contrast, Bakhtin considers the life of works of art in *great time*: "Works break through the boundaries of their own time, they live in centuries, that is, in *great time* and frequently (with great works, always) their lives there are more intense and fuller than are their lives within their own time."[6] The re-accentuation of novelistic images is an important aspect of this idea of *great time*. And no novelistic image has generated as much re-accentuation as Cervantes's Don Quixote. The image of Don Quixote is known throughout the world, even by millions who have never read the novel. It has appeared in literature, art, and music more than any other. If one wants to meditate on the concept of re-accentuation, there is no better place to begin than with Don Quixote.

This book is a unique scholarly attempt to examine *Don Quixote* from multiple angles to see how the re-accentuation of the world's greatest literary hero takes place in art, film, theater, and literature. To achieve this end, we drew upon colleagues from North America—the United States and Canada—and Europe—Spain and Great Britain—in order to bring the widest variety of points of view on the subject. But we also wanted this book to be more than just another collection of essays of literary criticism. For this reason, we also invited contributions by scholars and artists who have dealt with our hero's image in the visual arts, film, the theater, comic books, and television. We have included among our contributors a biologist, an art historian, a puppeteer, and a businessman. Some of these essays are not written in a typical academic, scholarly style. And that is as it should be.

One of our aims was to incorporate into this book another of Bakhtin's signature concepts: polyphony. The concept of polyphony comes originally from music, where it refers to musical lines sung independently and simultaneously but with each voice unique and not in harmony. For Bakhtin, a polyphonic novel is one in which the author's word has no privilege, where each character's voice, worldview, and consciousness receives equal representation in its own terms: "*A plurality of independent and unmerged voices and consciousnesses, a genuine polyphony of fully valid voices is in fact the chief characteristic of Dostoevsky's novels.*"[7] In our case, we have chosen to minimize the editors' voices; we have imposed no strict definition of re-accentuation on the contributors, but have given them complete freedom to discuss the concept in their own terms, in their own style, in their own voice.

Part I of the book consists of a single chapter that lays the theoretical groundwork for understanding the concept of re-accentuation. In chapter 1 Tatevik Gyulamiryan explores the meaning of *re-accentuation* in the trans-contextualization of a concept, a character, or a literary/visual work. As it is not uncommon to confuse the meaning and usage of the Bakhtinian concept with other notions such as adaptation and imitation, this chapter makes Miguel de Cervantes's masterpiece *Don Quixote* a central focus and discusses the term *re-accentuation* to demonstrate its importance in the scholarship of *Don Quixote*, as well as discusses its relation to other concepts such as adaptation, imitation, and parody.

Part II deals with imagery and ideology. Chapter 2, written by Eduardo Urbina and Fernando González Moreno, is the foundational work in this part. In it, the authors put forward the notion that these images must be considered not only as artistic ornaments, but also, and especially, as the reflection of how the novel was read in different periods, of how Cervantes's characters were reinvented by every society to transform them into icons of their own ideals. The authors analyze these key visual readings, beyond Doré and Dalí, and focus on other illustrators, less known in some cases, but for whom Don Quixote becomes a real obsession or a continuous inspiration. Among these reader-painters are Charles-Antoine Coypel, whose most important professional achievements were inspired by Cervantes; Robert Smirke, whose paintings and illustrations are the real first images of Don Quixote in the Romanticism; George Cruikshank, who illustrated two different editions recovering the humorist reading of the novel that previous English editions had relegated; and Savva Brodsky, whose mastery and personal interpretation of the novel is quite a symbol of hopelessness before crude reality.

In chapter 3 Emilio Martínez Mata turns our attention to the ideological interpretation of Quixote. He argues that although throughout the seventeenth century *Don Quixote* was generally interpreted as an aesthetic satire of romances of chivalry, two facts greatly contributed to turn *Don Quixote* into one of the most influential works in the eighteenth century. According to the author, the first fact was the ideological change that took place from the end of seventeenth century and brought about the Enlightenment; the second fact was the interpretation of *Don Quixote* spread by René Rapin in 1674 as a satire on Spanish aristocracy. Rapin's interpretation allowed *Don Quixote* to be understood as an ideological rather than literary satire, placing it in a key position for the great novelists of the eighteenth century, the one that laid the foundations of the modern novel by Fielding, Smollett, Sterne, and Diderot.

In chapter 4 Ricardo Castells introduces us to the world of the Classics Illustrated—the series of graphic novels in the United States that started in 1941, with a total of 169 literary adaptations and sales of over 200 million volumes. The author indicates that although Classics Illustrated were meant for children, the comic-book versions of *Don Quixote* and other chivalric tales were surprisingly sophisticated because contemporary young readers were exposed to adaptations of Arthurian romances from an early age. According to the author, Classics Illustrated presented a simplified but respectful adaptation of *Don Quixote* because it was created for a juvenile audience that would have appreciated the literary and artistic qualities found in this re-creation of the chivalric tradition.

In chapter 5 Stacey Smythe singles out a single minor "character," the wooden horse Clavileño, and looks at how it has been re-accentuated through time. She examines, interrogates, and problematizes the manifest and manifold ways in which images of Clavileño—in the context of Jean Baudrillard's third order of simulacra, simulation—has proliferated beyond the borders of Cervantes's narrative, and has been appropriated in ways that have made identification with the original all but impossible and/or irrelevant. From the lithographs of the twentieth-century surrealist painter Salvador Dalí to the aquatint etchings of the twenty-first century multi-media artist Tony Fitzpatrick, this chapter concerns itself with those images of Clavileño that not only re-accentuate Cervantes's original text for a contemporary audience, but also stand as works of art in their own right.

In chapter 6 Stephen Hessel analyzes the presence of portraiture in the early modern European and Muslim cultural imaginations, and its impact on re-accentuations of Cervantes. Through Cervantes's *Persiles* and Pamuk's *My Name Is Red*, the lack in the symbolic order is considered as a source of allure and danger. The desire to achieve aesthetic permanence and the aversion to an anthropocentric representation of the world is made clear in the Muslim context presented by Pamuk's novel. The problematic created by these opposing currents exhibits the lack that the symbolic order presents in the face of mimetic representation and re-accentuation's capacity to be coopted to efface evidence of that lack. This concept is then applied to Cervantes's portraits and to his legacy. Finally, the lack in the symbolic order is presented as a force that provides order to the interpretation and re-accentuation of meaning in the Cervantine universe, instead of threatening its existence.

Part III deals with the area that seems most appropriate to study the subject of re-accentuation: literature. J. A. Garrido Ardila argues in chapter 7 that the history of the novel has benefited enormously from the re-accentuation of *Don Quixote*. In the early twentieth century, some Spanish novelists (e.g., Unamuno and Azorín) again turned their attention to Cervantes's masterpiece while others (Ortega, Maeztu, and Unamuno) made it the fulcrum of some of their essays. The chapter further deals with Borges's short story "Pierre Menard, Author of *Don Quixote*" (1939) that stands out as perhaps the most enigmatic twentieth-century take on Cervantes's novel. Novelists from Fielding, Smollett, and Sterne to Austen and Flaubert had re-created in their fiction some of the most idiosyncratic features of *Don Quixote*, whereas Borges's fictional Menard re-writes it to produce the very same text as Cervantes. In this chapter the author revisits Borges's short story to explain how it implicitly parodies Unamuno's *Vida de Don Quixote y Sancho* to highlight the uniqueness of Cervantes's work. Furthermore, he also analyzes how Borges celebrates and re-creates the polyphonic perspectivism of *Don Quixote* as one of the essential features of the novel genre.

In chapter 8 Rachel Schmidt deals with World War I and how Don Quixote shows that meaning-making occurs through assimilating and reacting to other's words. She points out that many theories of the novel are based on strong misreadings of *Don Quixote* and argues that World War I threw into question the possibility of finding meaning with the other. She re-examines works of Ortega y Gasset, who insisted upon the illusive, atrophied nature of culture, and re-visits the works of Lukács, who probed the split between the individual and society. Further, she re-visits the essay "Meerfahrt mit *Don Quijote*" (1934) by Thomas Mann, the essay that opens with the question: "What is Germany?" The expelled *morisco* Ricote overlaps in Mann's essay with the Jews escaping on board the ship. Schmidt shows that in all cases Cervantes serves as the first speaker who dared to utter the European problem of conflict with the other, and thus raised the questions to which the modern European novel would respond.

In chapter 9 Howard Mancing takes up the 1973 argument that Don Quixote's attack on the windmills he perceives as giants is "a confrontation of man and machine, one of the earliest in literature, and one of the most perfect." There are several short stories and novels that play off this idea and explicitly involve Don Quixote, and Mancing carefully examines many of them. The two novels discussed at length are Kathy Acker's *Don Quixote*, in which a female Quixote has an abortion, and James McConkey's *Kayo, The Authentic and Annotated Autobiographical Novel from Outer Space* (1987), a complex metafiction involving word play, messages from outer space, and a critique of Jacques Derrida's deconstruction. The discussion of short stories includes works from Poul Anderson's "Quixote and the Windmill" (1950) to Rhys Hughes's "The Quixote Candidate" (2014). The essay ends with a brief mention of the recent discovery star that has been named Cervantes and that is circled by four planets named for the major characters in Cervantes's novel.

In part IV we turn to the subject of film. In chapter 10 Slav Gratchev focuses on the process of *re-accentuation* of the image of Don Quixote when the novel was adapted to the screen in 1957 by the famous Russian director Grigori Kozintsev. In light of Bakhtinian theory, the author explains the nature, the necessity, and the results of this *re-accentuation*. He also analyzes the diaries of Grigori Kozintsev and Eugenie Schwartz and their private correspondence while they both were contemplating the film and working on the script. According to the author, these invaluable materials that chapter relies upon are indispensable for Cervantes scholarship, but until today they have only been available in Russian and have never been translated to English.

William Childers in chapter 11 is concerned with the presence of *Don Quixote* in the work of the late screenwriter Waldo Salt, who, blacklisted during the McCarthy era, eventually went on to write several acclaimed screenplays for *Midnight Cowboy*, *The Day of the Locust*, *Serpico*, and *Coming Home*, developing an innovative approach that has been highly influential with later generations. It was an adaptation of *Don Quixote* that allowed him to make the transition from the frustrated fifty-year-old has-been-who-never-was to the triumphant dean of American screenwriters he became in the 1970s. The chapter begins with an overview of Salt's career, explaining his importance in the emergence of the New Hollywood. Next, the author examines Salt's unpublished *Don Quixote* adaptation, focusing primarily on the particular re-accentuation of Cervantes's novel. Finally, the chapter ends with a survey of the quixotic element of Salt's later work before concluding with broader claims for the significance of Quixote and Quixotism in U.S. cinema during the late twentieth century.

In chapter 12 Bruce Burningham deals with Ah Gan's 2010 Chinese film version of *Don Quixote* in order to demonstrate the ultimate accuracy of Cervantes's far-reaching prediction. Like many other re-accentuations of *Don Quixote*, Ah Gan's film liberally adapts the original text to its own needs. Where Cervantes's protagonist is an aging *hidalgo* who mostly fights imaginary enemies, Ah Gan's Don Quixote is a much younger man who makes a name for himself as a pre-modern Chinese knight-errant by battling and defeating the knights of a malevolent syndicate, thereby winning the hand of his real-life Dulcinea along the way. The author argues that Ah Gan's twenty-first-century (post-Maoist) Don Quixote is a revolutionary hero whose success ultimately stems from inspiring the masses to overthrow the syndicate in favor of a new order.

Jonathan Wade in chapter 13 continues the conversation about film and re-accentuation of Don Quixote with a closer reading of the 2001 French film *Amélie*. What has yet to be explored, ponders the author, is the Cervantine intertext that informs both the framing and the framed. The specific mention of Don Quixote in the film invites viewers to consider the various ways in which Miguel de Cervantes is implicated throughout the work. The author believes that there is the quixotic characterization of its protagonist; the character referred to as the glass man, recalling Cervantes's *El licenciado Vidriera*; and various shades of madness throughout. What is more, the film recollects the narrative structure and self-consciousness of the novel. Just as Cervantes created a story about stories and storytelling, *Amélie* presents viewers with a work of visual art about the visual arts that celebrates both their variety and their composition.

Chapter 14 is unique in many ways: first, it is written by Steven Ritz-Barr, a puppeteer, a real professional who got fascinated by Don Quixote as a universal idea. Don Quixote's story by Cervantes was the second of his series of films called Classics in Miniature®. The goal was to develop the story as a puppet performance for the film medium—a live-action animated film that captured the essence of the original text. How to transform such a long book into a thirty-minute program and yet retain the integrity of the story was no small task. The author discusses his choice of episodes that resonated more personally, while keeping in mind the limitations of puppet film. The problem was how to create a living Don Quixote in the mind of the viewers; how to make a film to be watched by young viewers and adults, those with more or less familiarity with Cervantes's novel.

Theater and television are the subject of the essays in part V. Margarita Marinova and Scott Pollard in chapter 15 explore the ramifications of Mikhail Bulgakov's authorial choices as he re-accentuated *Don Quixote*. They focus specifically on the heightened theatrical nature of the presented events, which will shed new light on several major themes introduced in the adaptation: (1) the symbiotic, and thus doomed in the Soviet context, relationship between the Artist and his community; (2) the character-building but also self-destructive consequences of the merging of theater and life; and (3) the creative Artist, his pupils, and the pursuit of self-expression in a highly restrictive society. Needless to say, Bulgakov's own experiences as a banned author in Stalin's Russia uniquely prepared him for taking on Cervantes's masterpiece. By the end of the 1920s, Bulgakov was not allowed to publish any of his own work, yet he stubbornly continued his quixotic quest to find sanctioned outlets for his creative talents. Adaptations of world literature provided one such venue. The chapter shows how Bulgakov's Дон Кихот (Don Quixote) dialogized the Spanish original in order to highlight its subtle links to his contemporary society.

In chapter 16 Victor Fet, who is a professor of biological science but has a great passion for literature, focuses on the screenplay of Grigory Kozintsev's *Don Quixote* (1957) that happened to be the last work of Evgeny Schwartz (1896–1958), one of the best Russian "re-accentuators." The

work of Schwartz is little known outside Russia. He was among enthusiastic, truly Quixotic creators of children's literature and theater in the
USSR. The chapter brings to us the classic play *The Dragon* (1944) written
in the midst of the darkest wartime. There, Lancelot—a Quixotic rather
than Arthurian knight errant—liberates a city from an evil Dragon only to
find the citizens corrupted into Dragon's spawn. Schwartz's re-accentuation captured the naïve and impossible hopes of a very brief, half-baked
"thaw" period with Khrushchev in power.

Finally, in part VI we step out of the traditional humanities and arts
and into the practical world of business. In chapter 17 Roy Williams
talks about visionaries who have always been attracted to Don Quixote's
pursuit of the impossible dream. In this chapter the author, another non-
academic contributor, examines Quixote as a symbol of the quest for a
better tomorrow. Included in this chapter are interviews with businesspeople who gather from around the world at Wizard Academy, a school
for entrepreneurs built upon Quixote's pursuit of a glorious beauty that
no one but him could see, and the Chapel Dulcinea—the school's gift
to the world: a free wedding chapel that hangs off the edge of a cliff in
Austin, Texas.

This is the book that we are pleased now to offer to your attention.

NOTES

1. M. M. Bakhtin, *The Dialogic Imagination: Four Essays*, ed. Michael Holquist,
trans. Caryl Emerson and Michael Holquist (Austin: University of Texas Press,
1981), 409.

2. Ibid., 421.

3. Ibid., 422.

4. Ibid., 422.

5. M. M. Bakhtin, *Speech Genres and Other Late Essays*, ed. Caryl Emerson and
Michael Holquist, trans. Vern W. McGee (Austin: University of Texas Press, 1986),
4.

6. Ibid., 4.

7. M. M. Bakhtin, *Problems of Dostoevsky's Poetics*, ed. and trans. Caryl Emerson,
intro. Wayne C. Booth (Minneapolis: University of Minnesota Press, 1984), 6; ital-
ics in the original.

I

RE-ACCENTUATION: THEORETICAL INTRODUCTION

1

On Re-accentuation, Adaptation, and Imitation of Don Quixote

Tatevik Gyulamiryan

Mikhail Bakhtin's works convey unprecedented interpretations of literary pieces, linguistic phenomena, philosophical approaches, and cultural practices. In his numerous studies, Bakhtin interprets the relationship between the new and the old, as well as cultural, social, and artistic tendencies to reuse and reclaim old trends. He highlights the importance of recycling familiar words, ideas, and concepts to create new ones; in fact, he states, more than half of what we claim as new has appeared in other contexts before.[1] As we progress through our lives, we come across numerous objects, ideas, and notions that are *re-accentuations* of previously known concepts. Re-accentuation—a term Bakhtin uses in reference to recycling discourses, literary characters, and works—carries a singular value in comparative studies. In this article, I focus on the notion of re-accentuation in quixotic literature. I define the term re-accentuation and its taxonomic relation to adaptation, imitation, and parody, as I explore examples of various metamorphoses of Don Quixote in literature and film. The numerous conscious transformations of *Don Quixote* and its protagonist reveal the uniquely generative nature of Cervantes's novel and the Manchegan knight's ability to transpose into the "hero of a thousand faces."[2]

RE-ACCENTUATION

Re-accentuation is a term that was first coined by Mikhail Bakhtin. Although Bakhtin mentions the term only briefly, it opens a platform of various possible interpretations and proves to be essential in comparative studies. Re-accentuation, according to Bakhtin, can be of multiple types. He outlines four of its major uses: linguistic and discourse re-accentuations as well as re-accentuations of characters and novels.

Linguistic re-accentuation occurs when the stress on a spoken word shifts depending on the part of speech. Some examples include: áccent/accéntuate, práctical/practicálity, sítuate/situátion. The accent changes its position and falls on a different vowel when a prefix or suffix is added to the root. In linguistics, this is an obvious and a common occurrence.

Bakhtin then defines the re-accentuation of discourse as something that occurs when the speech of a hero fuses with that of his or her author. He considers the fusion of the author and hero's discourse as the hero's re-accentuation of the author's thoughts. In Bakhtin's words: "The author encases his own thought in the image of another's language," while the hero encapsulates a "discourse about himself and about his world" intermixed with the author's view "about him and his world."[3] In Bakhtin's view, the characters are couriers between writers and readers; they re-accentuate the writer's original discourse through the personas they embody.

While Bakhtin mainly focuses on author-character discourse re-accentuation, it is common in literature to come across characters re-accentuating each other's discourse as well. One of the greatest examples of this kind of re-accentuation can be found in *Don Quixote*. When Don Quixote and Sancho are at the house of the Duke and the Duchess, they meet Countess Trifaldi, who greets them in a pseudo-sophisticated manner, her speech overflowing with superlatives.

> —Confiada estoy, señor poderisísimo, hermosísima señora y discretísimos circunstantes, que ha de hallar mi cuitísima en vuestros valerosísimos pechos acogimiento, no menos plácido que generoso y doloroso; porque ella es tal, que es bastante a enternecer los mármoles, y a ablandar los diamantes, y a molificar los aceros de los más endurecidos corazones del mundo; pero antes que salga a la plaza de vuestros oídos (por no decir orejas), quisiera que me hicieran sabidora si está en este gremio, corro y compañía, el acendradísimo caballero de don Quijote de la Manchísima, y escuderísimo Panza.[4]

> ("I am confident, most powerful lord, most beautiful lady, most discerning company, that my most grievous affliction will find in your most valiant bosoms a refuge no less serene than generous and pitying, for it is such that it would be enough to soften marble, and dulcify diamonds, and bend the steel of the hardest hearts in the world; but before I bring it to your hearing, so as not to say ears, I would be most happy if you would tell me if in this group, circle, and company there is to be found that most unblemished knight Don Quixote of La Manchissima, and his most squirish Panza.")[5]

Sancho rushes in to reply:

> —El Panza—antes que otro respondiese, dijo Sancho—aquí está, y el don Quijotísimo asimismo; y así podréis, dolorosísima dueñísima, decir lo que quisieridísimis; que todos estamos prontos y aparejadísimos a ser vuestros servidorísimos.[6]

("Panza," said Sancho before anyone else could respond, "is here, and Don Quixotissimo as well, and so, most dolorous duennissima, you can say whatever you wishissima, for we're all ready and most prepared to be your most servantish servantissimos.")[7]

Sancho parodies Countess Trifaldi's discourse, re-accentuating her superlatives and applying them not only to adjectives but to nouns and verbs as well. While Sancho's re-accentuation of Countess Trivaldi's words illustrates his attempt to parody her speech, it is obvious that Cervantes is the one who assigns the rhetoric to his characters. Sancho's comic re-accentuation of Countess Trifaldi's discourse prefigures the multiple re-accentuations that take place between *Don Quixote* and other works. Sancho is doing with nouns and verbs what later works will do with *Don Quixote*'s characters and themes.

Re-accentuation, therefore, is not limited to words and discourse. Bakhtin argues that novelistic themes and characters can be re-accentuations of earlier works. Re-accentuations of novelistic themes re-contextualize central ideas from an original novel in a new work. For example, *Monsignor Quixote* (1982) is a re-accentuation of *Don Quixote*, where the plotline primarily encompasses the adventures of Father Quixote (a re-accentuated Don Quixote) with his squire Zancas (a re-accentuated Sancho Panza) in his limping SEAT 600 (a re-accentuation of Rocinante). This novel offers an original story of a bishop and ex-mayor's travels through post-Franco Spain but lends itself to a quixotic reading due to various re-accentuations of characters and themes grounded in Cervantes's *Don Quixote*.

To re-accentuate a character, an author or producer takes an original character's image and places it in a different context. This kind of character re-accentuation requires that the character have a strong image and be easily recognized. Don Quixote is a highly recognizable character and has a series of eminent traits that define him. In particular, he is (1) a reader, (2) a dreamer, (3) an adventurer, and (4) a lover. Characters in other pieces of art who exhibit most of these quixotic traits can be seen as re-accentuations of Don Quixote.

Re-accentuation: What It Isn't

Before diving into specific examples of re-accentuations of Don Quixote in literature and film, it is important to mention that re-accentuation is related to, but not quite the same as, concepts such as re-writing, parody, imitation, and adaptation. For example, it is different from mere re-writing, since re-writing involves revision or copying without contextual changes. Borges's "Pierre Menard, Author of *Don Quixote*" is a brilliant illustration of the concept of re-writing. Borges's eponymous protagonist strives to re-create Cervantes's novel and immerses himself in *Don Quixote* with such dedication that he manages to re-write parts of the novel so accurately from his memory that they look like a copy of the original. Although Borges then ironically states that Menard's *Don Quixote* is far richer than Cervantes's, the reader realizes that, in Menard's version, there have been no contextual changes; therefore, his attempt to re-create the novel results in plagiarism. An author cannot achieve uniqueness by simply re-writing a character, because the context where the original and the newly created characters are represented remains the same. New contexts are essential components of re-accentuation as the fictional heroes, even if some of their characteristics appear to be re-written, now pertain to and represent a new world.

Parody also relates to re-accentuation but is not synonymous with it. Linda Hutcheon claims that parody is a type of imitation "but imitation characterized by ironic inversion."[8] She cites Bakhtin, saying that parody creates a "formal or structural relation between two texts" that amounts to "a form of textual dialogism."[9] For his part, Bakhtin sees parody as "an intentional dialogized hybrid,"[10] a concept that implies a dialogic relationship between the parodied and the original works. For example, Jane Austen's *Northanger Abbey* (1818) parodies gothic novels that enjoyed great popularity in England during the late eighteenth and early nineteenth centuries. At the same time, Austen's novel opens a dialogue between gothic fiction, in particular *Mysteries of Udolpho* (1794), and romance. While romance remains the central theme of *Northanger Abbey*, the love depicted in that novel goes through various trials in episodes influenced by gothic fiction.

Hutcheon asserts that parody does not always involve satire. As the case of *Northanger Abbey* attests, parody can generate ironic inversion or criticism, but it does not necessarily entail ridicule.[11] Similarly, Michael Scham sees parody as a tool to "salvage and revitalize,"[12] a definition that applies to the type of chivalric parody presented in *Don Quixote*, as well as most of the parodic literature derived from *Don Quixote*.[13] However, it is important to note that, "parodied genres do not belong to the genres that they parody."[14] For example, *Don Quixote* can be read as a parody of chivalric romances; however, the novel itself is not a chivalric romance. Another example is Ken Mitchell's *The Heroic Adventures of Donny Coyote* (2003), whose title already indicates the novel's parodic nature. *Donny Coyote* is a re-accentuation of *Don Quixote* and its characters, but it simultaneously parodies comic books as the eponymous protagonist strives to imitate superheroes.

Parody and imitation are closely related to each other,[15] the distinction being that a parody is grounded in a previous work (for example, *Don Quixote* parodying chivalric romances), while an imitation *derives* from a previous work (such as *Joseph Andrews* [1742], which explicitly imitates Cervantine narrative).[16] Imitation is a conscious intertextual reference that can be achieved at the character level or at the level of a full work. Don Quixote strives to imitate heroes from chivalric romances, especially Amadís of Gaul. However, he fails to become a re-accentuation of any character given that he possesses a number of unique traits that define him and only him.

Re-accentuation is also distinct from adaptation, although many mistakenly use the terms synonymously. This confusion derives from the fact that adaptation mostly refers to a shift between genres: from novels to movies, movies to TV shows, literature to art, etc. It is true that adaptation, like re-accentuation, is "not simply repetition; there is always a change."[17] However, adaptation often seeks a transformation across various genres of art (as when a novel is adapted for the screen) in order to present the original form in a new system. For example, Dale Wasserman's *Man of La Mancha* (1964) is an adaptation of Cervantes's *Don Quixote*. Although a Quixote, a Sancho, and even a Dulcinea perform in the musical, they are not re-accentuations of Cervantes's protagonists; the Quixote in *Man of La Mancha* is not a new character who tries to be *like* Cervantes's Quixote, he *is* Don Quixote brought into a new genre. Similarly, in Steven Ritz-Barr's puppet film *Quixote* (2010), the viewer watches adaptations of various episodes from the novel, such as the episode of the burning of the books, the episode with the little boy Andrés, or the part where Don Quixote is watching a puppet show himself.[18] Like *Man of La Mancha*, Ritz-Barr's adaptation of the novel does not present re-accentuations of Cervantes's characters. The characters do not strive to embody Quixote or Sancho; they *are* Quixote and Sancho in a different form of art. To recapitulate, adaptations of *Don Quixote* on screen or stage do not present re-accentuated protagonists. (And the converse is also true; works that employ re-accentuations of Quixote or Sancho are not adapted works of Cervantes.)

Conscious re-accentuations of *Don Quixote* and its characters take place when an author or producer determines the most defining features of Cervantes's protagonists and creates new characters who embody those traits. Re-accentuations of Don Quixote exhibit the most salient features defining the Spanish knight-errant—they are readers, dreamers, adventurers, and lovers. More often than not, re-accentuated Quixote characters undergo adventures as they strive to achieve dreams that have arisen in them due to voracious reading. They may also fall in love with unattainable or unsuitable beloveds, weaving a knotty love story. What follows is a more detailed look at the four quixotic traits and their forms of re-accentuation.

READERS

Don Quixote is well known for his frantic perusal of chivalric romances. However, the trait of the reader in Quixote is not only limited to the act of reading and delving into a fictional world for personal titillation; it also entails avulsing what belongs to that fictional world and material-izing it in reality.[19] Consequently, the books that Don Quixote reads turn into a lifestyle for him, as he intends to embody images of fictional characters in the real world. He refers repeatedly, for instance, to his fa-vorite chivalric romance, *Amadís of Gaul*. Given that behavior, language, clothes, and culture have evolved since *Amadís*, Quixote's inclination to embody every aspect of the book in his contemporary context comes across as lunacy. Don Quixote's rusty armor is outdated and demoded, his bookish language is archaic and funny, and his chivalric "pledge" to his lady is antique and strange for bystanders. While Don Quixote finds these styles appropriate for a knight-errant, he forgets to distinguish between the old reality presented in the books he enjoys and the con-temporary society around him that has long abandoned the trappings of the medieval lifestyle.

Re-accentuations of Don Quixote who embody the quixotic obsession for reading usually exhibit a dimmed ability to distinguish between real-ity and fiction. For example, Arabella, the protagonist of Charlotte Len-nox's *The Female Quixote* (1752), becomes overly obsessed with romance books. She imagines her life as a romance and acts as if she were a heroine similar to the ones she reads about. As expected, her society misunder-stands and misinterprets her behavior. Other exemplary literary works with a re-accentuated reader protagonist include Gustave Flaubert's *Ma-dame Bovary* (1856) and Jane Austen's *Northanger Abbey*. In these novels too, the heroines exhibit a powerful inclination toward reading and, like Arabella and their predecessor Don Quixote, interpret reality according to fiction—thus jeopardizing their reputations, their social images, and, above all, their judgments.[20]

In film, various protagonists feature quixotic devotion to reading. One of the many examples is *Matilda* (1996), a fantasy drama for young view-ers. The protagonist is a genius girl who exhibits exceptional interest in reading. Her brilliant knowledge and grasp of human nature, acquired from incessant reading, as well as her good will, save her school from a monstrous principal and free her from her ignorant parents. The movie plays on several elements originally found in *Don Quixote*, for example, by pairing Matilda's fantastic visions and abilities with realistic perspec-tives, an approach also widely found in magic realism.[21]

DREAMERS

The trait of the dreamer can be found in the unrealistic and idealistic vision of Cervantes's hero (as a result of excessive reading), combined with his endeavor to make the world surrounding him a better place. Thus, Alonso Quijano, a simple hidalgo who has devoured all literary fiction available to him, adopts a new identity and sets off on the roads of la Mancha with a goal to do good. He perceives himself as a knight-errant, adopts the archaic style of his favorite characters from chivalric romances, chooses a lady worthy of his love, "hires" a squire, and leaves home to fulfill his dreams. His irrational perception of himself and the surrounding world forms an exaggerated optimism, which in turn affects his ability to understand the consequences of his actions. Don Quixote refuses to see a possibility of failure and, despite his previous unsuccessful attempts, still undergoes a number of adventures expecting that others will acknowledge his chivalric identity.

Re-accentuated dreamers encountered elsewhere in literature exhibit similarly skewed perceptions of their situations, as well as similar perseverance in achieving their goals. Like Don Quixote, these "dreamer" characters often fail to distinguish reality from illusions, and their inability to acknowledge the unreasonableness of their goals leads them to failure. Some literary examples of re-accentuated dreamers include Captain Ahab from Herman Melville's *Moby Dick* (1851), Jay Gatsby from F. Scott Fitzgerald's *The Great Gatsby* (1925), and Daniel Quinn from Paul Auster's *City of Glass* (1985). The central characters of these novels[22] have dreams that later mutate into obsessive goals. Ahab searches for the white whale Moby Dick in order to take revenge for his lost limb; Gatsby spares no effort to reunite with his beloved Daisy; and Quinn is determined to solve a family mystery and protect Stillman Jr. from Stillman Sr. Despite these characters' almost deranged exertions, their respective quests fail and their dreams remain unrealized. Ahab's encounter with Moby Dick takes a deadly turn; the whale attacks and destroys Ahab's ship, leaving only one member of the crew alive. The day Jay Gatsby anticipates a new beginning with Daisy comes to a close with his murder. Quinn believes he has found the refuge of Stillman Jr., only to find an empty apartment and disappear himself. As in *Don Quixote*, at the very moment the protagonists of these quixotic novels feel they finally have come close to satisfying their dreams, the narratives twist in a sudden *peripeteia*, and the novels end in a minor key; Don Quixote renounces his identity as a knight-errant, Ahab and Gatsby are killed, and Quinn simply vanishes from the novel.

ADVENTURERS

The trait of the adventurer is perhaps the strongest and the most developed characteristic of the Spanish knight-errant. Don Quixote is in motion throughout most of the novel and takes any challenge arising in front of him. Although most of the ventures that Cervantes's protagonist undergoes end in disaster, Don Quixote's determination and motivation hardly ever recede, and his extensive travels and insane adventures lead other characters to notice and embrace his new identity.

In re-accentuated characters, the adventurer's trait is usually insatiable, voracious, and sometimes overambitious. Various authors who have re-accentuated Don Quixote have captured and recapitulated this core definition of the Spanish knight-errant's life: his adventures. Works like *The Heroic Adventures of Donny Coyote* (2003) by Ken Mitchell, *The Adventures of Tom Sawyer* (1876) and *The Adventures of Huckleberry Finn* (1884) by Mark Twain, as well as *The Savage Detectives* (1998) by Roberto Bolaño are comprised of travels. The heroes of these novels brilliantly re-accentuate the image of Quixote the adventurer as they travel extensively, stumbling upon various emprises along the way. Adrian Arancibia claims that "Every story is a travel story,"[23] but to me, *Quixote* is one of the two literary masterpieces—*The Odyssey* being the other one—where the core of travel and journey[24] stories dwells.

Movie protagonists who re-accentuate Quixote the adventurer mostly present a quest story. These quests often take the form of adventure movies, especially westerns. Although not all westerns present a quixotic story line or re-accentuated Quixotes, most of them depict some kind of Cervantine[25] pairing: Quixote-Sancho, Quixote-Dulcinea, Quixote-Sansón Carrasco, or Quixote-family. For example, *For a Few Dollars More* (1965) presents Manco and Mortimer as Quixote and Sancho, while in *Rango* (2011) the title character (a re-accentuated Quixote in the form of a chameleon) needs to prove he can fit in and help the residents of Dirt, while also finding his re-accentuated Dulcinea in an iguana named Beans. *Django Unchained* (2012) depicts both a freedom quest narrative and quixotic dedication and love between Django and Broomhilda. Like *Don Quixote*, these movies are identified by their abundantly adventurous plotlines and the visionary goals of their characters.

LOVERS

The trait of lover is Don Quixote's most versatile feature, encompassing idealization, obsession, and blindness, as well as loyalty and commitment. Dulcinea's imaginary presence in Don Quixote's life plays a crucial role in his successful embodiment of a knight-errant. Quixote acknowledges that his attempts to imitate knight-errantry would fail without a woman to whom he can pledge commitment. For this reason, he chooses Aldonza Lorenzo as his true love and names her Princess Dulcinea. Don Quixote's lover-like traits develop into loyal, idealized, and platonic feelings toward Dulcinea, a definition of love that resembles those highlighted in medieval romances and chivalric novels. Although Don Quixote never once encounters his beloved woman in the novel, the image of Dulcinea that he bears in his mind remains immutable for him. Dulcinea plays the role of a muse (as in the episode with the Basque merchants), an angel, and in some ways, even of God (as when Don Quixote evokes Dulcinea before an adventure). The Manchegan knight idealizes Dulcinea in so many ways that he eventually becomes obsessed with the creation of his own imagination.

The re-accentuated characters who exhibit the trait of the lover have one thing in common—all of them aspire to love and be loved by their partners. However, for most of these characters, like Don Quixote himself, their romantic feelings conceal self-serving motives as they fail to acknowledge and accept the dialogic nature of love. Most re-accentuated characters exhibit the quixotic definition of love, a love that is blind, ideal, and illusionary. Although their love appears romantic at first glance, it proves obsessive, overly idealistic, possessive, and jealous. *Anna Karenina* (1877), *Lolita* (1955), and *The Bad Girl* (2006) are examples of quixotic novels that present re-accentuated quixotic lovers. The central characters of these novels—Anna Karenina, Humbert Humbert, and Ricardo Somocurcio—illustrate that monologic or self-serving love toward an idealized partner takes love's most extreme form—obsession—and threatens to destroy the lover's mental health.

The list of works with re-accentuated characters featuring one or several of the four quixotic traits goes on, and because of limited space I have only been able to include a sparse sampling of works that present a Cervantine story line and quixotic characters.[26] We come across readers, dreamers, adventurers, or lovers in film and literature virtually every day, and we are constantly reminded of the prevalent presence of *Quixote* in our lives even after four hundred years since its publication. Research on Cervantes and especially *Don Quixote* is ever flourishing, and academics, as well as independent scholars, vigorously contribute to the bank of works dedicated to the Spanish master and his masterpiece. Analyses of quixotic literature have especially been abounding, including works such as *The Cervantean Heritage: Reception and Influence of Cervantes in Britain* (2009) edited by Garrido Ardila and his *Cervantes en inglaterra: El Quijote y la novela inglesa del siglo XVIII* (2014); Wood's *Quixotic Fictions of the USA, 1792-1815* (2005); Turkevich's *Cervantes in Russia* (1975); and Paulson's

Don Quixote in England: The Aesthetics of Laughter (1998), among numerous others. The vast number of scholarly works studying Cervantes and his novel's influence on literature and other forms of art can attest to one thing only; *Don Quixote* is and has been one of the most influential literary works ever written. With almost every rising quixotic novel[27] and film, the image of Don Quixote becomes more and more popularized in Spain and beyond its borders. Don Quixote is like No-man[28]; he can stand at his tower of faces, don the mask of a chosen character, and be reborn in any context.[29] As re-accentuated Quixotes keep re-appearing in places where readers need to discover them, Bakhtin provides us with an important tool that allows us to correctly define certain quixotic appearances in literature. While re-accentuation can provide essential clarification as we categorize quixotic works and define their characters, it also proves to be exceptionally valuable in many contexts in comparative studies.

NOTES

1. M. M. Bakhtin, *Speech Genres and Other Late Essays*, trans. Vern W. McGee, ed. Caryl Emerson and Michael Holquist (Austin: University of Texas Press, 1986), 87–89.
2. See Joseph Campbell, *The Hero with a Thousand Faces* (Princeton, NJ: Princeton University Press, 1972).
3. M. M. Bakhtin, *The Dialogic Imagination: Four Essays*, ed. Michael Holquist, trans. Caryl Emerson and Michael Holquist (Austin: University of Texas Press, 1982), 409.
4. Miguel de Cervantes, *Don Quijote de la Mancha*, vol. II, ed. John Jay Allen (Madrid: Cátedra, 2009), 347.
5. Miguel de Cervantes, *Don Quixote*, trans. Edith Grossman, intr. Harold Bloom (New York: Harper Collins, 2003), 705–6.
6. Cervantes, *Don Quixote II*, 347.
7. Cervantes, *Don Quixote*, trans., 706.
8. Linda Hutcheon, *A Theory of Parody. The Teachings of Twentieth-Century Art Forms* (New York: Methuen, 1985), 6.
9. Ibid., 22.
10. Bakhtin, *Dialogic*, 76.
11. Hutcheon, *Parody*, 6.
12. Michael Scham, "*Don Quijote* and *Lolita* Revisited," *Cervantes: Bulletin of the Cervantes Society of America* 26.1 (Spring–Fall 2006): 81.
13. *Don Quixote* revitalizes *Amadís of Gaul* (1508), which has long declined in popularity. Likewise, more modern works that exhibit quixotic features re-animate Cervantes's novel.
14. Bakhtin, *Dialogic*, 59.
15. Parody and imitation are also related to influence/intertextuality, since many works show influence from another work without necessarily parodying

or imitating it consciously. Turkevich suggests that "influence may be positive or negative, and may act directly or inversely. The positive effect is far more usual. It occurs when an author, favorably impressed by some feature of an earlier work, uses it consciously or subconsciously in his own." Ludmilla Buketoff Turkevich, *Cervantes in Russia* (New York: Gordian, 1975), x.

16. The title page of Fielding's *Joseph Andrews* indicates that Fielding wrote his novel in "imitation of the manner of Cervantes, who wrote *Don Quixote*." In addition, the narrative portrays various quixotic characters (including Joseph Andrews, who is a quixotic adventurer and lover, and Abraham Adams, who exhibits the traits of reader and dreamer). Henry Fielding, *Joseph Andrews*, ed. Martin C. Battestin (Middletown, CT: Wesleyan University Press, 1967).

17. Linda Hutcheon, *A Theory of Adaptation* (New York: Routledge, 2006), 176.

18. Note how ingeniously Ritz-Barr transforms Cervantine meta-fiction to the screen. The viewer is watching a film about a puppet show, where the puppets go to another puppet show. I am inclined to call this concept *meta-puppetry*.

19. Because of multiple examples of meta-fiction in this article, I refer to fiction as characters' reality and meta-fiction as their fictional world. (Don Quixote's intention to embody medieval knights-errant is his attempt to fictionalize his reality—the narrative setup of *Don Quixote*.) I do this in order to avoid overusing the word "fiction" and to simplify the discussion of multi-layered contexts.

20. I have chosen these three female re-accentuations of Don Quixote to draw attention to how reading affects gender. Those familiar with *The Female Quixote, Northanger Abbey*, and *Madame Bovary* can immediately identify one apparent difference between Don Quixote and his re-accentuated counterparts; although all of them are frantic readers and actors in their real-fictional world, Don Quixote is not confined to a specific social role. As for the women, Arabella is "cured" by a doctor so she can comply with her social responsibility and marry; Catherine realizes that her distorted interpretation of reality due to reading gothic fiction has jeopardized her relationship with Henry, so she has to control her active imagination in order for Henry to forgive and marry her; and Emma Bovary finds no way to recuperate the damage she has done to herself and her family, so she ends her life.

21. For interpretations of magic realism in Cervantes, see Arturo Serrano-Plaja, *"Magic" Realism in Cervantes:* Don Quixote *as Seen through* Tom Sawyer *and* The Idiot, trans. Robert S. Rudder (Berkeley: University of California Press, 1970).

22. *The Great Gatsby* and *Moby Dick* have been adapted for the screen, thus presenting the re-accentuated image of quixotic dreamers in cinematography as well.

23. Adrian Arancibia, "Postmodernity and the Latin American City: Mexico City and *The Savage Detectives*," *Black Renaissance* 2.3 (Winter 2009): 205.

24. For Don Quixote's personal journey, see Howard Mancing, "Embodied Cognition and Autopoiesis in Don Quixote," in *Cognitive Approaches to Early Modern Spanish Literature*, ed. Isabel Jaen and Julien Jacques Simon (New York: Oxford University Press), 2016, 37–52.

25. For a detailed discussion on definition and classification of *re-accentuation, quixotic*, and *Cervantine*, see Tatevik Gyulamiryan, "Homecoming Festivals: The Re-accentuated Image of Don Quixote in Western Novel" (PhD diss., Purdue University, 2015), 1–20.

26. See Bruce R. Burningham, *Tilting Cervantes: Baroque Reflections on Postmodern Culture* (Nashville: Vanderbilt University Press, 2008) for various references to re-accentuated Quixotes and Sanchos in postmodern film, and Gyulamiryan, *Homecoming,* for references to re-accentuated Quixotes in European and American novels.

27. Rainbow Rowell's immediately popular young adult novel *Carry On* (2015) depicts a re-accentuated Quixote named Simon Snow; his re-accentuation of Dulcinea, Tyrannus Basilton; and Penelope Bunce, his re-accentuated Sancho.

28. Homer, *The Odyssey,* trans. Robert Fagles, intr. and notes Bernard Knox (New York: Viking, 1996), 222–24.

29. *Game of Thrones,* dir. Alan Taylor et al., writ. David Benioff and D. B. Weiss, HBO, 2011–2018.

II

IMAGERY AND IDEOLOGY

2

Don Quixote Re-depicted

Eduardo Urbina and Fernando González Moreno

Almost since its publication, *Don Quixote* (1605–1615) has been a continuous source of inspiration for painters and illustrators who have tried to re-create into images Cervantes's text. These images must be considered not only as artistic ornaments, but also, and especially, as the reflection of how the novel was read in different periods, of how Cervantes's characters were reinvented by every society to transform them into icons of their own ideals.

Nowadays, Gustave Doré's illustrations (Paris: Librairie de L. Hachette et Cie. 1863), which popularized Don Quixote's image as a Romantic hero, or Dalí's (New York: Random House, 1946), who took the knight into his own Surrealistic universe, are recognized by most people, even by many who have never read the book. However, beyond these already well-known and popular visual readings, beyond Doré and Dalí, we can find many other illustrators, less known by the general public, for whom *Don Quixote* become a real obsession or a continuous inspiration.[1]

One of the first artists that we must include among these is, without any doubt, Charles-Antoine Coypel (1694–1752). *Premier peintre du Roi* and *Directeur de l'Académie Royale* since 1747, Coypel's first encounter with *Don Quixote* took place only one year after being accepted by the *Académie* in 1715 at the early age of twenty-one. In 1716, Coypel commissioned a series of twenty-eight tapestry cartoons for the *Manufacture Royale des Gobelins* under the general title of *Suite de Don Quichotte*, a commission that he carried out almost throughout his entire life, accomplishing it in 1751, just one year before his death. The subject chosen for the first tapestry was *Don Quichotte croit recevoir dans l'hôtellerie l'ordre de chevalier* (1715–1716).[2] Coypel designed twenty-three cartoons more before 1717; with another three executed in 1731, 1732, and 1734; and the last one, *Don Quichotte servi par les filles de l'hôtellerie*,[3] was painted in 1751. Designs to which we must add two more cartoons, traditionally not included in this *Suite de*

25

Don Quichotte, where Don Quixote and Sancho appeared seated in two pedestals (c. 1732, Banque de France).[4]

Along his brilliant and well-documented career, and under the influence of Watteau, Coypel's pictorial production was prolific, reflecting his interests in ancient history, mythology, religious scenes, allegories, and literary subjects. However, it was *Don Quixote* that became a recurrent topic in Coypel's pictorial and literary career. He found inspiration in Cervantes's novel not only for the already mentioned cartoons—considered together with his designs on Molière's comedies as his more relevant and renowned work—but for ornamental furniture—such as his canapé designs with motifs from *Don Quixote*[5]– and, in general, for the creation of his own work as a painter and as a playwright. The relation between Cervantes's novel and Coypel's work is easily recognized through the representation of episodes such as the shepherdesses' dance and the "speaking dance" of Love and Interest during Camacho's wedding (*DQ* II: 20) as well as his play *Folies de Cardenio* (1720), based on the character of the first part. Likewise, the connection is evident when comparing the cartoon where Don Quixote is delivered from Folly by Wisdom with his *Triomphe de la Raison* (1730), another of Coypel's plays (figure 2.1); or when analyzing the reiterative presence of Folly in his pictorial and literary productions. In this sense, as Ian Jamieson pointed out: "La note héroï-comique de don Quichotte convenait à merveille à Coypel qui possédait un sentiment du comique que les illustrateurs modernes n'ont jamais surpassé. Ici, il était sur son terrain. Sans exagérer un type que le poète espagnol avait déjà beaucoup chargé, il en fait très bien sentir le ridicule et il montra dans se tableaux de la grâce, de l'esprit et de la verve."[6]

Aware of the success that the Don Quixote cartoons were having, in 1721 Coypel decided to sign an agreement with the royal clockmaker Claude Martinot and Philippe Reboullet to engrave his designs, a way of giving them even a greater distribution. The prints were engraved and sold by Louis Surugue under royal privilege—*pour graver les estampes d'après les tableaux sur l'histoire de Don Quichotte*—since 1723 until 1744. Coypel supervised directly the engraving process after his designs—only twenty-five from the total of twenty-eight were engraved[7]—and chose some of the most notable burinists of the moment. Many of them were colleagues and friends from the French Academy: Louis Surugue *père* (*c.* 1686–1762), Charles-Nicolas Cochin *père* (1688–1762), François Joullain (1697–1778), Nicolas-Henri Tardieu (1674–1774), Simon-François Ravenet (1706–1774), Nicolas Charles de Silvestre (1700–1767), Jean-Baptiste Haussard (1679/80–1749), Nicolas-Dauphin de Beauvais (1687–1763), François de Poilly *le jeaune* (1671–1723), Louise-Magdeleine Horthemels (1687–1774), and Bernard Lépicié (1698–1755).

Coypel's cartoons and prints must be understood under a way of reading *Don Quixote* where the painter and playwright has tried to combine two different visions: one public and courtesan and another private, Coypel's himself. Regarding its public sense, many of these illustrations—Don Quixote knighted at the inn, the knight hanging from the inn window, Clavileño, the night encounter with doña Rodríguez—still reflect the continuity of the tradition that read Cervantes's novel mainly as a work of entertainment and humor, a burlesque reading;[8] now disguised with a more refined and courtesan appearance but still entertainment. On the other hand, certain illustrations—Don Quixote led by Folly, the theater during Camacho's wedding, Wisdom releasing Don Quixote from his madness (figure 2.1) show us the beginning of a new way of reading

Don Quichotte est delivré de sa Folie par la Sagesse.
a Paris chez Surugue rue des Noyers.

Figure 2.1. Charles-Antoine Coypel/Charles-Nicolas Cochin *père. Don Quichotte est delivré de sa folie par la Sagesse* (Paris: Louis Surugue, c. 1728–1730, burin engraving)

Don Quixote as a fable as allegorical theater, from which we can obtain a moral and didactic conclusion beyond the mere burlesque reading. In Coypel's designs Don Quixote becomes an allegorical image, which implies a deeper reading, in consonance with the didactic-moral value that this artist conferred to the allegory of Folly in others of his pictorial and literary works, transforming Cervantes's character into a metaphor of the perils that threaten us when we leave aside Reason and Prudence, and laying the foundations of the satirical-didactic reading that finally succeeded with Lord Carteret's edition and John Vanderbank's illustrations (London: J. & R. Tonson 1738).

While the eighteenth century was dominated by Coypel's rococo and allegorical images and by Vanderbank's academic and decorous designs—those last strictly to comply with John Oldfield's considerations about the role that illustrations should play to reinforce a higher and serious reading of *Don Quixote*[9]—the nineteenth century arrived with several novelties on the wake of Romanticism. In this sense, two illustrators monopolized most of the editorial market of the century: Tony Johannot (Paris: J.-J. Dubuchet et Cie., 1836–1837) and Gustave Doré (Paris: Librairie de L. Hachette et Cie., 1863); the second most popular and better known than the first.[10] Nevertheless, we want to focus now on a previous artist who deserves the merit of being the first to depict Don Quixote under this new aesthetic ideal: Robert Smirke (1753–1845).

Smirke had specialized as a painter of literary subjects, developing a characteristic format of monochrome and small-size paintings that made them particularly adequate to be used by the engravers to produce book illustrations. His designs, among many others, appeared in *The Picturesque Beauties of Shakespeare* (London: C. Taylor, 1783–1787), *The Arabian Nights* (London: Printed for William Miller by W. Bulmer and Co., 1802), Alain René Le Sage's *The Adventures of Gil Blas of Santillane* (London: Longman, Hurst, Rees, and Orme, and G. Kearsley, 1809), and illustrated the works of several British poets such as James Thomson. Regarding the focus of our study, Smirke had the possibility of illustrating *Don Quixote* for the London: T. Cadell and W. Davies, 1818 edition,[11] but this was not the first time that the painter approached Cervantes's novel. In 1793, as part of the process to be accepted as a full academician by the Royal Academy, he had chosen for his diploma *Don Quixote and Sancho Panza*. The painting, where both characters appear seated in the middle of a rocky landscape, may be alluding to the episode when they enter Sierra Morena (*DQ* I: 23). It already shows some of the novelties that Smirke would develop years later in his 1818 illustrations, such as the melancholic atmosphere that surrounds the characters, the feeling of loneliness that they emanate, and the increasing presence of nature, that now begins to be recognized as one more of the main characters in the novel.

Smirke transformed not only Don Quixote but Cervantes too in romantic and tragic heroes. In this sense, the headpiece of the "Preface" that shows Cervantes looking for inspiration in an austere setting recalling the prison in Argamasilla, a reminder of the lack of recognition suffered by the author; or another where Don Quixote appears alone, melancholic, and missing Sancho in the Duke's palace (*DQ* II: 44); or in the illustration that depicts the knight, thoughtful and meditating about his penance and Dulcinea, sitting on a cliff in Sierra Morena, a sublime, suggestive, and imposing landscape (*DQ* I: 26), are especially iconic (figure 2.2). Regarding this last print, for example, Givanel indicated: "El virus romántico no podía, en verdad, atacar más fuertemente al héroe cervantino."[12] Smirke's visual reading also allows us to explore for the first time Don Quixote's imagination. Till now, the illustrators had focused on the reality against which the knight's fantasies clashed with humorist consequences; instead, Smirke adopts Don Quixote's own point of view, empathizing with him and, therefore, feeling his frustration and despair with the impossibility of reaching his ideal reality. This is seen in the illustration and the headpiece dedicated to the Knight of the Lake, represented as Don Quixote imagines him (*DQ* I: 50), and the print with Montesinos introducing Durandarte to the knight, which reproduces Don Quixote's description as if it were real (*DQ* I: 23).

Another novelty to be noticed in the 1818 edition is the increasing interest in the interpolated novels of "The Impertinent Curious" and "The Captive." Both had been illustrated for the first time in the 1738 edition, when Vanderbank, following Oldfield's recommendations about variety, dedicated one design to each tale. The episode represented by Vanderbank on "The Captive," *Zoraida Discovered by Her Father in the Arms of the Captive* (*DQ* I: 41), had become habitual in English editions, such as London: Cooke, 1796 by Thomas Kirk, or London: William Miller, 1801 by Banks. Smirke also illustrated this episode in 1818, since the scene, including the image of a fainted Zoraida, allowed not only a melodramatic representation quite in keeping with the romantic taste, but also a chance to display an orientalist and evocative setting.[13] Moreover, Smirke illustrated for the first time the moment when Zoraida's father is abandoned in Cava Rumía, a scene of special drama and emotive nature that reinforces the romantic reading of this story. For "The Impertinent Curious," Smirke represents three episodes of the story; one of them, *Camilla's Artifice* (*DQ* I: 34), was also chosen by Vanderbank (1738) as the most representative of the novel. However, it is interesting to notice the different instant selected by both artists. While Vanderbank depicts Camila pretending to stab herself, and Lotario and Leonela "trying" to stop her, Smirke has represented the latter and more dramatic moment when Camila, held by a distressed Leonela, is already lying "dead" on his bed. The two other episodes

Figure 2.2.   Robert Smirke/Francis Engleheart. *Don Quixote's Penance on the Mountain* (London: T. Cadell and W. Davies, 1818, burin engraving)

illustrated by Smirke were a complete novelty: *Anselmo, Camila, and Lotario* (*DQ* I: 33) and *Anselmo Fallen on the Ground* (*DQ* I: 35). The first offers a bucolic and romantic image of the three friends at the beginning of the story, while the second focuses on the dramatic ending of the betrayed husband, dazed by his thoughts and tormented by anguish and despair.

During the nineteenth century when this romantic reading flourished, a very different visual interpretation was taking place too. Since the publication of the already mentioned Tonson 1738 edition, where Carteret and Oldfield defended a more serious and deeper reading of Cervantes's novel, the illustrators that had followed this tendency were forced to pay a very high price: to give up the humorous episodes in favor of those with dialogues and speeches. The first victim of this shift was the painter and engraver William Hogarth, precisely one of the most eminent English satirists. Recognizing the value of these humorous episodes as a fundamental part of Cervantes's novel to build up his satire, Hogarth offered seven designs to be included in the Carteret's edition, intent to reinforce the parodic image of some of the characters. Thus, Maritornes and the innkeeper's wife were both represented with grotesque features, as well as the priest in female clothes. Six of these designs, inappropriate and lacking decorum according to Oldfield's criterions, where dismissed, and only one was accepted: *Don Quixote Arrives at the Inn and Encounters the Ladies of Easy Virtue*.[14]

Although Hogarth might have lost this battle, he inaugurated in England a powerful new trend of satirical illustrators that were ready to bring humor back to *Don Quixote*. Two of the most remarkable followers of Hogarth's tradition were the English caricaturists Thomas Rowlandson (1756–1827) and George Cruikshank (1792–1878). Rowlandson was in charge of the illustrations for William Combe's *The Tour of Doctor Syntax in Search of the Picturesque* (1812),[15] a quixotic parody written to satirize the romantic literature of travel. However, for our current purpose, it is Cruikshank who interests us the most. His characteristic style, which goes from the most benevolent humor to the most grotesque satire, made Cruikshank a very adequate candidate to confront *Don Quixote*. The illustrator accepted the challenge twice,[16] first in 1824 for the London: Knight and Lacey edition with Charles Jarvi's translation. It included twenty-four illustrations by Cruikshank, wood-engraved by Sears and William Hughes, and it was reprinted in London: Jones & Co, in 1828 and 1831, and the second time, as part of "Roscoe's Novelists' Library," for the London: E. Wilson, 1833 edition with translation by Tobias Smollett. Cruikshank etched fifteen plates accompanied by three portraits (Don Quixote, Sancho, and Dulcinea), designed by Joseph Kenny Meadows and wood-engraved by J. Smith.

In both editions, Cruikshank selected episodes not according to the visual reading initiated by Oldfield and Vanderbank, but in accordance with the tradition of the early Flemish and Dutch editions (Dordrecht: Savery, 1657; Bruselas: Juan Mommarte, 1662; and Amberes: Geronymo y Juan Bautista Verdussen, 1672–1673). Thus, both sets of illustrations included scenes such as Sancho's blanketing, the fight against the windmills, Don Quixote's penance in Sierra Morena, the attack against the wine-skins, the encounter with the false Dulcinea, Don Quixote's "fight" with the lion, the adventure of Clavileño, the night visit of doña Rodríguez, and Sancho's dinner in Barataria island (figure 2.3)—scenes that we can consider as parodic, perfect examples of the burlesque mode displayed by Cervantes and representative of the laughter and humor exhibited by the novel.

Cruikshank was severely criticized for having made such a selection. Ashbee, in reference to the illustrations in the 1824 edition, declared "they are of not great merit."[17] And Río y Rico, now regarding the etchings of 1833, mentioned that "both artists [Cruikshank and Meadows] show they had not been able to understand the immortal novel,"[18] meaning they were unable to read *Don Quixote* in a deep manner, and thus were limited to the burlesque and comical interpretation. These illustrated readings may seem clumsy, exaggerated, and superficial, more in keeping with the first Flemish editions than with the latter academic, although such considerations are in themselves limited. Cruikshank, as a good caricaturist, recognized Cervantes as someone of his own profession, was able to see the parody in his sense of humor, and, therefore, the path that led to satire, as in the case of Givanel, for whom "Cruikshank is, undoubtedly, a great illustrator of modern times."[19] The English caricaturist, with his disproportionate and gawky Don Quixote, his sometimes exaggeratedly terrified sometimes ingenuously amazed Sancho, his mocking innkeepers and wenches, and his nearly grotesque servants, redeems humor and brings laughter back to *Don Quixote*, consistent with the means used by Cervantes to pierce his spear brilliantly.[20]

William Heath Robinson (1872–1944) was an outstanding follower of this satirical tradition, although his caricatures are not conceived to merely provoke laughter but as subtler parodies. "Not the least attractive feature of the peculiar kind of humour of which Heath Robinson is the chief, if not the sole, exponent—pointed out A. E. Johnson—is the wide range of its possibilities. It can be made the vehicle of satire, fierce or mild, as well as the expression of mere whimsicality."[21] For sure, he can be considered as one of those illustrators especially gifted to confront *Don Quixote*. All along his career he proved to have a remarkable talent for humor and irony, displaying an unparalleled imagination that can only be described as quixotic. We could recall here his well-known designs of

Figure 2.3. George Cruikshank. *The Don & The Duenna* (London: E. Wilson, 1833, etching)

complex inventions and rickety machines that achieved absurdly simple results, parodies of a world ruled by technology and progress that the artist refuses to accept. However, it is in his own works as a writer-illustrator where Heath Robinson shows more clearly his personal interest in Cervantes's novel. In this sense, Robinson's three children's books—*The Adventures of Uncle Lubin* (1902), *Bill the Minder* (1912), and *Peter Quip in Search of a Friend* (1922)—share with *Don Quixote* a fundamental idea: the main character embarking on a peculiar quest through a world where reality gets confused with fantasy.

Heath Robinson had the opportunity of illustrating *Don Quixote* three different times—first, for the London: Sands & Co., 1897 edition, when he drew fifteen black-and-white illustrations that still show Aubrey Beardsley's influence in Robinson's early works. Especially remarkable is the portrait dedicated to Sansón Carrasco, which evokes in a masterly manner his personality according to Cervantes's description: "he was a very great wag; he was of a sallow complexion, but very sharp-witted, somewhere about four-and-twenty years of age, with a round face, a flat nose, and a large mouth, all indications of a mischievous disposition and a love of fun and joke"[22] (*DQ* II: 3) (figure 2.4). The second set of illustrations

Figure 2.4. William Heath Robinson, *The Bachelor Sampson Carrasco* (London: Sands & Co., 1897, process)

was produced for the London/New York: Dent & Sons/Dutton & Co., 1902 edition, which included forty-three black-and-white designs. The third and last set of *Don Quixote* illustrations was composed of eight new scenes in color that, unfortunately, the artist did not see published. They appeared *post mortem* in the London/New York: Dent & Sons/Dutton & Co., 1953 edition, which also included a selection of twenty-six illustrations from the 1902 set. Heath Robinson offers us an outstanding catalog of expressions and human types, as we can see in the illustration titled *Here Don Quixote Could no Longer Contain Himself from Speaking* (DQ I: 45), where the inn guests and other characters mock the barber who was trying to defend the reality of his basin. Furthermore, the illustrator shows constantly a deep respect for the *hidalgo manchego*, avoiding to ridicule him. The images of Don Quixote represented by Heath Robinson suggest tenderness, just as we see in *They Found Him Sitting up in Bed* (DQ II: 1), and fine humor, as it happens with *We Will Turn Shepherds* (DQ II: 67).

Arriving at the twentieth century, we cannot conclude without mentioning, however briefly, another illustrator whose personal, outstanding, and original visual reading have passed unnoticed in comparison with others by better-known and more popular artists. We refer to the Russian book illustrator, architect, and sculptor Savva Brodsky (1923–1982). Brodsky's illustrations were included in the Moscow edition published by Molodaia Guardia in 1976. It included a Cervantes portrait, two frontispieces, headpieces for each chapter, and thirty-nine double page illustrations, all in black and white. Brodsky's style, a kind of expressionist realism with symbolistic tints, is especially suitable to illustrate *Don Quixote*. For the Russian artist, following the writer Ivan Turgenev, the Knight of La Mancha becomes a symbol of idealism, of the defense of higher eternal principles that deserve dedication and sacrifice; a symbol of faith in immutable Truth.

La Mancha is represented as a hostile desert that defeats Don Quixote once and again; a desolate landscape where, despite all the perils and menaces—the soldiers and the galley-slaves,[23] the enemies and monsters imagined by the knight; despite all those who laugh at him—the servants from the episode of Clavileño, the Dukes; the knight is able to pursue his destiny, riding toward a shining horizon of tolling bells. Brodsky does not forget either the comical elements from Cervantes's novel—the flocks of sheep, the herd of pigs, the windmills, Sancho's blanketing . . . nevertheless, these elements serve instead to reinforce Don Quixote's own tragedy. It is difficult to choose only one illustration as the most representative, but perhaps the most significant is the image of Don Quixote, defeated by the Knight of the White Moon, held in Sancho's arms just as a new *Pietà*. Don Quixote has been defeated for us; he has sacrificed himself for us. Aside, a bell still keeps tolling, symbol of the hope that has not died (figure 2.5).

Figure 2.5.   Savva Brodsky, _Don Quixote Defeated by the Knight of the White Moon_ (Moscow: Molodaia Guardia, 1976, process)

   Brodsky proved to have read _Don Quixote_ in such an extraordinary way that, thanks to these illustrations,[24] even the Real Academia de Bellas Artes de San Fernando decided to nominate him as "Académico correspondiente" in Moscow. The title was conferred in 1977, only one year after the publication of the edition, and allowed him to achieve an old dream, to visit Cervantes's homeland. And thus, we can finish our own journey with the words of his speech at the Royal Academy, which denote his absolute admiration for the novel and its characters: "creo que si en el mundo no quedara ni un solo Don Quijote, el mundo sucumbiría."[25]

NOTES

   1. All the editions and illustrations mentioned in this chapter can be consulted in http://dqi.tamu.edu/ (accessed July 15, 2016); for more information about the online project "Iconografía Textual del _Quijote_," see Fernando González et al., "La colección de _Quijotes_ ilustrados del Proyecto Cervantes: catálogo de ediciones y archivo digital de imágenes," _Cervantes. Bulletin of the Cervantes Society of America,_

XXV, 1 (2005): 79–104; and Eduardo Urbina et al., "Visual Knowledge: Textual Iconography of the Quixote," in *Don Quixote Illustrated: Textual Images and Visual Readings*, ed. Eduardo Urbina and Jesús G. Maestro (Pontevedra: Mirabel Editorial/Cátedra Cervantes, 2005), 15–38.

2. Don Quixote believes to be knighted at the inn.

3. Don Quixote served in the inn by the ladies of easy virtue.

4. See *Thierry Lefrançois, Charles Coypel. Peintre du Roi (1694-1752)* (Paris: Arthena, 1994).

5. Cupid wearing Mambrinos's helmet and Dulcinea separating the wheat from the chaff.

6. Ian Jamieson, *Charles-Antoine Coypel. Premier Peintre de Louis XV et Auteur Dramatique (1649-1752)* (Paris: Librairie Hachette, 1930), 70.

7. They were not engraved *Don Quichotte endormi combat contre les outres* (1716) or *Don Quichotte au ball chez don Antonio Moreno* (1731). For a complete study of this set see Fernando González Moreno, "*Don Quichotte Conduit Par La Folie*: la herencia de Charles-Antoine Coypel en las ediciones ilustradas del *Quijote*," *Anuario de Estudios Cervantinos* 4 (2008): 1–50.

8. See Rachel Schmidt, *The Canonization of Don Quixote through Illustrated Editions of the Eighteenth Century* (Québec: McGill-Queen's University Press, 1999), 38–46.

9. See Fernando González Moreno, "Aproximación a una teoría del arte de ilustrar libros: *Quijotes* del siglo XVIII," in *Teoría y literatura artística en España: revisión historiográfica y estudios contemporáneos*, ed. Nuria Rodríguez Ortega and Miguel Taín Guzmán (Madrid: Real Academia de Bellas Artes de San Fernando, 2015), 679–704.

10. See Fernando González Moreno, "Don Quijote en los albores del Romanticismo o el prodigio ilustrado de Tony Johannot," in *Don Quijote, cosmopolita. Nuevos estudios sobre la recepción internacional de la novela cervantina*, coord. Hans Christian Hagedorn (Cuenca: Empresa Pública Sociedad Don Quijote de Conmemoraciones Culturales de Castilla-La Mancha/Ediciones de la Universidad de Castilla-La Mancha, 2009), 343–68.

11. It includes forty-eight chapter illustrations and twenty-six head and tail-pieces engraved by Francis Engleheart, Richard Golding, Abraham Raimbach, James Fittler, John Scott, Anker Smith, James Heath, Charles Heath "the elder," Charles Turner Warren, James Mitan, William Finden, and Cosmo Armstrong. The Tate Britain keeps thirteen of the original paintings used for this edition plus two more canvases by Smirke depicting *Don Quixote* episodes: *The Countess Trifaldi Unveiling* and *Sancho Panza and the Duchess*. These two episodes also appear among the 1818 illustrations, but the compositions of the paintings are not the same as those of the prints; they are different versions.

12. The romantic virus could not, in fact, attack the Cervantine hero harder. Juan Givanel y Mas and "Gaziel," *Historia gráfica de Cervantes y del Quijote* (Madrid: Plus Ultra, 1946), 186–88.

13. This romantic interest in Orientalism can be also seen in the representation, for the first time, of the Arabian historian Cide Hamete Benengeli (*DQ* I: 9).

14. *The Funeral of Chrystom and Marcella Vindicating Herself, The Innkeeper's Wife and Daughter Taking Care of the Don after Being Beaten and Bruised, Don Quixote*

Seizes the Barber's Bason for Mambrino's Helmet, Don Quixote Releases the Galley Slaves, The Unfortunate Knight of the Rock Meeting Don Quixote, and The Curate and Barber Disguising Themselves to Convey Don Quixote Home.

15. Originally published in Rudolph Ackermann's *Poetical Magazine* (1809–1811). This first collaboration between Rowlandson and Combe was followed by *The Second Tour of Dr. Syntax: In Search of Consolation* (1820) and *The Third Tour of Dr. Syntax: In Search of a Wife* (1821).

16. Cruikshank also illustrated other quixotic works, such as George Buxton's *The Political Quixote, or The Adventures of the Renowned Don Blackibo Dwarfino, and his Trusty Squire, Seditiono: a Romance, in which are Introduced Many Popular Celebrated Political Characters of the Present Day* (1820), and Henry David Inglis's *Rambles in the Footsteps of Don Quixote* (1837). See Fernando González Moreno and Beatriz González Moreno, *Andanzas tras los pasos de don Quijote por H. D. Inglis* (Vigo: Editorial Academia del Hispanismo, 2012), 15–64.

17. Henry Spencer Ashbee, *An Iconography of Don Quixote, 1605-1895* (London: Printed for the author by the University Press, Aberdeen, and issued by the Bibliographical Society, 1895), 140.

18. "Ambos artistas demuestran que no habían sabido entender la inmortal novela." Gabriel-Martín del Río y Rico, *Catálogo bibliográfico de la sección de Cervantes de la Biblioteca Nacional* (Madrid: Tipografía de la Revista de Archivos, Bibliotecas y Museos, 1930), 497.

19. "Cruikshank es, indudablemente, un gran dibujante de los nuevos tiempos." Givanel, *Historia gráfica*, 198. We cannot avoid recalling here the use of this same expression by Charles Baudelaire in reference to Constatin Guys, declared as "painter of modern life."

20. Paraphrasing the *motto* used in the traditional allegory of Satire: "Irridens Cuspide Figo" (Mocking, I pierce the spear). In fact, the London: J. Cooke, 1774 *Don Quixote* edition included a frontispiece with this allegory and this *motto*, plus the poem: "When Whims and Madness had possess'd each Knight, / Who fancy'd he was only born to fight, / This well tim'd Satire with plain Truth combin'd, / At once gave Pleasure and Reform'd the Mind."

21. A. E. Johnson, *The Book of W. Heath Robinson. Brush, Pen, and Pencil* (London: Adam and Charles Black, 1913), 37.

22. "Muy gran socarrón, de color macilenta, pero de muy buen entendimiento: tendría hasta veinte y cuatro años, carirredondo, de nariz chata y de boca grande, señales todas de ser de condición maliciosa, y amigo de donaires y de burlas."

23. The image of the galley-slaves recall that of the *Burghers of Calais* by Rodin (1884–18-89), which commemorate an episode of self-sacrifice and mercy.

24. *Don Quixote* was not the only Spanish literary work illustrated by Brodsky, also Juan Valera's *Pepita Jiménez*, Manuel de Falla's *El sombrero de tres picos*, Benito Pérez Galdós's *Doña Perfecta*, and Vicente Blasco Ibáñez's *Sangre y arena*.

25. I believe that if there were not a single Don Quixote in the world, the world would succumb. Savva Brodsky's record and complete speech is kept in the Archive of the Real Academia de Bellas Artes de San Fernando (Madrid, Spain).

3

Don Quixote in the Rise of Modern Novel: The Satirical Interpretation[1]

Emilio Martínez Mata

It is well known that *Don Quixote* has been one of the most influential works in Western literature. That influence has been exerted through two very different ways. On one hand, from German Romanticism on, *Don Quixote* has become a myth used to express the duality of human souls, the fight between the spiritual, noble, profound part and the material one, that is, gross reality. That fight is known to be doomed to failure, which contributes to highlight its nobleness. According to that interpretation, Cervantes had shown us the unavoidable failure of the purest aspirations when confronted to stubborn reality. That is the origin of expressions used in many languages, such as *quixotic* and others, used even by people who have not read the novel to characterize endeavors unfortunately doomed to failure.

On the other hand, *Don Quixote* is in the origin of modern novel due to its influence upon the main British novelists of the eighteenth century—Fielding, Smollett, Sterne—who, on their behalf, laid the foundations for the great novel of the nineteenth century, in which the mark of *Don Quixote* is significant.[2] The list of the main nineteenth-century novelists that show a decisive Cervantine influence is impressive: Jane Austen, Dickens, Mark Twain, Herman Melville, Stendhal, Flaubert, Turgenev, Dostoyevsky, Tolstoy, Galdós, Clarín, and so many others.

The influence of *Don Quixote* is not limited to characters and episodes but it determines the conception of modern novel itself. The most important trace is doubtlessly the so-called "quixotic principle," the adoption of an identity according to literary characters,[3] which the novelists from the eighteenth and nineteenth centuries understood as the formulation of imbalance between literature and real life but was interpreted by Romantic novelists as the imbalance between the individual and the world (which gave cause for seeing the Cervantine novel as the first example of the struggle of the self against the external, hostile world as twentieth-century critics have understood it ever since the well-known formulation by Gyorgy Lukács).[4] Of course, we can also find other evident influences, such as the ambivalent portrayal of the characters (Don Quixote is sane and insane at the same time, Sancho is simple but witty, no character is totally good or bad),[5] the irony, or the two-way dialogue between the writer and the reader.

To achieve this result from the simple burlesque interpretation of *Don Quixote* in the seventeenth century, a decisive change was needed. It took place during the late seventeenth century and the early eighteenth century in England, due to the convergence of several factors. The spread of *Don Quixote* during the Age of Enlightenment, which turned it into one of the most influential works in Europe, cannot be explained just by the ideological and cultural changes that took place in this period, nor by the boom of the novelistic genre, as it has been traditionally accepted (that is the explanation by Paolo Cherchi and Anthony Close).[6] Those circumstances doubtlessly contributed to that spread, but they were not decisive by themselves, as shown by the fact that the process does not follow a parallel development in different countries and the interpretation of the Cervantine novel also differs.

The matter of which influence of *Don Quixote* was more decisive on eighteenth century novelists, those who would eventually be the basis for modern novel, has been widely discussed, but there has not been enough focus on why that influence occurred, the reasons why a burlesque work, pulp fiction at any rate, could trigger such a rich and complex process. I intend to analyze one of the factors that, in my opinion, became the causes of that process, which was so significant for the development of modern novel: the satirical interpretation of *Don Quixote* that spread in Britain during the late seventeenth century and the first half of the eighteenth century.

The interpretation of *Don Quixote* along the eighteenth century cannot be explained by neoclassical aesthetics and Enlightenment thought alone. Actually, those factors were practically common—to a greater or lesser degree—among intellectual elites throughout Europe; however, their consequences regarding the interpretation of *Don Quixote* were not the same. Proof of this can be seen in the fact that its interpretation in eighteenth-century Britain differs significantly from the interpretation in other countries such as France or Spain, although neoclassical aesthetics was common and their intellectual elite had also assimilated Enlightenment thought. What is going to provide the novel with that significance along the century is the confluence of a number of factors that took place in Britain during the late seventeenth century and in the early eighteenth century. In addition to its editorial success, *Don Quixote* achieved a much greater intellectual weight than any other fiction work along the Age of Enlightenment and eventually became a reference work beyond the field of novel.

There is an Enlightenment feature that played a relevant role in that process of change in the appraisal of *Don Quixote*. It is the huge importance given to critical thought, to the extent of defining the prevailing intellectual attitude during the Age of Enlightenment, in the same way as wit had prevailed during the Baroque period. That extraordinary dimension achieved by critical thought is explained by the fact of having become the basis of any cultural and intellectual endeavor. There are many proofs of that from the end of the seventeenth century. Boileau had stated in *L'Art poétique* (1674) that satire was the main genre and that he could not find a verse for praising but he could find a lot for condemning. Muratori demanded that men of letters or wise men, disregarding the particular field they devoted to (from poetry to optics or mechanics, including moral philosophy and even theology), have good taste, erudition, and critical capacity ("cio`si faccia con buen gusto, con critica ed erudizione").[7] That rise of critical attitude is also confirmed by those who show concern about it, like Mabillon and Bossuet, who complain that it is the illness of their time.[8] Even Lord Shaftesbury, perhaps as an explanation for its frequency at that time, finds a surprising addiction to satire in man, in spite of his natural tendency toward sociability (which would oppose to criticism of other men): "As fond as men are of company, and as little able to enjoy any happiness out of it, they are yet strangely addicted to the way of satire."[9]

In accordance with that spirit, British novelists express the critical or moral spirit of their creations, far from mere amusement as an objective. Richardson makes clear the instructive nature of his *Pamela* in its very title (*Pamela or Virtue Rewarded . . . In order to cultivate the Principles of Virtue and Religion in the Minds of the Youth of Both Sexes*).[10] Fielding, in the dedication page of *Amelia*, expresses the satirical purpose of the novel and how it is not addressed to individual faults but to social ones:

> The following Book is sincerely designed to promote the Cause of Virtue, and to expose some of the most glaring Evils, as well public as private, which at present infest the Country; tho' there is scarce, as I remember, a single Stroke of Satire aimed at anyone Person throughout the whole.[11]

In an article published in *The Covent Garden Journal* (1752), Fielding makes a defense of satirical purposes in novels as opposite to mere entertainment ("diversion is a secondary consideration"). Showing moral defects and emphasizing virtues should be the priority objective. That is why he praises the great satire masters, Lucian, Cervantes, and Swift, who had been able to combine it with humor:

> Few men, I believe, do more admire the Works of those great Masters who have sent their Satire (if I may use the Expression) laughing into the World. Such are that great Triumvirate, Lucian, Cervantes, and Swift. These Authors I shall ever hold in the highest Degree of Esteem; not indeed for that Wit and Humour alone which they all so eminently possess, but because they all endeavoured, with the utmost Force of their Wit and Humour, to expose and extirpate those Follies and Vices which chiefly prevailed in their several Countries.[12]

Fielding relies on Horace to criticize the interest in mere pastime, and at the same time he advocates humor as an instrument of satire:

> Writers are not, I presume, to be considered as mere Jack-Puddings, whose Business it is only to excite Laughter: This, indeed, may sometimes be intermixed, and served up, with graver Matters, in order to titillate the Palate, and to recommend wholesome Food to the Mind; and, for this Purpose, it hath been used by many excellent Authors: *for why* (as Horace says) *should not any one promulgate Truth with a Smile on his Countenance?* (159)

In that same writing, he also defends the usefulness of wit and humor in order to communicate a moral purpose, using Richardson's words:

> When Wit and Humour are introduced for such good Purposes, when the agreeable *is blended with the useful, then is* the Writer said *to have succeeded in every Point. Pleasantry* (as the ingenious Author of Clarissa says of a Story) *should be made only the Vehicle of Instruction.* (159)

It is therefore not surprising that, in the preface of *Joseph Andrews*, Fielding distances himself from *romances*, that is, novels like Honoré d'Urfé's *Astrea*, Calprenède's *Casandra*, or Scudéry's *Clelia* for their "very little instruction or entertainment."[13] In the same direction, Fielding proclaims Cervantes's satirical purpose together with the reader's entertainment: "Cervantes is to be considered as an Author who intended not only the Diversion, but the Instruction and Reformation of his Countrymen."[14]

The satirical purpose that people from the eighteenth century value in novels can be found in *Don Quixote* thanks to an interpretation widely spread throughout Europe, by French Jesuit René Rapin, who highlights *Don Quixote* within satire in his book about poetics *Réflexions sur la poétique d'Aristote et sur les ouvrages des poètes anciens et modernes* (1674), immediately translated to English and widely spread, to the extent of turning Rapin into the most influential French critic in the Britain of the late seventeenth and early eighteenth centuries.[15] Rapin interprets *Don*

Quixote as a satire, not on books of chivalry but on chivalric values, so deeply rooted in Spanish aristocracy. The result would then be a very subtle satire on the whole country because all the Spanish nobility was obstinate about it.[16]

The idea was adopted and disseminated by Louis Moréri in *Le Grand Dictionnaire Historique*, a work widely spread throughout Europe.[17] The result was the great acceptance it had, particularly in France, Germany, and Great Britain. In France, it was repeated, among others, by Madame de Lambert, Baudouin, Jean-François Peyron, and the Marquis of Mirabeau. In Great Britain, it was referred to by, at least, William Temple, lord Shaftesbury, Motteaux, Steele, *The Examiner*, William King, Daniel Defoe, lord Carteret, Warburton, William Collins, Fielding, Hurd, *The Monthly Mirror . . .* [18]

Rapin's interpretation ended up gaining unexpected political relevance when William Temple accused *Don Quixote* of being responsible for the decadence of the Spanish Empire by debilitating the virtues that had encouraged the Spanish people and made it possible. *Don Quixote* had been "A great Cause of the Ruin of Spain, or of its Greatness and Power" because "after Don Quixot appeared, and with that inimitable Wit and Humour turned all this Romantic Honour and Love into Ridicule; the *Spaniards* . . . began to grow ashamed of both, and to laugh at Fighting and Loving . . . this *Spaniard* would need have pass for a great Cause of the Ruin of *Spain*, or of its Greatness and Power."[19] The explanation for this surprising reasoning can be found in the words by Jean-François Peyron mentioning the risk of having debilitated the heroism that characterized the Spanish nation with this satire on chivalry: "He had corrected his country from their enthusiasm for great adventures; he had cast, by means of his *Don Quixote*, indelible embarrassment over the books of chivalry, and perhaps he should be censured for having weakened those heroic feelings, that energy of character, that greatness of soul which honoured the Spanish nation."[20] Still at the beginning of the nineteenth century, Navarrete would still consider the knightly spirit forged during the *Reconquista* war as the prime mover of Spain's overseas achievements during the sixteenth century.[21]

Peyron's explanation is connected to the supposed Spanish pride as a national cliché (expressed by Peyron in an ennobling manner as "energy of character") in a time when national clichés were considered fully truthful. This alleged Spanish pride is clearly linked to the chivalric —and aristocratic—idea of honor, which would justify, even demand, pride as a means of bringing it to bear socially. This would give credit to Rapin's symbolic interpretation of *Don Quixote* as a satire on Spanish aristocracy. This cliché had been current from the sixteenth century on, and Cervantes himself refers to it: "They seemed liberal and restrained with everyone, far from the arrogance commonly attributed to Spaniards" (*La señora Cornelia*) and "Spaniards are welcome and approved . . . the cause is that . . . they do not give rise to showing their condition, known as arrogant" (*Persiles*).[22]

That cliché was current in the eighteenth century. Montesquieu mentions the Spaniards' seriousness and hubris in his *Lettres persannes*, and Cadalso certifies the "vanity and pride commonly attributed to us [Spaniards] by strangers."[23]

Rapin's interpretation of *Don Quixote* as a satire on Spain will have very different consequences in Great Britain with respect to France. The centuries-old enmity between France and Spain is to blame for the propaganda against Spain developed by French authors. The so-called "Black Legend" against Spain focuses on the activities of the Inquisition and the cruelty and greed of Spaniards during the conquest of America. Consequently, in France Rapin's interpretation of *Don Quixote* would be one more element in that unfavorable attitude toward their neighboring country, with which so many military confrontations had taken place.

In Great Britain, on the contrary, the hostility toward Spain from the late sixteenth century had been substituted by political rivalry with France. The different historical and political context of Great Britain undoubtedly favored that Rapin's interpretation was not considered from a political perspective, the old confrontation between nations, but from an ideological one: the Spain supposedly satirized by Cervantes would represent, more than any other country (due to the specific circumstances or the Reconquest war, as Peyron explained), the aristocratic ideology, ultimately feudal, and consequently the "ancien régime" that they intended to leave behind.

The British novelists of the eighteenth century had noted, following Fielding's pattern, that *Don Quixote* showed itself as a parody just to pursue an objective of a totally different nature. For them, there was not the slightest doubt that *Don Quixote* started as a parody but, behind that appearance, its objective was, according to Rapin's interpretation, not a literary satire but an ideological one.

Fielding shows that he took René Rapin's interpretation very seriously. In his review of *The Female Quixote* (1752), by Charlotte Lennox, he identifies in *Don Quixote* a critical purpose with respect to a behavior controlled by chivalric codes, which he supposes generalized in Spain in Cervantes's time and describes as "a vicious Folly":

> Cervantes is to be considered as an Author who intended not only the Diversion, but the Instruction and Reformation of his Countrymen: With this Intention he levelled his Ridicule at a vicious Folly, which in his Time universally prevailed in Spain, and had almost converted a civilized People in a Nation of Cut-throats.[24]

On the other hand, in Spain Gregorio Mayans himself, the scholar who writes "Life of Miguel de Cervantes Saavedra" commissioned by lord Calteret as a preface for his edition of *Don Quixote* (London, 1738), refers to the satirical dimension of the novel in a very vague way (and, of course, noticing no objective of ideological nature). As he does not know Rapin's interpretation, he is unable to identify the target of that satirical interpretation (obviously apart from books of chivalry). That is to say, Mayans praises *Don Quixote* as a satire simply because it is a category esteemed by neoclassical authors, in the same way he also praises the simplicity of its style, its decorum and authenticity, qualities that meet the aesthetical principles generally accepted.

The quixotic model had already been used by Samuel Butler in the seventeenth century to satirize the excesses of Puritanism in his *Hudibras*, a narrative verse-satire in three parts (1663, 1664, and 1678). The success of *Hudibras* was remarkable, with more than eighty reprints along the seventeenth and eighteenth centuries, and it was translated to French and German.[25] But the model of satire that *Hudibras* represents differs from the one perceived in *Don Quixote* in the eighteenth century. Unlike the kind satire of the Cervantine novel, Butler's work shows a degrading criticism typical of the baroque style.

A sample of that new look on *Don Quixote* and the different appraisal of its protagonist in England from the late seventeenth century is Samuel Johnson's comment reproaching Butler for having turned his hero Hudibras into a mere object of scorn, far from the virtues that Cervantes attributes to don Quixote. While Cervantes had provided him with such good judgment and virtue as to retain our appreciation in spite of his generally ridiculous behavior (but never despicable thanks to the author's unrivaled skill), Butler had not been sensitive enough as to provide his hero with any quality to avoid laughter and scorn:

> Cervantes had so much kindness for Don Quixote, that, however he embarrasses him with absurd distresses, he gives him so much sense and virtue as may preserve our esteem; wherever he is, or whatever he does, he is made by matchless dexterity commonly ridiculous, but never contemptible.
>
> But for poor Hudibras, his poet had no tenderness; he chooses not that any pity should be shown or respect paid him; he gives him up at once to laughter and contempt, without any quality that can dignify or protect him. (119–20)

Samuel Johnson's opinion, when confronting Cervantes's satire to Butler's, reflects the different nature of Enlightenment and Baroque satires. While Baroque satire uses a cruel and insulting tone, addressing individual behaviors, Enlightenment satire, which originates at the beginning of the century in England with Addison and Steele, makes use of an ironic, even good-natured tone, and addresses an abstract objective.

Steele characterizes real satire as a result of the satirist's good nature, which leads to condemning bad habits without insulting persons:

> That Good-Nature was an essential Quality in a Satyrist, and that all the Sentiments which are beautiful in this Way of Writing must proceed from that Quality in the Author. Good-Nature produces a Disdain of all baseness, Vice, and Folly, which prompts them to express themselves with Smartness against the Errors of Men, without Bitterness towards their Persons (*Tatler*, no. 242, October 10th, 1710).[26]

On his behalf, Addison condemns personal satire along the same lines, referring to its harmful effects: "Lampoons and Satyrs, that are written with Wit and Spirit, are like poison'd Darts, which not only inflict a Wound, but make it incurable" (*Spectator*, no. 23, March 27th, 1711).[27]

William Temple praises Cervantes as a satirist, contrasting him to Rabelais for not having used in his satire the malice and obscenity that he reproaches in Rabelais, so, in his opinion, *Don Quixote* is the highest example of satiric style:

> The Matchless Writer of *Don Quixot* is much more to be admired for having made up so excellent a Composition of Satyr or Ridicule without those Ingredients [the malice and smut that he throws in Rabelais's face], and seems to be the best and highest Strain that ever was or will be reached by that Vein. ("Of Poetry," 102)[28]

That praise of Cervantes by William Temple takes place within the context of his negative opinion about the use of ridicule ("another Vein which has entred and helpt to Corrupt our modern Poesy is that of Ridicule," 3:101), which highlights the specific nature of Cervantes's satire, very different from Butler's, whose *Hudibras* he points at as an example of burlesque.[29]

The satirical interpretation of *Don Quixote* had already been shown by Fielding during his period as a playwright. In *Don Quixote in England*, which was performed in 1734 but whose writing had started in 1727, Fielding turns Don Quixote, moved to England in an electoral period, into an instrument to satirize the bad habits of British society: hypocrisy and corruption. Remembering the ambivalent nature of the Cervantine hero (mad regarding chivalry but wise and sane for everything else), Don Quixote's speeches are used to criticize general hypocrisy and interest for money (marriages of convenience).

That obsessive but trustworthy Don Quixote in *Don Quixote in England* corresponds to the Parson Adams in *Joseph Andrews* (1742). This novel begins as a parody—on Richardson's *Pamela* (1740)—thanks to the character who entitles the novel, *Pamela*'s main character's brother, passionate reader of his sister's letters (that is to say, the text of Richardson's novel, because, following the fashion of epistolary novels, *Pamela* is made up of the letters between the protagonist and her parents). Joseph is guided by his sister's moral model to turn down the seduction attempts by his mistress, a parallel situation in which the victim is not a young lady but a young man and the results are opposite. While in Richardson's *Pamela* the protagonist's virtue is rewarded with her marriage to her master, in Fielding's novel Joseph loses his job. From that moment on, Joseph becomes to some extent a Sancho Panza, the counterpart of quixotic Parson Adams for his prudence and pragmatism. In the manner of Don Quixote, Adams perceives the world through his literary models, although they are not the discredited and anachronistic books of chivalry but the classics and the Bible, models that are universally accepted although the adventures that happen to them show that real society is far from those theoretical models. As a consequence, satire takes place by the contrast between the hypocrisy and cynicism of that society and the theoretical model that society should follow, the Bible. It is Adams's ingenuity, constantly colliding with a society that is far from its model, what highlights that contrast and, as a result, the social faults that are satirized.

The satirical interpretation that British novelists perceived in *Don Quixote* following a particular path of the way opened by Rapin, that is, the satire of some ideological values they confront, rescued *Don Quixote* from the dead end where the burlesque interpretation had placed it, as a mere parody of the books of chivalry with no other function but entertainment.

Reading *Don Quixote* as a simple parodic novel did not bring about relevant consequences in the conception of the novel. As an example, that can be seen in Spain, where *Don Quixote* did not provoke any changes in the evolution of the novel as a genre (until the influence of French and British Realism arrived in the nineteenth century). In the seventeenth century it is seen, in the same way as in other countries, as a burlesque work, valued as an entertainment for its amenity but lacking any other significance.

Juan de Monmarte says so in his preface to his 1662 edition. Despite being interested, as its publisher, in highlighting the merits of *Don Quixote*, Monmarte is unable to note any other values apart from entertainment: "Minor in substance ['in its contents'] for being a book of chivalry, a mockery of the old ones and entertainment for the future, made up just to pass time in idleness."[30]

Until the late seventeenth century, *Don Quixote* is assessed in all countries as a minor work that has gained popularity, but it does not produce any interesting comments. It becomes a source of arguments, mainly for playwrights, but it has no significant effects on the novel. In Spain we have to wait for José Francisco de Isla's *Fray Gerundio* (1758) to find some relevant influence (apart, of course, from the second part of *Don Quixote* published in 1614 under the name of "Alonso Fernández de Avellaneda"). The very nature of *Fray Gerundio*, a parodic satire on the excesses of baroque preaching (in which the features of Gongoristic style were taken to the extreme of the most ridiculous paroxysm), shows to what extent the interpretation from the previous century remained in the Spain of the first half of the eighteenth century.

The editorial trajectory of *Don Quixote* shows the impact of its change in interpretation. In the sixteenth century, *Don Quixote* had achieved remarkable popularity but it had not been a relevant editorial success. Its twenty-six editions are far from, for example, Mateo Alemán's *Guzmán de Alfarache* (1599), with the same number of reprints just in the first five years, or other works such as Jorge de Montemayor's *Diana* (1559), a pastoral romance reprinted twenty-six times in forty years (proportionally two times those of *Don Quixote*).

After the initial success in the first years, *Don Quixote* soon begins an evident editorial decline, partly alleviated by its illustrated editions. Despite the rise due to the commercial attraction of illustrated editions, at the end of the century we find a thirty-year period without any edition in Spain.

On the contrary, during the Enlightenment a real editorial blooming takes place. Sixty-five editions are published in France, fifty-three in Britain (there had been only nine in the seventeenth century), thirty-seven in Spain, eleven in Germany, eight in Holland, four in Italy, three in Ireland, two in Russia, one in Portugal, Austria, Denmark, and Poland.

The extraordinary dimension achieved by *Don Quixote* in the eighteenth century would be inconceivable for a simple clownish work, a parody of an out-of-style literary genre, or a social prototype. The identification of transcendental contents in the Cervantine novel, transformed in a satire of the values of the Old Regime (especially identified with Spain), is the reactant that provides *Don Quixote* with a different consideration and a much higher consideration, which allows the British novelists of the eighteenth century to perceive the richness of the narrative resources used by Cervantes.

The satire of chivalric values that British novelists see in *Don Quixote* acquires a very different dimension from the conscience of a new dimension of the world, which wants to break away from the past. We know that, at the beginning of the eighteenth century, a noticeable awareness of the change of epoch takes place, from some social values to other new ones, formulated by means of very expressive images such as the one that gives the period its name: "the Enlightenment" is the light that banishes ignorance, prejudices, and substituted values. That image symbolically condenses that new ideological attitude and the awareness of an age that sees itself as very different from the past and oriented to social progress.

The aristocratic values of the "ancient regime" are rejected and sub-stituted by others that pursue "public happiness," incompatible with the aristocratic individualism of the knightly world. Role models are now social, oriented not to honor or fame (of individual character) but to common good, to the whole society. That is why the interpretation of *Don Quixote* as a satire of chivalric, feudal values gives the novel an un-expected harmony with these new times, which undoubtedly contributes to its extraordinary success during the Enlightenment and to the fact that its success goes together with the esteem of critics, unlike what had hap-pened in the seventeenth century.

The literalness of Don Quixote's formulations about his purposes ("do good to all, evil to none," "defend helpless maidens") has contributed to a great extent to the fact that we now see chivalric values in an idealized manner. But aristocratic, knightly values (bravery, pride, defense of honor sword in hand) are values of an individual nature, not collective, since they are oriented mainly to individual rather than social aims (personal glory). On the contrary, the Enlightment supports social values, oriented to the community and pursuing "common happiness," common welfare.

Spanish and French re-creations of *Don Quixote*—and the British ones from the seventeenth century—had used it, apart from as a source for epi-sodes or characters, as a model of parody of a literary genre, not of some principles. What those re-creations reflect is that, anyway, *Don Quixote* remained a burlesque work. British novelists, from Fielding on, provide it with a very different consideration when they interpret it as a satire with an abstract character and good-natured, accordingly with their concept of satire. That high esteem allowed them to go beyond the repertoire of episodes and characters and adopt a whole conception of the novel, in which the "quixotic principle" (the imbalance between literature and reality) was essential, but also other features, such as the ambivalent por-trayal of the characters, the irony and the accomplice dialogue between the author and the reader thanks to the autonomy and ironic capacity that Cervantes grants to the narrating voice, truly revolutionary. Those fea-tures had gone practically unnoticed when *Don Quixote* was considered a mere literary parody of an old-fashioned genre, but the British novelists of the eighteenth century admired them and so turned *Don Quixote* into the grounds for modern novel.

NOTES

1. This work has been funded by Spanish Economy and Competitiveness Min-istry (Ref.:FFI2014-56414-P).

2. The bibliography about the Cervantine influence on the British novel of the eighteenth century is very wide. A synthetic and accurate review of that bibliography can be seen in Pedro Javier Pardo García, "La tradición cervantina en la novela inglesa: De Henry Fielding a William Thackeray," in *Entre Cervantes y Shakespeare: Sendas del Renacimiento*, ed. Zenón Luis-Martínez y Luis Gómez Canseco (Newark: Juan de la Cuesta, 2006), 73–75. Now see John A. Garrido Ardila, "Las rutas del *Quijote* por la novela inglesa del siglo XVIII," *Cuadernos de Estudios del Siglo XVIII* (2016).

3. Harry Levin, "The Quixotic Principle: Cervantes and Other Novelist," in *The Interpretation of Narrative: Theory and Practice*, ed. Morton W. Bloomfield (Cambridge, MA: Harvard University Press, 1970), 45–66.

4. Gyorgy Lukács, *Teoría de la novela* (Barcelona: Edasa, 1971).

5. About this feature in the characters, see E. Martínez Mata, "La caracterización de los personajes en el *Quijote*," in *Cervantes y los cauces de la novela* (Madrid: Visor, 2014), 157–77.

6. Paolo Cherchi, *Capitoli di critica cervantina (1605-1789)* (Rome: Bulzoni, 1977). Anthony Close, *The Romantic Approach to "Don Quixote"* (Cambridge: Cambridge University Press, 1978).

7. Muratori, *I primi disegni della Repubblica Letteraria d'Italia* (1703), in Pedro Álvarez de Miranda, *Palabras e ideas: el léxico de la Ilustración temprana en España (1680-1760)* (Madrid: Real Academia Española, 1992), 511.

8. Mabillon, *Traité des études monastiques*, 1691, Bossuet, *Maximes et réflexions sur la comédie*, 1692 (quoted in Pedro Álvarez de Miranda, *Palabras e ideas*, 517–18).

9. Lord Shaftesbury, *The Moralists, A Philosophical Rhapsody*, in *Characteristics of Men, Manners, Opinions, Times*, ed. John M. Robertson (Indianapolis: The Bobbs-Merrill Company, 1964), II: 84.

10. *Pamela or Virtue Rewarded. In a Series of Familiar Letters from a Beautiful Young Damsel, to her Parents. In order to cultivate the Principles of Virtue and Religion in the Minds of the Youth of Both Sexes. A Narrative which has its Foundation in Truth and Nature* (1740).

11. Henry Fielding, *Amelia* (1751), ed. M. Battestin (Middletown, CT: Wesleyan University Press, 1984), 3.

12. *The Covent Garden Journal*, no. 10 (February 4, 1752), in *The Criticism of Henry Fielding*, ed. Ioan Williams (London: Routledge & Kegan Paul, 1970), 160.

13. "Such are those voluminous Works, commonly called Romances, namely, *Clelia, Cleopatra, Astraea, Cassandra*, the *Grand Cyrus*, and innumerable others, which contain, as I apprehend, very little Instruction or Entertainment," Henry Fielding, *Joseph Andrews*, "Author's Preface."

14. In his review of *The Female Quixote* (1752), de Charlotte Lennox: *The Covent Garden Journal*, 24 (March 24, 1752), in Fielding, *The Criticism . . .* , 191–92.

15. About this interpretation and its impact in France, Britain, Germany, and Spain, see Emilio Martínez Mata, "El *Quijote*, sátira antiespañola," *Voz y Letra* 16.1–2 (2005): 95–104.

16. "Ce grand homme, ayant ésté traité avec quelque mépris par le duc de Lerme, premier ministre de Philippe III, qui n'avoit nulle considération pour les sçavans, écrivit le roman de *Don Quichot*, qui est une satyre trés fine de la nation: parce que toute la noblesse d' Espagne, qu'il rend ridicule par cet ouvrage,

s'éstait entêtée de chevalerie." Translation to English: "This great man having been slighted, and received some disgrace by the Duke of *Lerma*, chief *Minister* of State of *Philip* III, who had no respect for Men of Learning, writ the Romance of *Don Quixot*, which is a most fine and ingenious Satyr on his own Country; because the Nobility of *Spain*, whom he renders ridiculous by this work, were all bit in the head and intoxicated with Knight-errantry," Thomas Rymer (1674).

17. "Il y fut traité avec quelque mépris par le Duc de Lerma, premier ministre de Philippe III, Roy d'Espagne. Pour se vanger de ce Ministre, qui n'avoit aucune consideration pour les gens de Lettres, il compose le roman de *Don Quichot*, qui est un ouvrage incomparable et une Satire trés fine de la nation, parce que toute la noblesse d'Espagne, qu'il rende ridicule par ce livre, s'etoit entêtée de Chevalerie. Le vers tronquez, qu'on y void au commencement, témoignent que cette piece regardoit principalment le Duc de Lerme, car son nom y est caché avec addresse," Louis Moréri, *Le Grand Dictionnaire Historique* (1681).

18. Apart from the German references mentioned in Martínez Mata, "El *Quijote, sátira antiespañola,*" see D. G. Mohorf (1700) and J. B. Mencke (1745), quoted in Carmen Rivero, *La recepción e interpretación del Quijote en la Alemania del siglo XVIII* (Argamasilla de Alba: City Council of Argamasilla de Alba, 2011), 116–17.

19. William Temple, "An Essay upon Ancient and Modern Learning" (1690), in *Critical Essays of the Seventeenth Century*, ed. J. E. Spingarn (Bloomington: Indiana University, 1957), 3, 71–72.

20. "Il avoit corrigé sa nation de son ardeur pour les grandes aventures; il avoit jeté par son *Don Quichote* un ridicule inéfaçable sur les romans de chevalerie; & peut-être doit-on lui reprocher d'avoir énérvé ces sentiments héroïques, cette énergie de caractère, cette grandeur d'âme qui distinguoient la nation espagnole," Jean-François Peyron, *Nouveau voyage en Espagne fait en 1777 et 1778* . . . , t. II, 233–34.

21. Martín Fernández de Navarrete, *Don Álvaro de Bazán, primer marqués de Santa Cruz* (1830). In *Marinos y descubridores* (Madrid: Atlas, 1944), 113.

22. "Mostrábanse con todos liberales y comedidos, y muy ajenos de la arrogancia que dicen que suelen tener los españoles," *Novelas ejemplares*, ed. J. García López (Madrid: Real Academia Española, 2013), 482; "Son bien vistos y recibidos los españoles . . . es la causa que . . . no dan lugar a mostrar su condición, tenida por arrogante," *Persiles*, ed. C. Romero (Madrid: Cátedra, 2002), 610–11.

23. Referred to in Emilio Martínez Mata, "El *Quijote*, sátira antiespañola."

24. Henry Fielding, *The Covent Garden Journal* 24 (March 24, 1752), in Fielding, *The Criticism* . . . , 191–92.

25. *Hudibras* had even been commented upon by Voltaire (in *Letters concerning the English Nation*, London, 1733: 212–13) and adapted by Thomas D'Urfey (*Butler's Ghost: or Hudibras. The Fourth part*) and Edward Ward (*The life . . . merrily translated into Hudibrastick verse*, 1710–1712). It also had a scholar edition with historical notes: *Hudibras in Three Parts, written in the Time of the Late Wars. Corrected and Amended with Large Annotations and a Preface by Zachary Grey, Ll.D.*, vol. I, (Dublin: Robert Owen and William Brien: 1744). A reference to the reprints of *Hudibras* in Agapita Jurado Santos, *Recorridos del Quijote por Europa (siglos XVII y XVIII)* (Kassel: Reichenberger, 2015): 11, 84, 127, 171–72, 203.

26. In Ronald Paulson, *Don Quixote in England* (Baltimore and London: The Johns Hopkins University Press, 1988), 23.

27. In Paulson, *Don Quixote in England*, 23.

28. William Temple, "Of Poetry," in *Critical Essays of the Seventeenth Century*, ed. J. E. Spingarn (Bloomington: Indiana University, 1957), 3: 102.

29. "In *English* by Sir *John Mince, Hudibras,* and *Cotton,* and with greater height of *Burlesque* in the *English* than, I think, in any other Language," William Temple, "Of Poetry," 3:102.

30. "Menor en la sustancia ['en su contenido'] por ser una novela de caballerías, toda burla de las antiguas y entretenimiento de las venideras, inventado sólo para pasar tiempo en la ociosidad." *Vida y hechos del ingenioso caballero don Quijote de la Mancha* (Bruselas, Juan de Monmarte, 1662), Dedication, 4.

4

Don Quixote and the Chivalric Ideal in Classics Illustrated Comics (1941–1971)

Ricardo Castells

For three decades Albert Lewis Kanter's Classics Illustrated comic books presented the first series of graphic novels in the United States, with a total of 169 different titles and sales of over 200 million volumes.[1] Kanter's family emigrated from Russia to escape the pogroms when he was seven years old, and even as a young man he was an avid reader and letter writer despite never finishing high school.[2] His Classics Illustrated collection—originally titled Classic Comics—consisted primarily of editions of forty-eight to sixty-four pages of well-known novels such as *Moby Dick*, *The Count of Monte Cristo*, and *The Last of the Mohicans*, but modern and traditional knights-errant were also an important part of the catalog. The series included *Knights of the Round Table*, a retelling of Thomas Malory's *Le Morte d'Arthur*; Sir Walter Scott's *Ivanhoe*, *The Talisman*, and *Castle Dangerous*; Robert Louis Stevenson's *The Black Arrow*; Sir Arthur Conan Doyle's *The White Company*; and two American novels, Mark Twain's *A Connecticut Yankee in King Arthur's Court* and Howard Pyle's *Men of Iron*.

This study analyzes the Classics Illustrated edition of Miguel de Cervantes's *Don Quixote*, published in May of 1943. Although Classics Illustrated comics were meant for children, the content of these chivalric tales was relatively complex because young readers from the 1940s to the 1960s were frequently exposed to new versions of this tradition. Whether from reading Hal Foster's *Prince Valiant* in the Sunday funny papers (1937–1971 in the original full-page format) or Sidney Lanier's *The Boy's King Arthur* (published in 1880, but reprinted for over a century), many adolescents were familiar with the conventions of Arthurian romances. Moreover, the most popular Classics Illustrated titles were repeatedly reprinted over the three decades of the company's existence, so *Ivanhoe*, for example, went through twenty-five different printings and was continuously available from 1941 to 1971.[3]

In addition, over the years American children would have seen numerous adaptations of chivalric literature in a variety of visual media, such as the fifteen-part movie serial *The Adventures of Sir Galahad* (1949); films like *A Connecticut Yankee in King Arthur's Court* (1949), *The Black Shield of Falworth* (1954), and *El Cid* (1961); the television shows *The Adventures of Sir Lancelot* (1956–1957) and *Ivanhoe* (1958); and the Disney full-length cartoon *The Sword in the Stone* (1963). There were also two popular Broadway musicals, *Camelot* (1960) and *Man of La Mancha* (1965), both of which were later adapted to film. Some children may have even seen Saturday-afternoon reruns of the 1934 color short *Don Quixote* by Ub Iwerks, Walt Disney's collaborator and the co-creator of Mickey Mouse, which ends with Alonso Quixano recovering his sanity after eight minutes of misadventures and returning to a padded cell in Ye Olde Bughouse to burn his own library.

Classics Illustrated was especially important to Kanter because he did not conceive of the series as mere stand-alone works, but rather as a child's first introduction to great literature, a characteristic that helped the company to weather the Comic-Books Scare of the late 1940s and early 1950s. Critics such as the psychologist Fredric Wertham believed that comics glorified wanton violence and corrupted America's youth, not only by presenting a possibly homoerotic relationship between Batman and Robin, but also because Wonder Woman's superhuman strength could encourage lesbian tendencies in young girls.[4] Nevertheless, as Meyer Kaplan, one of Classics Illustrated's editors, told the New York State Joint Legislative Committee on Comic Book Control in 1951,

> The taste for good literature and fine art must be cultivated in a child slowly. He must be made to understand it before he can like it. . . . [A] pictorial rendering of the great stories of the world which can be easily understood and therefore more readily liked would tend to cultivate that interest. Then, when he grows older, if he has any appetite at all for these things, he will want to know more fully those bookish treasures merely suggested in this, his first acquaintance with them. He will more eagerly read them in the original form because he will already have a mind's eye picture of what the author was trying to portray with words. . . . The name of D'Artagnan, Ivanhoe, Jean Valjean and other famous characters in the world of literature will be no strangers to him.[5]

Wertham disagrees with Kaplan, as he later writes in *The Seduction of the Innocent* that comics "emasculate the classics, condense them (leaving out everything that makes a book great) . . . [and] do *not* reveal to children the world of good literature. They conceal it."[6] Fortunately, the controversy petered out over time, especially after most publishers accepted the censorship of the Comics Code Authority in 1954. Despite the change in

attitudes toward comic books, Wertham's and Kaplan's views are particularly relevant to the case of *Don Quixote*. According to Wertham, one
of the principal problems with graphic novels is that they debase fine literature, while Kaplan claims that readers learn to appreciate great books
over time, a process that begins in childhood before young readers are
capable of understanding the original works. Cervantes would probably
side with Kanter, as he strongly criticizes Alonso Fernández de Avellaneda—or whoever used that pen name—for appropriating his literary
characters and for having written "so many and so great absurdities."[7]

Cervantes specifically claims sole possession of Don Quixote—or at
least joint custody with the fictional author Cide Hamete Benengeli—
which means that no one else should use the Manchegan knight in any
subsequent works. As Cide Hamete tells his pen, only it can say, "For me
alone was Don Quixote born, and I for him: he knew how to act, and I
how to write."[8] Nevertheless, Mikhail Bakhtin believes that Cervantes's
artistic achievement presents the possibility—or perhaps the certainty—
of later appropriations of his work. Bakhtin describes the *Amadís de Gaula*
and most earlier chivalric romances as novels of the First Stylistic Line,
which present "only a single language and a single style (which is more or
less rigorously consistent)."[9] *Don Quixote*, on the other hand, is one of "the
great exemplars of the novel of the Second Line"—works that incorporate
multi-voiced speech as an essential part of the narrative—although "the
author builds a superstructure over these languages made up of his own
intention and accents, which become dialogically linked with them."[10]

Bakhtin believes that as a result of this linguistic complexity, "In these
great seminal works . . . authentic double-voiced novelistic images fully
ripen, now profoundly differentiated from poetic symbols, and become
the unique thing they ultimately are."[11] Don Quixote exists within these
complex forms of speech, so Bakhtin believes that the image of the Manchegan knight produces "an open, living, mutual interaction between
worlds, points of view, accents. This makes it possible to re-accentuate the
image, to adopt various attitudes toward the argument sounding within
the image, to take various positions in this argument and, consequently,
to vary the interpretations of the image itself."[12] Since Don Quixote is not
a static and immutable character like the typical literary knight-errant,
Bakhtin concludes that over time he can be repeatedly reinterpreted as his
image comes into contact with new cultural contexts:

> The [double-voiced novelistic] image becomes polysemic, like a symbol.
> Thus are created the immortal novelistic images that live different lives in
> different epochs. The image of Don Quixote has been thus re-accentuated in
> a variety of ways in the later history of the novel and interpreted in different
> ways, for these re-accentuations and interpretations were an inevitable and

organic further development of the image, a continuation of the unresolved
argument embedded in it.[13]

Although Bakhtin discusses *Don Quixote* within the European literary
tradition, the knight's image also appears in new artistic forms in what
Caryl Emerson calls "an intergeneric shift."[14] Over the centuries, the
Manchegan knight's figure has appeared in films, plays, ballets, operas,
engravings and book illustrations, sculptures, paintings and lithographs,
television shows, educational apps, video games, children's books, and
any number of cartoons, manga, and comics. In the case of Classics Illustrated, *Don Quixote* is unique among the collection's re-creations of
chivalric novels because it comes out in May of 1943, which makes it the
only one entirely drawn and published during America's participation in
World War II. Popular genres such as movies and comics are especially
important after the December 1941 attack on Pearl Harbor because they
help to rally American public opinion and maintain morale on the home
front, but comic books exhibit a more innovative and uniquely American
form of proselytization than film.

Compared to the New York–based comic-book publishers, Hollywood
studios were far more cautious in presenting political themes before the
American declaration of war. Curiously enough, the principal reason for
this reticence is that most movie moguls were from Jewish immigrant
families, including Louis B. Mayer (Metro-Goldwyn-Mayer), Jack and
Harry Warner (Warner Brothers), Harry Cohn (Columbia Pictures), and
Darryl F. Zanuck (20th Century Fox). While many actors and screenwriters were alarmed by the outbreak of the Spanish Civil War and the
spread of totalitarianism in Europe,[15] Mark Harris writes that in the late
1930s most studio chiefs were hesitant to finance political films because
they were so concerned about the threat of anti-Semitism that they "approached politics haltingly and after agonized deliberation. While bot-
tom-line imperatives were unquestionably a part of their calculus, their
trepidation also emanated from an accurate understanding of their fragile
place in American culture; to confront any national or international issue
that might put the spotlight on their religion was to risk animosity or even
censure."[16]

The focus of American filmmaking changed dramatically at the end of
1941, but even before the American entry into World War II, the presence
of Jewish comic-book illustrators and editors had precisely the opposite
effect as it did in Hollywood. While movie moguls were wealthy and
successful executives who had to defend a vulnerable but very profitable
medium, Paul Hirsch notes that the "comic book industry . . . was run by
a colorful collection of ex-pornographers, former left-wing radicals, and
hustlers. . . . What unified the owners and creators was their status as so-

cial outsiders . . . [who were] shut out of more mainstream professions."[17] Since comic-books artists and publishers in New York had far less to lose than their Hollywood counterparts, they could afford to take more daring positions on controversial topics. For example, on February 27, 1940, *Look* magazine published a two-page comic-book spread on how Superman would end World War II by taking Hitler and Stalin by the scruff of the neck to a war crimes tribunal in the League of Nations.[18] Jerry Siegel and Joe Shuster, Superman's co-creators, were both from Jewish immigrant families, a fact that was promptly noted by indignant Waffen-SS propagandists in Germany.[19] Captain America's co-creators, Joe Simon and Jack Kirby, were also from Jewish immigrant families, and the front cover of the superhero's first issue from March 1941—fully nine months before Pearl Harbor—shows the Captain famously punching Adolf Hitler in the face to prevent the führer from sabotaging American industry.[20]

World War II presents an extraordinary commercial and creative opportunity for comic-book publishers, and as a result they respond with red, white, and blue-clad superheroes—such as Wonder Woman, the Shield, Yankee Doodle Jones, Flagman, American Crusader, and Miss Victory[21]—who participate directly in the war effort, either by fighting on the front lines, selling war bonds, or breaking up rings of Axis spies who are secretly operating in the United States. Because of the growing interest in comic books during the war years, sales rose to an astounding 25 million volumes per month by 1943.[22] As a result of this extraordinary popularity, "Comic-book houses worked at a breakneck pace to meet the demand of a growing audience."[23] In addition, many comic-book artists joined the armed forces, which meant that the artistic quality of the some of the editions suffered. Classics Illustrated was no exception, as between February 1943 and January 1944 the company "produced a string of loose adaptations that tarnished the reputation of the series in some quarters for decades to come. But the insistent individuality—indeed, the exuberant eccentricity—of the artists employed during the war years often triumphed over the less-than-faithful scripts."[24] There is no question that the 1943 edition of *Don Quixote* would be a disappointment to modern readers who value the Classics Illustrated series primarily because of its faithful reproduction of the original texts. Nevertheless, this study suggests that it is precisely the volume's quirky originality and its distortion of its literary source that help turn the comic-book *Don Quixote* into a successful re-accentuation of Cervantes's masterpiece.

Since Classics Illustrated respects the source texts for their graphic novels, the cover art for *Don Quixote* lists the author as Miguel de Cervantes, while the first page indicates that the story adaptation is by Samuel H. Abramson and the illustrations by Zansky.[25] At the beginning of the story, "In a Spanish village in the seventeenth century, Don Quixote, a quiet scholarly gentleman, lived in a strange world of his own, peopled by the knights and heroes about whom he read in his books of chivalry and adventure."[26] Don Quixote is not the product of Alonso Quixano's literary imagination, but is rather a Spanish nobleman who declares that his "mission is to revive the age of chivalry . . . to prove that honor and courage are not dead . . . to fight like brave Galahad."[27] Don Quixote therefore cleans up his great-grandfather's armor and renames his horse Rozinante, but when he arrives at the inn at the beginning of his first sally, the innkeeper decides to play along because "it may be great sport."[28] It appears that Abramson and Zansky also join in the merriment, as the innkeeper tells Don Quixote, "Enter. First you will enjoy the hospitality of my castle."[29]

This comment on the inn's hospitality occurs in the same picture frame that presents two young women in the foreground, accompanied by a second caption in which one of them laughingly says, "Tee-hee."[30] The young woman has a broom in her hand, so the two of them seem to be maids, but it is obvious that Abramson and Zansky are sharing a private joke about the two prostitutes in the original text and about the kind of hospitality that would be available at the inn. The episode ends with a feast and with the innkeeper knighting Don Quixote, but the fight with the muleteers is never presented. Moreover, it is not until Don Quixote leaves the inn that he realizes that he needs "a fair lady to inspire me to victory . . . I shall call her Dulcinea."[31] It is unclear whether he has re-named a young woman from the village or whether he has created her out of whole cloth, but there is no doubt about his next decision. Although Don Quixote knows that he needs "a handsome young squire to support [him] in battle," he ends up with "none other than Sancho, the village handyman."[32]

While the cultured gentleman and the illiterate peasant appear to make an unusual pairing, this sort of combination would be quite familiar to contemporary comic-book readers. Don Quixote attempts to imitate literary knights errant like Amadís, or characters who would represent the Renaissance equivalent of the modern superhero. In the early 1940s, however, many comic books featured a superhero as well as a sidekick, such as Batman and Robin, Wonder Woman and Etta Candy, Superman and Jimmy Olson, and Captain America and Bucky Barnes. While Don Quixote and Sancho are probably more similar to Mr. America and Fat Man, José Manuel Annacondia López writes that "the primordial couple of hero and sidekick in comic books, Batman and Robin, shar[e] almost all of the features of one of the most famous and seminal pairings of literature: Don Quixote and Sancho Panza."[33] In this way, Sancho—who inadvertently subverts the chivalric ideal in the source text—enjoys a far more conventional role as a comic-book sidekick because of the intergeneric shift to a graphic novel.

Once Don Quixote and Sancho leave the village, the gentleman decides that "First we shall go to Saragossa where the tournaments are held," although Sancho replies, "But, master, the tournaments ended years ago."[34] As we know, Cervantes writes at the end of the first part of the novel that he has been unable to find any additional documentation on the knight-errant's third sally, but that "Only fame has preserved in the memoirs of La Mancha, that Don Quixote, the third time he sallied from home, went to Saragossa, where he was present at a famous tournament in that city, and that there befell him things worthy of his valour and good understanding."[35] Nevertheless, in the second part of the text Don Quixote discovers that a modern writer has penned a spurious continuation of his adventures, which includes an episode in Saragossa. The Manchegan knight immediately declares that "I will not set a foot in Saragossa, and so I will expose to the world the falsity of this modern historiographer,"[36] and he therefore decides to go on to Barcelona instead. Since it would be extremely awkward for a twentieth-century re-accentuation of *Don Quixote* to mention Cervantes's criticism of this practice, it seems perfectly logical for Abramson to have the Manchegan knight continue on to his original destination, which appropriately enough follows La Mancha's oral traditions.

Much of the graphic novel is made up of *Don Quixote*'s best-known episodes, although in many cases the action is deliberately altered in order to make it more entertaining for a younger audience. For example, the beginning of the encounter with the Vizcaíno is similar to the original text, but rather than stopping the action with "Don Quixote . . . with his lifted sword, fully determined to cleave him asunder,"[37] Rozinante "take[s] things into his own hoofs" and kicks the opponent to the ground.[38] Soon afterward, Don Quixote and Sancho get off their mounts in order to rest, but Don Quixote comments, "Look! Rozinante is seeking greener pastures!"[39] Instead of attempting "to solace himself with the fillies,"[40] however, Rozinante shows his chaste affection for a single mare by standing next to her and licking her face. Unfortunately, all suffer the expected fate at the hand of the Yangüeses, but an undaunted Don Quixote ends the episode by proclaiming, "Bravo! Let us hurry to Saragossa."[41] Don Quixote and Sancho soon arrive at the second inn, where the squire tells the well-known lie that "My master fell on a rock and bruised his ribs."[42] During the night, they do not receive a visit from the repugnant Maritornes, but rather from an attractive maiden who wants to see "if the brave knight and his handsome squire are resting comfortably."[43] It would be impossible for Abramson to present the failed assignation between Maritornes and the muleteer in the graphic novel, yet Sancho mistakes the maiden for a thief and the evening ends in much the same way as in Cervantes's novel.

One of the curious aspects of the changes between the original text and the Classics Illustrated re-accentuation is how Abramson presents Sancho Panza as an important agent in the graphic novel's adventures, which demonstrates that the squire has successfully assumed the role of the comic-book sidekick. When Don Quixote and Sancho first see the windmills, the squire tells his master: "Sir, you must be mistaken. I see no giants. I see before me only windmills which do no harm to anybody."[44] Don Quixote still attacks the giants, but he becomes stuck in the sails and goes around several times until Sancho knocks him off. The knight gratefully tells him, "Sancho, you have saved me from a terrible fate,"[45] but the squire is more concerned about sewing Don Quixote's pants, which now have a large tear in the seat. Sancho saves his master a second time when he is locked up in the oxcart, which has been arranged by the curate to get him back to the village. Don Quixote asks Sancho to help him escape, but Sancho answers, "Wait until tonight, master. I will think of a plan."[46] Once they stop for the night, "The wily Sancho plies the guards with wine,"[47] and once they fall asleep Don Quixote and Sancho continue their journey to Saragossa.

The entire Cardenio episode is missing in the Classics Illustrated version of the novel, but Abramson includes the Duke and the Duchess as a clever way to arrange for the knight's return home. Much like the innkeeper at the beginning of the comic book, the Duke tells the Duchess that "It will be great sport" to have Don Quixote in their home.[48] They entertain the knight alone when Sancho becomes the governor of Barataria, but Don Quixote soon insists on leaving for the jousts in Saragossa. As a result, the Duke has to go on ahead to the Aragonese capital, where he informs the Viceroy and his retinue, "Gentlemen, my friend Don Quixote is bound here for the tournament. He knows not that there has been no tournament for a century . . . It will break his heart. We must induce him to return home . . . but how can we?"[49] Fortunately, a court jester comes up with a plan that recalls the episode in which the bachelor Sansón Carrasco assumes the role of the Knight of the White Moon in Barcelona. All the Viceroy has to do is arrange for "an old-time tournament" where Don Quixote "will be defeated by a knight, but his life will be spared on the condition that he give up arms for one year and return home."[50]

Perhaps the biggest contrast between the endings of Miguel de Cervantes's *Don Quixote* and the Classics Illustrated re-accentuation is that after his final defeat in single combat, the graphic novel's protagonist lives to fight another day, confidently asserting that "In one year Don Quixote will ride again."[51] The original Alonso Quixano, on the contrary, "amidst the plaints and tears of the bystanders, resigned his breath—I

mean, died."[52] While the new ending may seem to present a radical devia-
tion from Cervantes's source text, it is important to remember the graphic
novel's May 1943 publication date, which is only a year and a half after
Pearl Harbor. At the same time, all of the original Classics Illustrated's
editions end with a one-page author biography and several pages of
cultural materials, which in this case include two pages on the daring
wartime deeds of Captain Arthur Wermuth and his half-Filipino sidekick,
Sergeant Crispin (Jock) Jacob.

Even though Wermuth and Jacob had been taken prisoner following
the fall of the Philippines thirteen months earlier, Classics Illustrated
ends the two-page spread on the two wartime heroes with the question,
"Where is Wermuth now? . . . Somewhere in the South Pacific, still fighting gallantly. His exploits on our tropical battle fronts, have become almost legendary. Wermuth holds 3 medals . . . and will undoubtedly win
many others to keep them company!"[53] Never mind that Wermuth's feats
were greatly exaggerated by an American press desperate for military
heroes at the beginning of the war, and that when he was liberated from
a POW camp in 1945, the Army got rid of him by giving him the choice
between a court-martial and an honorable discharge.[54] Accepting some of
the more improbable aspects of Captain Wermuth's and Sergeant Jacob's
exploits as historical truths, Classics Illustrated seems to present the two
soldiers as modern American versions of Don Quixote and Sancho, all as
part of a deliberate pairing that would be easily understood by a wartime
comic-book audience. In the same way that Wermuth will supposedly
continue to battle "little slant-eyed devils" when he is really a prisoner of
war,[55] the graphic novel's Don Quixote is prepared to take up arms once
again, even though he should rightly be at home preparing his last will
and testament.

With the comic-book conclusion of the adventures of Don Quixote and
Arthur Wermuth, the central message for Classics Illustrated's juvenile
readers seems clear: all patriotic Americans must unite in a noble and un-
relenting wartime struggle, following the example of the inexplicably liberated Army captain and the aging Spanish squire who patiently awaits
his next sally. While it seemingly makes no sense for the comic book to
link Don Quixote's fate to that of two prisoners of war from the Pacific
theater, in reality this creative (and patriotic) license is part of the "exuberant eccentricity" that William B. Jones has observed in wartime Classics Illustrated comic books.[56] Moreover, we should keep in mind that any
cultural production from the most difficult period of the conflict should
be examined from a specifically wartime viewpoint. For example, as Mark
Harris has written, after Pearl Harbor the American government's interest
in cinematic propaganda was so great that prominent Hollywood directors such as John Ford, Frank Capra, and John Huston joined the armed

forces to make patriotic films with the Naval Photographic Unit and the Army Signal Corps.

Once the fighting was over, audiences and film critics soon lost sight of the directors' wartime motion pictures, but Harris indicates that to the end of their lives, all of these filmmakers "still count[ed] among their most meaningful accomplishments a body of work most of their admirers had long-forgotten or never seen at all. As long as they lived, the war lived in them."[57] There is no question that the stakes were higher and the responsibilities much greater for any artistic works created during the years of the conflict, so wartime films should not be judged by conventional critical standards. By the same token, the Classics Illustrated *Don Quixote* must be viewed through a different social and historical lens, even though the graphic novel does not represent an example of overt propaganda. Since this re-accentuation of Cervantes's novel served to entertain younger readers during World War II—both on the home front and those serving in uniform—and taking into account that it also emphasized the importance of the armed struggle, then it can be considered an artistic and cultural success despite any textual inaccuracies and aesthetic deficiencies it may have.

As Mikhail Bakhtin has noted, the image of Don Quixote allows for "an open, living, mutual interaction between worlds, points of view, [and] accents,"[58] and as a result of this interplay the Manchegan knight is refashioned as he comes into contact with a new historical context during World War II. Don Quixote is a perfect example of what Bakhtin calls "the immortal novelistic imag[e] that liv[es] different lives in different epochs,"[59] which means that he cannot be constrained by his inventor's desire to keep control of a literary figure that is no longer his exclusive property. Cervantes could have never imagined that the image of Don Quixote would still be evolving almost three and a half centuries later, and much less during a worldwide conflict, but the knight-errant's constant re-accentuations demonstrate that new generations of writers and artists simply cannot accept Cervantes's request "to suffer the wearied and now mouldering bones of Don Quixote to repose in the grave."[60] On the contrary, Don Quixote and Sancho live long enough in the collective imagination that they entertain and inspire the Greatest Generation during some of the darkest days in American history, an achievement that suggests that—in the immortal words of Winston Churchill—this was their finest hour.

NOTES

1. Eric Leif Davin, *Partners in Wonder: Women and the Birth of Science Fiction* (Lanham, MD: Lexington Books, 2005), 170.

2. Michael Sawyer, "Albert Lewis Kanter and the Classics: The Man Behind the Gilbert Company," *The Journal of Popular Culture* 20.4 (1987): 1.

3. King-Collector, "Classic Comic Books Identifying Reprints," www.kingcollector.com.

4. David Heer, "The Caped Crusader: Frederic Wertham and the Campaign Against Comic Books," slate.com.

5. Michael Sawyer, "Albert Lewis Kanter," 8.

6. Frederic Wertham, *The Seduction of the Innocent: The Influence of Comic Books on Today's Youth* (Waltham, NY: Rinehart and Company, 1954), 36.

7. Miguel de Cervantes, *Don Quixote de la Mancha* (Oxford: Oxford University Press, 1992): 2.74, 1049.

8. Ibid., 2.74, 1051.

9. Mikhail Bakhtin, *The Dialogic Imagination: Four Essays* (Austin: University of Texas Press 1981), 375.

10. Ibid., 409.

11. Ibid.

12. Ibid., 409–10.

13. Ibid., 410. As Howard Mancing has noted, the re-accentuation of *Don Quixote* occurs almost immediately, as the characters' images were promptly reproduced in popular festivities in Valladolid (1605) and Cuzco (1607), as well as on the Spanish stage in Guillén de Castro's *Don Quijote de la Mancha* and *El curioso impertinente* (1606). Howard Mancing, "Dulcinea del Toboso: On the Occasion of her Four-Hundredth Birthday" (*Hispania* 88. 1, 2005): 55.

14. Caryl Emerson, "Bakhtin and the Intergeneric Shift: The Case of Boris Godunov," *Studies in 20th Century Literature* 9.1 (1984): 145.

15. David Welky, *The Moguls and the Dictators* (Baltimore: Johns Hopkins University Press, 2008), 33–38.

16. Mark Harris, *Five Came Back* (New York: Penguin Press, 2014), 15–16. By 1940 Hollywood begins to satirize Hitler with the Three Stooges' *You Natzy Spy* (Columbia Pictures) and Charlie Chaplin's independently produced *The Great Dictator*.

17. Dan Turello, "War and Superheroes: How the Writer's Board Used Comics to Spread Its Message in WWII," *Library of Congress Insights*, https://blogs.loc.gov/kluge/2015/11/war-and-superheroes-how-the-writers-war-board-used-comics-to-spread-its-message-in-wwii.

18. See Julius Darius, "On 'How Superman Would Win the War'," www.sequart.org.

19. Two months after the *Look* spread, Siegel was the subject of a particularly harsh response from *Das Schwarze Korps*, the official newspaper of the SS, which called him an "inventive Israelite" and "intellectually and physically circumcised" (Calvin College, "Jerry Siegel Attacks!" German Propaganda Archive, research.calvin.edu).

20. The front cover often did not reflect the comic's content because it was only meant to attract attention and increase sales. For the cover art of *Captain America*'s first issue, see Bradford W. Wright, *Comic Book Nation: The Transformation of Youth Culture in America* (Baltimore: Johns Hopkins University Press, 2001), 32.

21. SuperHeroMultiverse, "World War II and the Superhero," superheromultiverse.com.

22. Bradford W. Wright, *Comic Book Nation*, 31.

23. SuperHeroMultiverse, *Ibid.*

24. William B. Jones, *Classics Illustrated: A Cultural History* (Jefferson, NC: McFarland & Company, 2011, Kindle edition), chapter 4.

25. *Don Quixote* is Abramson's only contribution to the series, but Louis Zansky (1921–1978) draws a total of seven editions (Lambiek Comiclopedia, "Louis Zansky"). Zansky—another artist from a Jewish immigrant family—stops collaborating with Classics Illustrated when he joins the Army in 1944, but he later becomes a successful painter and watercolorist (William B. Jones, *Classics Illustrated*, chapter 3).

26. Miguel de Cervantes, *Don Quixote* (New York: Classic Comics, 1943), 2.

27. Ibid.

28. Ibid., 4

29. Ibid.

30. Ibid.

31. Ibid., 6.

32. Ibid.

33. Ibid., 8.

34. Ibid.

35. Miguel de Cervantes, *Don Quixote* novel, 1.52, 510.

36. Ibid., 2.59, 952.

37. Ibid., 1.9, 73.

38. Cervantes, *Don Quixote* comic, 10.

39. Ibid., 11.

40. Cervantes, *Don Quixote* novel, 1.15, 115.

41. Cervantes, *Don Quixote* comic, 12.

42. Ibid., 13.

43. Ibid., 14.

44. Ibid., 18.

45. Ibid., 22.

46. Ibid., 31.

47. Ibid., 32.

48. Ibid., 40.

49. Ibid., 56.

50. Ibid., 57.

51. Ibid., 60.

52. Cervantes, *Don Quixote* novel, 2.74, 1050.

53. Cervantes, *Don Quixote* comic, 63.

54. Bill Yenne, *Tommy Gun: How General Thompson's Submachine Gun Wrote History* (New York: St. Martin's Press, 2009), 156.

55. Cervantes, *Don Quixote* comic, 62.

56. Jones, *Classics Illustrated*, chapter 4.

57. Harris, *Five Came Back*, 12.

58. Bakhtin, *The Dialogic Imagination*, 409.

59. Ibid., 410.

60. Cervantes, *Don Quixote* novel, 2.74, 1051.

5

A Horse of a Different Color: Salvador Dalí and the Re-imagining of Clavileño

S. Alleyn Smythe

It is the two-dimensional equivalent of the artist's mannequin, an articu-lated "doll": lifelike and life-imitating, but nonetheless lifeless; malleable and maneuverable, and yet manipulating—in so much as it is a miniature of the human figure it is meant to represent and yet lacks all the flesh and fluidity of the form; lithe and limber, it is nonetheless limited. It is a toy conceived in the child's fertile imagination, born of boredom and need, and constructed of discarded shoe boxes, used-up paper towel tubes, and last year's slightly misshapen birthday party hats half-heartedly re-inflated. Triangles on the precipice of maturing into pyramids unite to simulate ears, hind legs, and hooves. Squares flirting with the possibility of becoming cubes strain to suggest torso, hindquarters, and head. Circles that dream of one day growing into spheres insist on serving as nostrils and eyes. All are connected not by flesh and bone, but by a hint of an outline—waning and waxing in places, all but absent in others—resem-bling twisted and frayed pipe cleaners held together with bubble gum and rubber bands. Spools of thread and drinking straws, it is a Tinkertoy sculpture; see-through and stilted, it is a paper cutout whose form is de-termined as much by what is missing as by what is present. It is a three-dimensional idea whose every "muscle," "tendon," and "joint" struggles to break free of its two-dimensional reality. Despite every effort to reduce the figure to little more than the sum of its parts, we *see* a horse. Despite whatever pre-conceived tenuous notions we may hold regarding its iden-tity, we *know* it is Clavileño. So we are told; so it is written.

Low and away, the star-shaped silhouette cowers; dwarfed and dwarf-like, the five-pointed figure crouches. Whether it faces toward or away is disputable. Whether it comes or goes is indeterminable. Whether it advances or retreats is non-ascertainable. Lacking any detail, it is sim-ply an inky asterisk that calls attention as much to its puny self as to the towering but hollow structure above whose greater importance he seems to punctuate and yet remains moot. It is at once its own entity, solid and substantial, and yet is little more than an appendage of the attendant figure that turns away from it and whose breadth fills the airless space of the picture plane. It is ancillary and subordinate. Its presence seems but an afterthought, a necessity of compositional continuity and continuousness. The curve created by the meeting of pyramidal arm to trapezoidal torso and trapezoidal torso to pyramidal thigh traces that of the horse's hind leg. The triangle of negative space created by the spread of its equally triangular legs mimics that between the horse's back legs. The streak of black that begins as a skein and dissolves into a thread as its course runs toward the figure mirrors the line by which the horse's back leg is defined. It is but a placeholder, filling what would otherwise be a compositional void. It is but a distraction that relieves the horse, if only momentarily and temporarily, from the burden of focused attention. It is a jester that walks on stage at the moment when the tension has grown too taut. He is no more, nor no less, than an assemblage of the same commonplace household items with which the horse has been constructed but with no discernible post or purpose. Despite every effort to reduce the figure to little more than the sum of its parts, we *see* a man. Despite whatever pre-conceived tenuous notions we may hold regarding his identity, we *know*—by association and proximity—it is Don Quixote.

Streaks of yellow and bursts of orange emanate from the neck, torso, and hindquarters of the horse, flooding the space behind him. They are evocative of the cooler-burning ochre and saffron-colored flames of a dying wood fire gasping for oxygen in the final stages of its life. They surround and engulf the charred lump of coal of a man blinded by, and shrinking away from, the glow of the smoldering pyre—a half-scorched ember spewed from the volcanic eruption. Less like vibrant sparkly bursts of gunpowder released from the ignited firecracker and more like the strings of the marionette that, through their nuanced and controlled manipulation, command the horse to dance, these crimson and lemon pennants—suggesting but not defining a mane and a tail—rein in the animal and fix him in a state of suspended animation. A pinkish-brown tone washes over and through the figures like spilled chocolate milk dripping off the edge of the table where the glass once containing it was precariously perched leaving deep pools and shallow puddles in its wake; watery and fluid, it nonetheless does little to squelch the raging fire. Warm and dry, it is the hue of a smoke swirled with the dusty earth trampled beneath the hooves of the horse and stirred up as he rears. Taupe-tinged billows rise from the earth like steam from the tarry asphalt on an Alabama highway in August. Tangerine smears stain the sky like mosquitoes splattered on the windshield of a southbound eighteen-wheeler as it cruises down that same road. The swaths of blush and beige, translucent but not transparent, and the swatches of canary and pumpkin, glowing but obscuring more than they illuminate, are the early morning palette of a day just breaking, one that promises to be oppressively hot. Permeating the air and the composition, there is no escaping the inferno. Where we *see* smoke, we must too *see* flames. When we *know* this is Clavileño, we *know* this is fire.

We *see* that, conspicuous in its absence, is the wooden peg upon his forehead from which the horse derives his name and which determines his course, but we do *see* Clavileño. We *see* that missing is the familiar inverted shaving basin cum helmet that shades a mind shriveled like a raisin in the sun, but we do *see* Don Quixote. We *see* that nowhere is there to be found the fireworks with which the horse's belly was reportedly filled, but we do *see* fire. We *know* the passage the image references, and thus we *see* it (figure 5.1).

> Desiring to conclude the strange and carefully made adventure, they set fire to Clavileño's tail with some tow-cloths, and since the horse was full of fireworks, it suddenly flew into the air with a fearsome noise and threw Don Quixote and Sancho Panza to the ground, half-scorched.[1]

It would seem perhaps inane and illogical at worst—at best, incongruous and inappropriate—in this the year defined, delineated, and all but dominated by celebrations and commemorations marking the four-hundredth anniversary of Cervantes's death, to begin an essay exploring the re-accentuation of *Don Quixote* as it is manifested in Dalí's *Clavileño* with a comparison of the author to Hieronymus Bosch—the Dutch painter of the fantastical and phantasmagoric, the delightful and demonic, the pleasurable and the punishable—whose death, coincidentally, crosses the five-hundred-year mark in this same year and whose artistic contributions a Bosch-infatuated Spain has feted with no less fanfare than that which his literary peer, if not contemporary, has enjoyed. While the differences between the seventeenth-century Golden Age Spanish novelist and the late fifteenth-/early sixteenth-century Northern Renaissance Netherlandish painter are glaringly obvious, the similarities between Spain's native son and his adoptive brother, although more subtle, are no less substantial. Quixote imitates, emulates, and reinvigorates the chivalric traditions of medieval literature; Bosch reconfigures, reimagines, and reanimates the hybrid monstrosities of medieval manuscripts. To the former, windmills are giants to be subdued, to the latter they are but toys similar in nature to the whirligig the Christ Child clutches as he pushes a walking frame on the obverse side of Bosch's circa 1480 oil-on-panel painting, *Christ Carrying the Cross* (figure 5.2).[2] Dulcinea is whore turned virgin; Eve is virgin turned whore.

Figure 5.1. Salvador Dalí. *Clavilegnio (Clavileño)* (c. 1972, lithograph on paper)

Figure 5.2.   Hieronymus Bosch. *Christ Child with a Walking Frame* (Kunsthistorisches Museum, Vienna, c. 1480s, oil on panel)

The commonalities between the two grow all the more transparent when one considers the profound intellectual, artistic, and stylistic in-fluence each has had on Salvador Dalí, whose 1972 lithograph of the aforementioned Clavileño pays homage to the ersatz horse of Cervantes's novel—itself a re-accentuation of the "flying" wooden horse of European and Near Eastern folklore, with all the obscurity of a Bosch composition. While the image is devoid of the surrealistic tendencies (the ironic and/ or oftentimes perverse juxtapositions of seemingly innocuous but nev-ertheless incompatible objects in an ironic and yet convincingly "real" manner) inherited from Bosch as much as, if not more than, those of his contemporaries by whom he was influenced and with which Dalí is most associated, it remains clear that were it not for the eponymous title, determining the figure's identity would be all but impossible. This work alone illustrates that the propensity for rendering the enigmatic, the absurd, the dangerous, and the lurid bordering on the comic in literature and in art is both endemic to Spanish literary and artistic production and a legacy that Dalí not only embraced but upon which he expanded to such a degree that the very concept of "surrealism" has become synonymous with his name.[3]

Between 1970 and 1972 Salvador Dalí produced a twenty-five-plate series of lithographs entitled *Les Chevaux de Dalí.* Among the collection of predominantly fictional horses drawn from, and inspired by, classical mythology, medieval literature, folklore, and Christian iconography, Cervantes enjoys the distinction of having two images based on episodes from his narrative represented in the suite: *Don Quichotte*—wherein Rocinante is depicted not once, but twice in the same picture plane, and *Clavilegnio (Clavileño).* Having returned time and again to the horse motif throughout his long, prodigious, and oftentimes controversial career— an unpublished diary reveals pages upon pages of barely legible notes wrapped around doodled anatomically correct horses, rearing, galloping, and carrying women away—in this suite, Dalí assembled the most compelling examples of the diverse and distinct compositional, technical, and painterly styles with which he had frequently experimented.[4] Reflecting both the long-standing European tradition of horse painting—extending as far back as the near eighteen-thousand-year-old cave paintings in Lascaux, France, and represented by artists such as Da Vinci, Dürer, Delacroix, and Degas—as well as the centuries-old Spanish love of and admiration for the animal's sheer raw power (i.e., *La victime de la fete/ The Horse of Death*), tempered by a beauty of line and form (i.e., *Le cheval de troie/The Trojan Horse*), and cloaked in a veil of elegance and grace (i.e., *Lady Godiva*), Dalí's horses reference his nation's past and rank him among the most notable and noteworthy Spanish hippophiles and interpreters of the subject while maintaining the expression of a uniquely Dalinean perspective.

With the inclusion of *Clavileño* in the *Dalinean Horses* series, Dalí not only underscores the significance of Cervantes's contribution to the rich literary tradition of casting horses in roles equally as vital as, if not more important than, those who travel through adventure and adversity astride them and with whom their identities become inseparable, but canonizes him much in the way that Countess Trifaldi does when she rattles off the appellations of history's most notorious and noteworthy horses in response to Sancho's inquiry regarding the name of this mysterious, mystical, and magical creature of Merlin's making. As stated in the text:

"His name," responded the Dolorous One, "is not that of Bellerophon's horse, named Pegasus, or that of Alexander the Great, called Bucephalus, or that of the furious Orlando, dubbed Brillador, much less Bayarte, who belonged to Reinaldos de Montalbán, or Frontino, who was Ruggiero's steed, or Bootes or Pirithous, which, they say, were the names of the horses of the Sun, and his name is not Orelia, like the horse on which that unfortunate Rodrigo, last of the Visigoths, entered the battle in which he lost his life for his kingdom . . . but the name he has fits him, because he is called Clavileño the Fleet . . . and so, as far as his name is concerned, he can certainly compete with the famous Rocinante."[5]

Of those "famous names of well-known horses" listed by the Countess, only Bucephalus and Pegasus and, naturally, Rocinante gain membership into Dalí's elite club. From among the choice and the chosen, Clavileño has been carefully selected; among the privileged and prestigious, he has been deliberately placed.

Dalí was neither the first nor the last to illustrate episodes from *Don Quixote*. Long is the tradition of rendering the eponymous protagonist of Cervantes's epic "knight's" tale pictorially, either as an accompaniment to the text or as an independent work of art. As early as the mid-seventeenth century—just forty years after the first publication of Part II in the original Spanish and some thirty-five after the publication of the same in English—illustrated versions of Part I began to be put into production beyond the borders of the author's native land, primarily in Spanish-speaking territories. In fact, the first complete illustrated edition of Cervantes's novel appeared not in the original Spanish but in a Dutch translation, printed in the city of Dordrecht in the Netherlandish Low Countries. The twenty-four-plus engravings of this 1657 edition—along with the successive two versions—depicted those narrative passages best suited to visual representation, that is, those with emphasis on the more physical escapades of *el ingenioso hidalgo de la Mancha*, the selection of which set the standard for illustrated versions of the text for multiple successive generations.[6]

Although these images were among the first mass-produced, widely disseminated, and greatly expanded upon, it was the 1863 engravings of the nineteenth-century French illustrator, sculptor, and painter Gustave Doré (1832–1883) that remained most faithful to and best captured and rigidly codified the physical depictions of the pseudo-knight as described in the text: "[a] gentleman . . . approximately fifty years old; his complexion was weathered, his flesh scrawny, his face gaunt"[7]—and that served as the Quixotic prototype of subsequent iterations, both in illustrated texts as well as on film and in theater, for several decades thereafter. Moreover, Doré's handling of the "Clavileño the Swift" episode—the earthbound ersatz horse, on whose back rides the dynamic duo, and onto whose neck a blindfolded and blindly obedient Quixote clutches, "flying" through a star-strewn, inky-black nighttime sky—both exemplified, as well as reified, the popularly held image and widely reproduced rendering of the incident, an image Dalí eschewed in his own treatment of the same scene.

Dalí was neither the first nor the last to isolate a particular image or incident from the narrative and render it pictorially for purposes other than as a textual accompaniment. By far the most memorable, recognizable, and reproduced of these images is Pablo Picasso's 1955 black-and-white Indian ink sketch depicting the Spanish literary hero and his sidekick Sancho Panza astride their respective trusty mounts. The willowy, angular, gaunt-faced knight and his malnourished bag-of-bones nag—of whom Quixote seems to be an extension—grow reed-like among the miniaturized windmills planted at their feet. Beside him, his frequent foil and fair-weather friend Sancho sits like a lump of hastily affixed clay atop his equally pudgy and formless donkey and in disproportionate size and stature to his master's lean, lanky, elongated form. The loosely connected, seemingly casual, scribbles, dots, and dashes of which the figures are formed invigorate and animate what would otherwise be a lifeless pair and static composition. Featured in the August 18 issue of the French weekly journal *Les Lettres Françaises* in celebration of the 350th anniversary of the publication of *Don Quixote*, Part I, Picasso's rendering of the iconic duo quickly became the archetype, supplanting and all but obliterating all previous iterations (figure 5.3).[8]

Dalí was neither the first nor the last to wholly divorce a singular element, episode, or character from its narrative context and re-accentuate it. From commemorative stamps (issued by *Correos de España* in 1947 and again in 1966) to celebratory coins (ten euro denominations minted in 2005), from red wines (Clavileño Crianza from the Bodega Los Pozoz de Daimler) to gasoline brands ("El Clavileño": "*de fama mundial; la mejor para automoviles*"), from museums (Clavileño Chocolate Museum, Villajoyosa) to the souvenirs they hawk (chocolate bars and hot cocoa mix), in Spain the name Clavileño is synonymous not only with the iconic wooden horse of chapters 41 and 42 of *Don Quixote*, Part II, but with a host of unrelated objects, products, and services. Repackaged, repurposed, and re-appropriated, Clavileño paint has been applied to countless facades, but the structures beneath remain largely unaltered. Despite the best and most admirable of efforts to associate peddled products with a literary classic in a testament to tradition and as proof of patrimony and pedigree, the two-year-old *tinto* affixed with a "Clavileño" label is no more a fine bottle of perfectly aged vintage wine, than the baby with the baboon heart is an ape. To his credit, the "donor" image Dalí transplants proves a compatible, if not a bit awkward, fit with its recipient.

Figure 5.3. Pablo Picasso. *Don Quixote* **(c. 1955, vectorization of Picasso's 1955 drawing** *Don Quixote***)**

The images of Clavileño and Don Quixote of the "Dalinean Horses" suite were neither Dalí's first nor his last engagement with the text of *El ingenioso hidalgo don Quijote de la Mancha*. In addition to having already produced numerous etchings, lithographs, paintings, and sculptures independent of the narrative, in 1946 he developed a suite of black-and-white sketches and offset watercolors to accompany a Random House English translation of Part I. Although criticized for having borrowed elements of the imagery of the eighteenth-century Romantic English poet, painter, and printmaker William Blake (1757–1827)—particularly pertaining to issues of palette and composition in the watercolors—Dalí, in depicting Don Quixote as a burlesque caricature of the medieval knight-errant of chivalric literary tradition, departs from the Romanticism convention established by Doré of representing the *hidalgo* as a heroic figure.[9] More likely, and more easily discernible, is the recycling of Dalí's own iconic imagery as can be observed in several of the plates from his 1963 illustrated *Divine Comedy*—a prime example of which is *Virgil's Admonishment*. By contrast, the 1972 lithographs in no way resemble Blake's romantic sensibilities or mimic Doré's heroic iconography. They exhibit none of the frenzied energy of Dalí's own free-standing etchings: the Slinky-like torsos, arms, and legs of tightly wound coils, loaded and ready to spring by which Quixote's figure is defined, the loose flowing cascade of curlicues that denote Rocinante's mane and tail, the whirling, twirling, spinning discs that suggest his shield. They contain none of the surrealistic imagery of his paranoiac paintings juxtaposing different and disparate objects in a provocative and thought-provoking way: flying tigers and burning giraffes, balloon-light, spindly-legged elephants walking on water, melting watches, and boats with butterfly mainsails. Amidst an oeuvre of the bizarre and the absurd, the unexpected and the illogical, Dalí's image of Clavileño persists in remaining enigmatic, distinct, and singular in conception and in execution. Cartoon-like in its simplicity, but neither comic or simple, what we *see* and what we *know*, remain unclear and irreconcilable. It is noted:

> The way we see things is affected by what we know or what we believe. Yet this seeing which comes before words, and can never be quite covered by them, is not a question of mechanically reacting to stimuli. We only see what we look at. To look is an act of choice. As a result of this act, what we see is brought within our reach.[10]

He rears like a well-trained Lipizzaner pony performing a *levade*. A multi-colored frame of interlocking square beads functions as a thin and fragile mosaic beam on which he balances on hind legs—the right, conjoined smoke stacks belching bluish-gray smoke and emitting lemon-yellow flames; the left, a series of pipes and pressure valves connected by plastic tubes and rubber hoses. The bent and elevated forelegs are the metal plates of a child's Erector Set, fitted together with nuts and bolts, pins and posts; the hooves are the scooping buckets of a Tonka Toy earthmover. His torso is but a tangle of coils; his breast is a hodgepodge of gears and teeth—both connected to a robotic head by pulley and wheel. His mechanical innards whiz and whir, but he remains idle. Through the cherry-red lips of a perpetually open mouth, he expires a fiery crimson and canary breath; from his bread-box head crackles a fiery crimson and canary mane; from his aerosol can hindquarter explodes a crimson and canary tail. He is bound to and by a metal grid of spindly bars to which the objects that swirl about him—hand-drawn models of hydrogen atoms, heart-embossed playing cards, and swatches of graph paper and lemon-yellow legal pads—are affixed, immovable, and permanent. Through the unobstructed open "windows" burning targets float in an inky void. A turquoise blue, star-studded orb radiates an ochre light that does nothing to illuminate the objects below. We *know* the horse is not Clavileño and yet—in this posture, in this pose, in this place—it is Clavileño we *see* (figure 5.4).

In 2001, autodidactic graphic artist, actor, poet, raconteur, and Chicago native Tony Fitzpatrick collaborated with his son Max and his daughter Gaby—then ages eight and six respectively—in the production of a suite of twenty-six etchings, each rendered in "a brilliant palette that recalls the vivid hues of early color television and all-American comic books" and inspired by one letter of the alphabet.[11] The image described above is the central figure in the composition representing the "H"; "horse" is simply the obvious choice when considering animals whose moniker begins with the same letter. It is neither Clavileño, nor is it intended to be evocative of Clavileño—Dalí's or otherwise, and yet it somehow is. Once we have had Clavileño "brought within our reach," once we have made the choice to look, we have little choice but to *see*, despite what we *know*. If "it is seeing which establishes our place in the surrounding world," it is knowing—or the illusion of knowing—that makes us secure in that place. It is argued that:

> An image is a sight which has been recreated or reproduced. It is an appearance, or a set of appearances, which has been detached from the place in which it first made its appearance and preserved—for a few moments or a few centuries . . . our perception or appreciation of an image depends also on our own way of seeing.[12]

In this context, the images produced for the original illustrated version of *Don Quixote* were already re-accentuations of Cervantes's vision in so much as they attempted to render with pictures what had been painted with language; the written word had already been transferred to the graphic image and thus re-accentuated. The first engravers were already bringing their own perspectives—their individual and collective ways of seeing—to bear on their visual interpretations of the narrative. No one passage is ever read, interpreted, or appreciated in the same way by any

Figure 5.4. Tony Fitzpatrick. *H Is for Horse*, from *Max and Gaby's Alphabet* (c. 2000, four-color etching with aquatint on paper)
© Tony Fitzpatrick, 2000. Gift of Janice and Mickey Martin.

two people; no one image ever accurately or adequately captures the way any two people envision it. It matters little, if at all, what the artist intends for us to see or what the author intends for us to glean, as reception is perception and as such, it can neither be predicted nor dictated. Even for a particular individual, perception of an event—witnessed or relayed—evolves, devolves, or morphs over time, for it is neither the image itself nor the context in which it is situated that changes but rather our relationship to that image and/or its context. Every experience is tainted and tinted by that which was experienced before. As such, when Dali, almost four hundred years after the first illustrations hit the open market, introduced a new generation to a new iteration of Clavileño in a new context, it was only fitting that he himself would have approached the task with an altered perspective. Isolating Clavileño from the *Dalinean Horses* suite and placing him under a microscope reveals no more about Dalí's intentions or his perspective—for any theories proffered would, naturally, be based on a personal agenda—but simply provides the opportunity to revisit the image, and by association, the text. As noted: "The past is never there waiting to be discovered, to be recognized for exactly what it is. History always constitutes the relation between a present and its past."[13] Enigmatic and obscure, Dalí's lithograph mandates a return to the narrative—to the past, to history, for further exploration. Thus, Cervantes is kept alive and well.

It is the nature of writings such as the argument presented herein to reference elements of images, reproductions of which are included in either the body or at the conclusion of the text. Tradition dictates that examples of the works discussed be provided. While this essay has maintained that convention, it has also intentionally deviated from the norm. By beginning with a lengthy descriptive passage rather than privileging the visual image, a deliberate attempt has been made to re-accentuate the very image deconstructed. Painting with words that which was rendered in pictures re-accentuates the re-accentuated image; the graphic is transferred to the written and thus the image is re-imagined. As the American Pulitzer Prize–winning poetess Anne Sexton wrote, "It doesn't matter who my father was; it matters who I remember he was." It matters not how an artist or an author re-accentuates an image, it matters only how the individual perceives that re-accentuation. What we *see* (and/or what we *want* to see) is what we *know*; what we *know* (and/or what we *think* we know) always influences what we *see*. But the choice to look is always ours—and ours alone.

NOTES

1. Miguel de Cervantes, *Don Quixote,* trans. Edith Grossman (New York: Ecco, 2003), 724.

2. This strikingly odd, slightly ghostlike, and rather haunting image on the reverse side of Bosch's *Christ Carrying the Cross* (c. 1480, oil on panel, diameter 28 cm, Kunsthistorisches Museum, Vienna) depicts a young, naked child pushing a walking frame. The figure is, presumably, the Christ Child, whose early tentative and awkward steps clearly prefigure his Passion, while the toy windmill/whirligig clutched in his right hand is an allusion to both the Cross itself, as well as his inevitable crucifixion. Bosch renders a touching yet unsentimental, if somewhat unusual, image of Christ in all his human fragility as he sets out on the journey that will ultimately lead to his death. Despite the fact that Bosch's death predates Cervantes's birth by some thirty years, in the context of the current discussion it is all but impossible not to see the resemblance of the whirligig-wielding Christ Child pushing the three-legged walking frame to the lance-wielding Don Quixote pushing on the bandy-legged Rocinante as he embarks on his own ill-fated quest.

3. It is possible, although not provable, but certainly delicious to consider, that Dalí may have even "borrowed" his iconic mustache from an image in the midsection of the left wing ("Eden") of Bosch's *Triptych of Garden of Earthly Delights* (c. 1500, oil on panel, 220 x 97 cm, Museo del Prado, Madrid).

4. Maev Kennedy, "Salvador Dalí Diary Up for Sale in Auction of Surrealist Artifacts," *The Guardian*, April 19, 2016, accessed September 10, 2016, https://www.theguardian.com/artanddesign/2016/apr/19/salvador-dali-diary-auction-surrealist-dada-artists-artefacts.

5. Cervantes, *Quixote*, 715–16.

6. Geoff West, "The Early Illustrated Editions of *Don Quijote*," *European Studies Blog*, British Museum, March 29, 2016, http://blogs.bl.uk/european/2016/03/the-early-illustrated-editions-of-don-quixote-the-low-countries-tradition.html.

7. Cervantes, *Quixote*, 19.

8. A. G. Lo Ré, "A Possible Source for Picasso's Drawing of Don Quixote," *Cervantes: Bulletin of the Cervantes Society of America* 12.1 (1992): 105.

9. Daniel Holcombe, "Salvador Dalí as Surrealist Illustrator of Don Quixote," *News and Events* (blog), ACMRS, n.d., https://acmrs.org/news/salvador-dal%C3%AD-surrealist-illustrator-don-quixote.

10. Berger et al., *Ways of Seeing* (London: British Broadcasting Corp., 1972), 8.

11. Tony Fitzpatrick, *Max & Gaby's Alphabet* (Chicago: Museum of Contemporary Art, 2001), 10.

12. Berger et al., *Ways*, 10.

13. Berger et al., *Ways*, 11.

6

Image Not Found: Portraiture, Identity, and the Future of Cervantismo

Stephen Hessel

This chapter's approach to re-accentuation departs from the traditional Bakhtinian definition. Instead of focusing on the re-accentuation of literary characters, such as the world-famous knight-errant and his squire, Cervantes the author will be considered as a character that undergoes this transformative process. Furthermore, visual representation constitutes the medium of re-accentuation in this case, instead of more common narrative-driven media. I aim to show the inherent re-accentuability of portraiture and its subjects, the consequences of this characteristic of that artistic genre, and then bring it to bear upon our contemporary representations of the author of *Don Quixote*.[1]

The goal of this chapter is *not* to describe who Cervantes was. Instead, I outline through an analysis of portraiture how a combination of his works, fragmentary biography, and interpretations of these materials constitute the many operative accentuations of the author active at the moment. In a sense, a consideration of the role of portraiture as an aesthetic tradition and an epistemological force will facilitate this reflection upon Cervantes's "identity" and how his role as author lends itself to constant re-accentuation. This will be accomplished through a psychoanalytic reading of two texts: *Los trabajos de Persiles y Sigismunda* by Cervantes and Orhan Pamuk's *My Name Is Red*. This foundation will anchor a metacritical examination of the history and present state of Cervantes studies while commenting on the possible futures of Cervantismo and how Cervantes and his works may be re-accentuated in the future. Investigation of four topics is essential to achieving this goal: (1) the emerging power and popularity of the portrait in the early modern world, (2) the role of portraiture in the production and re-accentuation of identity and legacy through its contact with the Other, (3) the impact of the Lacanian "lack" within the symbolic order of this genre, and finally (4) the future of Cervantes studies and Cervantismo in light of attempts to paint a clearer picture of the historical author.

Approaching Rome at a pace dictated by the frequency of their misadventures and felicitous encounters, Periando/Persiles and Auristela/Sigismunda, accompanied by their fellow pilgrims, stumble upon a bizarre scene. A portrait of a beautiful woman hangs from the branch of a willow tree. The ground is drenched in gore—the traveler's shoes stained with "warm blood"—and Auristela finds her own visage staring back at her.[2]

Further investigation reveals the presence of two gravely wounded men lying among the rushes, both known to the pilgrims from previous encounters on their long voyage from the barbaric periphery to Rome. In parallel scenes, Arnaldo the prince of Denmark, and the Duke of Nemurs recount their bloody encounter incited by a portrait of Auristela. It appears that both men are desperately in love with the subject of the painting, but on a deeper level their words and actions suggest that ownership of the portrait is worth dying and killing for despite the supposed primacy of the love they hold within the deepest reaches of their being; are they in fact in love with Auristela or have they instead become infatuated with her image? Is there a difference?

The Duke exclaims, "Whoever you may be, you'd have done well, mortal enemy of my rest, if you'd raised your hand a little higher and struck me in the center of my heart, for there you'll unquestionably find a more vivid and true portrait than the one you made me take from my shirt and hang on the tree so it shouldn't help me as a sacred relic and shield during our combat."[3] Despite arguing that the true portrait of Auristela is found in his heart, he refuses to give the physical portrait to Arnaldo without a fight. Arnaldo likewise associates the image with his soul, "You won't take it away, traitor, because the portrait is mine, part of my soul! You've stolen it, and though I haven't offended you in any way you want to take my life."[4] Both claim to hold Auristela's image within their hearts, but the portrait must also stay in their possession to vindicate their right to this love, functioning much like a sacred relic.

Ignacio López Alemany's study of representations of Auristela/Sigismunda in portraiture sheds light on this apparent paradox by contrasting the love arising from the enjoyment of beauty, in accordance with a Petrarchan model, with the "true love" that is founded upon post-Tridentine values of fidelity to the soul of the beloved. Alemany describes Petrarchan love thusly, "Following the Petrarchian [sic] and Neoplatonic convention of 'love's fatal glance,' the viewer will feel compelled to possess the image and transfer his love to it/her [. . .] [T]he Petrarchian [sic] lover is trapped in the contemplation of the *phantasm* impressed in his soul, and instead of a step toward divinity, woman becomes, rather, the principal obstacle on the path to God."[5] Contrarily, the post-Tridentine love embodied by Persiles and Sigismunda is based in Neoplatonic thinking that, despite the persistence of "love's fatal glance," allows the lover to transcend the image in order to encounter a concept of love and beauty beyond the initial infatuation with the image. Instead of an obstacle it becomes a stepping-stone by re-accentuating the role of the image within the framework of desire. The phantasmal lack transforms into a transcendent presence.

Cervantes makes the case against the love shown by both Arnaldo and the Duke when, shortly after arriving in Rome, Auristela is poisoned and loses her beauty. Both suitors reveal that they were enamored of her image, not her soul, and promptly abandon their pursuit of her affections when confronted with her altered appearance. Alternatively, Periandro's love for her remains unwavering and could represent the Neoplatonic resolution of representational infatuation.[6]

In the end, neither suitor ends up with Auristela, but the bloody scene along the pilgrim road to Rome and Auristela's portrait speak to a larger issue within this novel, within Cervantes's literary corpus, and within the social and literary construct of identity during the Spanish Golden Age. The road to love and desire for the Other is paved with images that simultaneously facilitate and threaten the realization of "true" love through their various re-accentuations within the interpretive field.[7] Representation, identity, and portraiture are inextricably linked to love, desire, and self-realization on each of the aforementioned levels, making a nuanced understanding of the role of this genre in the field of Cervantes studies an essential topic of discussion, especially considering recent trends and the quatercentenary of the author's death. What love, what desire, what truth can be found in a portrait?

There is something disconcerting about portraits. Borges in "Tlön, Uqbar, Orbis Tertius" comments on the monstrous nature of mirrors—the reflection they produce an ephemeral portrait—and their multiplication of images, "We discovered [. . .] that there is something monstrous about mirrors. That was when Bioy remembered a saying by one of the heresiarchs of Uqbar: *Mirrors and copulation are abominable, for they multiply the number of mankind.*"[8] Portraits go further because they maintain the reflected image and inscribe it on a surface that can exceed the durability of human experience and existence. Portraits play at presence, but signal back to a lack. This durable presence threatens to become dislodged from its original context, allowing it to be re-accentuated in ways unimaginable to the portrait's artist or subject.

One of the best-known critiques of portraiture dates to the same century as Cervantes's final years. In "A su retrato," Sor Juana Inés de la Cruz attacks the supposed miracles of this genre, but by doing so she also unintentionally signals toward its rising popularity. While the sacral realm of representation is authorized to visually represent religious figures through the tradition of Christian iconography, its extension to the profane could threaten to usurp the prerogative of God.[9] As the sonnet shows, it is not representation that troubles Sor Juana, but rather its pre-sumptive and false durability. Yet despite her eloquent sortie against the value of portraiture, she would shortly become a target of it: re-accen-tuated against her wishes. Posthumous portraits of her began to appear within a half century of her death. Even Sor Juana was unable to escape the genre she so strongly critiqued.

In fact, the macabre and blasphemous defiance of death inherent in the genre may have been part of its popularity. David Castillo's thoughts on Hans Holbein's painting *The Ambassadors* point to a peculiar synthesis of materialistic possessions in the form of the props that surround the two human figures, the materialism of representation in the form of the portrait, and its foil in the critique of worldly materialism ironically made through the distorted representation of a material artifact; a hidden ob-ject/image in the painting. The portrait of two men contains what appears to be a smudge. Further investigation reveals, through anamorphosis, the image of a skull in the space once occupied by the aforementioned aberra-tion. As Castillo states, "[t]he ghostly skull that smears the portrait of the two French ambassadors is intended to remind us of the fact that earthly possessions, power, and knowledge are nothing but illusions that hide the face of death."[10]

Later he identifies the "moralistic drive" of the painting and ties it to the narrative voice of *Guzman de Alfarache, atalaya de la vida humana*, but I find an implicit irony, and perhaps inevitability, in the use of material ar-tifacts to critique the perceived value of other such objects. From another perspective, instead of a moralistic critique, this piece, like Cervantes's *Quixote* is for literature, could be considered an illuminating simulacrum of both the value and the danger of portraiture. Cervantes's masterpiece, like Holbein's portrait, plays at being two apparently opposed things: representation and its own critique—chivalric romance and a satirical attack on it. Don Quixote is simultaneously accentuated and contrarily re-accentuated by Cervantes.

In this way, portraiture may have appealed to the zeitgeist of the later Renaissance and Baroque. The omnipresence of the "illusion/disillusion" motif, the popularity of "wonders" and "novelty," and the incessant flux of perception with regard to Baroque cultural artifacts signal toward this unsettling play with the symbolic order as a source of enjoyment and an object of desire.[11] The paradoxes of portraiture and its critiques of itself allow the spectator to experience the dangers of symbolic lack in a simulated fashion that attempts to project risk while anchoring itself to safety or, in the case of *Guzman de Alfarache* and much of the picaresque tradition, to a moralizing subtext. But this begs the question of what is the purpose of the desire to subvert the symbolic order: risk or its moralizing potential?

This discomfiting quality of portraiture was even more powerful during the Renaissance and Baroque. The move away from the half-face portrait toward the three-quarter-face portrait or full portrait constituted a break from trends in portraiture popularized during antiquity and the medieval period. The added realism of this perspectival technique was bolstered by other advances in aesthetics and, combined with the evermore-flexible parameters with regard to acceptable subject matter, portraiture became dislodged from its lofty place within sacred and regal art. Similar to the rise in print media during the period, the increased accessibility to portraiture constituted a sea change in not only perspectival approaches to the world but also in the role and value of the portrait.

Before venturing into the world of *My Name Is Red*, it is important to emphasize the shift of art from sacred to profane in a way that recognizes both the continued moralizing priority of some works and its marked absence in others. The use of representations of profane subjects as weapons against moral turpitude was commonplace in the literature of the Renaissance and Baroque. The picaresque is replete with "wicked" deeds framed by a moralizing narrative voice in the post–*Lazarillo de Tormes* era: *Lazarillo castigado*, *Guzmán de Alfarache*, *La pícara Justina*, etc. This phenomenon is made possible in writing due to the diegetic nature of narrative, but it finds itself limited in mimetic representation because little context can be proffered beyond the imprecise semiotic framing at times realized through the inclusion of symbols, icons, and emblems. Mimetic representation frequently lacks the context necessary to present a clear critique of the subject matter it represents, allowing for a wide range of accentuations and re-accentuations that depart from the original critical intent.

Therefore, representing the profane through mimesis leaves too much room for a spectator to go astray. Like "love's fatal glance" the image out of context could bring the viewer closer to God, but instead it could become an obstacle. This threat may explain why medieval art was frequently presented as an extra-literary accompaniment to text, thereby minimizing misinterpretation, or as a work of sacred iconography implicitly tied to piety. Consequently, modern art's estrangement from text multiplies its interpretive possibility, which is anathema to a banking approach to the transmission of meaning or moral didactics.[12]

To better understand the impact of the portrait and frame its power in relation to lack, an analysis from a non-Eurocentric perspective may be of use. This can be provided by considering the impact of portraiture on traditional Islamic art, a world Cervantes may have been acquainted with due to his captivity in Algiers. The exaggerated reaction it displays elucidates the similar yet somewhat subterranean phenomenon in Christendom. The question of perspective and portraiture in Islamic art of the sixteenth century makes explicit many of the implicit consequences of the portrait boom in early modern Europe.

Orhan Pamuk's novel *My Name Is Red* does just that. It begins with another bloody scene catalyzed by a portrait—that of the Ottoman Sultan Murat the III. A murdered Ottoman miniaturist, Elegant Effendi, laments his fate from the bottom of a well where his murderer has dumped his body. He warns the reader of the conspiracy that led to his death and still threatens the world, "My death conceals an appalling conspiracy against our religion, our traditions and the way we see the world."[13] The reader, who is addressed directly by a series of voices throughout the novel, soon becomes aware that this threat is a secret book that Enishte Effendi, a painter whose travels to Venice have left him enamored of Western portraiture, has been compiling at the Sultan's request. The book's use of Western artistic techniques to depict the Sultan and his realm immediately reminds us of the Holbein painting and most Western portraits from the sixteenth and seventeenth centuries, but the reaction we hear from the mélange of voices signals to the threat this genre posed to the Muslim worldview.

One of these voices, a miniaturist called Stork, tells a story that details the origins of an aspect of Islamic art that makes Western portraiture a pernicious force due to its perspectival tendencies. Stork narrates the actions of Ibn Shakir, a renowned calligrapher and scribe who witnessed the fall of Baghdad to the Mongols:

> Ibn Shakir ascended the minaret of the Caliphet Mosque in the coolness of morning, and from the balcony where the muezzin called the faithful to prayer, witnessed all that would end a five-centuries-long tradition of scribal art [. . .] [H]e was struck with the desire to express his pain and the disaster he'd witnessed through painting, which until that day, he'd belittled and deemed an affront to Allah; and so, making use of the paper he always carried with him, he depicted what he saw from the top of the minaret. We owe the happy miracle of the three-hundred-year renaissance in Islamic illustration following the Mongol invasion to that element which distinguished it from the artistry of pagans and Christians; that is to the truly agonizing depiction of the world from an elevated Godlike position attained by drawing none other than a horizon line.[14]

This story reveals that visual representation in Muslim cultures was already a delicate issue. Depictions of Allah and the Prophet were violations of Islamic law according to several "hadith," and this prohibition hung like a shadow over the visual arts.[15] Ibn Shakir's adoption of a perspective akin to Allah's, instead of being seen as a dangerous usurpation, becomes an authorizing feature of artistic endeavors because the perspective of the Almighty was inherently sacred and sufficiently contextualized to minimize the work's subversive capacity. Art from this perspective was made sacred by being presented through the eyes of God. Western portraiture, with its proximity to the subject, the absence of a horizon line in many cases, and nonlinear perspectives was seen as an affront because it ignored the perspective of Allah and authorized an anthropocentric representation of the world.

Enishte Effendi's portrait of the Sultan is also deemed heretical because it lacks the context typically provided by the books that, as a rule, contained the works of the Islamic miniaturists. Though part of a book, this portrait threatens to free itself from the diegetic, becoming dangerously mimetic and re-accentuable beyond acceptable limits. One of the many voices that populate the novel is that of an image of a tree who laments its circumstances:

> As a tree, I need not be part of a book. As the picture of a tree, however, I'm disturbed that I'm not a page within some manuscript. Since I'm not representing something in a book, what comes to mind is that my picture will be nailed to a wall and the likes of pagans and infidels will prostrate themselves before me in worship [. . .] The essential reason for my loneliness is that I don't even know where I belong. I was supposed to be part of a story, but I fell from there like a leaf in autumn.[16]

The issue does not lie with the painting's subject but rather the fact that it is a representation, a decontextualized image whose semiotic ambiguity is dangerous to the dominant order. Possible misinterpretation is at the core of its problematic existence.

Another dangerous feature of Western portraiture mentioned in *My Name Is Red* is tied to a characteristic of the genre still found in contemporary society: prolonging presence through the absence inherent in representation. Enishte tells his nephew Black about his encounters with Venetian portraiture and marvels at its power, "If your face were depicted in this fashion only once, no one would ever be able to forget you, and if you were far away, someone who laid eyes on your portrait would feel your presence as if you were actually nearby. Those who had never seen you alive, even years after your death, could come face-to face with you as if you were standing before them."[17] While attractive to Enishte, this preservation of artificial presence in the world after one's demise would be deemed an insult to the authority of the Almighty.

All this frames the concerns of Enishte's fellow miniaturists, but it does not justify the enactment of the violence found throughout the novel. Ferma Lekesizalin's psychoanalytic reading of *My Name Is Red* provides a window into the psyche of the murderer but also speaks to how a portrait could nurture homicidal tendencies within a person and galvanize them to action. By appealing to the Lacanian "lack" in the symbolic order,

Lekesizalin shows how images can both suppress this lack or exacerbate its presence, which is a representation of absence:

> In Lacan, the symbolic system works in such a way that it produces a left-over, a remainder that cannot be fully absorbed in it. The non-symbolizable element, that is, the lack, underlies the subject's relationship with the symbolic system. The subjective realization involves alienation due to the lack. To participate in the symbolic order means to internalize the lack and to be split up with the imaginary ego which is complete and perfect. Lacan emphasized the fact that the subject always realizes itself through the Other that is also affected by the lack.[18]

As Lekesizalin claims, when properly contextualized "icons or representations continue to fascinate us insofar as they fix the hole in the symbolic network."[19] The fascination, enjoyment, and affirmation that come from the properly contextualized image, though tinged with lack, mitigate the anxiety produced by the hole in the symbolic order, but the process must be repeated in order to continue concealing its hollow center. This opens representation up to an ongoing process of re-accentuation that must be properly corralled in order to facilitate the effacement of lack, but this process is inherently capable of shaking off its bonds and creating re-accentuations that threaten the dominant order due to insufficient framing of the image.

Consequently, an insufficiently contextualized image uncovers the lack in the symbolic order and must itself be coopted or effaced. Again, Lekesizalin makes this clear:

> The way the murder demonizes Western art shows what Žižek terms the 'construction of a point which effectively does not exist, but which, nonetheless must be presupposed in order to justify our negative reference to the other' [. . .] Western art, the art of 'the infidels' becomes a fantastic monster created to alleviate the Islamic artist's *angst*; his fear of being faced with the lack in the symbolic order.[20]

For the murderer and other miniaturists, the mimetic game of visual representation within the symbolic order has taken a turn and exceeded the acceptable parameters of its socially sanctioned role. The pleasure that was once derived from artistic representation has soured, and the spectator is now aware that the abyss is staring back. Through the portrait and the varied reactions to it, *My Name Is Red* frames the genre as both alluring and dangerous. Both intratextual spectator and extratextual reader orbit the painting like moths circling the flame of an oil lamp; remove the lamp chimney and it's only a matter of time.

That said, how can these insights illuminate the many and at times contradictory images of Cervantes? Why does consensus seem unattainable?

Why not ponder Cervantes's portrait and context to fix the hole in this particular symbolic network?

But "aye, there's the rub." There is no authentic portrait of Spain's most famous author. His works are adorned with portraits, but they are merely facial composites produced by inference and a healthy dose of conjecture—re-accentuated approximations without an original accented artifact. Ilan Stavans's recent book *Quixote: The Novel and the World* grapples with this issue and claims, "[t]he 'likeness' of Cervantes [. . .] is important because, in the pictorial representations that have been created of the two over time, Cervantes is indeed made to look like Don Quixote and vice versa: they are, in some way, doppelgängers."[21] This may explain the common features shared among the various portraits that grace the front matter of many editions.

This tradition began with forgeries, further complicating the issue and image of the author.[22] Though numerous, I will focus on one portrait because it is the most important and widespread since its discovery in 1910. Attributed to Juan de Jáuregui y Aguilar, *Cervantes c. 1600* claims to be the Jáuregui portrait of Cervantes mentioned in the prologue to the *Novelas*. Cervantes begins the prologue by wishing he could provide his portrait, but after blaming an unnamed friend for its absence he writes, "Anyway, since the occasion has passed, and I am left blank and without figure, I must make use of my own tongue [pico], which though it stammers, may suffice to state truths that even if presented by gestures could be understood" (my translation).[23]

The portrait from his "pico" probably served as the inspiration of the forged portrait, but the description's brevity provides an ambiguous sketch that does not fully match the painting: "lively eyes," the fact that the forgery conceals Cervantes's teeth—which he writes about at length—and the full-length verbal description becoming a quarter-length portrait. Just as Avellaneda attempted to capitalize on the delay in the publication of Cervantes's second part of the *Quixote*, it appears the parties that attempted to pass this painting off as a true portrait of Cervantes were initially successful.

As a consequence, most representations of Cervantes have continued to preserve the similarities between Don Quixote and his author, forever linking not only their physical representation, but also the image and reputation of the author to the book's place in the world. The author is re-accentuated in accordance with the perceived value of his literary works. At first glance this may not seem to be of importance because taking an author at their "word" is not an uncommon practice, but trends in Cervantes studies show that determining what Cervantes was trying to convey is a sticky issue.

James Parr's work on the narrative levels in *Don Quixote* in conjunc-
tion with many subsequent studies shows that identifying the many
speaking voices within the text is almost a Gordian knot. Furthermore,
this multiplicity of voices tends to proffer contradictory information,
begging the question of whom to trust. Finally, the pièce de résistance
is certainly that the whole work, both volumes in fact, are prefaced by
opposing commentaries on plagiarism, the ultimate usurpation of narrative authority.

Therefore, the seminal project undertaken by Américo Castro in 1925
with *El pensamiento de Cervantes*, though immensely important in ques-
tioning both the "romantic approach" and the "ingenio lego" approach to
Cervantes, which dominated the field for over three centuries, finds itself
standing on shifting sands, and as a consequence so does much contemporary criticism as it is strongly found upon Castro's work.[24] It convincingly appeals to the tenes of humanism in order to explain both the author
and his masterpieces, but the nature of the text, despite its diegetic attributes, presents an irresolvable lack whose deconstructive power reduces
the text and its constitutive parts to an empty signifier; a series of poorly
contextualized tableaus whose disconcerting portent simultaneously ef-
faces and uncovers the lack in the symbolic order.

Any reader is faced with this lack, and attempts at filling the void are
subject to the same subversive influence. This lack is a central feature of
both representation and a spectator or reader's interaction with the representational artifact. This is no more obvious than in the genre of portraiture where aesthetics intertwines with metaphysical concerns regarding
authenticity and legacy. The fact that Cervantes's portrait lacks authenticity serves to suggest that all representations and re-accentuations of the
author must grapple with this lack on a level that transcends the custom-
ary baseline found in mimetic depiction.

Can readers avoid becoming Petrarchan lovers and transcend the image to arrive at a catholic and Tridentine love of Cervantes? Or are they
doomed to squabble among the rushes and inter the rejected Other at the
bottom of desolate wells? Perhaps the answers lie somewhere between
the natural impulse to defend the integrity of the symbolic order and attempts to erase what threatens it. Re-accentuation, as understood in this
project with regard to portraiture, may provide a middle ground.

Four centuries after the death of Cervantes, scholars stand at a cross-
roads and the conditions have never been more favorable to reevaluating
the way identities are constructed around the empty signifier that constitutes the core of this iconic author. The theory-based Cervantes scholars
of the American academy and the philologically informed scholars of
Spain—reductive characterizations, to be sure—have begun to grapple
with each other's hypotheses. Cross-pollination has begun perhaps

most interestingly in Spain. Serious challenges to generally accepted ha-
giographic biographies have begun to appear less than a year after Cervantes's remains were supposedly found in the Iglesia de las Trinitarias
in Madrid.

José Lucía Megías, in a biography of Cervantes's early life titled *La
juventud de Cervantes: Una vida en construcción*, has argued that Cervantes
the writer is greatly responsible for the images of him found in contemporary society, but also that much of the information he provided is patently
false (for example, he wore glass, he did not stutter,[25] he was most likely
not a heroic participant in the battle of Lepanto but rather a "soldado
bisoño" or novice soldier,[26] etc.). This work constitutes a major challenge
to the general accepted biography, but in the end, it falls victim to the
problem of portraiture we've already discussed at length. In an interview
Lucía shows that his project is still grounded on a desire to encounter
the true Cervantes, "I wanted to remove the layers of myth in order to
discover the real Cervantes" (my translation).[27]

Despite the opening of many avenues of investigation and interpretation, this impulse may fall short due to its desire to lay claim to an elusive
and illusory authenticity—an unrealizable accurate representation may
be valued over a deeper understanding of the multiplicity of re-accentuation. Furthermore, the meaning and value of the text is variable when
other issues are taken into account. The quatercentenary has given rise to
various re-imaginings and re-accentuations of Cervantes's life and works.
Yet not all aim to encounter the true Cervantes but instead sell products
and services. Cervantes and Don Quixote are not merely literary figures.
Their cultural pervasiveness makes them icons with all the baggage that
accompanies that status.

These appropriations show what many already of know; Cervantes
studies is not an island unto itself. It is a voice, or rather a series of voices,
involved in the larger cultural phenomenon that is Cervantismo. It is
not a unified movement but rather a series of projects orbiting around a
gravitational mass, a singularity; a partially representable lack never truly
captured.

So then what I propose is the adoption of the perspective Borges provides in "Pierre Menard, author of the *Quixote*" in which a French sym-
bolist attempts to write the *Quixote* word for word without copying it—by
being Pierre Menard and producing something different with the exact
same words. This perspective could serve as a point of contact between
the diverse projects that make up the Cervantine solar system.[28] Instead
of a black hole in the center of the symbolic order the omnipresent lack
creates the necessary gravity to produce meaning in almost infinite ways.
Without it the game of signification would be impossible because to fix
all meaning is to destroy its power. Re-accentuation would be impossible.

To conclude, the words of Brother William of Baskerville, the protagonist of Umberto Eco's *The Name of the Rose*, seem apropos. Speaking about another character's desire to destroy a book, William says that the murderous book burner "feared the [. . .] book [. . .] because it perhaps really did teach how to distort the face of every truth, so that we would not become slaves of our ghosts. Perhaps the mission of those who love mankind is to make people laugh at the truth, *to make truth laugh,* because the only truth lies in learning to free ourselves from insane passion for truth." And how can this be accomplished? "Er muoz gelíchesame die leiter abewerfen, so er an ir ufgestígen." "One must cast away [. . .] the ladder, so that he may begin to ascend it."[29]

NOTES

1. The process of re-accentuation, as described by Bakhtin in "Discourse of the Novel," plays an important role in this project. The question of how the rise of portraiture impacted the early modern world reveals a process of re-accentuation with regard to visual representation during the fifteenth to seventeenth centuries, but it also affords the opportunity to consider how present-day valuations and reevaluations of Cervantes and his works stem from specific conditions.

2. Cervantes, *Persiles,* 310.

3. Cervantes, *Persiles,* 311.

4. Cervantes, *Persiles,* 311.

5. López Alemany, "Portrait," 205 and 206.

6. Though I do not deny the possible Neoplatonic resolution, I do not feel that the novel frames it in such a way that it serves the didactic purposes of *exemplum,* which typically would foreground a morally lofty or condemnatory resolution in a work of Golden Age literature.

7. As will be seen, images, texts, and characters are re-accented through their placement within a new context, which may strengthen the fixity of meaning or create dangerously ambiguous parameters.

8. Borges, *Collected Fictions,* 68.

9. Beyond the parameters set by Christian iconography, portraiture enters a realm in which re-interpretation and re-accentuation multiple exponentially.

10. Castillo, *(A)wry Views,* 14.

11. Baroque literature and art are replete with unlikely pairs, characters out of their element, and representations that challenge the fixity of perspective. By re-contextualizing the object of the spectator's gaze, they suggest that the fixity of signs, images, and words is insufficient beyond considering the thing in and of itself. The thing and its representation are always further nuanced or accented by their context, which for the latter is twofold: the context of the signified within the frame of the work, and the context of the signifier and the work that contains it within the frame of existence of the spectator.

12. Freire, *Pedagogy,* 56.

13. Pamuk, *Red,* 5.

14. Pamuk, *Red*, 70.

15. "Hadith" are statements or actions of Muhammad not found in the Quran.

16. Pamuk, *Red*, 47.

17. Pamuk, *Red*, 27.

18. Lekesizalin, "Art, Desire, and Death," 91–92.

19. Lekesizalin, "Art, Desire, and Death," 94.

20. Lekesizalin, "Art, Desire, and Death," 96.

21. Stavans, *Quixote*, 17.

22. The use of "forgery" to describe these portraits should not be construed as moral condemnation. They do purport to be something that they are not but, as no original exists to challenge their authenticity, they are more fabrication than deceitful imitation.

23. Cervantes, *Obras*, 513.

24. Castro's work could be considered one of the most important re-accentuations of Cervantes as a character within the academic cultural imagination.

25. Lucía Megías, *La juventud*, 26–27.

26. Casillas, "Adiós,"

27. Casillas, "Adiós."

28. The Cervantes solar system does in fact now exist since Cervantes was chosen as the name for the star Mu Arae or HD 160691 in December of 2015. The orbiting planets are named after characters from *Don Quixote*.

29. Eco, *Rose*, 492.

III

LITERATURE

7

Borges and the
Hermeneutics of the Novel

J. A. Garrido Ardila

Jorge Gracia has described Borges's short story titled "Pierre Menard, autor del *Quijote*" (henceforth PM) as a work that "in particular seeks to address a set of very interesting and even profound philosophical questions,"[1] and suggested that "[it] is a literary work and text rather than a philosophical one"[2] on the grounds that "literary works are distinguished from philosophical ones in that their conditions of identity include the texts they express. Moreover, literary texts are distinguished from philosophical ones in that they express literary works."[3] Certainly, Borges's short story on the topic of *Don Quijote* is not short of sophistication, both philosophical and literary. In the long history of Cervantean and Quixotic re-accentuations, PM stands out as one of the most suggestive and intricate texts ever produced. It has been the source of countless interpretations and critical readings. Nadia Lie, for instance, has studied and highlighted the role of the reader;[4] Roberto González Echevarría has emphasized the relevance of the context in which it was written;[5] and Enrique Sacerio-Garí has studied Borges's intellectual world and how it shaped this short story.[6] Those and other readings (e.g., by Aguilar, Black, Efron, Matthews, Olea Franco, and Rodríguez Luis, among many others[7]) have repeatedly underlined and praised the formidable complexity of this text. In this chapter, I would like to discuss one central aspect of PM's literary sophistication: its understanding of *Don Quijote* as a text that has been mimicked and re-accentuated throughout the centuries and yet remains always, in its entirety, meaningful to readers of all epochs. My reading of Borges's text will accordingly submit that, while the four-century history of imitations and emulations of *Don Quijote* is rich in titles of quality, Borges believed that Cervantes's opus magnum has remained perennially a contemporary masterpiece of timeless significance.

Don Quijote has inspired and generated countless imitations and emulations. Jean Canavaggio, for instance, has studied these transformations of the Don Quijote myth, in literature, film, and the graphic arts, explaining how its presence quickly became truly pervasive in world cultures.[8] These transformations and re-accentuations have proved particularly prolific in the field of fiction and very often outwith Spain. The most fertile ground for this was probably Augustan England, where many writers re-made and re-modeled the Quixote myth. I have called those English texts *Quixotic fictions* and *Cervantean fictions*.[9] Quixotic fictions are those that re-create the myth of Don Quixote the character (i.e., the monomaniac deployed commonly for satirical purposes), and Cervantean fictions those in which the author uses formal and aesthetic features of Cervantes's novel. Generally speaking, of course, the distinction between Cervantean fictions and Quixotic fictions applies to other national literatures beyond Britain. Borges's PM is quite a remarkable work in the *mare magnum* of fictions that mimic, in one way or another, *Don Quijote*.

The fulcrum of PM is the value and the diachronic validity of fiction. One needs to consider this short story as the work of an author who was also an active literary critic. To Sacerio-Garí this aspect of Borges's life proves instrumental to understand the inception of PM:

> It is not surprising that the man who wrote the pseudo-essay review, "The Approach to al-Mu'tasim," about an imaginary book, a man who spent three years writing a biweekly column on foreign books and authors, should write "Pierre Menard, Author of Don Quixote," a story whose narrator is the reviewer of an imaginary author's life works. It is not surprising that Borges' intertextually-rich critical fictions are based rhetorically on the art of book reviewing.[10]

Like many other authors, of course, Borges uses his own text aiming to reflect upon the nature of fiction. With his background as a literary critic, he chose *Don Quijote* to that purpose, doubtless because *Don Quijote* marks the dawn of modern fiction.

PM unfolds from a Cervantean text that makes conscious use of Cervantean narrative devices to a complex reflection, by Borges the literary critic, on *Don Quijote*'s literary value as a timeless classic. The reader will immediately notice the many Cervantean features in the first paragraphs of PM. The text, written as a literary review, begins with an observation that purports to assess the works of Menard:

> La obra visible que ha dejado este novelista es de fácil y breve enumeración. Son, por lo tanto, imperdonables las omisiones y adiciones perpetradas por madame Henri Bachelier en un catálogo falaz que cierto diario cuya tendencia *protestante* no es un secreto ha tenido la desconsideración de inferir a sus deplorables lectores —si bien estos son pocos y calvinistas, cuando no masones y circuncisos. Los amigos auténticos de Menard han visto con alarma

ese catálogo y aun con cierta tristeza. Diríase que ayer nos reunimos ante el mármol final y entre los cipreses infaustos y ya el Error trata de empañar su Memoria . . . Decididamente, una breve rectificación es inevitable. (41)[11]

(The *visible* work left by this novelist is easily and briefly enumerated. Impardonable, therefore, are the omissions and additions perpetrated by Madame Henri Bachelier in a fallacious catalogue which a certain daily, whose *Protestant* tendency is no secret, has had the inconsideration to inflict upon its deplorable readers—though these be few and Calvinist, if not Masonic and circumcised. The true friends of Menard have viewed this catalogue with alarm and even with a certain melancholy. One might say that only yesterday we gathered before his final monument, amidst the lugubrious cypresses, and already Error tries to tarnish his Memory . . . Decidedly, a brief rectification is unavoidable.)

Like in *Don Quijote*, a number of narrators and editors co-exist in PM. *Don Quijote* was, intratextually, the story written by Cide Hamete, translated by the Toledan boy and then edited by a third person, also with references to Avellaneda, the author of an apocryphal sequel to Part I. In *Don Quijote*, characters and editor engage in constant metafictional commentaries. PM is "written" by an anonymous literary critic who defends the work of Menard and rectifies the malignant work of another critic, sounding like Cervantes himself defending the authenticity of his work against Avellaneda's spurious sequel. The text written by the fictional critic also records the epistolary comments by Menard, and both voices (the writer's and the critic's) alternate to resonate in heteroglossia dialogue. Like in Cervantes's prologue to Part I of *Don Quijote*, where Cervantes turns to the opinions of a (very likely fictional) friend of his, in Borges's story Menard and the critic are introduced to the reader as friends. The fictional author of PM thus sets out to write a text that shares the multiple narrative voices and metafictional components of *Don Quijote*.

After producing a list of Menard's "obra visible" (known works), a total of nineteen works, the fictional critic brings to the reader's attention Menard's *Don Quijote* and calls it "Esta obra, tal vez la más significativa de nuestro tiempo" (45) (This work, perhaps the most significant of our time). He then explains the principles Menard followed when he penned his *Quijote*. The first of these is Novalis's "total identificación con un autor determinado" (45) (a *total* identification with a given author). The second is the rejection of "esos libros parasitarios que sitúan a Cristo en un bulevar, a Hamlet en la Cannebiére o a don Quijote en Wall Street" (45) (those parasitic books which situate Christ on a boulevard, Hamlet on La Cannebière or Don Quixote on Wall Street). Conversely, Menard prefers Daudet's idea of "conjugar en una figura, que es Tartarín, al Ingenioso Hidalgo y a su escudero" (45) (to conjoin the Ingenious Gentleman and his squire in *one* figure, which was Tartarin), although he regards Daudet's plan "de ejecución contradictoria y superficial" (45) (though contradictory and superficial of execution). Yet essentially, the anonymous critic places Menard in the same or similar spot where many other authors have found themselves: writing fiction that somehow emulates *Don Quijote*. Immediately after, the critic unveils Menard's aspirations: "No quería componer otro Quijote—lo cual es fácil—sino *el Quijote*. Inútil agregar que no encaró nunca una transcripción mecánica del original; no se proponía copiarlo. Su admirable ambición era producir unas páginas que coincidieran palabra por palabra y línea por línea con las de Miguel de Cervantes" (46) (He did not want to compose another Quixote—which is easy—but *the Quixote itself*. Needless to say, he never contemplated a mechanical transcription of the original; he did not propose to copy it. His admirable intention was to produce a few pages which would coincide—word for word and line for line—with those of Miguel de Cervantes). This plan differs considerably from those of the legion of emulators and imitators who wrote prose fiction inspired by Cervantes's novel. Menard seeks to write a *Don Quijote* that overshadows the original. This conception reminds of Unamuno's *Vida de don Quijote y Sancho* (1905, The Life of Don Quixote and Sancho). PM and *Vida de don Quijote y Sancho* are, of course, different in many ways and on many levels. Yet both their authors attempt to re-write *Don Quijote* under the same preconceptions.

Unamuno often declared that *Don Quijote*, the book, and Don Quijote, the character, were independent from his creator Cervantes. The fictional Don has lived (and lives eternally) in the imagination of readers and is independent from his creator. There is an allusion in PM that is, in all likelihood, a reference to Unamuno. The sixth work in the list of Menard's oeuvres is "Una monografía sobre el *Ars Magna Generalis* de Ramón Llull" (43) (A monograph on Raymond Lully's *Ars magna generalis*). Llull's *Ars Magna Generalis* calls to mind Unamuno's novel *Amor y pedagogía* (1902, *Love and Pegagogy*), where the character Don Fulgencio is engaged in the writing of an essay titled *Ars magna combinatoria*. Bénédict Vauthier has argued rather convincingly that Don Fulgencio's treatise mimics Llull's *Ars Magna Generalis*.[12] Vauthier explains minutely the implications of this intertextual instance for the understanding of *Amor y pedagogía*. Overall, the resemblance of Fulgencio's title to Llull's are certainly striking, and it is not impossible that Borges was, when he lists Llull, thinking of Unamuno's *Amor y pedagogía*. If so, Borges's literary experimentation goes further than Daudet's Quixotic-Sanchesque Tartarín or any other previous imitations and emulations: indeed, like Unamuno, Borges believes *Don Quijote* (the text and also the character) to live immortal and free from its creator. Novalis's dictum advising the emulator's "total identificación" (supra) with the author is therefore overridden. Like Unamuno,

Borges does not seek the identification with the author, but with the text and the character themselves. PM is hence a deeply Unamunesque take on *Don Quijote*. However, while Unamuno re-wrote *Don Quijote* explaining it, Borges will make Menard re-write Cervantes's text not as a critical reader, but as an author of fiction instead. This, in itself, is a tremendously innovatory endeavor.

Borges's fictional critic states the difficulty of Menard's project: "El método inicial que imaginó era relativamente sencillo" (46) (The first method he conceived was relatively simple). However, soon he acknowledges that "la empresa era de antemano imposible" (46) (but the undertaking was impossible). The following reflection is written in sheer Unamunian fashion: "Ser, de alguna manera, Cervantes y llegar al *Quijote* le pareció menos arduo por—consiguiente, menos interesante—que seguir siendo Pierre Menard y llegar al *Quijote*, a través de las experiencias de Pierre Menard" (46–47) (To be, in some way, Cervantes and reach the *Quixote* seemed less arduous to him—and, consequently, less interesting—than to go on being Pierre Menard and reach the *Quixote* through the experiences of Pierre Menard). Like Unamuno, Menard approaches *Don Quijote* not with the "total identificación" with the author, but with a total identification with Menard himself. At that precise point, Borges has proclaimed, like Unamuno in *Vida*, what we could call the death of Cervantes the author. Although the task is, in the words of the critic, "imposible," Menard proceeds with his plan and writes segments of chapter I.38 following a method explained in a letter he addresses to his friend the critic and is included, partially at least, in PM. "El *Quijote* es un libro contingente, el *Quijote* es innecesario" (48) (The *Quixote* is a contingent book; the *Quixote* is unnecessary), writes Menard in his letter, before extolling other works by Cervantes, namely *La Galatea*, the *Exemplary Novels*, *Persiles*, and *A Trip to Parnassus*, but states that his memory of *Don Quijote* is "simplificado por el olvido y la indiferencia" (48) (simplified by forgetfulness and indifference). Menard proclaims,

> Yo he contraído el misterioso deber de reconstruir literalmente su obra espontánea. Mi solitario juego está gobernado por dos leyes polares. La primera me permite ensayar variantes de tipo formal o psicológico; la segunda me obliga a sacrificarlas al texto "original" y a razonar de un modo irrefutable esa aniquilación . . . A esas trabas artificiales hay que sumar otra, congénita. Componer el Quijote a principios del siglo diecisiete era una empresa razonable, necesaria, acaso fatal; a principios del veinte, es casi imposible. (49)

> (I have taken on the mysterious duty of reconstructing literally his spontaneous work. My solitary game is governed by two polar laws. The first permits me to essay variations of a formal or psychological type; the second obliges me to sacrifice these variations to the "original" text and reason out

this annihilation in an irrefutable manner . . . To these artificial hindrances, another—of a congenital kind—must be added. To compose the *Quixote* at the beginning of the seventeenth century was a reasonable undertaking, necessary and perhaps even unavoidable; at the beginning of the twentieth, it is almost impossible.)

The task is, as both the fictional author and the critic-narrator warn us, impossible. Yet Menard manages to write sections of his *Quijote*. So imposing the feat is, that he will not be capable of writing any more. Yet the critic celebrates Menard's insightful version, that he judges "más sutil que el de Cervantes" (49) (more subtle than Cervantes's). The reason is,

Éste, de un modo burdo, opone a las ficciones caballerescas la pobre realidad provinciana de su país; Menard elige como "realidad" la tierra de Carmen durante el siglo de Lepanto y de Lope. ¡Qué españoladas no habría aconsejado esa elección a Maurice Barrès o al doctor Rodríguez Larreta! Menard, con toda naturalidad, las elude. En su obra no hay gitanerías ni conquistadores ni místicos ni Felipe II ni autos de fe. Desatiende o proscribe el color local. Ese desdén indica un sentido nuevo de la novela histórica. Ese desdén condena a *Salammbô*, inapelablemente. (49)

(The latter, in a clumsy fashion, opposes to the fictions of chivalry the tawdry provincial reality of his country; Menard selects as his "reality" the land of Carmen during the century of Lepanto and Lope de Vega. What a series of *espagnolades* that selection would have suggested to Maurice Barrès or Dr. Rodríguez Larreta! Menard eludes them with complete naturalness. In his work there are no gypsy flourishes or conquistadors or mystics or Philip the Seconds or *autos da fé*. He neglects or eliminates local color. This disdain points to a new conception of the historical novel. This disdain condemns *Salammbô*, with no possibility of appeal.)

The critic then proceeds to quote from both Cervantes's and Menard's texts, thus revealing that the Frenchman's version is identical to that of the Spaniard. But before, he has warned "El texto de Cervantes y el de Menard son verbalmente idénticos, pero el segundo es casi infinitamente más rico" (50) (Cervantes's text and Menard's are verbally identical, but the second is almost infinitely richer).

The richness of Menard's version seems to lie, as the critic has suggested above, in the fact that it is "written" outside the context of seventeenth-century Spain. The importance of the authorial context in PM was highlighted by Mancing, who has noted that "The brief segments he actually produced . . . are indeed the very words MC [Miguel de Cervantes] originally wrote, but are radically different in their meaning and effect on the reader because of the different context in which they were written . . . and read."[13] Shortly after Mancing, Howard Giskin suggested:

Through Menard's recreation of the *Quixote* in a different time and place from Cervantes' original, Borges implies the simple yet disturbing supposition that the meaning of literary works is entirely dependent on the varying historical and social contexts in which they are read. Simple because it seems obvious that context plays an enormous part in the determination of meaning of texts; complex and disturbing in its suggestion that literary meaning is constructed through mental processes irrevocably tied to location and period.[14]

Location and period, or "the context," determine the act of reading. Today, in 2016, the idea immediately brings to mind Andrés Trapiello's translation of Cervantes's text into present-day Spanish,[15] an effort that has not been appreciated by all Cervantes scholars.[16] While Trapiello has sought to cleanse *Don Quijote* from the language of its context to bring it close to twentieth-century readers, Menard attempts the same with an eye on its essence. Indeed, Menard mentions in his letter to the critic, "No en vano han transcurrido trescientos años, cargados de complejísimos hechos. Entre ellos, para mencionar uno solo: el mismo *Quijote*" (49). The key to understand Menard's *Don Quijote* lies in the reader's perspective, as Menard himself reveals to his critic and friend when he notes the three hundred years that have elapsed since 1605–1615.

Menard presents the 1940s reader with a version of *Don Quijote* that, being a word-by-word transcription of Cervantes's original, was still highly meaningful in the mid-twentieth century, as it is today, seventy years after. It is, to the reader in Borges's times, "infinitamente más rico" (50) (almost infinitely richer) because Menard's text is written by a contemporary writer, thus proving that the text is *contemporary*, whereas Cervantes's is not. In other words, the most contemporary version of *Don Quijote* is still the 1605–1615 original version. In order to highlight this, the fictional critic ponders upon a number of issues.

In his commentary of the passage "la verdad, cuya madre es la historia, émula del tiempo, depósito de las acciones, testigo de lo pasado, ejemplo y aviso de lo presente, advertencia de lo por venir" (50) (truth, whose mother is history, rival of time, depository of deeds, witness of the past, exemplar and adviser to the present, and the future's counselor), the critic notes that,

> La historia, *madre* de la verdad; la idea es asombrosa. Menard, contemporáneo de William James, no define la historia como una indagación de la realidad sino como su origen. La verdad histórica, para él, no es lo que sucedió; es lo que juzgamos que sucedió. Las cláusulas finales—*ejemplo y aviso de lo presente, advertencia de lo por venir*—son descaradamente pragmáticas." (51)

(History, the *mother* of truth: the idea is astounding. Menard, a contemporary of William James, does not define history as an inquiry into reality but as its origin. Historical truth, for him, is not what has happened; it is what we judge to have happened. The final phrases—*exemplar and adviser to the present, and the future's counselor*—are brazenly pragmatic.)

To Cervantes, *history* (in Aristotelian literary terminology) was a fundamental element of fiction. When the critic-narrator reminds us that Menard is a contemporary of William James, he underlines the fact that realism as understood by Cervantes was still relevant to great contemporary authors like James. The comment is decidedly not gratuitous, since realism, as a literary concept, was of the utmost importance in the transition of literature into the twentieth century.[17] (In many ways, Borges's allusion to James thus predates Carlos Fuentes's comparison between *Don Quijote* and James Joyce's *Ulysses*.[18]) In many ways, Menard's conception of "historia" is the same as Cervantes's was: the origin or source of "realidad" in fiction. When Borges employs the term "verdad histórica," he uses the same wording as writers in sixteenth-century Spain under the distinction of "historia" and "fábula."[19]

In the following paragraph, the critic recalls an observation Menard made to him:

No hay ejercicio intelectual que no sea finalmente inútil. Una doctrina es al principio una descripción verosímil del universo; giran los años y es un mero capítulo—cuando no un párrafo o un nombre—de la historia de la filosofía. En la literatura, esa caducidad es aún más notoria. El *Quijote*—me dijo Menard—fue ante todo un libro agradable; ahora es una ocasión de brindis patriótico, de soberbia gramatical, de obscenas ediciones de lujo. La gloria es una incomprensión y quizá la peor. (51)

(There is no exercise of the intellect which is not, in the final analysis, useless. A philosophical doctrine begins as a plausible description of the universe; with the passage of the years it becomes a mere chapter—if not a paragraph or a name—in the history of philosophy. In literature, this eventual caducity is even more notorious. The *Quixote*—Menard told me—was, above all, an entertaining book; now it is the occasion for patriotic toasts, grammatical insolence and obscene de luxe editions. Fame is a form of incomprehension, perhaps the worst.)

Borges points to the tendency in Spain, at the time, to read *Don Quijote* as a book about the Spanish nation and its people, e.g., in Ramiro de Maeztu's *Don Quijote, Don Juan y La Celestina* (1926) and Unamuno's *Vida de don Quijote y Sancho* and *Del sentimiento trágico de la vida* (1913). For Borges and Menard, however, *Don Quijote* is still relevant to authors of fiction owing to its treatment of realism, of the "verdad histórica."

The critic who writes PM tells that Menard "Multiplicó los borradores; corrigió tenazmente y desgarró miles de páginas manuscritas" (51–52)

(He multiplied draft upon draft, revised tenaciously and tore up thousands of manuscript pages). Yet the fact that Menard's version is identical, word by word, to Cervantes's original proves that the original *Quijote* is still (in 1941 and today) highly significant from a literary point of view. The critic then declares, "He reflexionado que es lícito ver en el *Quijote* 'final' una especie de palimpsesto, en el que deben traslucirse los rastros—tenues pero no indescifrables—de la 'previa' escritura de nuestro amigo. Desgraciadamente, sólo un segundo Pierre Menard, invirtiendo el trabajo del anterior, podría exhumar y resucitar esas Troyas . . ." (52) (I have reflected that it is permissible to see in this "final" *Quixote* a kind of palimpsest, through which the traces—tenuous but not indecipherable— of our friend's "previous" writing should be translucently visible. Unfortunately, only a second Pierre Menard, inverting the other's work, would be able to exhume and revive those lost Troys). *Don Quijote* thus becomes over time a palimpsest of itself, but one that regenerates constantly. The expression brings to mind José Ortega's claim that "Toda novela lleva dentro, como íntima filigrana, el *Quijote*, de la misma manera que todo poema épico lleva, como el fruto el hueso, la *Ilíada*"[20] (All novels have inside of them, like an intimate filigree, *Don Quijote*, like all epic poems have in them, like a piece of fruit has its bone, the *Iliad*). In PM Ortega's idea gains new meaning, since Borges has argued convincingly and cleverly that both the original *Don Quijote* and any other subsequent versions are palimpsests in as much as Cervantes's novel lives immortally, defying the test of time.

PM closes with this reflection voiced by the fictional critic:

Menard (acaso sin quererlo) ha enriquecido mediante una técnica nueva el arte detenido y rudimentario de la lectura: la técnica del anacronismo deliberado y de las atribuciones erróneas. Esa técnica de aplicación infinita nos insta a recorrer la *Odisea* como si fuera posterior a la *Eneida* y el libro *Le jardin du Centaure* de madame Henri Bachelier como si fuera de madame Henri Bachelier. Esa técnica puebla de aventura los libros más calmosos. Atribuir a Louis Ferdinand Céline o a James Joyce la *Imitación de Cristo* ¿no es una suficiente renovación de esos tenues avisos espirituales? (52–53)

(Menard (perhaps without wanting to) has enriched, by means of a new technique, the halting and rudimentary art of reading: this new technique is that of the deliberate anachronism and the erroneous attribution. This technique, whose applications are infinite, prompts us to go through the *Odyssey* as if it were posterior to the *Aeneid* and the book *Le jardin du Centaure* of Madame Henri Bachelier as if it were by Madame Henri Bachelier. This technique fills the most placid works with adventure. To attribute the *Imitatio Christi* to Louis Ferdinand Céline or to James Joyce, is this not a sufficient renovation of its tenuous spiritual indications?)

The critic, friend, and advocate of Menard's has understood that the Frenchman's *Don Quijote* has "enriched" the art of reading by means of a new technique. One needs to remember, again, Andrés Trapiello's recent version of *Don Quijote*, updated linguistically to the modern reader. Borges believes that Cervantes's *Don Quijote* is such a rich literary masterpiece, rich as a literary artifact, both aesthetically and philosophically, that Menard or anyone else could only re-write it word by word in his attempt to compose an updated version. Cervantes's original text is, on the basis of its literary perfection, the best possible version of *Don Quijote* for readers in 1941 and at any other time in the history of humanity.

To Borges's mind, Cervantes's *Don Quijote* is so rich a text that every single word in it is still powerfully meaningful and relevant to us today, despite those three hundred years "transcurridos" (supra). Cervantes's novel, in its original form, is, as the critic claims, "las más significativa de nuestro tiempo" (supra). The fictional reviewer here refers to Menard's *Quijote*, but the fact that in order to compose the most meaningful work of our time Menard needs to re-write Cervantes's *Don Quijote* verbatim is testament to Cervantes's novel's status today as the most relevant of literary works. The Borgesian thesis in PM is, in sum, that in the wake of all that enormous quantity of emulations and imitations, the original *Don Quijote* will always be the most readable and contemporary of all, and that the best contemporary adaptation/imitation/emulation of *Don Quijote* is *Don Quijote* itself. For Borges, therefore, *Don Quijote* offers itself to the readers of all times as the masterpiece of fiction of the deepest meaning, and whose meaning always interests and speaks to readers regardless of their historical and cultural contexts. Timeless is the greatest literature, and in the depths of the greatest fiction lies its capacity to become timeless, like Cervantes's *Don Quijote*, perhaps even more so than any other novel.

NOTES

1. Jorge J. E. Gracia, "Borges's Pierre Menard: Philosophy or Literature?" *The Journal of Aesthetics and Art Criticism* 59.1 (2001): 45–57, 45.

2. Gracia, "Borges's Pierre Menard: Philosophy or Literature?" 46.

3. Gracia, "Borges's Pierre Menard: Philosophy or Literature?" 46.

4. Nadia Lie, "Who Is the Reader of Pierre Menard? Borges on Cervantes Revisited," in *International Don Quixote*, eds. Theo D'haen and Reindert Dhont (Amsterdam: Rodopi, 2009), 89–108.

5. Roberto González Echevarría, "The Novel after Cervantes: Borges and Carpentier," in *Love and the Law in Cervantes* (New Haven, CT: Yale University Press, 2005), 231–49.

6. Enrique Sacerio-Garí, "Towards Pierre Menard," *MLN* 95.2 (1980): 460–71.

7. Jesús Aguilar, "Can Pierre Menard Be the Author of *Don Quixote*?" *Variaciones Borges* 8 (1999): 166–67; Georgina Dopico Black, "Pierre Menard, traductor del *Quijote*; or Echo's Echoes," *Cervantes: Bulletin of the Cervantes Society of America* 31.1 (2001): 27–49; Arthur Efron, "Perspectivism and the Nature of Fiction: Don Quixote and Borges," *Thought* 50 (1975): 148–75; Steven Matthews, "Jorge Luis Borges: Fiction and Reading," *Ariel* 6 (1989): 62–67; Rafael Olea Franco, "La lección de Cervantes en Borges," *Inti* 45 (1997): 99–103; Julio Rodríguez Luis, "El *Quijote* según Borges," *Nueva Revista de Filología Hispánica* 36 (1988): 477–500.

8. Jean Canavaggio, *Don Quijote del libro al mito* (Madrid: Espasa-Calpe, 2006).

9. J. A. Garrido Ardila, *Cervantes en Inglaterra: El Quijote y la novela inglesa del siglo XVIII* (Alcalá de Henares: Centro de Estudios Cervantinos, 2014) and "The Influence and Reception of Cervantes in Britain, 1607-2005," in *The Cervantean Heritage: Reception and Influence of Cervantes in Britain*, ed. J. A. Garrido Ardila (London: Legenda, 2009), 2–30, 12.

10. Sacerio-Garí, "Towards Pierre Menard," 464.

11. All references in Spanish are from Jorge Luis Borges, "Pierre Menard, autor del *Quijote*," in *Ficciones* (Madrid: Debolsillo, 2012), 39–53. The translations are from Jorge Luis Borges, "Pierre Menard, Author of the *Quixote*," *Labyrinths* (New York: New Directions, 2007), 36–44.

12. Bénédicte Vauthier, "Ejercicio(s) de estilo(s) en *Amor y pedagogía* de Miguel de Unamuno: el *Ars magna combinatoria* del gran mixtificador unamuniano," in *Miguel de Unamuno estudio sobre su obra I: actas de las IV Jornadas unamunianas, Salamanca, Casa-Museo Unamuno, 18-20 de octubre de 2001*, ed. Ana Chaguaceda Toledano (Salamanca: Universidad de Salamanca, 2003), 113–22, 216.

13. Howard Mancing, "Jorge Luis Borges (1899-1986)," in *The Cervantes Encyclopedia* (Westport, CT, and London: Greenwood Press, 2004), I, 81–82, I, 81.

14. Howard Giskin, "Borges' Revisioning of Reading in 'Pierre Menard, Author of the Quixote'," *Variaciones Borges* 19 (2005): 103–23, 101.

15. Andrés Trapiello, *Don Quijote de La Mancha* (Madrid: Destino, 2013).

16. J. A. Garrido Ardila, "El *Quijote* hoy," *Bulletin of Hispanic Studies* 92.8 (2015): 855–60, 859.

17. J. A. Garrido Ardila, "Itinerario de la novela modernista española," *Revista de Literatura* 75.150 (2013): 547–71.

18. Carlos Fuentes, *Cervantes o la crítica de la lectura* (Alcalá de Henares: Centro de Estudios Cervantinos, 1997).

19. J. A. Garrido Ardila, "Cervantes y la novela moderna: literatura experimental y realismo en el Quijote," *Cervantes: Bulletin of the Cervantes Society of America* 33.2 (2013): 145–72, 165.

20. José Ortega y Gasset, *Meditaciones del Quijote / Ideas sobre la novela* (Madrid: Espasa-Calpe, Austral, 1969), 125. This translation is mine.

8

World War and the Novel: Responding to *Don Quixote* in 1914 and 1934

Rachel Schmidt

World War I and World War II cast into doubt the axiomatic belief that Europe was the cradle of civilization, and spurred its intellectuals to question the notion of "European civilization." In 1914, the Hungarian, Georg Lukács (1885–1971), and the Spaniard, José Ortega y Gasset (1883–1955), writing from the peripheries of the war zone, sought answers to the dissolution of European civilization through interrogating the genre of the novel. In 1934, while entering into exile for his criticism of the Nazi regime, the German Thomas Mann (1875–1955) undertook a similar exercise. But what would the novel reveal about the nature of a political-cultural unit, Europe, and a socio-political phenomenon, war? The answer lies in the fact that these authors believed Cervantes to be the initiator of the modern novel, this genre being understood as the literary form unique to modernity and thus giving form to its social structure and dilemmas. In short, for these authors, Cervantes poses the question: What is Europe, and, more specifically, what is European conflict?

There exists, in Bakhtinian terms, dialogic communication by these authors with Cervantes through his novel, and also between the authors in their readings of Cervantes and their notions of the novel. Ortega, Lukács, and Mann approach the image of Cervantes and his *Don Quixote de la Mancha* as "another, alien consciousness and its world, that is, another subject ('Du')."[1] In this dialogue with the early-modern Spanish novel, the twentieth-century authors gain the "gift of indirect speaking," making themselves an object in relationship to their interlocutor, Cervantes, and thus acquire double-voiced speech by introducing into their own thought Cervantes's nuanced analysis of the relation of the European world to its perceived enemies.[2] Through destabilizing the epistemological relation between cultural construct and physical reality in Don Quixote's clash with his surrounding world, Cervantes serves for Ortega as a model for critiquing the epic mode of thought that is leading Europe into war. In a

Bakhtinian sense, Ortega "enrich[es] the other [Cervantes] from outside," making him "aesthetically significant" as an alternative sort of hero.[3] Lukács also sees Cervantes as a model for the critique of modern society, although the Hungarian views the modern dilemma in ontological terms as an irredeemable split between the individual and society caused by a meaningless world. Mann explores Cervantes's incorporation of official discourse justifying the expulsion of the *moriscos* from Spain as an example of the incisive political critique made possible by double-voicing. Moreover, Mann achieves a doubling of double-voicing, as he respeaks Cervantes's already double-voiced speech. Although this effect could appear vertiginous as meaning sways beneath the reader, the unsettling of meaning was one of the themes all three authors sought to explore. An advantage of double-voiced speech, which incorporates the words of the other into the speaker's mouth, becomes salient in times of conflict and war. Uttered in ironic tones, double-voicing serves simultaneously as a weapon for critique and a shield for self-defense.

I. JOSÉ ORTEGA Y GASSET

Ortega wrote his *Meditations on Don Quixote* in the summer of 1914 in El Escorial, far from the brewing conflict but well aware of what was to come. Spain being officially neutral, Ortega was caught between the Francophile Spanish political left to which he belonged and the German colleagues with which he had studied and now dialogued.[4] Ortega's essay on the novel can be read as a response—from Spain—to this feverish embrace of bellicosity by these very same intellectuals. Ortega y Gasset focuses on the question of Europe first through the lens of Spain, and specifically "that we concentrate through *Don Quixote* the great question: for God's sake, what is Spain?"[5] For Ortega, Mediterranean culture grew up around the shores of the Mediterranean Sea, thus predating Europe.[6] The idea of Europe begins with the Germanic incursions into the disintegrating Roman Empire, the movement of trade routes into the continent, and the movement of Greek thought toward Germania. Italy, France, and Spain are Germanized, meaning Europe includes the Mediterranean and the Germanic, which Ortega defines in a series of binary oppositions that can be reduced to these: Spain/Germany, impression/concept. Insistent on an evolutionary notion of nationhood within Europe, Ortega argues that each state must develop its inherited traits for the better good of the whole, but yet at the same time within the whole, thus balancing out the extremes of the parts. Spain "represents in the moral map of Europe the extreme predominance of the impression. . . . We would be unfaithful to our destiny if we abandoned the energetic affirmation of impressionism latent in our past. I do not propose this but rather the opposite: an integration."[7] This integration is an act of patriotic criticism that involves the rejection of all that has been considered traditionally Spanish to find what is truly Spanish.[8]

Whereas Germanic thinkers excel by thinking profoundly and clearly through the concept, Latin thinkers excel through the clarity (and profundity, one could add) of vision. Cervantes, as a Spanish and European artist, integrates concept and impression in the novel. To find the key to a Spanish philosophy, morality, politics, and science, would be to find the Cervantine approach to these.[9] *Don Quixote* exemplifies the realist novel, which calls into question the existence of the ideal realm that motivates human action. Writing about Don Quixote's famous attack on the windmills, Ortega notes that the windmills have a meaning or "sentido" (also meaning *direction* in Spanish) for whoever gives them meaning. For Don Quixote they are giants. But they also have a material reality, being windmills. The realist novel breaks the mystification wrought by Don Quixote's interpretation by showing the windmills' materiality. Yet Ortega asks a larger question:

> But the others? I mean, the other giants in general? From where did people get giants? Because there never were and never have been giants *in reality.* However it may have come about, the occasion in which someone first thought up a giant was not in any essential way different from Cervantes's scene.[10]

This insight is crucial for understanding Ortega's argument that Cervantes destabilizes abstract thought. All ideal thought, that is to say abstract thinking about cultural concepts, lacks grounding in material reality. "Even justice and truth, all the work of the spirit, are mirages produced in matter. Culture—the material vector of things—intends to establish a separate and self-sufficient world to which we can move our internal organs."[11]

Rather than arguing for a nihilistic rejection of culture, Ortega calls for a Cervantine ability to hold in mind both the irreality of culture and the material circumstances of human existence. Maese Pedro's puppet play in *Don Quixote* Part II, chapter 26, and Velázquez's painting *Las Meninas* exemplify this ability to show the ideal vision and the material creation of the ideal in the same artistic image. Cervantes enfolds in the puppet play the sphere of the impossible mythic world of the chivalric adventure, as seen in the tale of Gaiferos and Melisendra in the room inhabited by "naïve men, of the type that we see at any time occupied in the miserable toil of living."[12] Between these two worlds, one ideal and one material, stands Don Quixote, who breaks the barrier as he loses sight of the fictional nature of the puppet play and attacks to protect the damsel's honor. But Ortega notes that the room itself is placed within a book, "in a theatre stage even grander than the first."[13] In this way culture and material reality are for the modern human irretrievably intertwined to such an extent that the greatest clarity is to see the interconnection. In this sense the greatness of Velázquez's *Las Meninas* is that "at the same time that he paints a portrait of monarchs, he puts his studio in the painting."[14]

Ortega ironizes the notion of heroism and defines the novel by describing two vectors for interpreting human action.[15] Using the example of the desert mirage, Ortega writes that one way of seeing is naïve, direct, and linked to the epic: "then the sun effectively paints water."[16] The other is ironic and oblique, showing the visual illusion: "through the water's freshness we see the earth's dryness that feigns the illusion."[17] This oblique seeing corresponds to the realist novel. Ortega, like Lukács, sees the epic hero as one with his environment. The modern hero wants to be himself, thus initiating a split with his ancestors and his present society. For Ortega, Don Quixote is not an epic hero, for he is doubtlessly split from his society, but he is a hero for he clearly expresses the will to be himself, translated into the will for action and adventure.[18] To will to be oneself implies a desire for an ideal, and the necessarily tragic inability to acquire it. According to Ortega, everyone has in himself the stump of a hero, not least of all, the reformer or the innovator who looks toward a better future.[19] The comic perspective laughs at the hubris, which, according to Ortega, serves a useful purpose: "for each hero it wounds, it crushes one hundred charlatans."[20] Comedy arises from the self-delusion inherent in the tragic inability of the hero to achieve his ideal: "From wanting to be to believing that one already is, there is the distance between the tragic and the comic."[21] The tragic aspiration is already present, either in the fall of the hero such as Don Quixote, or in the mere limiting horizon, but the comic element will link it to material reality.[22]

In the summer of 1914, Ortega sees laughing at heroism as largely salutary. In 1916 Ortega published a review of Max Scheler's *The Genius of War and the German War* (1915), in which the German thinker defended the hero in epic terms as the individual who incarnated national essence.[23] Expressing the widespread (but short-lived) German enthusiasm for the war, Scheler maintained that the heroism wrought by war gives the occasion for reinvigorated culture and unique heroes reflecting each nation's values. He even found in war a chivalric principle that affirmed the enemy combatant as an Other, and stated that countries, such as Belgium, that did not distinguish between the chivalric death of the soldier in war and vulgar murder were weak, sensual, and cowardly. Ortega replies that he feels shame ("vergüenza") that passion and lies have poisoned a fellow philosopher's thought.[24] Agreeing with Scheler that the desire for domination and the will to power are the spiritual vectors for war, he points out that the German has fallen into "irrealismo," or unreality, by losing sight of war's material vector: physical violence. Turning to an image from Cervantes, Ortega refers to an object that caused a fight in *Don Quixote* Part I, chapters 44–45, for the maddened knight-errant saw it to be Mambrino's helmet, but its rightful owner, the barber, insisted that it was his basin, an implement of his trade: "If the barber's basin, that has an element of the helmet, were nothing but helmet, no one would argue over it."[25] Likewise, war is not only the assertion of a state's will to power but also the physical commission of state violence. Thus, Ortega argues for a new ideal of justice: a system of international law by which states would resolve conflicts by non-violent means.

II. GEORG LUKÁCS

In his introductory preface to the 1962 edition of *The Theory of the Novel*, the mature Lukács set forth some guidelines for reading this youthful work. Now a confirmed communist, he advises against taking seriously the reactionary nature of his writings, beholden as it was to German Romanticism. Nonetheless, he shares a telling anecdote about the inspiration for the essay in September 1914, at the beginning of World War I, when Max Weber's wife, Marianne, asks him: Who will save us from Western civilization? Marianne described in 1916 the spirit of community that overcame many in the German-speaking world as "in the collapse of the ego and in its special existence in its living unity we felt ourselves become part of a higher ethical dignity, which exists in the complete willingness to sacrifice oneself for the good of the whole."[26] As Lukács wrote in 1962, "The prospect of final victory by the German of that time was to me nightmarish,"[27] but neither was the prospect of the victory by the West (from which he excluded Germany) appetizing. Instead, he took up the question: What, indeed, is the problem of Western civilization? Thus his essay is to be read as a despairing critique of the faults of Western, understood as European, civilization.

For Lukács, as for Ortega, the epic represented the ancient world, in which the individual hero expressed his society's values. The insistence that the epic hero is bygone takes on political overtones given that the German-language press was popularizing the notion of Pan-Germany in words such as "the whole German people stands today on the stage of history as did earlier Frederick the Great. The whole has become the hero."[28] To the contrary, for Lukács, the novel is the heterogeneous form of transcendental homelessness, in which the individual lives unanchored in a society bereft of meaning.[29] The individual becomes a problem, for his ideals cannot survive in the contingent world in which they are

unreal and impossible. The brokenness of the modern world as well as
the broken relationship between the world and the modern individual
is reflected in the essential aesthetic quality of the modern novel: irony.
Irony functions on many levels. As the "self-abolition of subjectivity"
noted by the early Romantics, it lends the novel its strengths, making
of the world's heterogeneous fragmentation the connected web of mis-
understandings that is the novel.[30] The writer who submits to the ironic
viewpoint through an attitude of *docta ignorantia*, acknowledging the loss
of ideals and meaning (in some passages, God), is thus able to achieve ob-
jectivity in the novel.[31] In this way, Lukács preserves the mimetic capacity
of the novel as a broken, self-reflexive form that reflects for him a broken,
meaningless, and grotesque world.

In Lukács's view, violence renders the writer's melancholy reflexiv-
ity objective, making "form-giving," that is to say creative production,
possible.[32] The novel is the form of "mature virility," for through it the
author confronts life while also accepting his limitations in the face of
reality. Lukács defines Cervantes's era as the time when meaninglessness
breaks forth: "when the Christian God began to forsake the world; when
man became lonely and could find meaning and substance only in his
own soul, whose home was nowhere."[33] The resulting abandonment of
the world—that is to say, the loss of transcendental meaning—leads to an
irredeemable split between the individual and society that renders epic
heroism grotesque: "the purest heroism is bound to become grotesque,
the strongest faith is bound to become madness, when the ways leading to the transcendental home have become impassable; reality does
not have to correspond to subjective evidence, however genuine and
heroic."[34] One possible fate of the modern individual in a God-forsaken
world is to insist that reality must conform to his or her ideal of it, causing what Lukács terms the narrowness of the soul in the abstract idealist,
of which the character Don Quixote is the example par excellence. Don
Quixote is still a hero insofar as his "interiority succeeded, not only to
emerge unblemished from the fray, but even to transmit some of the
radiance of its triumphant, though admittedly self-ironising, poetry to
its victorious opponent [reality]."[35] The other possibility is that the soul
becomes wider than the social world can encompass, resulting in the disillusioned romantics such as Wilhelm Meister.

It is worth noting in Lukács's characterization of Cervantes as author
a slippage between the image of an unconscious genius and an authorial
force behind the form that is the novel. For Lukács the individual is, in
the fullest sense of the term, a creation of his/her time, so that Cervantes
must be dual insofar as he comes from a dual moment. Cervantes, the
"naïve artist" and the "intuitive visionary," corresponds to "watershed of
two historical epochs": the epic world rounded by meaning and the mod-

ern world of the novel, a world bereft of meaning. Cervantes, as seen by Lukács, "creatively exposed the deepest essence" of his period's problematic, this being the split between the subjective world of the modern subject and his/her society.[36] He also praises Cervantes's "creative criticism of the triviality of the chivalrous novel" that "leads us once more to the historico-philosophical sources of this genre."[37] Yet Lukács pictures Cervantes as "the faithful Christian and naïvely loyal patriot," thus stripping from the Spanish author either the consciously critical viewpoint that Ortega attributes him or the willfully ironically and politically engaged position Mann will attribute him.[38] Lukács's ultimate dismissal of Cervantes's agency might be due to the Hungarian's belief—at this point in his life—in the "true world of ideas."[39] Lukács personifies another speaker in Cervantes's novel, "the profound melancholy of the historical process, of the passing of time that speaks through this work a truth more powerful than the hero: that time brushes aside even the eternal."[40] Making the novel a mouthpiece for historical time not only minimizes the agency of the human being, including but not limited to the author, but also leads to the assertion that historical time wields the power to overcome the eternal, associated with the realm of ideas and ideals.[41]

In response to Marianne Weber's attempt to lighten his mood in 1914 by regaling him with tales of individual heroism, Lukács responded, "The better the worse!" In 1914 the young Hungarian despaired of finding answers to his questions about Europe's fate, giving up hope for human agency in the face of what he viewed as history's overwhelming power. It is not surprising that he would turn to Marxism in 1918. But on the eve of 1914—in the face of total war—it seemed that the literary genre that held clues to explaining the convulsion of socially sanctioned violence gripping Europe was the one instituted on the parody of socially sanctioned violence: *Don Quixote.*

III. THOMAS MANN

Thomas Mann's essay, "Voyage with *Don Quixote,*" is set on his trip to the United States in May 1934.[42] The essay opens with the question: What is German? The structure of the essay parallels Ortega's encircling technique used in the *Meditaciones*, by which the essayist approaches his topic indirectly, as the train of thoughts flows from the surroundings but leads to central insights.[43] Mann also alludes to Ortega's concept of human living as a shipwreck, held afloat by the security systems, both ideological and technological, that are civilization and culture.[44] Elusive and ironic in its political references, it has been called Mann's credo in this difficult time, and was the final essay in his last volume to be published in Germany during the Nazi period.[45] A critic of the Nazis from the early 1930s onward, Mann had written to the Reichsministerium des Inneren on April 23, 1934, to defend himself from the charge of dishonoring Germany, indicating his fear of symbolic and physical eradication from his country.[46]

Mann's reading of *Don Quixote* hinges on humor, history, irony, and European civilization. For Mann, Don Quixote is a *Narr*, a bookish fool pushed into madness by reading chivalric romances.[47] Sancho Panza's affection for his master renders him lovable, but also "Volkstümlich," that is to say, representative of the Spanish people.[48] Noting that Spain's greatness is long past, Mann alludes to Germany's present by contrasting the history of might and power ("großmächtig") to human-sized history, associated with freedom and an ironic view of one's self. Human history links to Sancho's (and Spain's) ability to embrace the sad deflation of Spanish chivalry in Don Quixote's figure. As Mann notes ironically, the lighthearted view of one's place in history probably "does not ensure a people a prominent role in history,"[49] but it does grant the Spanish people charm, good taste, and, most importantly, a good conscience, resulting in the final defeat of brutality. In this way a people does not forget the ugliness of humanity, violent injustice, or the brutality in their midst, nor grant support to those who drive toward power through violent means.[50] Mann echoes Ortega's notion of shipwreck to figure the concept of adequation to reality, understanding the shipwreck to undo hubristic claims upon grandiose history. As he clarifies, "History is ordinary reality, to which one is born, to which one must be adequate. Upon it Don Quixote's inept loftiness of soul suffers shipwreck."[51] This image of the shipwrecked knight-errant Mann finds winning and laughable. Nonetheless, he allows himself to imagine a much darker image, one he notes that Cervantes did not imagine: the Don Quixote of brutality, who in his opposition to idealism is a pessimistic believer in force or violence ("pessimistisch-gewaltgläubiger Don Quixote").

Mann sees in Cervantes a model for the author writing in a repressive regime.[52] The German novelist's admiration for the Ricote episode in *Don Quixote* Part II, chapter 54, links to both his own exile and the fate of the Jewish exiles aboard the *Volendam*. Sancho Panza meets his former neighbor, Ricote, exiled during the Morisco expulsion of 1609–1613, but who has returned to Spain disguised as a pilgrim to find a treasure he left buried there. Mann admires the way in which Cervantes shrewdly mixes "professions of loyalty and of the author's strict adherence to the church, his blameless submission to the great Philip III—and the most lively human sympathy for the awful fate of the Moorish people . . ."[53] Cervantes wins the reader's sympathy for Ricote by letting his character voice longing for his home country, Spain, and express the sufferings endured in exile. By linking the official phrases denouncing the *moriscos* as the "snake in the bosom" and the "enemy in the house" to other phrases expressing love for Spain, Cervantes shows the calumnies to be lies (*Lügen*).[54] Moreover, Cervantes's heart ("das Herz des Dichters") speaks in this second part of Ricote's speech, as he sympathizes with the persecuted and banned *moriscos* who are equally as good as he and the other Spaniards.

Mann's reading of Ricote's praise for Philip III's expulsion of his people depends on introducing irony into Cervantes's voicing of the official discourse. Indeed, Mann inflects Cervantes's words with his own practice of "stille Kritik" during the first years of his exile.[55] Through his "silent criticism," as opposed to his earlier *and* later "militant humanism," he had hoped, in vain, to maintain contact with German readers.[56] Mann practices this silent criticism interpreting the Ricote episode, for not only does he demonstrate how Cervantes achieves speaking for an expelled people obliquely, but he also points out Ricote's praise of Germany, where he found freedom of conscience. As Smith remarks, Mann's "criticism is as indirect as Cervantes': the Spaniard criticizes Spain by portraying the loyalty and homesickness of the Moor; Mann criticizes Germany by emphasizing Cervantes' understanding and sympathy for the plight of the (Moorish) exiles."[57]

Mann's analysis of the *morisco* episode invites reconsideration of the offhand references to the Jewish passengers aboard the *Volendam*. Married to the Jewish-born Katia Pringsheim, Mann vocally opposed Nazi anti-Semitism already in 1930 when he signed a petition "Against Anti-Semitism," and knew about the concentrations camps by 1933 or 1934, denouncing them publicly in 1936 in his "Down with the Concentration Camps."[58] Given this knowledge and his public stance against Nazi anti-Semitism, his representation of the Jewish passengers as merely fellow shipmates is ironic, for he places in his own mouth the judgmental asides of urbane anti-Semitism. In the May 21 entry are two such examples. A Dutch woman from Rotterdam travels with twins to South Carolina to visit their grandmother. The essayist judges the grandmother as "furchtbar egoistisch"—a surprisingly colloquial turn of phrase—for bidding her family to come to the American South in the heat of summer. He excuses himself for such indiscreet cattiness: "It is no affair of ours; but when one shares the same horizon with such proceedings, one has one's thoughts."[59] He then remarks offhandedly that a Jewish nanny accompanies her who reads modern books. The reader is left wondering about both the nanny, spoken of so condescendingly, and the possibility of her escape to America.

With a similarly supercilious tone, Mann presents an American male traveling first-class who socializes with the Jewish refugees. In the May 21 entry Mann describes the American as the "Enfant terrible" of the traveling society, sporting an Anglo-Saxon fish mouth.[60] The American here appears as a sort of Sancho, who dares to mingle with the exiled Ricote; indeed, this would explain the grotesque imagery with which Mann describes his mouth. The American's customs irritate the author, who views him as ignoring his fellow first-class passengers, preferring to read while he eats and socializing at other times with the Jewish passengers in tourist class. In his aloof nature and implicitly haughty disregard for the first-class bourgeoisie, the American calls to mind Lukács's characterization of Don Quixote as an abstract idealist as he seeks to live out higher ideals than those of his social class. His presence unsettles the bourgeois mindset that Mann chooses to critique in his self-representation. Mann confesses jealousy of the Jews with whom the American socializes and envies the American's focus and purposefulness. When the American does not deign to view a Hollywood movie with the first-class passengers, Mann describes him as disturbing, or "beunruhigender," literally unsettling the peace.[61] In his diary entries from the time that he wrote this essay, Mann wrote a quatrain titled "To Put Myself at Peace" ("Zu meiner Beruhigung"), in which the verse read: "You lack only peace, nothing more!"[62] The American can be seen, then, as a figure of conscience, who unsettles Mann in his own complacency. As Mann complains of the American, "People ought to know where they belong. People ought to keep together."[63] In short, Mann takes a daring turn on ironic double-voicing, for he chooses to use himself as the mouthpiece for a sort of petty, chauvinistic, and judgmental mindset that allowed anti-Semitism to flourish, and then poses the silent American as the upright actor whose actions critique the Nazi policy that forces the Jewish passengers into exile.

Although Mann does not allow himself to picture a Nazi or Fascist Don Quixote, he does dream of a Don Quixote that shifts into the face of Zarathustra, boasting the features of Nietzsche, on the morning the ship pulls into New York City.[64] Here Zarathustra repeats one of the final characterizations of Don Quixote in Cervantes's text: that as both Alonso Quijano and Don Quixote, he was always amiable and kind, and therefore beloved by all—in short, not a man of brute force. Earlier in the text, Mann criticizes Nietzsche for his "hectic attack" upon the Christian ethics that exalt and abase the hero. Defending Europe and implicitly the Jewish people, Mann insists that Christianity is the flower of Judaism, and comprises, along with Mediterranean antiquity, one of the two pillars of Western culture. To eliminate either Christianity—and by extension, Judaism—or Mediterranean antiquity would mean to break from Europe, resulting in an "inconceivable, impossible diminishment" of the "human stature" of any community.[65] In the context of 1934, the elimination of the Jewish people from Germany means the destruction of one pillar of Western culture, and thus the destruction of Germany. Mann demystifies the myth of the Jew as the enemy within, just as Cervantes demystified the myth of the *morisco* as the serpent in the breast.

CONCLUSION

On the eves of both World Wars, authors from Spain, Hungary, and Germany turn to *Don Quixote* looking for answers to their impassioned questions: What is the problem of (Spanish, German, European) civilization, and how has it given rise to the horrors of war? For both Ortega y Gasset and Lukács, reacting to a feverish German nationalism that equated death on the battlefield with chivalric heroism, Cervantes's novel demystified the notion of epic heroism in modern society. Focusing on the tragicomic aspects of the novel, Ortega dialogued with a Cervantes who questioned not only the ideals of chivalry but also justice and culture itself. Lukács opposed the hero of the epic to the anguished protagonist of the novel, who lives in a world bereft of meaning and is destined either to dedicate his life toward abstract, idealist, and ultimately nonsensical pursuits as did Don Quixote, or to a life of disillusionment and pleasure-seeking. For Lukács, the novel as the modern genre expressing the essential split between the individual and society sets forth the problem of Europe. Mann, slowly accepting his exile from Nazi Germany, finds in the Ricote episode an alternative Germany that is open and tolerant, as well as a model for writing in an oppressive political situation. Indeed, as I have written this essay in 2016 and 2017, I have found myself wondering—at times even aghast—at the ways the social and political problems signaled by these three twentieth-century writers through their dialogue with Cervantes have emerged yet again in Europe and North America. Through his parody of violence enacted in the name of chivalric/military justice and through his double-voicing of the political discourse scapegoating a minority population within early-modern Spain, Cervantes presents a text from which to open a critique of Western nation-states and their contingent political and economic order.

 Don Quixote has become the site of a speech genre encompassing essays on the novel that seek to comprehend and criticize—albeit obliquely—European national bellicosity. In "The Problem of Speech Genres," Bakhtin notes that the native speaker is fluent in these genres, being able to recognize them spontaneously and participate in them fully without even recognizing their existence.[66] Fluency involves the assimilation of the words of others as well as the re-accentuation of these words.[67] Although all three authors worked in written genres, their conscious choice to adopt essayistic forms that are more fluid, experimental, and informal made present a stronger, essayistic authorial voice impassioned by the strong emotions of the politically fraught moment and openly impressed by the contingent surroundings. So doing, they responded to an *image* of Cervantes based on the author's interpenetration with his characters, be they Don Quixote, Sancho, or Ricote. As Bakhtin notes, the author "enters into these images as an indispensable part of them (images are dual and sometimes double-voiced)."[68] Thus, Cervantes as an ironist, or in Bakhtinian terms, a master of double-voicing, becomes the author who asks the questions to be answered: what is European civilization? What are the national identities of its constituent states? And why does it fall into such brutal conflicts with its perceived enemies within?

NOTES

1. M. M. Bakhtin, "The Problem of the Text in Linguistics, Philology, and the Human Sciences: An Experiment in Philosophical Analysis," in *Speech Genres and Other Late Essays*, trans. Vern W. McGee (Austin: University of Texas Press, 1986), 111.

2. Bakhtin, "The Problem of the Text," 110.

3. M. M. Bakhtin, "Author and Hero in Aesthetic Activity," in *Art and Answerability: Early Philosophical Essays by M.M. Bakhtin*, eds. Michael Holquist and Vadim Liapunov, trans. Vadim Liapunov (Austin: University of Texas Press, 1990), 129.

4. The fragmentary nature of Ortega's text has led to speculation that the outbreak of war caused him to publish it prematurely. Expressing his personal bind vis-à-vis Germany, in an anonymous depiction of his teacher Hermann Cohen published in 1915, Ortega cautioned the need to distinguish between German politics and science (Rachel Schmidt, *Forms of Modernity:* Don Quixote *and Modern Theories of the Novel* [Toronto: University of Toronto Press, 2011], 207–8).

5. "Razón de más para que concentremos en el *Quijote* la magna pregunta: Dios mío, ¿qué es España?" (José Ortega y Gasset, *Meditaciones del Quijote* [Madrid: El Arquero, 1975], 88). All translations are mine unless otherwise indicated.

6. Ortega y Gasset, *Meditaciones del Quijote*, 62.

7. "Representamos en el mapa moral de Europa el extremo predominio de la impresión . . . seríamos infieles a nuestro destino si abandonáramos la enérgica afirmación de impresionismo yacente en nuestro pasado. Yo no pongo ningún abandono, sino todo lo contrario: una integración" (Ortega y Gasset, *Meditaciones del Quijote*, 86).

8. According to the "parable" Ortega offers, Admiral Parry urged his sled dogs north one day only to find how far south he had traveled (Ortega y Gasset, *Meditaciones del Quijote*, 92).

9. Ortega y Gasset, *Meditaciones del Quijote*, 93.

10. "¿y los otros?, quiero decir, ¿y los gigantes en general? De dónde ha sacado el hombre los gigantes? Porque ni los hubo ni los hay *en realidad*. Fuere como fuere, la ocasión en que el hombre pensó por vez primera los gigantes no se diferencia en nada esencial de esta escena cervantina" (Ortega y Gasset, *Meditaciones del Quijote*, 125–26).

11. "También justicia y verdad, la obra toda del espíritu, son espejismos que se producen en la materia. La cultura—la vertiente ideal de las cosas—pretende establecerse como un mundo aparte y suficiente, adonde podamos trasladar nuestras entrañas" (Ortega y Gasset, *Meditaciones del Quijote*, 126).

12. ". . . hombres ingenuos, de estos que vemos a todas horas ocupados en el pobre afán de vivir" (Ortega y Gasset, *Meditaciones del Quijote*, 118–19).

13. ". . . en otro como retablo más amplio que el primero" (Ortega y Gasset, *Meditaciones del Quijote*, 119).

14. ". . . al tiempo que pintaba un cuadro de reyes, ha metido su estudio en el cuadro" (Ortega y Gasset, *Meditaciones del Quijote*, 119).

15. According to Ortega, the Renaissance squeezed the possibility of adventure, putting physical limits to the world (effectively bracketing out the supernatural) and psychological limits on the human imagination (Ortega y Gasset, *Meditaciones del Quijote*, 122–23).

16. ". . . entonces el agua que el sol pinta es para nosotros efectiva. . . ." (Ortega y Gasset, *Meditaciones del Quijote*, 124).

17. ". . . a través de la frescura del agua vemos la sequedad de la tierra que la finge" (Ortega y Gasset, *Meditaciones del Quijote*, 124).

18. Ortega y Gasset, *Meditaciones del Quijote*, 135.

19. Ortega y Gasset, *Meditaciones del Quijote*, 140.

20. "Es una risa útil; por cada héroe que hiere, tritura a cien mixtificadores" (Ortega y Gasset, *Meditaciones del Quijote*, 142).

21. "De creer ser a creer que se es ya, va la distancia de lo trágico a lo cómico" (Ortega y Gasset, *Meditaciones del Quijote*, 142).

22. Cervantes take the term *tragicomedia* from Fernando de Rojas, who originally titled his *Celestina* (1499) the *Tragicomedia de Calisto y Melibea*, to define the novel.

23. Ricardo Gibu Shimabukuru, "En torno a la esencia del poder. Un estudio comparativo entre Max Scheler y José Ortega y Gasset," *Franciscanum* 163.57 (2015): 133. See Max Scheler, *Der Genius des Krieges und der deutsche Krieg* (Leipzig: Verlag der Weißen Bücher, 1915), 59.

24. José Ortega y Gasset, "El Genio de la guerra y la Guerra alemana (Der Genius des Krieges und der deutsche Krieg, por Max Scheler. 1915)," in *Obras completas*, vol. 2 (Madrid: Revista de Occidente 1963), 202.

25. Ortega y Gasset, "El Genio de la guerra y la Guerra alemana," 204.

26. Jeffrey Verhey, *The Spirit of 1914: Militarism, Myth, and Mobilization in Germany* (Cambridge: Cambridge University Press, 2000), 130.

27. Georg Lukács, *The Theory of the Novel*, 11.

28. Jeffrey Verhey, *The Spirit of 1914: Militarism, Myth, and Mobilization in Germany*, 176.

29. The German phrase is "transzendentalen Obdachlosigkeit" (Georg Lukács, *Die Theorie des Romans* [Darmstadt and Neuwied: Hermann Luchterhand, 1982], 32).

30. Georg Lukács, *The Theory of the Novel*, trans. Anna Bostock (Cambridge, MA: The MIT Press, 1989), 74–75.

31. Lukács, *The Theory of the Novel*, 90.

32. Lukács, *The Theory of the Novel*, 85.

33. Lukács, *The Theory of the Novel*, 103.
34. Lukács, *The Theory of the Novel*, 104.
35. Lukács, *The Theory of the Novel*, 104.
36. Lukács, *The Theory of the Novel*, 104.
37. Lukács, *The Theory of the Novel*, 103.
38. Lukács, *The Theory of the Novel*, 104.
39. Lukács, *The Theory of the Novel*, 105.
40. Lukács, *The Theory of the Novel*, 104.
41. As Georg Lukács readily admitted in his 1962 preface, *The Theory of the Novel* was based on German Romantic aesthetic theories as well as Hegelian philosophy, and was enthusiastically received, including by Thomas Mann. Lukács's notion of romantic irony and his definition of the novel were deeply indebted to the young Friedrich Schlegel (Schmidt, *Forms of Modernity*, 96–101).
42. Although the essay takes the form of diary entries written on ship, Mann wrote it several months later, starting on August 31, 1934 (Volker Hage, "Mit '*Don Quijote*' nach Amerika. Über Thomas Manns 'Seitensprung' im Jahre 1934," *Thomas Mann Jahrbuch* 10 [1997]: 59). When it first appeared in a volume titled *Leiden und Größe der Meister* (Berlin: Gottfried Bermann Fischer, 1935), the meditation on *Don Quixote* replaced an intended essay on Gerhard Hauptman that Mann decided not to publish after his contemporary declared political sympathy for the Nazi party (Anne-Kathrin Reulecke, "Voyage with Don Quixote: Thomas Mann between European Culture and American Politics," in *Escape to Life: German Intellectuals in New York: A Compendium on Exile after 1933*, eds. Eckhart Goebel and Sigrid Weigel (Berlin and Boston: Walter De Gruyter, 2012), 379.
43. According to a diary entry, Mann considered it both a feuilleton and a work rich in associations (Hage, "Mit '*Don Quijote*' nach Amerika," 59).
44. On Ortega's notion of culture, civilization, rafts, and shipwreck, see John T. Graham, *The Social Thought of Ortega y Gasset: A Systematic Synthesis in Postmodernism and Interdisciplinarity* (Columbia: University of Missouri Press, 2001), 1, 115.
45. Hage, "Mit '*Don Quixote*' nach Amerika," 61, 63. Living in exile in Germany at the time, Mann made his first Atlantic crossing to promote his novel, *Joseph and His Brothers*. Nonetheless, this text is fraught with the foreboding of a future American exile from 1938 to 1952. During the 1934 Atlantic crossing, "his personal state was one of transition, doubt, and uncertainty" (Gabriele Eckhart and Meg H. Brown, *Shifting Viewpoints: Cervantes in Twentieth-Century and Early Twenty-First-Century Literature Written in German* [Newcastle upon Tyne: Cambridge Scholars, 2013] , 41).
46. Reulecke, "Voyage with Don Quixote," 385.
47. Thomas Mann, *Meerfahrt mit Don Quijote* (Wiesbaden: Im Insel Verlag, 1956), 17.
48. Mann, *Meerfahrt mit Don Quijote*, 18.
49. Thomas Mann, "Voyage with Don Quixote," in *Essays*, trans. H. T. Lowe-Porter (New York: Vintage, 1957), 336.
50. "Aber sie vergißt im Grunde das menschlich Unschöne, das Gewalttättig-Ungerechte und Brutale nicht, das in ihrer Mitte geschehen, und ohne ihre Sympathie ist zuletzt kein Macht- und Tüchtigkeitserfolg haltbar" (Mann, *Meerfahrt mit Don Quijote*, 19).

51. Mann, "Voyage with Don Quixote," 336.

52. Goethe often served as an alter ego in Mann's writings (Hermann Kurzke, *Thomas Mann*, trans. Leslie Wilson [Princeton, NJ: Princeton University Press, 1999], 435).

53. Mann, "Voyage with Don Quixote," 359.

54. Mann, *Meerfahrt mit Don Quijote*, 52.

55. Mann's reading of Cervantes's ironic voicing of Ricote's speech is now largely accepted among Cervantes scholars. For example, see Francisco Márquez Villanueva, *Personajes y temas del Quijote* (Madrid: Taurus, 1975), 241. Nonetheless, it was unique in Mann's time.

56. Michael Allen Smith, "Thomas Mann's 'Meerfahrt mit *Don Quijote*: The Case against a Formalist Approach to Essay Criticism," *The German Quarterly* 49.3 (May 1976): 325.

57. Smith, "Mann's 'Meerfahrt mit *Don Quijote*'," 324.

58. Kurzke, *Thomas Mann*, 426.

59. Mann, *Meerfahrt mit Don Quijote*, 23; Mann, "Voyage with Don Quixote," 339.

60. Thomas Mann, *Meerfahrt mit Don Quijote*, 24.

61. Thomas Mann, *Meerfahrt mit Don Quijote*, 43.

62. The German reads, "Dir fehlt nur Ruhe, weiter nichts!"(Hage, "Mit 'Don Quijote' nach Amerika," 59).

63. Mann, "Voyage with Don Quixote," 354.

64. Gene R. Pendleton and Linda L. Williams, "Themes of Exile in Thomas Mann's 'Voyage with Don Quixote'," *Cervantes: Bulletin of the Cervantes Society of America* 21.2 (Fall 2001): 82.

65. Mann, "Voyage with Don Quixote," 356.

66. M. M. Bakhtin, "The Problem of Speech Genres," in *Speech Genres and Other Late Essays*, trans. Vern W. McGee (Austin: University of Texas Press, 1986), 78–79.

67. Bakhtin, "The Problem of Speech Genres," 89–91.

68. Bakhtin, "The Problem of the Text," 116.

9

The Don Quixotes of Science Fiction

Howard Mancing

INTRODUCTION

Don Quixote is the world's first science fiction novel.

Or at least that is what Robert Plank suggests in his 1973 article "Quixote's Mills." His argument is that Don Quixote's attack on the windmills he perceives as giants is "a confrontation of man and machine, one of the earliest in literature, and one of the most perfect."[1] Plank is, of course, only partially right: the windmill scene does indeed prefigure the classic man-machine relationship that is so characteristic of much science fiction. But a single scene does not define the entire novel. *Don Quixote* is a great novel in so many ways: it is a profoundly realistic, metafictional, psychological, ironic, satiric, comic, parodic novel. It is the novel that has given us the single most recognizable character of all time,[2] and it is the novel that has most influenced the subsequent development of the genre of the modern novel that emerged in the Renaissance. But it is not the first science fiction novel. The windmill scene is paramount in the man-machine (or man-technology) relationship, but it is far from the only important event in the novel. As Iván Jaksić has stated, "Not only do several episodes revolve around the protagonist's confrontation with a variety of machines and technological instruments, but also the entire book concerns Don Quijote's inability to come to terms with a modern world increasingly characterized by technology."[3]

There is, however, one scene in which Don Quixote and his squire Sancho Panza travel into outer space. Well, almost. In chapter 41 of the second part of the novel (1615) an elaborate ruse is played on the mad knight-errant and his squire. In order to rescue a damsel in distress, a magical flying horse named Clavileño is sent to transport knight and squire to the scene of the captivity, located halfway around the world. The horse is constructed of wood and is steered by a wooden peg on its head. After Quixote and Sancho, blindfolded, mount the device, they are made to believe that they are flying through the air at great heights. Torches are used to create the heat of the stars and bellows to create the sensation of moving through the air. When the two adventurers are brought crashing back to earth they learn that they have won a victory in the adventure simply by undertaking it. But the mischievous Sancho, turning the tables on those who set up the joke, claims that during the voyage he peeked from under his blindfold and saw the earth below him no larger than a mustard seed and the people who walked on its surface were no larger than hazelnuts(!). Further, he claims that when they passed the constellation of the Seven Little Goats, he dismounted for a while and romped with the goats. An original anticipation of space travel? Hardly, even though some critics have hailed it as such.[4] The scene is no more than another of the several bad practical jokes played on the chivalric pair for laughs. But still, *Don Quixote* anticipates the man-machine encounter and space travel. Not bad for an early seventeenth-century novel.

The character of Don Quixote, however, has been an inspiration for a modest number of science fiction short stories and novels, and it is this group of works that I want to discuss in this essay. In the remainder of this essay I will trace the appearance of a dozen novels and short stories that feature some version of a re-accentuated Don Quixote. This is as much an inventory as an exploration of aesthetic re-accentuation.

JOHN MYERS MYERS, *SILVERLOCK* (1949)

In Myers's novel, the protagonist A. Clarence Shandon is shipwrecked off the imaginary island of Commonwealth (of Letters). In his travels throughout this strange land, Shandon takes the name of Silverlock and has encounters and adventures with Beowulf, Till Eulenspiegel, Anna Karenina, Prometheus, and many more historical, literary, and mythological personages, including, of course, Don Quixote and Sancho. Silverlock's guide absurdly and incongruously introduces him to "the noble, puissant, and chivalrous Don Quixote de la Mancha, conqueror of High Utopia and Low Cockaigne, savior of Lubberland, shield of Dun Coba, protector of Saffron-Walden, prince of paladins, squire of dames, and dean of knights errant."[5] Among other things, Don Quixote agrees to assist in the search for the giant John Bunyan and the blue ox. Cervantes's hero is not essential to this novel, but he does put in an interesting cameo appearance.

Forerunners

I have begun with Myers's novel because it is, I believe, the first obvious work of science fiction that includes Don Quixote as a character. But there are other, much earlier, works involving Cervantes's protagonist that have been classified as science fiction (or speculative fiction, or fantasy). They deserve at least brief mention here. The earliest work of this sort with which I am familiar is Jacques Alluis's almost completely ignored *L'Escole d'amour ou les heros docteurs* (1666; *The School of Love, or The Doctor Heroes*), in which the characters go to the *Pays des Romans* (*Land of Novels*), where they meet characters like King Arthur and the famous Spanish knight-errant Amadís de Gaula in a burlesque of chivalric and heroic fictions.[6]

Quite singular is Eaton Stannard Barrett's *The Heroine, or Adventures of Cherubina* (1809), a romance about a book-inspired young woman who calls herself Cherubina and tries to live a life in imitation of the heroines of the romances she reads. Only after admitting her error and marrying happily does she read *Don Quixote* and realize that Cervantes's novel had been the prototype of her life. In the second edition, 1814, there is a metafictional prologue titled "The Heroine to the Reader," written from the Moon in which the Heroine, now "a corporeal being, and an inhabitant of another world," informs the reader that after a work is written the characters described in it take form on the Moon.[7] These Lunarians, or Moonites, continue to live until they are completely forgotten on earth. The first figure whom the lunar Cherubina meets is Don Quixote, who becomes her guide to the new world, introducing her to the Lady of the Lake, Achilles, Tristram Shandy, and many others.

In the early twentieth century, one of the more interesting works with a similar sort of literary metafictional theme and plot is Walter de la Mare's *Henry Brocken* (1904). The protagonist spends his youth reading fiction and then one day, he writes, "a little before eleven I saddled my uncle's old mare Rosinante (poor female jade to bear a name so glorious!) and rode out . . ."[8] Brocken meets and talks with characters such as Jane Eyre, Lemuel Gulliver, and Annabel Lee, but not with Don Quixote.

Kenneth Morris's "The Last Adventure of Don Quixote" (1917) tells how Quixote does not die in the final chapter, but arises stronger than ever, mounts his beautiful steed Rocinante, and rides out, soon to be accompanied by another great knight as his squire. The two conquer their powerful enemies, and at the end of the story the identity of the other knight is revealed: "Side by side in pleasant converse they rode forward then to the palace gates of their sovereign: Don Quixote of La Mancha and Don Michael Archangel: each wondrously pleased with the nobility and high bearing of his companion."[9]

In G. L. van Roosbroeck's "How Don Quixote Was Defeated in Moronia" (1929), Quixote, who has for centuries continued his adventures, summons great knights from the past—Roland, King Arthur, Amadís, and many others—to attack the castle of Moronia, "the rallying place of all those who denied the Dream and proclaimed the exclusive rule of Reality."[10] The great army slays countless numbers of the silent enemy, described as a "limitless number of the blind, deaf and dumb Moronians, without brains or blood, but more powerful than the combined kings of the earth,"[11] but eventually they are overwhelmed and succumb to these forces of reality. All the heroes perish in the dungeons of Moronia: "But their pale ghosts sped, with no uncertain gait, for a hiding place between the covers of chronicles and picture-books—from where they ride forth, occasionally, to haunt children's rooms and University Halls."[12] Works like these can be very entertaining for book lovers and scholars, and they anticipate a certain strand of science fantasy in which literary and historical figures are real and mingle with newly created characters in strange worlds.

There is also a very long history of novels and stories in which Don Quixote lives on, is reincarnated, is brought back to life, and so forth, to continue his adventures in more modern times. The novels by Myers and Simak and the story by Donnelly included in this essay are of this variety, but set in an obviously science-fiction context. I should note, too, that there are dozens of fictions of this sort written in Spanish. They range from Padre Valbuena's *La resurrección de Don Quijote* (1905; *The Resurrection of Don Quixote*) to Armando de Miguel's *Don Quijote en la España de la reina Letizia*[13] (2016; *Don Quixote in the Spain of Queen Letizia*). This is a minor strain of re-accentuation that merits a study of its own.

POUL ANDERSON, "QUIXOTE AND THE WINDMILL" (1950)

The most interesting early appearance of Cervantes's character in science fiction is a story by one of the more prolific and popular writers of the mid-twentieth century, Poul Anderson. In the story two men, a manual laborer and a technician, who have lost their jobs to machines, are getting drunk and complaining about their fate. As they talk, the first and only robot—a general-purpose, man-like machine—passes by. For the men, the robot represents the future in which the human race will be replaced by such machines. They try to take out their aggression on the robot, throwing stones at it and kicking it; one of the men says, "We can't hurt you. We're Don Quixote, tilting at windmills. But you wouldn't know about that. You wouldn't know about any of man's old dreams."[14] But the robot surprises the men by telling them that there are useful machines for very many specialized tasks, but there is no role for a general-purpose machine. Ever since its creation the robot simply wanders around, with nothing to do, and will continue to do so until it wears out—in about five hundred years. Human beings have one great advantage, the robot says: at least they can get drunk.

"Quixote and the Windmill" anticipates, at a fairly early date, one important aspect of the eventual effect of technology on human society: the displacement of human workers by machines. Further, Anderson saw what many other science-fiction writers failed to see: that specialized robot arms, assembly machines, and other kinds of single-purpose devices would be extraordinarily useful in many areas, but an all-purpose, mobile, humanoid-like robot would have little reason to exist. At the time the logical but naïve conviction was that what was easiest for us—physical locomotion, vision, strength—would be the first things we would craft robots to perform, while what was hardest for us—advanced mathematical and scientific thought—would take more time. As we now know only too well, this sort of (quixotic?) speculation about the future of robotics was fundamentally in error. History has validated Anderson's basic premise about the nature of the robot–human being relationship.

KATHY ACKER, *DON QUIXOTE: WHICH WAS A DREAM* (1968)

Punk novelist Kathy Acker, a student of the classics, consistently selected canonical works and authors as pretexts and intertexts for her own irreverent, aggressive, obscene, and outrageously satirical fictions. Her *Don Quixote* is not mainstream science fiction, but it is clearly some sort of postmodern phantasmagorical vision of twentieth-century America; it certainly is one of the most radical re-accentuations of Don Quixote ever written.[15] Acker describes her technique as follows: "I write by using other written texts, rather than by expressing 'reality,' which is what most novelists do. Our reality now, which occurs so much through the media, *is* other texts. I'm playing the same game as Cervantes."[16]

Acker read Cervantes's novel when she was preparing for an upcoming abortion, and she has commented, "I couldn't keep my mind off the abortion so I started writing down what I was reading, but the abortion kept getting into it."[17] So it is that the first section of the three parts into which the novel is divided is titled "Don Quixote's abortion" and begins, "When she was finally crazy because she was about to have an abortion, she conceived of the most insane idea that any woman can think of. Which is to love."[18] These words are a paraphrase of one of the famous lines of the first chapter of Cervantes's novel—"he had the strangest thought any lunatic in the world ever had"[19]—and the rest of this part is a sustained paraphrasing, adaptation, re-contextualization, and playful reproduction of the opening chapters of *Don Quixote* I (with a few allusions to the second part).

The protagonist's equation of abortion with quixotic madness, self-referential word play (catheter/Kathy; hack/Acker), vision of men as evil giants, a speaking dog (sometimes named St. Simeon) as her Sancho Panza, the reference to Amandia of Gaul, the many references to evil enchanters, and much more, make this part of the novel one of the most outlandish of all quixotic fictions. The remainder of the novel consists of a parody and pastiche of other literary works, political and religious criticism and satire, feminism, sex and gender, violence, autobiography, literary theory, and much more. Only toward the end of the novel does the Don Quixote rewrite come back. This is especially true of a relatively long section based on the Cave of Montesinos from *Don Quixote* (II, 23).

Acker is perhaps the best known of the writers discussed in this essay. She was an important figure in both feminist and postmodernist writing of the second half of the twentieth century. She is not an important figure in the literature of science fiction, but Don Quixote is her point of entry in that field and her accomplishment is certainly one to be recognized and appreciated.

EMIL PETAJA, *THE NETS OF SPACE* (1969)

Ex-astronaut Donald Quick frequently reads from Cervantes's novel: "Don Quixote was his ideal and his alter ego. Perhaps Don's name had something to do with it (his father had admired the Woeful Knight, too) or perhaps it was his facility for getting himself into the damndest scrapes by trying to help whenever he saw anything that needed helping. . . ."[20] The woman he loves is his nurse, named Donna Elena Dulce, whom he makes into his Dulcinea. After an accident in which Quick is exposed to a large amount of "time-space gas" he begins to have dreams in which he interacts with species from other worlds. In the first he has been swept up in an exploratory net deployed by a species of giant crabs who discover that living humans make excellent food. In the second he finds himself on a world of tiny cricket-like humanoids where he identifies himself as Don Quixote and where he is considered a menacing god-like creature. This clearly recalls the voyages of Lemuel Gulliver but on a galactic scale. It turns out that the crabs really exist and are about to use their nets to scoop up all of humanity for their nutritional needs, but our hero manages to return to the other planet where he trades his beloved copy of *Don Quixote* for a weapon that will kill the crabs. He thus manages to save his own world and bequeath to another one the greatest of mythical stories.

As the novel ends, he and his Dulcinea embrace and kiss; the final words are "Somewhere Cervantes smiled" (128). The way in which Petaja literally makes the quixotic Quick into Don Quixote and the way in which the physical book titled *Don Quixote* plays a decisive role in the dénouement are quite original and interesting for readers of Cervantes's novel.

LEE HOFFMAN, *ALWAYS THE BLACK KNIGHT* (1970)

This is the story of a far-future traveling entertainment group that features a scene of singular combat between two knights. The protagonist, Kyning, plays the evil knight (riding a robot horse) dressed in black in a show always scripted for him to lose to his hated rival. A serious accidental injury during a performance leaves him stranded on the planet Elva. It turns out that everyone on the planet is always mildly sedated, and the entire world lives a monotonous and boring life without realizing the possibility of an alternative. Kyning recruits a man named Riker to stop taking the sedative, teaches him sword-fighting, and encourages him to read books, especially those of chivalry and knighthood.

Eventually Riker, who had "addled his wits by reading too many romances."[21] (114), becomes obsessed with the idea of taking over the planet in order to restore the inhabitants to their true humanity. But in the process he himself becomes violent and megalomaniac, actually seizes power and proclaims himself emperor, and is confronted by Kyning, who defeats him in single combat, but who also dies in the process. Kyning reads and quotes from books throughout the story and at one point contemplates the fine line between reality and fantasy.[22] *Don Quixote* is never mentioned in the novel, but Kyning dubs the woman he loves Dulcinea, once refers to himself as Riker's Sancho, and at the end when is about to die he thinks that there is "no Balsam of Fierabrás for this wound,"[23] making it clear that *Don Quixote* is the single most influential of the books he reads and that it is on the figure of Don Quixote that he has modeled himself.

CLIFFORD D. SIMAK, *OUT OF THEIR MINDS* (1970)

Horton Smith tries to retire from the busy world in order to write a book, but he suddenly finds himself in what he dubs "the Land of Imagination," which is "forged of all the fantasy, all the make-believe, all the fairy tales and folk stories, all the fictions and traditions of the race of Man."[24] He comes into contact with dinosaurs and werewolves, comic-strip characters, and even finds himself present at the battle of Gettysburg. There is a brief encounter with Don Quixote, who takes a comic pratfall, and, of course, Horton meets a beautiful woman and falls in love. It turns out that the whole thing is organized by the Devil, who complains that whereas in the past mankind sent gods and noble heroes to this land, for a long time now the only new creatures are vapid figures from popular culture. In the real world the Devil brings all traffic to a stop and threatens to do more when Don Quixote suddenly arrives and pins down the Devil with his lance while Sancho Panza throws holy water on him. The Devil surrenders, promises no more mischief, and all the imaginary characters disappear.

The novel is not very coherent, it is badly plotted and hard to follow, and it starts too slowly and ends far too abruptly. As discussed above in the section on *Silverlock*, the idea of bringing together real and imaginary figures from a variety of sources has a long and illustrious history. In many ways, this concept seems to be made for science fiction and fantasy.

STEPHEN ROBINETT, "THE LINGUIST" (1976)

This story is not about Don Quixote, the character, but involves *Don Quixote*, the novel itself. It deals with a man paid to read the novel in the original Spanish so that his engram (a stored memory trace) of that experience—not the novel itself, but the experience of knowing enough Spanish in order to pass an examination—can be completely removed from his brain and downloaded into the brain of a student who pays for the knowledge. The protagonist is thus a sort of neuroscientific version of a professional note-taker. (Interestingly, the crass downloader is named Plagio: *plagio*, "plagiarism" in Spanish.) There is no real re-accentuation of the character here, but it is interesting that the classic chosen for this example is that of Cervantes.

ALEXIS A. GILLILAND, THE *ROSINANTE* TRILOGY (1981–1982)

There is no knight-errant, squire, or skinny horse in these three novels. Don Quixote, Sancho Panza, and Rosinante are three *munditos* (small worlds; here, space stations) located near two asteroids. The plots involve national, international, and extraterrestrial business and politics. When the *munditos* projects are to be abandoned, those who run Rosinante rebel and win its political independence from a despotic North American Union. The novels mostly involve project managers, scheming politicians, super-intelligent robots (one of which begins its own religion), and sexual misadventures. There are some obvious intertextual references to popular culture and films, as well as a few allusions to Cervantes's novel; for example, the banner of Rosinante is "a rickety green horse on a white field."[25] This trilogy is included in this survey simply because of the names.

CHET WILLIAMSON, "ROSINANTE" (1984)

An astronaut called simply Don (later we learn his last name, Quentin: Don Q) is on a multi-year interstellar voyage accompanied by three *humanels*, beings "born from cell vats, fleshy computers programmed for living DNA."[26] The first, Sancho, is a technician/mechanic; the second is a domestic/mechanic named Rosinante; and the third is a beautiful female companion who provides emotional and sexual comfort, and her name is of course Dulcinea. The narrator is Rosinante, and she begins by describing her long, lanky, bony body with an equine face, a long bulbous nose, and loose flesh; its name seems perfectly appropriate. At one point, during the long return to earth after the mission is completed, Dulcinea malfunctions and is destroyed. Over a period of time Don turns to Rosinante for sexual and emotional companionship, and as the years pass Rose (as he calls "her") loses her original horse-like appearance, becoming ever more beautiful and human-like, as the two fall deeply in love. But this relationship is put to an end by the inevitable return to earth, with an unforgiving society, the astronaut's wife, and Rosinante's pre-planned destruction. At the very end it is clear that Rose's change in appearance was more perceived or imagined than physical. In their final meeting, before Rosinante is returned to the cell vat, Don secretly takes a small amount of DNA, hoping somehow to re-create a clone of his beloved Rose.

So here Don Quixote is re-accentuated as a human astronaut accompanied by three biological beings who complete the set from Cervantes's novel. The slow transformation of the horsey humanel servant into a beautiful lover—not real but as truly perceived by both beings—actually recalls what Don Quixote says about his beloved Dulcinea when talking with Sancho: "I depict her in my imagination as I wish her to be in beauty and in distinction."[27] As Roy H. Williams (who has an essay elsewhere in this volume) has written, "Every groom is Don Quixote. And every bride, his Dulcinea."[28] It may be only a slight transformation to see a Don Quixote of the future as an astronaut, but to re-accentuate Dulcinea as a non-human, horsey-looking sexual partner and beloved is truly extraordinary.

JAMES MCCONKEY, *KAYO, THE AUTHENTIC AND ANNOTATED AUTOBIOGRAPHICAL NOVEL FROM OUTER SPACE* (1987)

McConkey's novel is the most eccentric, quirky, and technically complex of the works discussed in this essay. A literature professor begins to communicate via computer with a person named Ohcnas Aznap (Sancho Panza spelled backward), who is in a more-or-less parallel or mirror world. This communicator is usually referred to as Kayo, from OK (backward, of course), from the first letters of his name, Ohc. Kayo is both a direct descendant of the famous author of his world's greatest novel, *The Authentic Adventures of Kayo Aznap* (which Kayo has never actually read and knows only through the Cliffs Notes version) and a character in that novel. Kayo refers to his earthling communicator as Sid, his equivalent of Cid (Hamete Benengeli).

Kayo's life story, his autobiographical confession, is far too complicated and bizarre to go into here, but much of it involves his relationship to Nod (Don spelled backward) an overweight, eccentric farmer who read too many westerns and believed himself a cowboy. He quixotically attempted to rescue his Dulcinea, a prostitute who works in the Golden Nugget Hotel and whom he calls Diana, who is persecuted by the enchanters who are the card sharks of the saloon. But Nod also became a famous professor named "Michael, or Miguel, Quexana, sometimes spelled Quixada or Quesada."[29] He has recently given up on his quest to rescue Diana because he is bedeviled by a new set of enchanters, the poststructuralists and deconstructionists who have convinced him that there is no reality and that everything is text. At the same time that Nod is a person in Kayo's life story, both of them are also characters in *The Authentic Adventures of Kayo Aznap* and are very much aware that they are literary characters. At one point Nod comments to Kayo that "I realized, to my horror that what I have done, as one who gave up his banal persona of Professor Michael Quexana to become Nod, the grand and quixotic character of a work by an ancestor of yours, is simply to prove I am living in nothing but a text; and that, of course is the sine qua non of poststructuralist belief."[30]

Meanwhile, the narrator, who receives Kayo's messages and writes and annotates his novel/autobiography, the professor of literature who receives Kayo's messages and whose favorite book is *Don Quixote*, is also plagued by the deconstructionists of his department. In a final irony, the book ends with a Note written by John ("Jack") Jones, Professor of Deconstructionist Criticism and Head of the Department of Poststructuralist Thought, who describes how he came by Kayo's work as transcribed and annotated by the anti-deconstructionist scribe Sid, here called Professor "M." Jones (who has never read *Don Quixote*), and smugly shows how "the author unintentionally has built with his Chinese boxes as good a model of the <u>self-contained, self-referential</u> text as any deconstructionist could."[31]

Throughout the novel primary themes are truth versus fiction, appearance versus reality, and the unreliability of any narration. Virtually every character is a version or a double of others, just as *The Authentic Adventures of Kayo Aznap* is a mirror of the inferior earth novel *Don Quixote*. Much of the novel is an allegorical denunciation of American politics, as every president is really just one man named Teddy who keeps getting reelected under different names and constantly devised ways to keep the citizens, called Unitedians, content or, at least, distracted. The levels of metafiction and intertextuality are multiplied repeatedly and dizzyingly in a unique and sometimes very funny retelling of *Don Quixote* in which every aspect of the characters, plot, theme, and narrative technique are radically re-contextualized and re-accentuated. McConkey's comic, satiric, academic, postmodern novel is one that any fan or scholar of Cervantes's work can enjoy.

ROBERT SILVERBERG, "ENTER A SOLDIER. LATER, ENTER ANOTHER" (1989)

Don Quixote is a minor player in this story of holographic existence, in which computer programmers re-create historical figures in a vat. The story begins when the Spanish explorer Francisco Pizarro (the first soldier) is brought to electronic life and then when he confronts none less that Socrates (the second) in an interesting and amusing philosophical debate. As part of the backstory, it turns out that it was a group of French programmers who invented and developed the project. But they abandoned their work after re-creating not a historical personage but a fictional character: Don Quixote. The re-creation was made for a celebration of the arrival of the king of Spain in Paris. The problem was that the holographic figure they produced was "a Don Quixote who was hopelessly locked to the Spain of the late sixteenth century and to the book from which he had sprung. He had no capacity for independent life and thought—no way to perceive the world that had brought him into being, or to comment on it, or to interact with it."[32]

The whole point of the Quixote episode is that a fictional character can be brought to holographic life more perfectly than historical characters because we already know everything about him/her, whereas real people always involve things we don't know and are more unpredictable. So here, Don Quixote is re-accentuated as—himself, nothing more. This idea is secondary to the main story of the Pizarro-Socrates debate, but it deals with the complex relationship between literary characters and real and/or historical human beings.

MARCOS DONNELLY,
"THE RESURRECTION OF ALONSO QUIJANA" (1992)

This story is presented as a translation from an old manuscript of *Don Quixote* found by the author's brother in Montreal, Canada. The author claims only to be the translator and editor, making no claims for the text's legitimacy. In a foreword, Cervantes explains why now, although he is long dead, he has decided to write this brief text from the afterlife in order to set straight the record about his protagonist. In an echo of a famous statement from the last chapter of the second part of *Don Quixote*, he claims that "Don Quijote was born for me alone," and then he adds that modern readers "have bastardized my grand theme," by creating a Quixote who "possesses lips that would burst into enchanting melody" (probably an allusion to Dale Wasserman's musical *Man of La Mancha*) rather than one who "Sports a mouth that spews vomit in the face of his idiot squire.[33]

The text consists of six short supplements to the very last chapter of *Don Quixote*, in which Alonso Quijana el Bueno renounces knight-errantry and then has a dream. In the dream Don Quixote finds himself in the desert of *Sudúrabu* (Saudi Arabia, and not South Hampton) during what is obviously the 1981 Gulf War, where he meets an American soldier named Santiago Rojas (Saint James the Red, for Don Quixote), who has a habit of exclaiming "Sacred Feces" (although an alternate translation for that phrase is also proposed). There he has a series of encounters with Iraqi and American troops and with modern military technology. Throughout, there are a number of editorial footnotes in which the author attempts to clarify the sometimes confusing text; e.g., the exact significance of and translation for the term *Airachis* is not clear: is it *Iroquois*, or *Iraquis*? In a brief afterword, Cervantes muses over the significance of his supplement.

An interesting combination of clever intertextuality, comedy, and social criticism, Donnelly's story of Don Quixote is quite unlike any other. The story is a sly commentary on the 1981 war, an intertextual spoof, and a comic play on the technique of the discovered and translated manuscript. Along with Chet Williamson's "Rosinante," it is perhaps the best and most original of the short stories discussed in this essay.

WALTER JON WILLIAMS, "DADDY'S WORLD" (1999)

This is another story in which Don Quixote makes only a cameo appearance. A little boy died in the hospital and the family reproduced him as hologram computer program, creating a wondrous world of playmates for him. One of the figures brought into Jamie's world is Don Quixote, whose main purpose seems to be falling off his horse in order to make the little boy laugh. The story turns dark when Jamie learns the truth of his condition, takes control of his own computer program, and creates his own context. It becomes his wish to die again, this time definitively, but when his father dies and returns as a computer program, daddy's world is re-created again—presumably forever.

ROBERT SHECKLEY, "THE QUIXOTE ROBOT" (2001)

Robert Sheckley, best known for his many humorous science-fiction/ fantasy novels and short stories, has said that he wrote this story as a "a little tribute to Cervantes and Don Quixote de la Mancha, that ingenious gentleman."[34] The story begins with the Quixote Robot riding his mechanical Rocinante, carrying his head under his arm, a result of a recent battle in which he defeated the giant Macadam, the evil road-maker of the Wasteland. With the help of a man named Laurent, who becomes his Sancho Panza (and who rides a mechanized donkey, assembled from pieces in the Quixote's saddlebags), the Quixote Robot heads for the Robot Factory. This is where Quixote hopes to "rid the world of the monstrous evil of industrialization"[35] by killing the Boss Robot, who also holds prisoner the Quixote's lady, Psyche, daughter of his creator Madigan. After defeating the Feral Locomotive that guards the factory, and with the further assistance of a mechanical rat named Randy, the Quixote Robot succeeds in destroying the Boss Robot—but is himself crushed in the battle and dies. Laurent and Psyche immediately fall in love and the story ends with a promise of the further adventures of the two of them, together with the mechanical Randy and Rocinante. Apparently, no such sequel has yet been written.

Lovers of Cervantes's characters can read with amusement this mechanization of Don Quixote. Interestingly, this re-accentuation of Don Quixote harkens back to Poul Anderson's quixotic robot at the beginning of this essay. It is clear that the concept of the computerized mechanical man-like metal creature is still as much at the heart of much current science fiction as it was over a half century ago. And it is also clear that the image of Don Quixote attacking a machine is still as much at the heart of science fiction as it was in 1605.

CARRIE VAUGHAN, "DON QUIXOTE" (2012)

This story is set in Spain, just outside of Madrid, in the final days of the Spanish Civil War, in 1939. Two American reporters are about to leave the city and return home, as it has become clear that Franco's Nationalist Army is about to overrun the city and end the war. But they make a startling discovery: two soldiers of the Republican forces have created a super-destructive tank-like machine that can destroy any conventional force it comes across. In effect, it is a kind of superhero: a single man within a powerful armored machine that can wreak havoc among an entire army. The soldiers have named the machine "Don Quixote." The reporters see the machine in action and are convinced that such a super weapon has the potential to change the nature of warfare forever. But they also fear that a weapon like this, in the hands of someone like Hitler, would be worse than if the Republican side won the war in Spain. So they destroy the device, tear up their notes, and vow to tell no one of what they had seen.

The story was published in an anthology of original science fiction stories about "power armor," a kind of full-body armor that increases a soldier's strength and endurance. In science fiction, the concept was originally explored in Robert A. Heinlein's classic novel *Starship Troopers* (1959). It is most popular in comics and movies about superheroes like *Iron Man*. Imagine Don Quixote, in Cervantes's novel so worried that the new infernal firearms are putting an end to the valor of armor-clad knights-errant, now thought of as a machine that can resist the strongest gunfire. With this recent re-accentuation of Don Quixote in science fiction we have come full circle. In 1605 Cervantes's Don Quixote attacks a windmill, believing it is a giant; in 2012 Don Quixote is the giant.

RHYS HUGHES, "THE QUIXOTE CANDIDATE" (2014)

This is a final, very borderline, story that re-accentuates Don Quixote in an unusual way. The story takes the form of an interview, with the questions omitted, but obvious, based on the answers. The narrator tells of his obsession with a certain Nuno Cotter, who has seen so many films that he believes that real life is nothing more than a movie and that he is the director. So he interrupts people on the street, tries to get them to perform their scenes in different ways, and of course both gets into trouble and becomes increasingly detached from reality. But it also becomes clear that the narrator himself is mad, obsessed in making a film about Cotter, a film he plans to title *The Quixote Candidate*. The levels of fiction and metafiction, quixotic madness and obsession, as told by a very unreliable and easily distracted narrator, make this one of the stories discussed here that best captures the spirit of quixotic fiction. Like Kathy Acker's novel, this story is on the borderline of science fiction, but its inclusion in science fiction bibliographies justifies its inclusion here.

CONCLUSION: ESTRELLA CERVANTES

It should be no surprise that Cervantes's Don Quixote, along with Sancho, Dulcinea, and Rocinante, should appear in fiction involving the future, and especially outer space, because now they literally are there. In 2015 the International Astronomical Union, which is responsible for naming newly discovered stars and exoplanets (planets that orbit stars outside our solar system), held a contest to name a newly discovered star located some 49.8 light-years from earth. The winning name was Cervantes, and the four planets that circle the star are named Dulcinea, Rocinante, Quijote, and Sancho.

One of the scientists who promoted the idea of naming this star and planetary group after Cervantes and his characters is Benjamín Montesinos.[36] Montesinos has stated that "It has been a great pleasure and an honor for a Manchegan astronomer like me to have been able to contribute to putting Cervantes and his characters in the heavens. When we re-read Don Quixote, we can imagine Clavileño flying and reaching the Cervantes star and the planets Dulcinea, Quixote, Rocinante, and Sancho. A luxury."[37] It only seems right that fact should catch up with fiction.

NOTES

1. Robert Plank, "Quixote's Mills: The Man-Machine Encounter in SF," *Science Fiction Studies* 1.2 (1973): 69.

2. For discussions of the way Don Quixote has become the most often and most easily recognized literary character of all time, see E. C. Riley, "*Don Quixote*: From Text to Icon," *Cervantes* special issue (winter 1988): 103–15, and Howard Mancing, "Don Quixote Miscellany," in *The Cervantes Encyclopedia*, 2 vols. (Westport, CT: Greenwood Press, 2004), I, 241–42.

3. Iván Jaksić, "Don Quijote's Encounter with Technology," *Cervantes* 14.1 (1994): 76.

4. Chad Gasta, "Cervantes's Theory of Relativity in *Don Quixote*," *Cervantes* 31.1 (2011): 51–52.

5. John Myers Myers, *Silverlock* (New York: Ace Books, 1966), 138.

6. See the interesting description and discussion of this work in Thomas DiPiero, *Dangerous Truths and Criminal Passions: The Evolution of the French Novel, 1569-1791* (Stanford, CA: Stanford University Press, 1992), 163–67.

7. Eaton Stannard Barrett, *The Heroine, or Adventures of Cherubina*, second ed., 3 vols. (London: Henry Colburn, 1814), vii.

8. Walter de la Mare, *Henry Brocken: His Travels and Adventures in the Rich, Strange, Scarce Imaginable Regions of Romance* (London: Faber and Faber, 1942), 18.

9. Kenneth Morris, "The Last Adventure of Don Quixote," in *The Dragon Path: Collected Tales of Kenneth Morris* (New York: Tor Books, 1995), 171.

10. G. L. van Roosbroeck, "How Don Quixote Was Defeated in Moronia," in *Grotesques* (New York: Living Art, 1929), 100.

11. Ibid., 102.

12. Ibid., 103.

13. Padre Valbuena, *La resurrección de Don Quijote* (Barcelona: Antonio López, 1905); Armando de Miguel, *Don Quijote en la España de la reina Letizia* (Barcelona: Stella Maris, 2016).

14. Poul Anderson, "Quixote and the Windmill," in *Strangers from Earth* (New York: Ballantine Books, 1961), 33.

15. The inclusion of Acker's novel here can be debated, but, importantly, it is included in many bibliographies of science fiction, including the prestigious International Speculative Fiction Database, http://www.isfdb.org.

16. Quoted by Lori Miller, "In the Tradition of Cervantes, Sort Of," *New York Review of Books* (November 30, 1986), 10.

17. Ibid.

18. Kathy Acker, *Don Quixote: Which Was a Dream* (London: Paladin, 1968), 9.

19. Ibid., 21.

20. Emil Petaja, *The Nets of Space* (New York: Berkeley Medallion Books, 1969), 15.

21. Lee Hoffman, *Always the Black Knight* (New York: Avon Books, 1970), 114.

22. Ibid., 70–71.

23. Ibid., 160.

24. Clifford D. Simak, *Out of Their Minds* (New York: DAW Books, 1983), 145.

25. Alexis A. Gilliland, *The Revolution from Rosinante* (New York: Ballantine Books, 1981), 89.

26. Chet Williamson, "Rosinante," *The Magazine of Fantasy and Science Fiction* (April 1984), 44.

27. Miguel de Cervantes, *Don Quixote*, trans. Edith Grossman (New York: Ecco, 2003), 201.

28. "Wedding Chapel Dulcinea," *The Monday Morning Memo* (March 1, 2005), http://www.mondaymorningmemo.com/newsletters/wedding-chapel-dulcinea/.

29. James McConkey, *Kayo, The Authentic and Annotated Autobiographical Novel from Outer Space* (New York: Dutton, 1987), 83.

30. Ibid., 157. The use of underlining for emphasis is frequent in the novel.

31. Ibid., 203.

32. Robert Silverberg, "Enter a Soldier. Later: Enter Another," in *Time Gate*, ed. Robert Silverberg, with Bill Fawcett (New York: Baen Books, 1989), 13.

33. Marcos Donnelly, "The Resurrection of Alonso Quijana," *The Magazine of Fantasy and Science Fiction* (March 1992), 32.

34. Robert Sheckley, *Uncanny Tales* (Waterville, ME: Five Star, 2003), 121.

35. Robert Sheckley, "The Quixote Robot," *The Magazine of Fantasy and Science Fiction* (December 2001), 145.

36. Montesinos is, appropriately, also the name of a famous cave in La Mancha, which is the scene of one of Don Quixote's most famous adventures (II, 22–23).

37. *Estrella Cervantes*: http://estrellacervantes.es; translation mine.

IV

FILM

10

The Art of Re-accentuation: *Don Quixote* by Grigori Kozintsev

Slav N. Gratchev

> The process of re-accentuation is enormously significant in the his-
> tory of literature. Every generation re-accentuates in its own way the
> works of its most immediate past. The historical life of classic works
> is in fact the uninterrupted process of their social and ideological re-
> accentuation.[1]

This essay will focus on the *re-accentuation* of the image of Don Quixote
while the novel was adapted to the screen in 1957 by the famous Russian
director Grigori Kozintsev. In light of Bakhtinian theory, we will try to
explain the nature, the necessity, and the results of this *re-accentuation*. We
will also conduct an analysis of Kozintsev and Schwartz's[2] diaries and
their private correspondence while they both were contemplating the film
and working on the script. We believe that these invaluable materials are
indispensable for Cervantes scholarship, but, unfortunately, until today
these documents have only been available in Russian and have never
been translated to English.

The film *Don Quixote* became a turning point in the career of both Evgeny Schwartz and Grigori Kozintsev. For Schwartz, the script for this film
became his very last work; Schwartz died in 1958 without seeing the film.
For Kozintsev, *Don Quixote* became the first of a glorious series of films
(*Don Quixote* in 1957, *Hamlet* in 1971, and *King Lear* in 1974) that made
his name immortal on the horizon of Russia's greatest directors, together
with Sergey Eisenstein and Dziga Vertov.[3]

Don Quixote came after many years of Kozintsev's artistic downtime—a
period that was forced on him by the declining regime of Stalin's suspi-
cions of everything and everyone. Kozintsev, for many years, was not
welcome at any film studios in the country (possibly due to his recommendation of the KGB) until 1954, right after the death of Stalin, when
he received a phone call from the LenFilm (Leningrad Film Studio, the
second largest studio in the country) with the invitation to make nothing

less than the classic *Don Quixote*. Overnight the disgraced and practically
forgotten Grigori Kozintsev all of a sudden became the most sought-after
film director in the country. With fair doses of certainty, we can conjecture
that Kozintsev's new appointment was the result of the direct interference
and personal recommendation of Nikita Khrushchev,[4] who tended to
think of himself as a very liberal and intelligent person who was predes-
tined to bring from obscurity all those disgraced and persecuted by Stalin.

This is what we read in Schwartz's diary: "Вчера звонил Козинцев.
Ему предлагают ставить "Дон Кихота." Он позвонил мне, и мне вдруг
захотелось написать сценарий на эту тему. Хожу теперь и мечтаю."[5]
(Kozintsev called yesterday. He got an invitation to film *Don Quixote*. He
called me about this, and all of a sudden I felt that I really want to write
a script. Now I cannot stop thinking and dreaming about it.) [All translations are mine, unless otherwise noted].

Certainly it was not accidental that Kozintsev chose Schwartz to write
the script; leaving aside the fact that Kozintsev was a friend of Schwartz,
he knew better than anyone how capable Schwartz was for this unusual
and arch-difficult task. Kozintsev also knew that Schwartz, with everything he did, always put on his own creative accents—he always *re-
accentuated* any well-known masterpiece, making it more contemporary,
more understandable for readers and spectators of the twentieth century.

Now, during the period of "Khrushchev's thaw,"[6] when artistic freedom seemed to become a reality, the adaptation to the screen of one of the
most famous novels had to become a real *re-accentuation* of Don Quixote
as a literary image. Kozintsev and Schwartz were certainly those inquisi-
tive "readers" who perceived *Don Quixote* in a far different way than it
was read and interpreted in the Soviet Union for the last thirty years,[7] and
definitely their *re-accentuation* of the image of Quixote could be extremely
productive. As Bakhtin put it, "in the re-accentuation of this kind there is
no crude violation of the author's will. It can even be said that this process
takes place within the image itself, i.e., not only in the changed conditions
of perception."[8]

The new project made Schwartz extremely excited; reading his correspondence with his closest friends, with Kozintsev, and with his wife,
we can see that Schwartz could not stop thinking about the book and the
image of Don Quixote. This is, for example, what we find in Schwartz's
diary: "Продолжаю думать о "Дон Кихоте." Необходимо отступить
от романа так, как отступило время. Ставить не "Дон Кихота," а
легенду о Дон Кихоте. Сделать так, чтобы, не отступая от романа,
внешне не отступая, рассказать его заново."[9] (I continue to think about
Don Quixote. It is necessary to distance from the novel, as time distanced
itself from it, too. We have to stage not *Don Quixote* but a legend about

Don Quixote. And we have to do it so that, without distancing too much from the novel, we tell the novel in a different way.)

It draws immediate attention that Schwartz certainly was making a clear distinction between *Don Quixote* as a novel and Don Quixote as a hero; the goal of the new film, as it was seen by Schwartz, was to tell a new legend about Don Quixote but, at the same time, distance it as much as possible from the novel or, in other words, "tell the novel in a different way" by means of cinematography. If we turn to the script, we will see that the beginning of the script is totally different from the novel, and so is the film:

Село в Ламанче. Летняя ночь приближается к рассвету. Два огонька медленно движутся вдоль заборов, поднимаются вверх по крутой улице. Это спешат с фонарями в руках два почтенных человека: священник, лиценциат Перо Перес, и цирюльник, мастер Николас.[10]

(Village in La Mancha. Summer night is approaching the dawn. Two lights move slowly along the fences, climb up the steep street. They are in a hurry with lanterns in their hands, two respectable men: the priest, Pero Perez, and the barber, master Nicholas.)

This is how Schwartz sees the beginning of the film; during the night in a small Spanish town, two persons walk toward the house of Don Quixote talking about his insane passion for books. They gossip about how he burns candles as if he were a rich man while his niece recently could not find enough money to call the doctor. Then they enter into the house of *hidalgo,* and they are greeted by two women who cordially invite them into the room of Don Quixote. There are many books there; books lean on the walls. We see books, but we do not see Don Quixote, as he has just gone through the window that remains still open.[11]

As we can see, there is a striking difference between the "practical" beginning of the film and the "romantic" beginning of the novel: "En un lugar de la Mancha, de cuyo nombre no quiero acordarme, no ha mucho tiempo que vivía un hidalgo de los de lanza en astillero, adarga antigua, rocín flaco y galgo corridor."[12] (In a village of La Mancha, the name of which I have no desire to call to mind, there lived not long since one of those gentlemen that keep a lance in the lance-rack, an old buckler, a lean hack, and a greyhound for coursing.) While the author talks in great detail about the life and the new passion of his hero, Schwartz's script immediately immerses us into real life where people gossip about their neighbors, where even the closest family members, instead of being understanding and supportive, invite strangers to help them condemn the "faulty" passion of Don Quixote that he experiences toward books.

It is no wonder that in the script the future Knight leaves his own house through the window; he is not as naïve as many may think him, and he is certainly bitterly aware of his family's disapproval of his passion and dream. The different dynamic of the beginning, the decisive look into the reality of life, all that, undoubtedly, make Schwartz's Don Quixote more contemporary and, certainly, even more alive.

Kozintsev, in turn, also ponders about Don Quixote's image:

> не то важно, что он решил стать рыцарем (это десятое дело), а важно то, что у него появилась идея [my emphasis] справедливости. Он решил, что так жить нельзя, взял копье, щит, на котором изображено пламенное сердце, и поехал на поиски, но не только на поиски рыцарских подвигов, а на поиски утерянной справедливости.[13]

> (It is not that important that he decided to become a knight [it's the tenth thing], but what is important is that he got *an idea* of justice. He decided that it was not right to live like he did, and he took a spear, a shield with an emblem that showed a flaming heart, and he went off in search of not only knightly deeds but also lost justice.)

As the cinema, according to Kozintsev, cannot simultaneously transmit the tragic and the comic sides of life, the director always has to make a choice between the comic and the tragic; in other words, he has to *re-accentuate* the literary character accordingly. For Kozintsev, Don Quixote is a deeply tragic figure that, perhaps, symbolizes death of the humanist dream. Kozintsev's extensive correspondence with Schwartz and Nikolay Cherkasov[14] reveals to us a wide range of nuances that are instrumental in the process of *re-accentuation* of the literary image. As noted:

> Вы уже дважды играли эту роль, и эти прошлые работы не только не помогают вам, но, напротив, мешают. . . .[15] Иного, совершенно иного хочется теперь. И как будто вы тоже увлеклись этим иным толкованием . . . Конечно, Дон Кихот смешной, но не только потому, что он тощий и нелепо говорящий, но, прежде всего потому, что он слишком честный и слишком святой для реальной жизни . . . И вот именно в выражении этих свойств и заключена наша задача. Здесь все трудности. Нужно найти эту святость, и эту честность - невозможные, не встречающиеся в реальной жизни. . . . Человечность - основа образа Дон Кихота.[16]

> (You have played this role twice, and this past experience not only does not help you but, on the contrary, it interferes. . . . We want different, absolutely different now. And, it seems to me, that you also are very much interested and fascinated with this new interpretation. . . . Of course, Don Quixote is funny, but not only because he is so skinny and often so ridiculously speaks;

he is funny because he was too honest and too holy for the real life. . . . And our problem is how to express these properties of his character. This is where all our difficulties are. We need to find this sanctity, and this honesty—yes, impossible in real life. . . . Humanity is the essence of the image of Don Quixote.)

Now we have to turn to the film to see the results of Schwart / Kozintsev's double *re-accentuation* of the image. Let's see how Schwartz, at the very beginning, changes our entire notion about one of the most unusual literary images, Dulcinea of Tobosso:

Рыцарь шагает по улице селения. Перед бедным крестьянским домиком с покосившимся забором он вдруг останавливается и почтительно снимает свою широкополую шляпу. "Я слышу звуки труб. Сейчас опустят подъемный мост, и Дульсинея Тобосская выйдет на балкон." (. . .) Дон Кихот подходит к забору. Через двор к коровнику пробегает молоденькая миловидная девушка. Рыцарь, увидев Альдонсу, вспыхивает, как мальчик. Прижимает руки к сердцу и роняет их, словно обессилев. "О дама моего сердца, - шепчет он едва слышно вслед Альдонсе. - Рыцарская любовь сжигает в своем огне чувства низменные и свинские, и направляет силы к подвигам О, Дульсинея!"[17]

(The Knight walks down the street of the village. Before the poor peasant house with the rickety fence, he suddenly stops and respectfully withdraws his wide-brimmed hat. "I hear the sound of trumpets. I know they will lower the drawbridge, and Dulcinea of Toboso will come on the balcony." [. . .] Don Quixote comes close to the fence. Across the yard to the barn runs a pretty young girl. The Knight sees Aldonsa and blushes as a boy. He presses his hands to his heart and then drops them in exhaustion. "The lady of my heart,"—he whispers faintly,—"the Knight's love burns in its fire all low and bad feelings and calls for heroic deeds. Oh, Dulcinea!")

Why would Schwartz and Kozintsev change the entire disposition of one of the most unusual characters of world literature—Dulcinea? We think that this is a part of their plan for re-accentuation of the main hero, Don Quixote; the re-accentuation is being done indirectly, through the development and elaboration of another arch-important, but still secondary, image, that of Dulcinea. As we know, Cervantes's Dulcinea never made her personal appearance in the book, nor did she pronounce a single word. In contrast, Schwartz / Kozintsev's Dulcinea appears as a "young pretty girl" running across the yard toward the barn. Somewhere in the background we hear the bleating of goats, the mooing of cows, and the voice of her father shouting loudly: "Aldonsa! Where are you, damn girl?" The rustic and prosaic landscape certainly does not correspond with the romantic encounter between the "knight" and his "Dame de Coeur." Let's listen to their first conversation:

> Сеньор Кехано! Как рано вы поднялись, словно простой мужик. Ох, что я говорю, простите мою дерзость Я хотела сказать - как птичка божья![18]

(Señor Quixana! How early you got up like a simple peasant. Oh, what do I say, please forgive my impertinence. I wanted to say—like a bird of God!)

Kozintsev/Schwartz's Dulcinea/Aldonsa knows perfectly well who she is talking to; this is señor Quixana, the nice gentleman living next door, who is so good-hearted and understanding that she is excited to share with him some good news:

> У нас такая радость, сеньор, корова принесла двух телят разом! И оба такие здоровенькие, только худенькие, как ваша милость. Ох, простите меня, необразованную. Я плету от радости сама не знаю что.[19]

(We have such pleasant news, sir: our cow brought two calves at once! And both of them are so healthy, but slender, as Your Grace. Oh, excuse me, uneducated girl. Because of joy, I say something foolish.)

Again and again, the image of Don Quixote is presented to us through the honest and unspoiled perception of another real individual that lives beside him—our "re-accentuated," so to speak, Aldonsa/Dulcinea who has known "señor Quixana" for many years, probably from her childhood. By comparing him to the calves, she simply meant to tell him how much she really likes him.

It is also significant that Schwartz and Kozintsev do not give Don Quixote a chance to talk to his "Dulcinea"; there will be another, much more important moment in his life when their conversation will be absolutely necessary, but for now the soliloquy is enough. When Aldonsa/Dulcinea runs away, Don Quixote, now alone, whispers after her:

> До свидания, о Дульсинея Тобосская, благороднейшая из благородных. Ты сама не знаешь как ты прекрасна и как несчастна. С утра до ночи надрываешься ты - так сделал Фрестон, и никто не благодарит тебя за труд. Нет. Только бранят да учат . . . О, проклятый вошебник! Клянусь, не вложу я меча в ножны, пока не сниму чары с тебя, о любовь моя единственная, дама моего сердца, Дульсинея Тобосская![20]

(Goodbye, oh, Dulcinea of Toboso, the noblest of the noble. You do not know how beautiful you are, and how unhappy. From early morning till night you work hard—this is what Freston did to you, and there is no one to thank you for all the work. No one. Only scolding . . . Oh yes, wreaked magician! I

swear, I will not thrust my sword into the sheath until I take the spell off of
you, my love, the only lady of my heart, Dulcinea of Toboso!)

From the very beginning of the film, the image of Don Quixote is
thought to become incredibly romantic, and, perhaps, it manages to reach
heights that have never been achieved by Cervantes himself. The comic
part of the hero is certainly downplayed; neither the script-writer, nor the
director shows a single intention to make us smile or laugh when we see
Don Quixote stopping and respectfully withdrawing his wide-brimmed
hat in front of the "poor peasant house with the rickety fence," or when he
whispers to himself, blaming the malicious Freston for all the misfortunes
of Dulcinea/Aldonsa.

This romantic image of Don Quixote initiated by Schwartz continues to
be elaborated by Kozintsev. His correspondence with Nikolay Cherkasov
is revealing; Kozintsev tries to share with the great actor his thoughts and
ideas about Cervantes's hero. As noted:

> Вот и задача для вас. Полюбить этот образ. Полюбить за чистоту и
> святую простоту. Так, чтобы прошибли слезы. Полюбить как реального
> человека, а не как предмет для комических карикатур и риторического
> пафоса. Наш ключ к роли: Алонсо Добрый.[21]

> (Here lies the challenge for you: you must love this image. Love it for his pu-
> rity and his holy simplicity. So that tears would come out of your eyes. Love
> him as a real person and not as a subject for comic cartoons or any rhetorical
> pathos. Our key to the role is: Alonso the Good.)

At first sight, it may seem that this, as we called it, *double re-accentuation*
of Don Quixote's image can be viewed as a violation of the author's will.
Or that this double re-accentuation may change the initial idea of the image to such an extent that it will be impossible to talk about Don Quixote
of Cervantes but only to talk about Don Quixote of Schwartz/Kozintsev.
It may be so, but we still tend to agree with Bakhtin who notes the following:

> In re-accentuation of this kind there is no crude violation of the author's will.
> It can even be said that this process takes place within the image itself . . . and
> such conditions merely actualize in an image a potential already available to
> it . . . we could say with justification that in one respect the image has become
> better understood and better "heard" than ever before.[22]

It is obvious that the image of Don Quixote in the script, as well as
in the movie itself, undergoes, perhaps, one of the most significant reevaluations, and Schwartz/Kozintsev's extensive re-interpretations of the
well-known image are, perhaps, the most revolutionary that have ever

been applied to Don Quixote. But we believe that there are a few important reasons for that. The first reason is that the two great artists—Kozintsev and Schwartz—were *simultaneously* interpreting and re-interpreting
the book of Cervantes while they were both contemplating the film. The
second reason, of no lesser importance, is the context of Russia's political
situation; the country that was awake after a lethargic intellectual sleep[23]
desperately needed some new interpretation of many moral, religious,
and literary values. Now, when individual and intellectual freedom
seemed to become a reality, these good old values had to be re-thought
or, to say it better, *re-accentuated*. Like everything in a country that was
for many years living under the yoke of dictatorship, even the immortal
image of Cervantes's hero was reduced to a simple, petty, and comical
figure, and the book of Cervantes, for a few decades, from schools to the
halls of academia, was treated as no more than a comic novel. Now it was
time to change the perception of the novel and time to *re-accentuate*, by
means of cinematography, the main character, Don Quixote.

It has been argued that:

> Within certain limits the process of re-accentuation is unavoidable, legiti-
> mate and even productive. But these limits may easily be crossed when a
> work is distant from us and when we begin to perceive it against a back-
> ground completely foreign to it.[24]

Kozintsev's understanding of the literary image of Don Quixote is certainly different. His free-spirited imagination easily "crosses the limits"
of the novel; Kozintsev plays, and very successfully, on the fact that the
novel itself is distant from us. Nowadays the contemporary spectator,
argues Kozintsev, will, in fact, better perceive the novel when adapted to
the screen. The same spectator will perceive the novel as well as its main
literary character "against a background completely foreign to it." Thus,
the contemporary spectator, reasons Kozintsev further, does not want to
see on the screen a crazy man; he will not believe in such an image. Nor
will the spectator believe in the message of a character that is perceived
to be mentally ill. From the text:

> Отвратительно умиляться и разыскивать сентиментальные места
> для того, чтобы разжалобить зрителя. Это образ рыцаря. Пусть у
> этого рыцаря нет ни рыцарской повадки, ни рыцарской поступи, ни
> рыцарских интонаций (и весь смысл именно в том, что всего этого нет
> ни крохотной тени!), но он добр, благороден, честен и строг к себе.
> Он застенчив в век развязности, целомудрен среди блуда и, наконец,
> возвышенно мечтателен в век расчета и власти чистогана.[25]

(It is disgusting to always look for the sentimental places to soften the heart
of a viewer. *This is the image of a knight* [emphasis mine]. And even though

this knight does not have chivalry habits, no chivalrous gait, or chivalry intonations [and this is most important, that he, in fact, does not have even the tiny shadow of all that!], he is kind, generous, honest, and strict with himself. He is shy in the age of familiarity, sober among fornication, and, finally, his dreams are pure in the age of calculation and power of lucre.)

Let's now see how Kozintsev and Schwartz *re-accentuated* "the image of the knight" in the final and, perhaps, the most important scene of the film. Here as well will take place the most interesting dialogue between Don Quixote and Dulcinea—the dialogue that, in our opinion, is the culmination of the *re-accentuation* of Cervantes's novel. As stated:

Комната пустеет. Вдруг снежная буря прекращается. Окно распахивается настежь. Снега как не было. Цветущее миндальное дерево заглядывает в комнату. Полная луна стоит в небе. Раздается шорох, шепот. "Сеньор, сеньор! Не оставляйте меня!" Дон Кихот садится на постели. "Кто меня зовет?" "Это я, Дульсинея." Перед ним в богатейшем бархатном наряде, сияя серебром и золотом, стоит Альдонса. "Спасибо вам, сеньора, за то, что приснились мне перед моей кончиной." "Я запрещаю вам умирать, сеньор. Слышите? Повинуйтесь даме своего сердца!"[26]

(The room empties. Suddenly a blizzard stops. A window swings open. The flowering almond tree looks into the room. The full moon is on the sky. You hear the rustling, whispering noise. "Senor, senor! Do not leave me!" Don Quixote sits on the bed. "Who is calling me?" "It's me, Dulcinea." Before him, in the richest velvet dress, shining with gold and silver, appears Aldonsa. "Thank you, my dear, for letting me dream about you before I die." "I forbid you to die, sir. Do you hear me? Obey the Lady of your heart!")

The soliloquy that started from the first encounter of Don Quixote with Dulcinea/Aldonsa now has developed into a *dialogue* between two major characters, a dialogue that changes altogether our perception of the knight as well as his "Dame de Coeur." All of a sudden, both literary characters acquire more life and reality than they had in the book; we feel that we have known these two people all our lives and that we are ready to join Aldonsa in her plea to Don Quixote and beg him not to die. This is when the art of *re-accentuation* shows all its tremendous potential; if many years ago upon closing the book of Cervantes, we felt sad that the story had finished, now, while watching the film and listening to the dialogue between these two eternal lovers, we feel that we are just about to say goodbye forever to a best friend without whom this life will never be the same, and we want to cry because of that. As noted:

"Вы устали? Да? А как же я?" Исчезает парча и бархат, и Алдонса стоит перед рыцарем в своем крестьянском платье. "А как же я? Нельзя, сеньор, не умирайте. Простите, что я так говорю, но только не умирайте.

Пожалуйста. Я понимаю, как болят ваши натруженные руки, как ломит спину. Не умирайте, дорогой мой, голубчик мой!"[27]

("Are you tired? Yes? But what about me?" Gradually her brocade and velvet disappear, and Aldonsa is facing the knight dressed in her peasant dress. "And what about me? You cannot, sir, do not die. I'm sorry to say so, but do not die, please. I understand how hurt your work-worn hands are, how your back is aching, but still, do not die, my dear, my darling!")

This unusual dialogue between two characters, one of which has never made a personal appearance in the book, is what we consider to be a pinnacle of the art of the double *re-accentuation* of *Don Quixote* by Schwartz and Kozintsev. We would like to call this moment a *point of maturity of the idea—the idea* of Don Quixote as universal literary image. Bakhtin believed that every literary *idea* would eventually mature into its full potential (in other words, would come to its "great time"), but she (*the idea*) always needs time and some kind of stimulating reception from the audience. This is precisely what she gets now from the new audience of cinema viewers. Given these two things being present—the time and the stimulus—the *idea* can finally be viewed from a productive distance, and she can enter into productive dialogue with other *ideas*—one related to Dulcinea, in our case. This is why we consider this dialogue to be arch-liberating in the process of re-accentuation, to be one that can unexpectedly reveal the new and surprising facets of the "good old idea" as it enters into global communication with each and every one around herself.

Before we end the article, we would like to show how, in their quest for the ultimate re-accentuation of every literary character in the book, Schwartz and Kozintsev changed the final scene of the book drastically by crowning it with a last and seminal dialogue between Don Quixote and his faithful squire Sancho Panza:

"Ах, не умирайте, ваша милость, мой сеньор! А послушайтесь моего совета и живите себе! Умереть - это величайшее безумие, которое может позволить себе человек. Разве кто убил вас? Одна тоска. А она баба. Дайте ей, серой, по шее, и пойдем бродить по свету, по лесам и лугам!" Дон Кихот оказывается вдрух в рыцарских доспехах. Он шагает черз подоконник, и вот рыцарь и оруженосец мчатся по дороге под луной. "Сражаясь неустанно, доживем мы, Санчо, до золотого века. Мир, дружба и согласие воцарятся на всем свете. Вперед, вперед, ни шагу назад!" Все быстрее и быстрее скачут под луной славный рыцарь Дон Кихот и его верный оруженосец Санчо Панса.[28]

("Oh, do not die, your honor, my liege! Take my advice and live yourself. To die is the greatest folly that a person can do to himself. Did someone kill you? Just the longing. Break her neck and let's continue to wander the world, through the forests and meadows!" Don Quixote is suddenly in a knight's armor. He walks over to the sill, and the knight and the squire rush onto the road in the moonlight. "Battling tirelessly, we will live, Sancho, to the golden age. Peace, friendship and harmony reign in the whole world. Forward, forward, not a step back!" Faster and faster the glorious knight Don Quixote and his faithful squire Sancho Panza gallop under the moon.)

Love and empathy between literary characters is what invariably unifies any great literary work, and this is what has always been of great importance for Bakhtin. In his view, only the answerable empathy can become a unique unifying power creating the desired "unity of answerability."[29] And this is what both masters, Schwartz and Kozintsev, in our opinion, have successfully achieved; they collaboratively managed to *re-accentuate* the image of the world's greatest literary hero to the extent of his elevated realness. By means of cinematography, they managed to bring this image closer to us but, at the same time, they did not distort the main idea of Cervantes's masterpiece: "Человечность - основа образа Дон Кихота.[30] (Humanity is the essence of the image of Don Quixote.)

NOTES

1. Mikhail Bakhtin, *The Dialogic Imagination: Four Essays*, ed. Michael Holquist, trans. Caryl Emerson and Michael Holquist (Austin: University of Texas Press, 1981), 421.

2. Grigori Kozintsev (1905–1973) was one of the most renowned Soviet film directors. His most famous adaptations are *Hamlet*, *King Lear*, and *Don Quixote* (1957). Evgeny Schwartz (1896–1958) was a Soviet playwright mostly famous for his theatrical adaptations. His last work, the script for *Don Quixote* (1957), was solicited by Kozintsev himself. Schwartz did not see the film; he died before the film was released.

3. Dziga Vertov (1896–1954) was a Soviet pioneer documentary filmmaker and cinema theorist. His filming techniques as well as his theories made a profound impression around the world on documentary movie-making, and his film *Man with a Moving Camera* is considered the eighth best film ever made.

4. Nikita Khrushchev (1894–1971) was a prominent Russian political leader from 1953 to 1964. He is remembered for his contribution to the de-Stalinization of the Soviet Union, for backing the progress of the Soviet space program, and for a number of liberal reforms.

5. E. Schwartz, *Pozvonki minuvshih dnej. Proizvedeniya 40-50 godov* (Moscow: Korona-print, 1999), 153.

6. Khrushchev's thaw (early 1950s–early 1960s) was a period in the Soviet Union when repression and censorship were reversed and many prisoners returned home from Gulag labor camps.

7. During Stalin's era, the book of Cervantes did not enjoy much popularity in the Soviet Union, nor did it receive much scholarly attention. It was viewed as

merely a comic book about a madman who lost his mind, did not have any "class-consciousness," and, as a consequence, could not deserve more than laughter.

8. Bakhtin, *Dialogic Imagination*, 420.

9. Schwartz, 153.

10. E. Schwartz, *Izbrannoe* (Saint Petersburg: Kristall, 1998), 793.

11. Regarding this, see E. Schwartz, *Izbrannoe* (Saint Petersburg: Kristall, 1998), 793–94.

12. Miguel de Cervantes, *Don Quijote de la Mancha*, ed. Juan Bautista Avalle-Arce, 2 vols. (Madrid: Alhambra, 1979).

13. G. Kozintsev, *Sobranie sochinenij*, 5 vols. (Leningrad: Iskusstvo, 1982), v. 1, 249.

14. Nikolay Cherkasov (1903–1966) was one of the most prominent Soviet actors. His major roles in cinematography include Alexander Nevsky, Ivan the Terrible, and Don Quixote.

15. Here Kozintsev refers to the two famous theatrical performances of Don Quixote by Cherkasov. One was in 1933 in Pushkin's Academic Theatre in Saint Petersburg; another one was in June 1941, just two weeks before the beginning of the Great Patriotic War, when Cherkasov played Don Quixote in Mikhail Bulgakov's play staged also in Pushkin's Academic Theater.

16. G. Kozintsev, *Sobranie sochinenij*, 5 vols. (Leningrad: Iskusstvo, 1982), v. 5, 441–42.

17. Schwartz, *Izbrannoe*, 797–98.

18. Schwartz, *Izbrannoe*, 798.

19. Schwartz, *Izbrannoe*, 798.

20. Schwartz, *Izbrannoe*, 799.

21. G. Kozintsev, *Sobranie sochinenij*. v. 5, 500–501.

22. Bakhtin, *Dialogic Imagination*, 420.

23. Stalin died in 1953. From the "Great Purge" that started in 1933 and went up to Stalin's death, the intellectual freedom in the USSR was reduced to next to nothing. Afraid to be sent to one of the countless labor camps, the intelligentsia preferred to avoid any type of intellectual discussion.

24. Bakhtin, *Dialogic Imagination*, 420.

25. Kozintsev, *Sobranie sochinenij*. v. 5, 500–501.

26. Schwartz, *Izbrannoe*, 860–61.

27. Schwartz, *Izbrannoe*, 860.

28. Schwartz, *Izbrannoe*, 861–62.

29. Regarding this, see M. Bakhtin, *Art and Answerability: Early Philosophical Essays*, ed. Michael Holquist and Vadim Liapunov, trans. Kenneth Brostrom (Austin: University of Texas Press, 1990).

30. Kozintsev, *Sobranie sochinenij*, v. 5, 501.

11

Surviving the Hollywood Blacklist: Waldo Salt's Adaptation of *Don Quixote*

William Childers

Duchess: Are you really mad?
Don Quixote: Only a madman would insist he's sane when the whole world
says he's mad. Since I consider myself sane, I must admit I'm mad, I suppose . . .

—Waldo Salt, *Don Quixote* (January 25, 1967), p. 68

At the end of his life, Waldo Salt (1914–1987) was a recognized master of the adaptation of novels to the film medium, with two screenplay Oscars (for *Midnight Cowboy* and *Coming Home*) and another nomination (for *Serpico*), a Writer's Guild Laurel award, a teaching appointment at NYU, and writing workshops under his direction at the newly founded Sundance Institute.[1] But that was not how his career began. He had only a few screenwriting credits, most notably for *The Shopworn Angel* (1938), when his name appeared in a list published in *The Hollywood Reporter* of known Communists. The following year, having just completed the screenplay for *Rachel and the Stranger* (1948), based on a story by Howard Fast, he was subpoenaed as one of nineteen unfriendly witnesses by the House Un-American Activities Committee (HUAC) in October 1947. He traveled to Washington, DC, to appear before the Committee, but when the Hollywood Ten were found in contempt, those hearings were suspended without Salt's having been called to testify. The ink was scarcely dry on his script for the Burt Lancaster vehicle *The Flame and the Arrow* (1950), however, when he was brought before HUAC again, on April 13, 1951.[2] He pled the Fifth and was blacklisted for over a decade. Even after the blacklist collapsed, he could not get the kind of work to which he aspired. In 1964 he found himself at fifty, separated from his wife, Mary Davenport, his career going nowhere, wondering what he was doing with his life. His sense of failure was perhaps not unlike Cervantes's own at about the same age, which is also the age of the *ingenioso hidalgo* when he takes the road on Rocinante. As Salt explains to Eugene Corr and Robert

153

Hillmann in their documentary *Waldo Salt: A Screenwriter's Journey* (1990), he received a visit at that time from his daughter Deborah, who said to him, "Daddy, no one would mind if you were doing something you really wanted to do, something really important to you." Stunned by her words into taking responsibility for his art, Salt vowed that from then on, "I was going to write everything as well as I could." He put everything else aside and worked for the next two years on the ambitious project that would mark the defining shift in his career: a screen adaptation of *Don Quixote*. Producer A. Ronald Lubin paid him a few thousand dollars in exchange for the right to produce it, if they ever found backing, then left Salt to his own devices; the fact that there was no immediate prospect of filming the screenplay gave him the freedom to develop what would become his mature and highly influential technique of screen adaptation. It was in the process of creating his *Don Quixote* that Waldo Salt became the screenwriter who triumphed in the New Hollywood of the late 1960s and 1970s.

Although public acclaim for *Midnight Cowboy* was still five years away at the time, the decision to adapt *Don Quixote* was the true turning point in Salt's fifteen-year struggle to reassert himself as a writer. After the blow handed him in April 1951, he had initially turned his back on Hollywood, collaborating with folksinger-songwriter/composer and fellow Communist Earl Robinson (best remembered today as author of "Joe Hill" and "The House I Live In") on *Sandhog*, a folk opera based on a story by Theodore Dreiser about the men who built the tunnels under the Hudson and the East River. For three years, from 1951 until its debut on November 23, 1954, at the Phoenix Theater in New York, they labored on this musical drama, whose protagonist, in keeping with the two men's political philosophy, was collective, rather than individual. Striving for authenticity, Salt imitated the characters' Irish working-class dialect; concern with accurately depicting their dangerous profession led the authors to hold meetings with real-life "sandhogs" from the Hod Carriers Union. The result, reviewers had to admit, was a polished, professional show that nonetheless struck most as outdated in its social-realist aesthetic. The unsigned review in *Theatre Arts* (off-Broadway edition) for February 1955 described it as "the class struggle set to music," rebuking the authors' Marxism: "the class struggle [. . .] is unfashionable, and in one variety, illegal. But had *Sandhog* been written and produced in the Federal Theatre era of the thirties, it would surely have been one of the most talked-about productions of the season. It came too late for its own good" (Waldo Salt Papers, UCLA, Box 90, folder 6). As a bid for acceptance as a serious writer, intended to impress people whose opinions mattered to Salt and rebuild his reputation despite the blacklist, *Sandhog* was neither a complete failure nor a resounding success. Earl Robinson believed in the musical and worked tirelessly for years to promote it. It found a receptive audience abroad in East Germany, in Australia, and in a radio version in Czechoslovakia. But the royalty checks were meager, and paying the bills was a real concern. Salt did not repeat the experiment.[3]

To support his wife and two young daughters, he took whatever screenwriting work he could, mainly swashbuckling TV adventure stories focused on individual heroes, ideologically about as far-removed from *Sandhog* as could be imagined. He wrote for British television, penning several episodes for a pirate show starring Robert Shaw, *The Buccaneers* (1956–1957), and for a series based on Sir Walter Scott's historical novel of chivalry *Ivanhoe* (1958–1959), starring Roger Moore. In the United States, for over ten years he could only write for television under a pseudonym. The one he used most often was his wife's maiden name, Davenport, with Mary shortened to M. or replaced with Mel. Another frequent pseudonym was Arthur Behrstock. Under these names, he wrote for such series as *The Adventures of Robin Hood* (1955–1958) and *The Sword of Freedom* (1957–1958), as well as the made-for-television film adaptation of *The Swiss Family Robinson* (1958).[4] While writing conventional action-adventure dramas may have been beneath his ability, it prepared him well for adapting the great parody of the chivalric genre, *Don Quixote*, where he drew upon this experience in creating action scenes to turn conventional Hollywood duels and jousts into slapstick comedy.

However exasperating it may be to accept second-rate work, at least one can rationalize it, during a period of internal exile, by attributing the failure to find better offers to the fact that one is the victim of a regime of censorship. When the blacklist began to weaken, however, Salt still did not find doors opening to him in Hollywood, or at least, not the ones he had hoped. One producer willing to hire him was Harold Hecht, who used him on *Taras Bulba* (1962), an adaptation of Gogol's novel, starring Yul Brynner and Tony Curtis. It is unmemorable, but not as bad as Salt later felt it to be. To be sure, it is hard to imagine its glorification of military prowess and nationalism could have appealed much to the writer who later penned socially and politically critical scripts like *Midnight Cowboy* and *Coming Home*. Above all, it is filmed in a style that is about ten years out of date. It participates in the stagnant mediocrity into which Hollywood was mired by self-censorship, rendering it incapable of keeping up with new developments in cinematic art, let alone upheaval in U.S. society. Like the many talented writers and directors younger than he was who would soon create what became known as the New Hollywood, Salt was chomping at the bit in his desire to do something innovative.

One example of this ambition is the detailed treatment he wrote for a biopic on Simón Bolívar, preserved among his papers, dated July 12, 1963, two years after he completed *Taras Bulba*. It is not clear for whom it was written or what exactly inspired him to write it. He researched the topic, reading several books on the Liberator, including Waldo Frank's 1951 study, *Birth of a World*, which he particularly admired. Salt describes Bolívar's life as "a story for our time, a story that has intense contemporary meaning" (Waldo Salt Papers, UCLA, Box 61, folder 4, 2). "He is a man of the early Nineteenth Century who foreshadows the whole Twentieth Century dilemma: Can human freedom become a reality? Can the spirit of man triumph over chaos and bring order to the dark forces that threaten destruction?" (9) It is interesting to note how quixotic he makes his hero out to be:

> Bolivar's personality is infinitely attractive, puzzling, contradictory. The problem of the film must be stated simply— the problem of a romantic idealist, an aristocrat and dreamer, who decided (without logical justification or practical means of fulfilling the task) to liberate his native land and all the countries of Latin America, a man who walked through blood and suffering and terror and despair, arousing millions of people to share his dream. (1)

Indeed, he quotes William Whately Pierson, who called Bolívar a "new Quixote" (8); two years later, more disillusioned than ever, he would be ready to take on Cervantes's hero directly.

After *Taras Bulba*, Salt wrote two more screenplays for Hecht, both of which resulted in forgettable films: *Flight from Ashiya* (1964) and *Wild and Wonderful* (1964). In Corr and Hillmann's documentary, Salt comments ironically on his embarrassment at having his name associated with these projects. He does not explain, however, that Hecht, to use him at all, required him to supply a letter acknowledging he was formerly a member of the Communist Party and had long since rejected Communism. In hopes of steadier employment, he continued writing for the networks. NBC took his script for an episode of their series *Espionage*, but they still insisted, as late as October 1963, on crediting it to Mel Davenport (Waldo Salt Papers, UCLA, Box 63, folder 8). Was the blacklist over or not? At this point, Salt sought the help of a lawyer, Jerome B. Lurie, who guided him through the process, as he had others before him, of sending an affidavit to HUAC admitting to having been a Communist, and explaining that he had left the Party years ago. Lurie warned him that the Committee would reject the affidavit unless he agreed to come before them and name names, but assured him that just submitting it would satisfy the big three networks, to each of which he provided a notarized copy (Waldo Salt Papers, UCLA, Box 77). While this affidavit was calculated to clear his name and is therefore not entirely reliable, it is revealing of his disenchantment with both sides in the Cold War. On the one hand, he affirms his commitment to democratic principles and individual freedom, to which he attributes his gradual disaffection with Communism. On the other, he accuses participants in 1950s anti-Communist "witch hunts" of curtailing civil liberties in a fashion not fundamentally different from Stalinist show trials:

> In particular as a writer I could not and cannot tolerate a system which requires and enforces unanimity of purpose and expression since these are individual by nature and cease to be purposeful or expressive when they are dictated by any external policy.
>
> In the end, I could not reconcile words of peaceful intention with the ruthless suppression of democracy and civil rights in Communist countries. I could not reconcile slogans about the greater good and human brotherhood with totalitarian despotism, persecution, torture and murder of political dissenters.
>
> I did not formally or officially terminate membership in the Communist Party or issue any public statement because I felt at the time it would appear to be a forced disavowal, too suggestive of the enforced confessions and recantations I found so degrading and reprehensible in the Communist Party, in the Soviet Union and other countries where thought control is permitted to compel conformity of opinion. (Waldo Salt Papers, UCLA, Box 77, folder 4, p. 3)

Exactly as Lurie had warned him to expect, HUAC rejected his letter and returned the affidavit. It seems it did the trick with the networks, however; he wrote an episode for the CBS series *The Nurses* the following year, under his own name.[5]

Yet in 1965, after nearly thirty years as a professional writer, his position was as precarious as it had ever been. He was not getting steady work, and what he could get was unworthy of his talent. He found himself, as George Litto, his agent, puts it in *A Screenwriter's Journey*, "at the bottom of the writing profession." Had his affidavit only partially cleared him? Something had to give. He knew the craft as well as anyone, but what did he really have to show for his decades of experience? He was a serious writer who could do more than just entertain his audience; he could make them think, given half a chance, but where was he going to get that chance? At fifty, he must have felt the time growing short. He had to show what he could do before it was too late. He entered a downward spiral combining failure, depression, alcoholism, and self-loathing. His daughter's challenge to "do something really important to you" provoked him into recognizing he had to save himself, not wait for someone else to do it. In this hour of need he turned to the characters who had saved a greater writer than he, in similar circumstances three and a half centuries before: a fiftyish skinny madman who thinks he is a knight, and the earthy, rotund peasant he drags along to be his squire.

The choice of *Don Quixote* was far from arbitrary. There is a long history in the United States of considering Cervantes's masterpiece as *the* representative book from Spain; and due to their identification with the

Loyalist cause in the Spanish Civil War, Spain held a special place in the hearts of American Leftists of Salt's generation.[6] Frequently, those called to testify before HUAC cited their sympathies with the Spanish Loyalists as the main reason for their involvement with the Communist Party. Indeed, Salt and his first wife had sponsored a Spanish teenager in a French refugee camp.[7] Among those who share this experience of defending the Spanish Republic, Cervantes and *Don Quixote* are venerated by association. For example, they are evoked in a cameo role as the symbolic defenders of Madrid in the Hemingway-narrated documentary *The Spanish Earth* (1937). Alvah Bessie, the only member of the Hollywood Ten who had served in the Abraham Lincoln Brigades, read *Don Quixote* during the year he spent in a federal prison for contempt of Congress for refusing to testify in 1947 (Nelson 181–83). So did Howard Fast, the blacklisted novelist who also wrote, during his prison stay, *Spartacus*, the novel that, adapted to the screen, broke the blacklist (Sorin 210; Buhle and Wagner 206). Another association with Cervantes was that blacklistees considered HUAC an "Inquisition" and could therefore view as relevant to their situation the entire context of Spanish history during which the Inquisition flourished. In his testimony before HUAC, Salt insisted that by means of the Fifth Amendment the Founding Fathers "intended particularly to protect individuals against political inquiry, against inquiry into heresy" (Waldo Salt Papers, UCLA, Box 77, folder 4, p. 19). In a prepared statement he brought to the hearing that he was not allowed to read, Salt criticized the proceedings in similar terms, noting that "the techniques of inquisition are as old as history" (Waldo Salt Papers, UCLA, Box 77, folder 10).[8] This association between HUAC and the Spanish Inquisition is borne out by Salt's incorporation of the Inquisition into his adaptation as Don Quixote's pursuers, discussed below. Finally, Salt's own personality, as it emerges from talking to those who knew him, is recognizably quixotic; or at least it became so, perhaps in part as a result of the very experience of being blacklisted.[9] He would be drawn to Cervantes's book for the rest of his life, and continue to incorporate it in subtle ways into his subsequent writing and artwork, as will be detailed in the concluding section of this essay.

Salt began working on *Don Quixote* in June 1965, allowing himself absolute freedom. Initially, he made a token effort to remain faithful to Cervantes's text in the literal, line-by-line sense, but that was short-lived. By the end of July he accepted that he must create his own screen equivalents for Cervantes's narrative inventiveness. At that point he met with an old writer buddy and fellow blacklistee, Abe Ginnes; Salt's notes on that conversation were the first of many on the key interpretive issues underlying the adaptation: character motivation, historical context, identification of the modern audience with the hero:

> Primary problem is identity of audience with Quixote. Identity with his initial impulse to take to the road. It is obviously not madness in the overall, but taking that for granted is not enough.
>
> The audience must understand from the beginning that they are not laughing *at* the infirmities of an old man, but with the awkward explosion of vitality in a man who has allowed himself to become old before his time. The causes for his dehydration may be sufficient as they stand: for purposes of modern identification—the smothering, mothering housekeeper—which would also be a lousy marriage to the greedy widow with her narcissistic daughter (the niece) and the unemployed hustler who's trying to carve his way into the family with his pruning hook (the stable boy).
>
> There is, I feel, a certain limitation to this simple explosion. Note for consideration the more profound motives in Cervantes—as they emerge later—but were probably more apparent to a reader of his day, even at the beginning—include:
>
> 1. The cultural aridness of the time.
> 2. The geographical aridness of the countryside, which I assume is related to the prairies of America or the New England rock-bound farmer.
> 3. Related to this, the aridness of a declining great power, economically, reducing the country gentleman and small landowners with the decline of Spain's overseas empire.
> 4. Related to this, the decline of glory—admired by Cervantes and Quixote with highest, noblesse oblige idealism.
> 5. Quixote is the total idealist, in that he overlooks and refuses to accept the sordid material motivations for imperialist militarism. He only follows the propaganda code of the Conquistadors as promulgated in the fiction of chivalry—the obligation to right wrongs and aid the helpless. This accounts for Quixote's philosophy about the real Golden Age, before gold became a base metal of exchange. His constant heroic failure represents the collapse of the high-flown aims in the face of grim materialist reality. Quixote, however, simply refuses to surrender the principles, even though they are constantly defeated by self-interest chicanery and myopic reality.
> 6. The religious mission aspect of Cervantes' Quixote is related to this.
>
>   He sets out—as a clown—to give leadership in a spiritual vacuum. This was true of Spain of his day, rising out of the collapse of Spain's leadership in Europe and the world. This leadership was real—considering such things as Columbus, El Greco, Velasquez, as well as the Armada and the Conquistadors—not to mention the Inquisition. The need for a new kind of virility and spirituality is the basis for the Quixote two-sided character—the need for a set of principles which allow of heroism in poverty and defeat—a mode of action for human beings

regardless of their circumstances. All of this is the background against which the Cervantes-Quixote operated.

It is important to consider the same moral quandary in its present aspect related to audiences of today. (Waldo Salt Papers, UCLA, Box 23, folder 8, July 30, 1965)

Salt tries out a lot of different things, initially working on a very large canvas: his first decisions, a very unusual situation for a Hollywood screenwriter. But then, he was not really working for anyone; the film had no backing at that point. There is no definitive, final version; plan called for an intermission between Part I and Part II, leading to a screenplay that ran to 249 pages and would have meant at least a three-hour movie. Then he began paring it down. In that process, he kept some ideas, discarded others. He maintained complete control over those rather, the whole project is an experimental screenwriting laboratory in which ideas are invented, reshaped, and recycled, or abandoned in favor of others, successively. There are half a dozen complete versions of the screenplay among the Waldo Salt Papers at UCLA, not to mention numerous discarded scenes, notes on characters and continuity, and artwork intended to aid in visualization of the final script.

Thus the material Salt produced for his adaptation of *Don Quixote* is much more voluminous than a simple screenplay. His rigorous mature technique for adapting fiction to film, which first appears here, consisted of three main stages: (1) meditation on the principal characters and their motivation, written up in dozens of typed pages; (2) creative outpouring of extended scenes and copious dialogue, much more than could finally be incorporated in a single feature film; (3) tightening of plotlines, elimination of extraneous scenes, whittling down the screenplay until it acquired its own internal unity. This was the approach he would use in all his subsequent projects. The result, though it might take longer to produce, has the advantage of being more than a mere scene-by-scene translation from words into images; Salt transposes the entire problematic underlying the text he adapts and then re-creates it in accordance with the demands of the film medium. Moreover, he understands the characters so well that he can ring seemingly endless changes on the scenarios he has created, giving his screenplays a flexibility and adaptability that makes him an ideal collaborator as filming proceeds.[10]

Without being avant-garde, the approach taken does not shy away from obtrusive techniques reminding viewers they are watching a film, in much the same way as Cervantes's narrative intrusions remind readers they are reading a work of fiction. Here are a couple of examples. As Don Quixote passes a windmill on his first sally, the frame freezes and there is an *on-screen footnote*, telling the audience that while some claim his first adventure was a windmill, "the camera cannot lie" (box 11.1). Freezing the frame and adding a footnote are already ways of drawing viewers' attention to the filmic apparatus, but on top of that comes the reference to the camera, which combines anachronism and self-referentiality, since it would have been impossible to *film* Don Quixote in the seventeenth century, even if he had ever really existed. This shot is part of a larger effort, by the way, to employ the windmill as a motif, incorporating it into the screenplay in multiple ways—as a setting for various scenes, and a backdrop to others. Given the symbolic importance that has accrued to the episode of the windmills over the centuries, Salt seems to want to give them a larger presence than they could have in a single brief scene. He is trying, as it were, to mitigate the anticlimactic effect the windmills scene tends to have on stage or screen.

BOX 11.1.   A MOMENT FROM THE FIRST SALLY, 2/7/1966
(WALDO SALT PAPERS, BOX 29, FOLDER 1, P. 9)

EXT. FIELD OF WINDMILLS DAY

Quixote and the stallion follow the path of least resistance, plunging headlong down a rocky hillside toward a scattering of windmills on a barren field. For a moment, it appears as though Quixote may be—intentionally or not—charging the nearest and largest windmill.

All action freezes momentarily. A large black asterisk appears, high on screen right, near the tip of the windmill. A second asterisk follows immediately, low on screen left, directing our attention to a subtitle:

FOOTNOTE: SOME CLAIM THAT DON
QUIXOTE'S FIRST EXPLOIT WAS A
WINDMILL. BUT THE CAMERA CANNOT
LIE...

A similar example is the use of reverse motion to convey a sense of Sancho's perplexity between his two sallies as the mad knight's squire. Rebuffed when he goes to see him by Alonso Quijano's housekeeper, a partially quixotized Sancho intervenes altruistically in a number of situations on his way home; but in his pensive frustration, he undoes it all when he gets there (box 11.2). Running the film backward draws the viewer's attention to the artifice, precisely at a moment in which what is at stake is the juxtaposition of the cynical/picaresque and altruistic/chivalric modes of representation. The facile solution of simply reversing the direction of the film to "undo" what he had done only a moment before reflects Sancho's simplistic thinking, but it does so by means of twentieth-century technology with which Sancho was unfamiliar. This is another example of a meta-cinematic technique Salt invented as equivalent to the meta-literary dimension of Cervantes's original.

Naturally in trying to give coherent form as a single feature-length film to a long, episodic novel, Salt combines and condenses a lot of material, even as he excludes and abridges. One instance of this that follows the lead of other adapters is the elevation of Sansón Carrasco to a leading character in the narrative, right from the beginning.[11] More innovative is the expansion of Ginés de Pasamonte's role into that of a bemused observer of the would-be knight's rise to prominence and his entire career. Salt cleverly recasts the puppet show Ginés does as Maese Pedro into a condensed presentation of the first two sallies, with a puppet Sancho, a puppet Quixote, a puppet Dulcinea, etc. In eminently Cervantean fashion, moreover, he uses this moment to distance himself from Dale Wasserman and Joe Darion's romantic idealism in *Man of La Mancha*, much as Cervantes does in Part II vis-à-vis Avellaneda's continuation. When "the puppet Don brags that he undertakes only the impossible," Salt's Quixote comments, "The man's a sentimental fraud. Only a fool or a madman would undertake the impossible" (Waldo Salt Papers, UCLA, Box 29, folder 7, p. 81). Thus Quixotism to Salt is emphatically *not* a purely abstract, unrealizable ideal, "The Impossible Dream," but an active commitment to making a real difference in this world. Having incorporated a puppet show about the characters into the film, Salt reprises it in the deathbed scene, as a way of talking about the posterity that awaits them, right down to the present, where we, the audience, are sitting watching them on a movie screen—"a puppet show the size of a wall"(box 3). Through deliberate anachronism, Salt ties the representation to the present, even going to the point of having Don Quixote discourage his squire with a line whose economy downplays the brilliance of its self-reflexivity: "Don't be quixotic, Sancho." This is another subtle anachronism that gestures ironically toward the larger-than-life quality of the characters. What better line for Alonso Quijano to employ in a twentieth-century adaptation to the film medium?

Salt's approach to the introduction of political content into his adaptation is oblique. He avoids the deliberate evocation of present-day politics, but he is definitely aware of and concerned with relevance to contemporary issues. His goal, as we saw above, was to guide his audience to

BOX 11.2. WALDO SALT PAPERS,
BOX 29, FOLDER 2, PP. 96–97 (7/10/66)

EXT. COUNTRY ROAD DAY
Sancho rides slowly, his hat feathers drooping. Passing a pasture, he
sees a village lad baiting a bull. The bull charges suddenly. The boy
runs in panic. Sancho jumps from Rucio, shouting:
            SANCHO
        I'll save you!
Sancho slides under the fence, waving his feathered hat. The bull
charges toward Sancho. The boy escapes. Sancho ducks back under
the fence just in time to avoid the bull's horns.

Sancho rides on whistling, his hat at a jaunty angle. He hops down
as he sees a mangy hound with a cowbell tied to his tail, chased by
the lad Sancho saved. Sancho removes the cowbell, scowling at the
boy.
            SANCHO
        You should be ashamed!
            (pats dog)
        You're free—go in peace. . .
Sancho rides on humming, high in the saddle. He slaps Rucio's
flanks as he sees a jack rabbit bounding crazily across the field,
pursued by the mangy hound. Sancho chases the hound and beams
benignly after the escaping rabbit.
            SANCHO
        Pax vobiscum . . .

EXT. PANZA FARM DAY
Sancho is singing as he rides into his farm. He explodes in a bellow-
ing shout as he sees the jack rabbit nibbling in the turnip patch.
            SANCHO
        Ingrate!
In a furious flash of fantasy, Sancho rolls the whole scene backward:
The rabbit races backward into the snapping jaws of the hound—the
hound backs his tail into the cowbell—the boy races backward onto
the horns of the bull and is tossed high in the air.
Sancho jerks the turnip from the ground, wipes it on his sleeve and
starts to eat it. Across the yard, Teresa appears, yelling:
            TERESA
        Sancho . . . ?

BOX 11.3.   FROM THE DEATHBED SCENE, 10/16/1966
(WALDO SALT PAPERS, BOX 29, FOLDER 3, PP. 174–75)

SANCHO
I see it—beyond the horizon—like an apocalypse—every generation—new Quixotes—like grasshoppers. Every puppet maker without a play—making up new Quixotes. Bigger Quixotes. I see puppet
shows the size of a wall . . .

In reverse—the scene in the pavilion fills the entire screen. Sancho
stares directly into camera, creating the illusion that we are the audience at the puppet show of his imagination.

SANCHO
Thousands of people out there watching a puppet Don Quixote dying in his bed. And some puppet Sancho Panza saying—if you want
my advice, you'll stand up! Get out of that bed! There's things to be
done! Rivers to be crossed! Lost causes to be won!

QUIXOTE
Don't be quixotic, Sancho . . .

make the applications to current political and moral realities themselves.
To help the spectator relate the "moral quandary" of Quixotism to the
present, he makes his hero an outlaw wanted by the Inquisition, which
plays a central role, as the following summary shows. The Holy Brother-
hood pursues Don Quixote from the moment he leaves on his first sally,
at first just to bring him home because his family is worried about him;
soon enough, though, they are chasing him in the name of the Inquisition,
for he claims the defense of the faith as part of his mission, which the Inquisitors interpret as a usurpation of their prerogative. Salt constructs an
elaborate scene to end the second sally, in which the proud Basque who
Don Quixote defeated and sent to find Dulcinea actually seeks her out
and is mistaken for the mad knight himself, since he is going around El
Toboso asking people there if they have seen her, and who else would do
that? After torturing him, the Inquisitors organize an Auto-de-Fe to punish him, but Don Quixote, arriving in El Toboso himself, interrupts the
proceedings. Along with Pasamonte, the Duke and Duchess are present
for this, and are immediately taken with the bold lunatic. This time the

"real" Quixote is captured. The Inquisition confines him to a madhouse, from which he escapes with Sancho's help, and is taken in by the Duke and Duchess at their palace. They head finally for Barcelona, since neither of them has ever seen the ocean. When Don Quixote fights the "Knight of the White Moon" in Barcelona, it is because he has challenged the Inquisition itself to judicial combat, and Carrasco has agreed to be their champion. Dulcinea arrives and tries to dissuade Quixote from fighting, but he refuses and is defeated at an elaborate joust. His deathbed scene takes place in Barcelona.

As explained above, the use of the Inquisition here is undoubtedly a veiled reference to HUAC, often referred to by blacklistees among themselves as "this Inquisition." Yet it is also central to the whole reorganization of the episodic narrative into a tightly bound plot, which as it advances circles around two poles: the confrontation with the Inquisition and the desire to reach Barcelona. Salt explains the reasons for this plot structure in his superb "Notes on Polish" from September 16, 1966, where he develops an analogy between the absurdity of reviving chivalry and the counterculture rejection of prevailing values as a way to "clarify for modern audiences exactly what 'chivalry' stands for in Quixote's mind":

> Quixote is opposed to the materialism of this Iron Age in which gold is prized so highly.
> A man—or student—rebelling today could say he is against conformity, the Establishment, the corruption, the computer, Madison Avenue, status symbols, Puritanism, atomic war, etc. He would be understood by everyone whether they agreed or not—because the environment is the same for everyone. A beard, sandals, a guitar would be immediately recognizable in the same way that Quixote's armor was recognizable in Cervantes' day. In a mild way, Bob Dylan put on Woody Guthrie's armor. We need a way to define Quixote's armor—motive and aspiration—as immediately and clearly as a picket sign, a bumper sticker or a button defines rebellion today.
> Barcelona is the objective. It should be more specific. Out of his naiveté and ignorance Quixote should invest Barcelona with some magic quality—which seems quite realistic to him—as realistic as the island seems to Sancho. He has to reach Barcelona in order to find the Holy Grail, the Sword Excalibur, the Magic Elixir, the secret—or—to lay a rose on the tomb of Guinevere, pay his respects to the ashes of El Cid, consult the Hermit—or—find a Forum large enough to encompass his ambitions. Obviously the village, even La Mancha or all of Spain is too small a pond for his ambition. [. . .]
> If a lovable crackpot today decided to revive the spirit of the frontier—or start a march—his objective would be Washington or New York. It would be as beautiful and ridiculous as the feeling of the audience varied about the possibilities of accomplishing what he intended. This comes nearer to Quixote. He wants to revive chivalry—as opposed to the Iron Age—translated into specific related modern terms. He is motivated by the things he sees

around him, reflected in himself . . . This is very important . . . the specifics
are all in Quixote. He wants to defeat the petty selfishness and discover the
greatness in himself. It isn't necessary to show the conditions against which
he is fighting if he is rejecting the reflection of those conditions in himself.
Bearded beatniks are rejecting Gillette, Right Guard, discrimination, Puritanism in themselves—reflecting the social scene which produces them. A one
act dialogue between two kids in the East Village could be a visual and accurate description of the entire social and political scene today. Artful Dodger
[referring to Salt's next project, discussed below] for instance. So—for real
consideration—what are the human conditions in Renaissance Spain which
correspond today—which Quixote is rejecting in himself?

The Inquisition is certainly key. (Waldo Salt Papers, UCLA, Box 28, folder
5)

The Inquisition is key because it is the authority behind the conventional
morality holding in place the status quo. Don Quixote's struggle, in this
version, is not for an abstract Ideal, but for social justice and freedom from
authoritarian control, not just in early modern Spain, but as applicable to
the mid-twentieth-century United States.

Salt endowed his hero with a backstory explaining his decision to
become a knight. In an early version, Quixote tells Sancho, "Once I saw
a Moor beaten to death by bullies who called themselves Christians. I
didn't do anything . . ." (Waldo Salt Papers, Box 29, folder 2, p. 18). That
is, he had witnessed a lynching and was wracked by guilt at not having intervened, an experience with which the U.S. audience circa 1965
could undoubtedly identify. Eventually, however, this backstory was
changed so it could also serve to motivate the choice of Aldonza Lorenzo
as Dulcinea: she became the one bullied—she was stoned and ostracized
as a punishment for promiscuity, as Quixote stood by and watched, a
traumatic experience that would be repeated in fragmentary flashbacks
throughout the first half of the final versions (Waldo Salt Papers, Box
29, folders 5 and 7). Eventually, in a version now preserved among the
Robert Altman Papers at the University of Michigan, Salt transformed
that scene into an Inquisitorial *auto-de-fe*, further reinforcing the animosity
between Don Quixote and the Inquisition, which thereby even pre-dates
his vocation as a knight (Robert Altman Papers, University of Michigan,
Box 541). Though such fragmentary flashbacks are commonplace today,
it was an innovative technique at the time, and was precisely the solution
Salt found to resolve the problem of how to present Joe Buck's traumatic
backstory in *Midnight Cowboy*, the most important example in the New
Hollywood of an obtrusive film technique used effectively to convey a
character's deep-seated emotions.[12]

Thus Salt's version of *Don Quixote* implies a full-fledged analysis and
interpretation of Cervantes's vast novel, inseparably bound up with the

restructuring necessary to make the episodic story more appealing for a movie audience, since his goal was to make a Hollywood movie, not, ultimately, an experimental or avant-garde film. While he understood *Don Quixote* to be a profoundly ambiguous work, in his reading it was essentially anti-imperialist and vigorously opposed to authoritarianism, using the parody of knight-errantry to mock the militarism of the Spanish Crown and intolerance of the Church, while simultaneously upholding what is truly noble in chivalry's moral outlook. At the same time as he restored the mad knight's "mission" to its historical context, Salt sought to provoke his audience to recognize its applicability to current political and moral realities.

In January 1967, while still putting the finishing touches on his *Don Quixote* adaptation, Salt threw himself into a new project, *The Artful Dodger*, an original screenplay about a charismatic youth named Billy Shine, who goes through a series of creative ideas for avoiding the draft for the Vietnam War before finally deciding to fake mental illness, though it ultimately appears his madness is not entirely feigned. This brilliant script is essentially the updating of *Don Quixote* Salt described in "Notes on Polish" a few months earlier, as a portrait of contemporary America through the perspective of a "lovable crackpot." The reference in those notes to "the Artful Dodger" shows Salt already had it in mind as his next project. Had the film been made in 1967 or 1968, it could have provided a satire of urban America equivalent to the one *The Graduate* (1967) became for the suburbs.[13] What happened instead was that Salt's agent brought the first forty pages or so to producer Jerome Hellman, who showed them to British director John Schlesinger. Schlesinger immediately recognized the bold innovation in screenwriting technique of the pages in front of him. It was marvelously visual, imagined in filmic terms, so that it was simply a matter of transferring what was on the page to the screen. Rather than offer a deal to make *The Artful Dodger*, however, Hellman hired Salt to replace Jack Gelber in their current project, the adaptation of James Leo Herlihy's novel *Midnight Cowboy*. This was the break that jump-started Salt's career, and his work on *Don Quixote* had prepared him to take full advantage of the opportunity. The freewheeling satirical image of New York City from *The Artful Dodger* found its way into *Midnight Cowboy* instead, with the well-known impact on U.S. film culture that ensued.[14] In 1970, Salt won an Oscar for best adapted screenplay, which, along with Dalton Trumbo's Writer's Guild Laurel Award that same year and Ring Lardner Jr.'s best adapted screenplay Oscar for *M*A*S*H* the following year, constituted a rash of honors for former Communists that finally consigned the blacklist era definitively to the past.[15] Over the next ten years Salt was sole or lead writer on four completed features: *Serpico* (nominated for an Oscar), *The Day of the Locust*, *The Gang That Couldn't Shoot Straight*, and *Coming Home* (for which he won his second Oscar), as well as a number of unfinished pictures. In this triumphant final phase of his career, Salt profoundly influenced the understanding of the screenwriter's craft within the emerging independent film movement by lecturing, teaching, and mentoring younger writers. After his death in 1987, the annual Waldo Salt Award for screenwriting was established at the Sundance Festival, where he had given screenwriting workshops from its founding in 1981.

Though no version of his *Don Quixote* has yet been filmed, it has gone into pre-production twice. The first time was in 1971, with a leaner version of the script trimmed down to ninety-seven pages by Salt himself, Robert Butler directing, Richard Burton to star, and Chaim Topol to play Sancho.[16] In the mid-1990s, after Salt's death, the script was revived by Hollywood agent Jon Levin, with revisions by Susan Shilliday. At first, Sean Connery was to play Don Quixote, then focus shifted to John Cleese with Robin Williams as Sancho Panza. Fred Schepisi was enlisted to direct, and brought John Guare onboard to do further re-writes. They got as far as a read-aloud with the lead actors, but the production was never greenlighted. One of the producers, Elisabeth Robinson, turned her experience into an entertaining epistolary novel, *The True and Outstanding Adventures of the Hunt Sisters*, in which she indulges the fantasy of the film being completed. The narrator comments that Cleese "embodies the baffled elegance of this Knight of the Sad Countenance" (274) and that he and Robin Williams "are heartbreakingly funny together" (281).[17]

After Phoenix Productions pulled the plug on the project in January 1997, Steven Haft still tried to find someone to back it. He and agent Ken Kamins (the latter apparently representing Quincy Jones Entertainment) sent two versions of the screenplay to Robert Altman, presumably hoping to interest him in producing and perhaps even directing the film. One of these, undated, with only Waldo Salt given as the author, is a lightly revised version of the January 25, 1967, draft at UCLA. Only the *auto-de-fe* scene mentioned above has been added. The other is a "combined draft" listing Salt, Shilliday, and Guare as authors. It is dated February 14, 1997. As compared with the Susan Shilliday revision of February 27, 1994, which was very respectful of Waldo Salt's original, this 1997 version has been aggressively re-written in ways that render it much less coherent. Scenes from Cervantes's novel that Salt had finally chosen to leave out have now been reintroduced, along with other new scenes, rendering the whole plot more episodic (Robert Altman Papers, University of Michigan, Box 541). These changes, introduced by John Guare, may have led to the project's collapse.[18]

Despite never having been filmed, indirectly this screenplay has had a decisive impact on cinema in the United States. Within the constraints that come with being a Hollywood screenwriter, Salt was an innovator who did much to bring the self-reflexive techniques and detached narrative style of the French New Wave to American mainstream cinema.[19] It was in the experimental laboratory of his *Quixote* adaptation that he first allowed himself this freedom. As Salt moved on from this "failed" adaptation to his well-known series of triumphs, an undercurrent of Quixotism persisted in his work; Cervantes's hero became a permanent fixture in his imagination. This is clear in the approach he took to the friendship between Joe Buck and Ratso Rizzo in *Midnight Cowboy*, of which Jon Voight has said, "I used to tell Dusty, 'We're Don Quixote and Sancho Panza.'" In adapting the real-life crime drama of Frank Serpico's stand against corruption in the NYPD, Salt consciously noted his quixotic side in notes on the character and his motivation:

> In his need for reassurance and confirmation, he must constantly seek new loyalties and symbols but none of them are obviously able to live up to Serpico's standards. Their betrayal of him—human as it may be and it must be made far more understandable and human than it would appear to be—offers Serpico his way out in each instance. It is his peculiar passion and need which somehow refuses to accept the fact fiction (fact perhaps) of man's innate corruption. [. . .] In this sense, he is Quixotic—driven by a need which he cannot define exactly, called psycho by most sensible people—laughed at because he is in fact the epitome of human absurdity. (Waldo Salt Papers, UCLA, Box 6, folder 5, 11/10/72, pp. 4–5)

A bit later, in the same notes, Salt specifically links Serpico's Quixotism to the Beats by way of Unamuno:

> Still pushing for a specific definition of Serpico's need—universal, human—the catholic word used by Unamuno to describe Quixote's quality his "glory"—the need for glory as applied to Sainthood, God, Jesus and Mary. True glory, not simply fame and fortune. A concept was certainly very much alive and well in the Village at that time. Ginsberg and Kerouac characterizing generation as Beat for beatific, producing a decade of diggers, levelers, ranters and holy fools—barefoot superstars in the park seeking glory. (Waldo Salt Papers, UCLA, Box 6, folder 5, 11/21/72, p. 3)

For this reason, in an early draft of the script he incorporated a scene in which a character tells Serpico he's being a Quixote. Perhaps feeling it was a bit heavy-handed, he replaced that reference to Cervantes with another, in a different part of the script, where Serpico is taking a Spanish class, and the professor recommends Unamuno's book on *Don Quixote* to the students as "background reading" (Waldo Salt Papers, UCLA, Box

7, folder 2, 3/12/73, p. 33). In *Coming Home* as well, Luke Martin (Jon Voight) and John Hyde (Bruce Dern), the male protagonists, can both be said to be quixotic figures, each in opposite fashion. Their confrontations with militarism and their resulting disillusionment reflect a position not unlike Cervantes's own, which led him to mock the heroic values that sent him to war in the first place, in terms that resonate powerfully with Luke's monologue to a group of high school students at the end of the film:

> I know some of you guys are going to look at the uniformed man and you're going to remember all the films and you're going to think about the glory of other wars and think about some vague patriotic feeling and go off and fight this turkey too. And I'm telling you it ain't like it's in the movies. That's all I want to tell you, because I didn't have a choice. When I was your age, all I got was some guy standing up like that, man, giving me a lot of bullshit, man, which I caught. [. . .] And I *wanted* to be a war hero, man, I *wanted* to go out and kill for my country. And now I'm here to tell ya that I have killed for my country, or whatever. And I don't feel good about it. [. . .] I'm here to tell ya it's a lousy thing, man. I don't see any reason for it. And there's a lot of shit that I did over there that I find fucking hard to live with. And I don't want to see people like you, man, coming back and having to face the rest of your lives with that kind of shit. It's as simple as that. I don't feel sorry for myself. I'm a lot fucking smarter now than when I went. And I'm just telling you, there's a choice to be made here.

Salt's Quixotism can also be observed in the many images he created of the mad knight. From his youth he had always cultivated visual art; more than just a hobby, it was part of how he was able to visualize film sequences so powerfully. While working on *Don Quixote*, he created a number of watercolor sketches of characters and scenes, some of which were featured in *A Screenwriter's Journey*. He drew a self-portrait he sent his daughter, Deborah, "after one especially long stretch of work on Don Quixote," of himself as "the happy knight—bloody but unbowed." In the typically six-by-eight-inch "doodle books" Salt kept for decades, which served as a kind of mental gymnasium to help him focus or distract him when he was blocked, drawings and paintings of lone knights occur with regularity.[20] Sometimes they are easily identifiable as drawings of Don Quixote, such as figures 11.1 and 11.3, in which the barber's basin with the cutout for the chin is clearly visible; in other instances, such as the drawing in figure 11.2, it is less clear, though given Salt's Quixote fixation, it seems reasonable to assume that these are also portraits of Cervantes's anti-hero. There are occasional notes, carefully lettered across an entire page, such as "WAS DON QUIXOTE an ACTER or ACTOR?" or "Don Quixote was outraged by the wrong of aging—of a virgin life an unful-

Figure 11.1. *Don Quixote and Sancho*. From a notebook by Waldo Salt, circa 1970–1980
Courtesy of Jennifer Salt.

Figure 11.2. *Portrait of Don Quixote.* From a notebook by Waldo Salt, circa 1970–1980
Courtesy of Jennifer Salt.

Figure 11.3. *Don Quixote and Dulcinea*. From a notebook by Waldo Salt, circa 1970–1980
Courtesy of Jennifer Salt.

filled death." (The second of these was written in what is believed to be his last notebook, found in his Malibu cottage, kept during 1986–1987.)

Several unfinished film projects of his last years had a quixotic side to them as well: a biopic about Hemingway, an adaptation of Mark Twain's *A Connecticut Yankee at King Arthur's Court*, and a film about General Joseph Stilwell's Burma Road. The Hemingway project occupied Salt nonstop from early 1977 until at least August 1979, about two and half years, and was canceled in 1981. He did a tremendous amount of research on Hemingway, who fascinated him, though he deplored his macho egotism. On the other hand, there was Hemingway's connection to Spain and the Spanish Civil War, on which Salt naturally spent a good deal of effort (Waldo Salt Papers, UCLA, Boxes 35 and 36). Like Hemingway, General Joseph Stilwell was a strong-willed individualist who forged his own path in life—literally, in the case of his determination to construct of a road out of Burma through the jungle to obviate the need for a supply airlift. The Stilwell project was his last, and it kept Waldo busy through 1985 and most of 1986. Twain's *Connecticut Yankee*, which he worked on between *Hemingway* and *Stilwell*, juxtaposes the chivalrous world of medieval knights and the debased modern world, only it does so by transporting a modern person back in time through the device of science fiction, rather than transporting a (would-be) medieval knight forward in time through the device of mental illness.[21] Among Salt's papers, finally, there is also a contract with Lubin to revive the *Quixote* project, splitting the proceeds 50/50. This contract was drafted in 1981 and revised in 1983, but is unsigned, and it is not known whether the two men finally reached agreement, and if so, what steps they undertook to film it.[22]

In assessing the ultimate importance of his work on *Don Quixote* to Salt's development as a screenwriter and therefore to the emergence and consolidation of the New Hollywood, there is a broader concern to address than technique in adaptation, approach to character, or even thematics *per se*. The blacklist marks a before and after for Salt and for the film industry in general, in terms of how we understand the relationship between Hollywood movies and public life, especially political life. During his early years in Hollywood, Salt was both a screenwriter with a social conscience (as evidenced by, say, *Rachel and the Stranger*), *and* an activist engaged in a range of political activities. Based on his own papers, questions put to him by HUAC in 1951, his 1963 affidavit, and the response to it from Congressman Edwin E. Willis dated January 17, 1964, it is possible to reconstruct the following partial list (though the dates are often difficult to pin down):

- Member, Los Angeles Committee of the Communist Party
- Delegate, Communist Party Convention

- Treasurer, Southern California Branch, National Federation for Constitutional Liberties
- Executive Committee, Eva Shafran Educational Foundation
- Delegate, People's Educational Center, Los Angeles
- Faculty member, School for Writers founded by the League of American Writers
- Board of Directors, The Actors' Laboratory
- Member, Hollywood Democratic Committee
- Candidate for Executive Board, Hollywood Arts, Sciences, and Professions Council
- Sponsor, Statewide Conference on Civil Rights in San Francisco, 1941
- Member, Agricultural Aid Committee of the United Cannery Workers Union
- Organizer for release of Morris U. Schappes (jailed for refusing to name names)
- Supported Albert Maltz for Executive Board of the Screen Writers Guild
- Sponsored adolescent refugee of the Spanish Republic, Juan Campuzano Solans
- Worked to establish peace conference in California, 1949

Many of the organizations to which he belonged were labeled "Communist fronts" in *Red Channels*, a pamphlet pooling information from such sources as the U.S. Attorney General, HUAC, and California's "mini-HUAC." But they also fought against lynching, defended civil rights and workers' rights, protected civil liberties, and engaged in adult education that was not necessarily limited to political propaganda. Salt's being listed as treasurer, delegate, executive committee member, etc., bespeaks an active role. In the case of The Actors' Laboratory, he was on the board of directors of a progressive theater group that came under attack from Red-baiting columnist Hedda Hopper for violating the color line by organizing social functions where Blacks and Whites could dance together (Frost 107–8). The portrait that emerges of Waldo Salt circa 1947 is of a committed, progressive writer, pursuing issues of social justice both in his screenplays and through organized political and community activism. It is true that the Communist Party provided a framework for this activity, and, as Jennifer Salt points out in *A Screenwriter's Journey*, it also provided a "family." The best example of this might be screenwriter Richard Collins, Waldo Salt's closest friend in those years, the best man at his wedding, and the one who first recruited him to join the Party. In 1951, Collins was among the "stoolpigeons" who named Salt before HUAC—in fact, Waldo sat in the hearing room and watched his former friend testify the day before he faced the Committee himself. How painful this must have been is hard for those who have not experienced it to imagine. What we can say is that this betrayal of friendship is just one example of how Cold War fearmongering and red-baiting undermined artistic and intellectual community across the United States after World War II.[23]

The Waldo Salt who emerged triumphant from the blacklist era in 1969 was a very different person from the one who entered that hearing room in 1951. Still committed to promoting social justice in his writing through the impact he might be able to have on his audience's understanding, he no longer put as much stock, it would seem, in collective action and political involvement. In the New Left of the 1960s, cultural work to some extent replaces direct, organized political engagement. Those who had been stung by the betrayal of fellow Communists and deprived of ideological clarity by the revelations about Stalin's Soviet Union were still committed to freedom of speech and above all freedom of thought. The defense of individual nonconformity against both Cold War conformism in the United States and Stalinist Party discipline leads to a paradoxical and ambivalent quixotism. Salt's quixotic turn thereby can be seen as part of a larger phenomenon, whereby Cervantes facilitated for many the journey through the contradictions of U.S. cultural politics during the Cold War. The renewal of interest in *Don Quixote* that led to the watered-down idealism of *Man of La Mancha* was the product of a crisis of faith in the life of our nation. In his recent book connecting Cervantes's life to the most original, pioneering aspects of his work, his "invention of fiction," William Egginton explicitly ties his maturity as a writer to his loss of youthful belief in the professed values of his society. "The man who emerged from that prison [in 1598 Seville] no longer believed in the ideals that Spanish society and its government had been promoting his entire life" (155). He developed his ironic and ambivalent style of fiction writing as a response to "the challenge of portraying the world according to the dictates of a society whose version of the truth he had once accepted but now knew to be false" (171). Egginton sums up his whole trajectory in these terms:

> As a young man, Cervantes bought into the religious and political doctrines of his day. He dueled for honor, risked his life for his country, spent long years in captivity, and returned fueled with hope for a comfortable and honorable old age. These hopes were dashed as he found that, in the eyes of his society and his government, he was not much more than an aging cripple whom they would rather be rid of than reward. His early attempts at prose and theater showed sparks of literary genius and critical wit, but it was only as his life progressed and his hopes and pains turned to naught that the real genius we now recognize came alive, that Cervantes became, as it were, Cervantes. (183)

Equally, Waldo Salt became Waldo Salt as a result of the blacklist. He underwent a similar transformation as a result of being treated like a criminal by his own government and an outcast by his own professional community. Like Cervantes, he learned to make uplifting art out of it, though he also came to accept the role of the artist as that of a loner, eccentric and misunderstood for the most part. Thus at the end of his life, Salt became, like Cervantes three centuries before him, a countercultural figure, who used his art to support progressive movements in his society such as opposition to the war and the defense of a nonconformist lifestyle emblematic of social changes that he hoped would help liberate his audience. All this, Quixote stood for in his mind, at the same time as he replaced the earlier belief in collective action and a shared community of artists that could never be recovered.

NOTES

1. Many thanks are due to those who have helped me piece together the account offered here of Waldo Salt's life and career, and *Don Quixote's* place therein. Jennifer Salt, first and foremost, generously shared with me her father's "doodle books" and other materials, as well as her own recollections and point of view. I have also benefited from conversations with Robert Hillmann, Jon Levin, and Susan Shilliday, who sent me the revised version of Waldo Salt's screenplay she completed in 1994. In addition, my account is based on what I have gleaned from Salt's papers, housed at UCLA, and the film *Waldo Salt: A Screenwriter's Journey*.

2. Salt also worked on *The Crimson Pirate* before being blacklisted, but the film was not released until 1952, and his name does not appear in the credits. Both *The Flame and the Arrow* and *The Crimson Pirate* were produced by Harold Hecht, who hired Waldo Salt again as soon as the blacklist was broken to write screenplays for three notoriously mediocre films in the early 1960s.

3. My account of *Sandhog* is a composite of materials in Box 90 of the Waldo Salt Papers at UCLA. According to the letters remitting checks from the management of the Phoenix Theatre, the original six-week run brought Salt $1,435.65 in earnings (about $13,000 in today's dollars); not a flop, exactly, but certainly not a hit, either. And not enough remuneration for three years' work. Salt's share of the East German royalties came to $300. He got just $34.64 for the Prague radio broadcast (Waldo Salt Papers, UCLA, Box 90, folders 11, 13, and 14).

4. Dates refer to the period when Salt wrote for each show. The partial list of credits is based on the scripts and correspondence in Salt's own papers, supplemented by examination the IMDb page on him. At times he used the pseudonyms when sending material to U.K.-based productions as well, at least when it was expected that these would air in the United States.

5. Lester Cole was a blacklistee who never renounced his Communist views and was never able to write for Hollywood again under his own name. In 1979, while working on his memoir of the blacklist, *Hollywood Red*, he sent an aggressive letter to Salt to inquire whether he had made a secret deal of some sort in order to be able to work again. "When did you return to writing in Hollywood? Was it with or without clearance? Since a public confession such as [Ring] Lardner's in the *Sat Eve Post* (1961) was required to return to work, and never having seen

yours, did you write one? Was it agreed to be held private, since I cannot find it in any archives?" (Waldo Salt Papers, UCLA, Box 77, folder 19). Salt did not answer and Cole drew his own conclusion, which was that he, like other blacklistees who wrote under their own names after 1961, had made a sworn statement that he had been a Communist and was one no longer. "I was forced to conclude that the fanfare of some writers breaking the blacklist was a myth—the blacklist broke *them*" (*Hollywood Red* 400). The difference between them, though, is that Salt could honestly swear he had abandoned Communism years before, while Cole could not. He did, however, correctly deduce that Salt had made a "confession."

6. Ralph Waldo Emerson, for example, held the view that Spain as a nation subsisted just on *Don Quixote* and the chronicles of the Cid (125). For the Left's abiding love of the Spanish Republic, see, most recently, Hochschild's *Spain in Our Hearts*.

7. For example, Richard Collins insists that was what drew him to Communism in his HUAC testimony, 4/12/51 (Waldo Salt Papers, Box 77, folder 3), especially pp. 18–19. The youth's name was Juan Campuzano Solans, and Salt kept the letters, photos, and drawings he sent them until his death (Waldo Salt Papers, Box 81, folder 9).

8. This also is evidenced in various letters and writings by Salt and fellow blacklistees preserved in Waldo Salt Papers, Box 77, which concerns the HUAC hearings. Indeed, the comparison seemed so obvious to Ceplair and Englund that they titled their study of the blacklist *The Inquisition in Hollywood* with no further explanation.

9. This observation is based on conversations with his daughter, Jennifer Salt, and with the co-director of the documentary about him, Robert Hillmann. In Hillmann and Corr's documentary, Jennifer Salt explains her father's attraction to Don Quixote in terms of his "intolerance for reality" and wonders, "Why didn't he just give up?"

10. This cannot fully be appreciated only by reading the final version of Salt's justly famed *Midnight Cowboy* screenplay. The multiple versions and notes for *Midnight Cowboy* conserved among his papers at UCLA (Waldo Salt Papers, UCLA, Boxes 1–4) attest to the parallels between the process he employed on that film and his *Don Quixote*. Another valuable source of insight into Salt's role as a collaborator in the filming process is the running commentary on *Midnight Cowboy* recorded by John Schlesinger and Jerome Hellman for the Criterion Laserdisc release, in which Salt's invaluable contributions on set are amply attested.

11. Pabst did this, for example, in his film version from 1933, making Carrasco the niece's fiancé.

12. The technique of the fragmentary flashback is used to incorporate scenes from Joe Buck's childhood and adolescence, culminating in Crazy Annie's rape, a traumatic experience motivating Joe Buck's bizarre choice of mission, that of becoming a gigolo to save the sex-starved maidens and widows of New York City. Biskind discusses the importance of this technique for the film's success in "Midnight Revolution."

13. *The Artful Dodger* was based on a young man Jennifer Salt was seeing at the time. There is overlap between Salt's script and some of the material in Brian de

Palma's *Greetings* (1968), but this could be a coincidence—the draft and the desire to avoid it were topical at the time. *The Artful Dodger* could still make a nice film, though of course it would have to be a period film now.

14. I follow the account in *A Screenwriter's Journey*, supplemented by Salt's own papers. *Midnight Cowboy's* significance for the New Hollywood is emphasized by Peter Biskind in "Midnight Revolution."

15. It was when he received the Laurel Award that Trumbo gave his controversial "only victims" speech. Trumbo also wrote Salt a charming pre-congratulatory letter in February 1970, for "the Oscar you will get if God remains as just as he was when I knew him" (Waldo Salt Papers, UCLA, Box 81, folder 10).

16. Richard Burton's connection to the project through producer A. Ronald Lubin dates back to 1966, as attested in *The Richard Burton Diaries* (126). Burton wrote on June 21, 1970, that they were to begin shooting in Colombia early in 1971 with Burton as Quixote, "Hoffman or Finney or Topol" as Sancho, and Sam O'Steen directing. "They want E[lizabeth Taylor] to play Dulcinante [sic] but I don't think the part good enough for her" (376). Notices in trade publications concerning the 1971 production can be found in the Waldo Salt Papers, UCLA, Box 80, folder 14. On December 14, 1970, Peter Noble declared in *The Hollywood Reporter* that filming was to begin in Almeria in April 1971, now directed by Peter Yates (who, perhaps not entirely coincidentally, did eventually direct an unremarkable adaptation of *Don Quixote* in 2000 for Hallmark, starring John Lithgow). In December 1971, it is definitely in pre-production, with producer Lubin and director Robert Butler scouting locations in and around Belgrade, and Chaim Topol to play opposite Burton. It fell apart for reasons I have yet to uncover.

17. Jon Levin told me he has not given up, for he made a "deathbed promise" to Lubin that he would someday film it. He said he still hopes to complete the project, perhaps by going back to Shilliday's version (which is quite sound, in my opinion). Levin admitted, though, that a successful completion of Terry Gilliam's *The Man Who Killed Don Quixote* would make it tougher to get the funding together.

18. Susan Shilliday was kind enough to send me a copy of her 1994 revised screenplay. She told me that after completing it, she no longer had any input into the project, nor was she ever told anything about why Phoenix withdrew. My assumption is therefore that the differences between her screenplay and the 1997 version at University of Michigan are John Guare's handiwork. Jon Levin told me he thinks it was the Guare re-write that killed the project. This is consistent with Fred Shepisi's comment, in an online interview, that the U.S. backers were put off by the screenplay's being too "episodic."

19. Robert B. Ray, *A Certain Tendency of the Hollywood Cinema, 1930-1980*, chapter 8.

20. Catherine Breslin did a very well-written piece on the doodle books for *New York* magazine in 1972.

21. See Monserrat Ginés, 34–44.

22. In a notebook from around 1982 or 1983, Salt wrote down some cryptic remarks on his and Lubin's last attempt at doing *Don Quixote* together. "We need Milty—Don't blow it. First new and possible approach (combining film and tape)

will require rewrite to sell new process (written in). Will require period of learning the state of the art then applying it to script. Milty ready to go whenever our deal is clear—Ours must be a new deal, will require funds for me."

23. Collins features prominently in Navasky's discussion of the social consequences of the blacklist in terms of friendships lost (371–83).

12

Crouching Squire, Hidden Madman: Ah Gan's *Don Quixote* and Postmodern China

Bruce R. Burningham

In 1615, in his dedication of Part II of *Don Quixote* to Don Pedro Fernández Ruiz de Castro, Count of Lemos, Miguel de Cervantes invents a playful anecdote about a supposedly recent visit from a Chinese emissary. During the visit, the emissary delivers a letter from the Emperor of China asking—nay, begging—Cervantes to send a copy of *Don Quixote* to China because the Emperor wants to establish a College for the teaching of Spanish, and wants to not only use Cervantes's novel as the primary textbook, but also want Cervantes himself to serve as rector of the College.[1] Cervantes asks the emissary whether the Chinese Emperor has provided funds for the Spanish author's travel expenses. But when he learns that offering such travel funds did not even cross the Emperor's mind, Cervantes sends the emissary packing, telling him that not only is he too poor and infirmed to travel, but also that he already has a superior patron in the Count of Lemos, with or without fancy colleges and rectorships.[2]

This anecdote, of course, is pure fiction and is designed to achieve two immediate goals. First, by claiming a worldwide fame for his renowned protagonist, Cervantes explicitly responds (without mentioning names) to the publication just a year earlier of the unauthorized sequel to *Don Quixote* by the pseudonymous "Alonso Fernández de Avellaneda" (whose treatment of the character is decidedly less than generous and was correctly understood as a personal attack on Cervantes himself). Second, by explicitly comparing his own patron to Zhu Yijun, the thirteenth emperor of the Ming dynasty, Cervantes seeks to flatter a man who was not only a patron of the arts, but who had also had a hand in the establishment (in Naples, Italy) of the Palazzo dei Regi Studi, a college whose official dedication occurred in the same year as the publication of Part II of *Don Quixote*.

While this story is clearly meant to be taken ironically, it does nonetheless tell us something important about Spanish imperial culture in the

early years of the seventeenth century. A hundred years earlier, such
an anecdote would have been largely unthinkable. In 1515, Columbus's
fourth and final voyage to the New World had barely occurred some thirteen years before. And while Hernán Cortez had already arrived in the
Caribbean by 1504, he would not commence his march on Tenochtitlán
(today's Mexico City) until 1519. Meanwhile, Francisco Pizarro, who had
also already arrived in the Caribbean by 1509, would not finally succeed
in toppling the Inca empire in the highlands of Peru until 1532–1534.
Thus, in 1515 the Far East would still have existed in the Spanish imaginary in much the same state as it had existed at least since the publication
of Marco Polo's *Travels* in 1300: as a largely mythical space of unimaginable riches inhabited by cynocephali and watched over by Prester John.
A visit by a Chinese emissary from Beijing to a Spanish novelist in Madrid
during the earliest years of the sixteenth century would have seemed
much more as fantasy than irony.

By 1615, however, the world had undergone a radical transformation. The Spanish Empire now stretched from the Philippines (so named
for Spain's King Felipe II) across the Pacific to Mexico and Peru (with
various viceroyalties extending north and south from what is today the
western United States all the way down to the Southern Cone of the
Western Hemisphere), and from the Caribbean across the Atlantic to
the Iberian Peninsula, southern Italy, and the Netherlands. Along with
the Portuguese Empire (which at that time stretched from Brazil to various colonies along the western coast of Africa and the Malabar coast of
India), Habsburg Spain had created a network of commerce and communication that, in the words of Charles Mann, literally "began the era
of globalization."[3] Indeed, Carmen Hsu has noted that Felipe II sent two
separate letters to the Emperor of China, one in 1580 that only made it as
far as Mexico City, and one in 1581 that took so long to reach Manila that
its overdue arrival in 1583 had vacated its purpose.[4] Moreover, Mann's
book *1493: Uncovering the New World Columbus Created* provides a very
useful world map featuring the Spanish empire circa 1600 that shows the
western routes by which silk, spices, and slaves from China and Japan
flowed through Manila and then across the Pacific on their way to Mexico
City (and eventually Europe) in exchange for silver mined in Potosí, Bo-
livia. The map also shows the eastern routes by which slaves, spices, and
manufactured goods from the Portuguese empire flowed from India and
Africa and across the Atlantic into the Caribbean in exchange for sugar,
rum, tobacco, and silver that was then shipped back to the Old World
ports of Lisbon and Seville.[5] Cervantes's seventeenth-century conceit that
a Chinese emissary might easily make his way to Madrid is underscored
by Mann when he discusses the extent to which Asians were already an

important presence in the Spanish New World, where they established the "first real Chinatown in the Americas" in the heart of Mexico City:

> They came via the galleon trade: sailors, servants, and slaves disembarking in Acapulco and scattering across New Spain. [. . .] Known collectively as *chinos*, Asian migrants spread slowly along the silver highway from Acapulco to Mexico City, Puebla, and Veracruz. Indeed, the road was patrolled by them—Japanese samurai perhaps in particular.[6]

Within this cultural context, the notion that the Emperor of China might be interested in establishing a school dedicated to the teaching of Spanish in order to facilitate entry into the early modern global marketplace is not that far-fetched (and certainly not that far-removed from the economic arguments we continue to make today for the study of English or Spanish or Mandarin). Still, Cervantes's conceit is just that, and the world would have to wait for another three hundred years or more before the citizens of a completely different empire (i.e., the United States), during the middle of what Henry Luce called the "American century," would truly make *Don Quixote* the centerpiece of its Spanish-language pedagogy.[7] Whatever role Cervantes's novel played in the cultural history of China between 1605 and today, the importance of his famous protagonist for Chinese cultural history re-emerged in 2010 with the release of Ah Gan's film adaptation of *Don Quixote*.

Starring Guo Tao as Don Quixote, Wang Gang as Sancho Panza, and Kar Yan Lam as "Princess Fragrante" (the film's Dulcinea), Ah Gan's Chinese production of *Don Quixote* forms part—whether deliberately or not—of a series of worldwide cultural events held during the past decade to commemorate the four hundredth anniversaries of the publication of Part I of Cervantes's novel in 1605; of the publication of Part II in 1615; and of the death of Cervantes himself in 1616 (among others). The film was produced by Filmko Pictures and Shenzhen Golden Shores Films with a reported budget of 11 million U.S. dollars. The oral language of the film is Mandarin, but it also provides subtitles in both English and traditional Chinese. The movie was billed as the first Chinese film to be completely 3D, and was aided in this regard by both the Chinese Academy of Sciences (which lent 3D camera equipment to the production) and German 3D consultants.[8] Utilizing a great deal of computer-generated imagery (especially in several panoramic scenes whose expansive vistas are aesthetically related to traditional Chinese landscape painting), much of the film looks and feels like a video game. Visually, the film quotes, pays homage to, or even borrows liberally from such earlier films as Ang Lee's 2000 *Crouching Tiger, Hidden Dragon* (whose title Ah Gan explicitly references and from which he most immediately borrows his martial arts, wire-fighting aesthetic).[9]

Like all cinematic adaptations of *Don Quixote*, but especially those that "translate" the text for other linguistic, temporal, and cultural contexts, Ah Gan's version follows the basic plotline of Cervantes's original novel, but takes a number of liberties with the text. Such a connection to *Don Quixote* is facilitated by the existence of a long, autochthonous tradition of literary "knight-errantry" within Chinese culture itself.[10] Set in what is clearly seventeenth-century China (even though the film still calls it La Mancha), Cervantes's basic skeletal structure is recognizable. Don Quixote is introduced as a man inspired by his voracious reading of chivalric narratives to imitate the exploits of the knights-errant he has read so much about. Donning his famous grandfather's suit of armor and naming his old hack of a horse Rocinante, he sets off in search of meaningful adventures through which he can prove his worth and better the world around him. Along the way, he convinces his peasant neighbor Sancho Panza to ride as his squire, and he spends most of the film attempting to rescue "Princess Fragrante," who has been kidnapped by an evil knight named El Fox, one of a triumvirate of knights that includes Sir Westgate and the Venerable Knight of the East who form part of the "Northern Sky Sect" led by a powerful character known only as "Godfather."[11] Other recognizable Cervantine components, even if they appear out of sequence, include (among others) the battle with the "army" of sheep; Don Quixote's naked penance á la Beltenebros; a knighting ceremony (of sorts); the attack of the windmills; a Cide Hamete figure named Sima Wan who offers to write up Don Quixote's adventures in exchange for a fixed price per volume;[12] Sancho's blanketing at the inn for Don Quixote's failure to pay the bill; an extended stay in a Ducal palace of sorts; and Sancho's time as governor of Barataria (here strangely rendered, at least in the English subtitles, as "Dreidel Island").

Ah Gan's *Don Quixote* swerves radically from Cervantes's original in a number of significant ways. First, where Cervantes's protagonist is an aging *hidalgo* whose only remaining family connection is his young niece, Ah Gan's protagonist is a relatively young man whose still-living father and mother chide him for not making something of himself in comparison to his three other brothers who have achieved success in both business and academia. It is precisely this guilt trip laid on him by his parents that spurs Don Quixote on to become a knight-errant. Second, where Cervantes's Dulcinea is an idealized woman whose reality (if it exists at all) is splintered among at least two genuine peasant girls (neither of whom is even aware of her role in this regard), Ah Gan's "Princess Fragrante" is a very real girl named Rosie, who is actually kidnapped by the film's villains, and whom Don Quixote eventually rescues from their clutches. Third, and even more importantly, where Cervantes's protagonist mostly faces a menagerie of merely accidental or even imagined enemies (like the evil enchanter Frestón, whom he constantly blames for his misfortunes), Ah Gan's Don Quixote does battle with very real knights armed with genuinely deadly weapons, and is thus more akin to Li Mu Bai, the warrior protagonist of *Crouching Tiger, Hidden Dragon*, than to Cervantes's mad knight.

Critical reception of Ah Gan's *Don Quixote* remains mixed. Among journalistic film critics, the reaction was quite tepid, and Ah Gan's treatment is not likely to go down in the annals of film history as one of the top 100 movies of all time.[13] Still, it *is* a worthwhile addition to the ever-expanding canon of *Don Quixote* adaptations, if for no other reason than each new perspective on what has truly become an archetypal figure only deepens our appreciation of the original and its worldwide impact. Scholarly reception of the film (at least so far; at least as far as I am aware) is more or less limited to a single academic article by Jorge Abril Sánchez published in 2013. Abril's approach is to read this film in connection with Sun Tzu's fifth-century BC treatise titled *The Art of War* (which, as readers may recall, enjoyed something of an ironic renaissance in late-1980s entrepreneurial circles after it was mentioned in the 1987 Oliver Stone film *Wall Street*). After spending several pages discussing the history of warfare and military strategy in ancient China, and then glossing *The Art of War*, Abril argues that Ah Gan's Don Quixote (protagonist not film) embodies the values of this earlier Chinese text. For Abril, Ah Gan "characterizes his hero as an individual who controls his enemy's mind by staying calm and not letting himself be driven by his anger and impulses." He is a character who "comes out victorious because he understands that the power of our mind is much greater than the strength of our body."[14]

While I do not necessarily disagree with Abril's assessment here of the importance of *The Art of War* in contributing to the underlying philosophy of Ah Gan's film, I would like to examine a little more closely an element that Abril mentions only in passing: that Don Quixote's final attack on the Godfather and his three corrupt knights serves to demonstrate "that people can achieve the impossible by joining forces."[15] And I want to do so by looking at two scenes in particular that diverge radically from Cervantes's original.

The first such scene takes place about one hour and twenty minutes into the film. Having rescued Princess Fragrante from El Fox's house where she has been held, Don Quixote encounters the villainous knights of the Northern Sky Sect on a high cliffside road that presumably leads back to La Mancha. This scene is in many ways the structural equivalent of Cervantes's original protagonist's encounter with Sansón Carrasco, the University of Salamanca student disguised as the Knight of the White Moon at the end of Part II of the novel. Readers will recall that Cervantes's Don Quixote had unexpectedly (even accidentally) defeated Sansón

Carrasco earlier in Part II when the latter was disguised as the Knight of the Mirrors. Upon Don Quixote's later defeat at the hands of the Knight of the White Moon, Cervantes's protagonist renounces his chivalric identity and returns home, where he soon dies as Alonso Quijano the Good. In Ah Gan's version of this decisive encounter, Don Quixote fights all three of the villainous knights at once. And, as a demonstration of his valor, he deliberately puts down his so-called "Lance of Invincibility" and offers not only to arm himself with just one small yellow flower, but to also give his opponents three unanswered blows before defending himself. Sir Westgate strikes first, knocking Don Quixote off his feet and onto the ground, but the mad knight gets back up, smelling the flower as he does. El Fox strikes the second blow, which is much more forceful; still, Don Quixote gets back up, blood spilling from his mouth, but still wielding his flower. The third blow comes as a full-scale assault by all three knights at once. This final blow knocks Don Quixote off the cliff and onto a protruding tree, where Sancho later finds him dangling unconsciously as the squire is returning home from his time as governor of Dreidel Island.[16]

But where Cervantes's Sancho is unable to revive his master following this physical and psychological defeat, Ah Gan's Sancho does nurse Don Quixote back to health, and along with Sima Wan convinces him to recommit himself to his chivalric mission rather than renounce his profession and release Sancho from his service. Says the scribe: "The great knight must know of the recent troubles. [. . .] El Fox's Godfather has become Prime Minister. The Northern Sky Sect is in power. There is nothing to stop them. They have no worthy opponents to fear. They grow more brazen, while the people suffer."[17] (And this is not to mention the fact that Rosie has already attempted suicide rather than submit to being the Godfather's wife.) Faced with a world of genuine evil, where even the apparatus of the state has turned against justice, Ah Gan's Don Quixote agrees to come out of retirement.

And this brings us to the second of the two scenes, which occurs roughly one hour and thirty-four minutes into the film. Here, a rejuvenated Don Quixote and Sancho arrive in the capital city, where amid the crowd in the busy marketplace, they announce their intention to physically oppose the Godfather and his three villainous knights. El Fox, speaking for the group, says, "Are you still alive? You're a lunatic!" To which Don Quixote defiantly replies (as the various camera shots cut away to close-ups of the Godfather and Rosie, but also [and more importantly] to various people in the gathering crowd):

> Yes. You are correct. I am a lunatic. I was born a lunatic. To people like you, I am nothing more than a useless lunatic. A simpleton. But someone has to do something. Since all the capable, intelligent people have gone into hiding, I

have no choice but to try my best. [. . .] If everyone here remains silent, then silence shall reign in the world. The reason we are here today is to show the capable, intelligent people of this world that there are still simple-minded idiots like me who will not stand idly by in the face of perils, and who believe that good shall overcome evil. You're right. I'm here to court death. But for Miss Rosie [whose real name he now recognizes], and more so for all these citizens, I came because I had to.[18]

At the end of this speech, El Fox accuses Don Quixote of fomenting a revolt and thus initiates an attack with a loud battle cry. However, what none of the triumvirate of evil knights expects is for the several members of the crowd—from little boys to a young woman to mature men trained in the martial arts to an older man armed with only a soup ladle—to begin to attack *them* instead, ultimately defeating each one in turn. This leaves only the Godfather, whom Don Quixote declares he will fight "mano-a-mano." Again dropping his "Lance of Invincibility," Don Quixote charges the mounted Godfather, knocking him from his horse, and the two engage in a lengthy fistfight that sprawls from one market stall to another on the dusty ground in between. At one point, the Godfather nearly manages to escape, but the encircling crowd deliberately holds him in place just long enough for Don Quixote to finish the fight by snapping the Godfather's neck with his legs during a wrestling hold—a notably violent moment in a film whose violence has been mostly cartoonish. This scene ends with a short sequence of images—deliberately designed to echo earlier images of Sancho's "blanket tossing"—of Don Quixote being thrown high into the air by the jubilant crowd.[19]

This culminating scene is significant for at least three reasons. First, I would suggest that Don Quixote's "inspiration speech" is somewhat unexpected in a post–Tiananmen Square Chinese film, given that its rhetoric—especially where Don Quixote says, "If everyone here remains silent, then silence shall reign in the world," and that he has come "to show the capable, intelligent people [. . .] that there are still simple-minded idiots like me who will not stand idly by in the face of perils"—could easily lead viewers (at least those viewers with some knowledge of the violent events of 1989) to think of the world-famous "Tank Man," whose own defiant confrontation with a line of tanks was more than just a little quixotic.[20] Second, while Don Quixote himself breaks the neck of the evil Godfather, he is aided in no small way by the entire crowd, which makes the toppling of the Northern Sky Sect a clearly collective endeavor rather than the accomplishment of a solitary hero (however brave and inspiring). And third, Sancho's role in this victory is significant, even if ambiguously constructed. During the first part of Don Quixote's "inspiration speech," Sancho is shown standing shoulder to shoulder with his master, equal in defiance and courage. Still, he is not shown to play any part in the struggle that ensues between the crowd and the various members of the Northern Sky Sect. Nevertheless, he is shown once again—along with Sima Wan—at the center of the crowd that throws Don Quixote high into the air. In this scene, Sancho asks the scribe why he is there, and is told that the scribe did not wish "to miss the opportunity to witness a legend," nor to record "this episode of knight-errantry." And when Sancho then inquires whether he, too, will appear in Sima Wan's history, the scribe simply replies, "We'll see."[21]

Sima Wan's response to Sancho represents a deliberate challenge to the squire to rise to the occasion and follow in the footsteps of his master. Such a challenge, of course, is tied to a narrative trajectory in Cervantes's original novel whereby Sancho is said to have been "quixotified" through his ongoing encounter with the mad knight. Readers of the novel will recall that in Cervantes's final chapter Sancho unsuccessfully attempts to delay the coming of his master's death by trying to convince Don Quixote to head out on yet another adventure. In contrast, a completely different cinematic adaptation of *Don Quixote*, the 1972 film *Don Quixote Rides Again* (starring Cantinflas as Sancho Panza and Fernando Fernán Gómez as the mad knight) shows a tearful Sancho successfully rekindling the chivalric enthusiasm of his disheartened master by telling him, "We have to continue. We have to continue, sir. Many people await us. The universe is filled with poor people who are calling us to do justice for them. We cannot abandon them. We cannot abandon the weak, the humble. [. . .] We have to ride, sir. For the good of mankind."[22] But where this Cantinflas version of *Don Quixote* shows a re-inspired knight and his squire riding off into the sunset on their way to other adventures, Ah Gan's Chinese version shows Don Quixote quietly settling down, with Rosie by his side, to enjoy his own happily-ever-after ending. Ah Gan's Sancho, meanwhile, is shown in the final scene wearing Don Quixote's knightly armor and charging full tilt (on his donkey) at his own set of CGI windmills.[23] Ah Gan's Sancho is a thoroughly quixotified defender of the poor and the downtrodden, in stark contrast to Cantinflas's Sancho, who remains nothing but a loyal sidekick. In short, Ah Gan's peasant Sancho ultimately has become a hero in his own right. And this brings us back to the importance of Don Quixote for postmodern China.

As many have argued (myself included), Don Quixote is an archetypal figure who seems to emerge as an important cultural touchstone at crucial moments in history.[24] He first emerged at the start of the seventeenth century within the context of Europe's geopolitical transition from the medieval to the early modern, as the Iberian empires first set the world on a crash course with globalization. He was there at the turn of the twentieth century when the "Generation of 1898" turned him into martyr, symbol of a defeated Spain that had lost its last colonies to the upstart United

States. He was there on the eve of World War II when Frank Capra's *Mr. Smith Goes to Washington* turned him into an American everyman who doesn't believe in impossible dreams. He was there in Cold War Russia in 1957 when Grigori Kozintsev saw in him—at least on some level—the idealistic figure of the postwar Soviet "New Man."[25] And he was there in 2010 when Ah Gan transformed him yet again into a symbol of a twenty-first-century China that is well on its way to becoming both the world's largest economy and a major player—economically, culturally, and militarily—in global affairs.

Following Frederic Jameson, I have use the term "postmodern" here to describe this moment in Chinese history.[26] Still, this Western term is obviously difficult to apply to a region of the world whose own history does not necessarily correspond to a system of periodization designed to describe a uniquely European trajectory. As Arif Dirlik and Zhang Xudong note with regard to contemporary China, "if the postmodern is indeed a condition of late capitalism, it does not make much sense to apply it to situations where even the modern, as an economic and political category, remains to be achieved."[27] Nevertheless, as Dirlik and Zhang also argue, it is contemporary China's "spatial fracturing and temporal desynchronization" that justifies the descriptor "postmodern," precisely because "postmodernity is not just what comes after the modern but rather what comes after particular manifestations of the modern in China's historical circumstances, [such that] the postmodern is also the postrevolutionary and the postsocialist."[28] Arguments like these are echoed by Sheldon Lu, who argues that "hybridity, unevenness, nonsynchronicity, and pastiche are the main features of Chinese postmodern culture."[29] Thus, my own use of the term here is meant to indicate a post-revolutionary, post-socialist, post-colonial society that has not only become a key supplier in the global, capitalist economy, but is also increasingly participatory as both creator and consumer of global pop culture.[30]

Like his various archetypal predecessors, Ah Gan's Don Quixote represents a cultural harbinger of his host country's transition into its next phase. Like his Cervantine counterpart he is a walking anachronism; he even admits as much following his initial defeat at the hands of the triumvirate of villainous knights.[31] However, Ah Gan's Don Quixote is an anachronism not because he is out of place in his *own* time, but rather because he is out of place in *our* time. He is a Ming-era paladin living in a world of video games and CGI movies that has abandoned traditional Chinese dress in favor of Western business suits. In this regard, he embodies what Wang Mingxian calls Chinese postmodernism's "spatial plurality, its hybridity, and its inclusiveness, in which various schools, theories, and ideologies coexist and compete in the same socioeconomic environment."[32] At the same time, and for this very reason, he also symbolizes the values of the socialist revolution on which the People's Republic of China is supposedly built: he defends the masses and then inspires them to organize themselves in order to throw off their corrupt, capitalist, gangster overlords; at which point, rather than seize power for himself as warrior's reward, he simply rides away to live a quiet life as a simple farmer with Rosie by his side, leaving matters of state (along with its potential withering away) to others.[33]

In sum, if Don Quixote embodies the fractured desynchronization of postmodern China, it is Sancho—the film's ultimate hero, its real "crouching squire, hidden madman"—who embodies China's restructured cohesion at the beginning of the twenty-first century. As Glenn Odom notes in his study of acting and subjectivity in postmodern Chinese film, twentieth-century socialist realism "tends to treat the individual not as a subject but as a spokesperson for the group."[34] Needless to say, of course, Ah Gan's *Don Quixote* could hardly be called a work of socialist realism. Nevertheless, in its final evocation of Sancho's attack on the CGI windmills (and among the several other components of its temporal, spatial, cultural, and ideological pastiche), the film does posit the peasant squire as the epitome of a proletarian quixotic higher consciousness. And it is this quixotic higher consciousness, the film suggests, that will determine the direction of China in the coming years as it enters what may turn out to be a very "Chinese century."

NOTES

1. Miguel de Cervantes, *Don Quixote*, translated by Edith Grossman and introduction by Harold Bloom (New York: Harper Collins, 2003), 453.

2. Cervantes, 454.

3. Charles Mann, *1493: Uncovering the New World Columbus Created* (New York: Vintage, 2012), 7. See also Marsha S. Collins, "Going Global: Cervantes' *Don Quixote* Rides into the Future," *Expositions* 6.2 (2012): 33.

4. Carmen Hsu, "Dos cartas de Felipe II al emperador de China," *eHumanista: Journal of Medieval and Early Modern Iberian Studies* 4 (2004): 194–95.

5. Mann, *1493*, 152–53.

6. Mann, *1493*, 413–14. On the East-West cultural exchange during this period, see also Carlos de Sigüenza y Góngora and Alonso Ramírez, *Infortunios de Alonso Ramírez*, ed. Estelle Irizarry (San Juan, PR: Editorial cultural, 1990); Christina Lee, ed., *Western Visions of the Far East in a Transpacific Age, 1522-1657* (Aldershot, UK: Ashgate, 2012); Carmen Y. Hsu, "Writing on Behalf of a Christian Empire: Gifts, Dissimulation, and Politics in the Letters of Philip II of Spain to Wanli of China," *Hispanic Review* 78.3 (2010): 323–44; and Carmen Y. Hsu, "La imagen humanística del gran reino chino de Juan González de Mendoza," *Bulletin of Hispanic Studies* 87.2 (2010): 187–201.

7. Henry R. Luce, "The American Century," *Life* (February 17, 1941): 61.

8. Karen Chu, "Filmko on a Quest to Make 3D 'Quixote'," *Hollywood Reporter*, online March 22, 2010, available August 15, 2016, n.p.

9. On Ah Gan's place within the cultural tradition of "ShanZhai" culture, see John Berra and Liu Yang, "Cheap Laughs: The Mass-Production of Low-Budget Chinese Comedies from *Feng Kuang De Shi Tou/Crazy Stone* (Ning Hao, 2006) to *Gao Xing* (Agan, 2009)," *Asian Cinema* 23.1 (2012): 45–58.

10. On the tradition of Chinese knight-errantry, see Liu Kang, "Popular Culture and the Culture of the Masses in Contemporary China," *Boundary 2: An International Journal of Literature and Culture* 24.3 (1997): 99–122.

11. The decision to name this character the "Godfather" confirms Shuqin Cui's assessment that many of the films coming out of post-colonial Hong Kong represent a "hybrid genre" of "Asian martial arts and Hollywood gangster-thrillers" (Shuqin Cui, "Stanley Kwan's *Center Stage*: The (Im)Possible Engagement Between Feminism and Postmodernism," *Cinema Journal* 39, no. 4 (2000): 61–62).

12. The character of Sima Wan is loosely based on the real-life figure of Sima Qian, China's most important and best-known historian, who lived during the Han dynasty in the first century BC.

13. See, for instance, Kozo, Review of *Don Quixote* [Ah Gan], LoveHKFilm.com, available August 15, 2016; and Todd Rigney, "Windmills Enter the Third Dimension in Agan's *Don Quixote* 3-D," BeyondHollywood.com, available August 15, 2016.

14. Jorge Abril Sánchez, "Ah Gan's Don Quixote (魔俠傳之唐吉可德, 2010): Sun Tzu, Sun Bin, and the Warrior Spirit of the Chinese Knight of La Mancha," *Don Quixote: Interdisciplinary Connections* (Newark, DE: Juan de la Cuesta, 2013), 134.

15. Ibid., 133.

16. *Don Quixote* [Ah Gan], 1:20:00–1:27:00.

17. *Don Quixote* [Ah Gan], 1:33:25–1:33:55.

18. *Don Quixote* [Ah Gan], 1:35:25–1:36:40.

19. *Don Quixote* [Ah Gan], 1:37:00–1:43:05.

20. See Liu Kang, "Popular Culture and the Culture of the Masses in Contemporary China," *Boundary 2: An International Journal of Literature and Culture* 24.3 (1997): 99–122; and Lu, "Postmodernity."

21. *Don Quixote* [Ah Gan], 1:43:05–1:43:30.

22. *Don Quixote Rides Again*, 2:07:07–2:07:55.

23. *Don Quixote* [Ah Gan], 1:43:50–1:45:50.

24. See Burningham, "Don Quixote in the American Imaginary," *Approaches to Teaching Cervantes's* Don Quixote (New York: Modern Language Association of America, 2015), 153–58; and *Tilting Cervantes: Baroque Reflections on Postmodern Culture* (Nashville: Vanderbilt University Press, 2008).

25. On Soviet cinematic adaptations of *Don Quixote*, see Antonio Martínez Illán, "Don Quijote en el cine soviético: Kozintsev y Kurchevski," *El telón rasgado: El Quijote como puente cultural con el mundo soviético y postsoviético*, ed. Jorge Latorre, Antonio Martínez y Oleksandr Pronkévich (Pamplona: Eunsa, 2015), 317–41.

26. See Frederic Jameson, *Postmodernism; or, The Cultural Logic of Late Capitalism* (Durham, NC: Duke University Press, 1991), 1.

27. Arif Dirlik and Xudong Zhang, "Introduction: Postmodernism and China," *Boundary 2: A Journal of Postmodern Literature and Culture* 24.3 (1997): 3.

28. Ibid., 3–4.

29. Sheldon Hsiao-peng Lu, "Global Postmodernization: The Intellectual, the Artist, and China's Condition," *Boundary 2: An International Journal of Literature and Culture* 24.3 (1997): 66. See also William J. Burling, "Periodizing the Postmodern: China Miéville's *Perdido Street Station* and The Dynamics of Radical Fantasy," *Extrapolation: A Journal of Science Fiction and Fantasy* 50.2 (2009): 326–44; Annie Hau-Nung Chan, "Fashioning Change: Nationalism, Colonialism, and Modernity in Hong Kong," *Postcolonial Studies* 3.3 (2000): 293–309; Xiaoming Chen, "The Mysterious Other: Postpolitics in Chinese Film," *Boundary 2: An International Journal of Literature and Culture* 24.3 (1997): 123–41; Shuqin Cui, "Stanley Kwan's *Center Stage*: The (Im)Possible Engagement Between Feminism and Postmodernism," *Cinema Journal* 39.4 (2000): 60–80; Guo Jian, "Resisting Modernity in Contemporary China: The Cultural Revolution and Postmodernism," *Modern China* 25.3 (1999): 343–76; Ning; Wendy Larson, "Women and the Discourse of Desire in Postrevolutionary China: The Awkward Postmodernism of Chen Ran," *Boundary 2: An International Journal of Literature and Culture* 24.3 (1997): 201–23; and Ning Wang, "A Reflection on Postmodernist Fiction in China: Avant-Garde Narrative Experimentation," *Narrative* 21.3 (2013): 296–308.

30. On postmodernity and popular culture in post-Tiananmen China, see Lu ("Postmodernity" 145–46).

31. *Don Quixote* [Ah Gan], 1:32:42–1:32:47.

32. Wang Mingxian [trans. Zhang Xudong], "Notes on Architecture and Postmodernism in China" *Boundary 2: An International Journal of Literature and Culture* 24.3 (1997): 163.

33. For another cinematic representation of global capitalism as gangsterism, see Juan Padrón's Cuban film *Vampires in Havana*.

34. Glenn A. Odom, "Socialist Realism and New Subjectivities: Modern Acting in Gao Xingjian's *Cold Theatre*," *Asian Theatre Journal* 31.1 (2014): 156.

13

Amélie as Re-accentuation of Cervantes

Jonathan Wade

Although generally described as a feel-good, fanciful comedy, closer readings of the 2001 French film *Le fabuleux destin d'Amélie Poulain* have had a more difficult time agreeing on its meaning and merit, casting it as a celebration of little things or *le petisme* (Scatton-Tessier); an endorsement (Bonnaud) or subversion (Oscherwitz) of a whitewashed France of yesteryear; a voyage of self-discovery (Morrissey); or even a facile, albeit pleasurable, throwback to 1930s Poetic Realism (Andrew). What has yet to be explored, however, is the Cervantine intertext that informs both the framing and the framed. The specific mention of Don Quixote almost a third of the way into the film invites viewers to consider the various ways in which the novel, and Cervantes's works in general, are implicated throughout. There is, for instance, the quixotic characterization of its protagonist; the character referred to as the glass man, recalling Cervantes's *El licenciado Vidriera*; and various shades of madness throughout. What is more, the film recollects the narrative structure and self-consciousness of the novel. Just as Cervantes created a story about stories and storytelling in *Don Quixote*, *Amélie* presents viewers with a work of visual art about the visual arts that celebrates both their variety and their composition. Hence, there are echoes of both his writing and his writings throughout the film. *Amélie* is not, however, a parody or a pastiche of Cervantes's works. Among the many terms that might be employed to describe the relationship between *Amélie* and Cervantes's writings, this paper explores the degree to which Bakhtin's concept of re-accentuation is applicable.

At the close of "Discourse in the Novel," the fourth and final essay of *The Dialogic Imagination* (1975), Bakhtin describes re-accentuation as a process of rapid transformation that literary texts (particularly novels) undergo as they are subsequently re-imagined outside of the context of their creation. As he explains, "every age re-accentuates in its own way

the works of its most immediate past."[1] For Bakhtin there is nothing inherently good or bad about this process. Shifting backdrops and lenses
(both social and ideological) alter the way we perceive a text by accen-
tuating it in ways that sometimes illuminate and other times obscure the
original: "In an era when the dialogue of languages has experienced great
change, the language of an image begins to sound in a different way, or
is bathed in a different light, or is perceived against a different dialogiz-
ing background. In this new dialogue, a proper, direct intentionality in
both the image and its discourse may be strengthened and deepened,
or (on the contrary) may become completely reified."[2] Jorge Luis Borges
explores these same outcomes in "Pierre Menard, Author of the *Quixote*"
and "The Library of Babel," respectively.

Bakhtin's discussion is more theoretical than concrete, although he
does put forward Don Quixote as an example par excellence of this process. Four centuries of re-accentuations have multiplied the character's
signifying potential, resulting in a multifaceted novelistic image: "The
image of Don Quixote has been thus re-accentuated in a variety of ways
in the later history of the novel and interpreted in different ways, for
these re-accentuations and interpretations were an inevitable and organic
further development of the image, a continuation of the unresolved argument embedded in it."[3] He continues:

> In any objective stylistic study of novels from distant epochs it is necessary to
> take this process continually into consideration, and to rigorously coordinate
> the style under consideration with the background of heteroglossia, appropri-
> ate to the era, that dialogizes it. When this is done, the list of all subsequent
> re-accentuations of images in a given novel—say, the image of Don Quix-
> ote—takes on an enormous heuristic signficiance, deepening and broadening
> our artistic and ideological understanding of them.[4]

In essence, Bakhtin is describing an approach to novels (and other art
forms) that is not unlike an etymologist's relation to words. The study of
re-accentuations would yield, then, a character history that expands existing knowledge about the character and the context in which they came to
light (or took on a new light). While he does not employ Bakhtin's concept in his work, Anthony Close's *The Romantic Approach to* Don Quixote
(1978) traces the evolution of a particular re-accentuation of Don Quixote,
to name only one of many previous studies that demonstrate this process
without actually borrowing Bakhtin's framework.

Even though his essay focuses on the novel, Bakhtin also acknowledges the importance of re-accentuated images as they are translated
from one art form to another.[5] A study that focuses on re-accentuations
as they develop within a series of novels over time will read differently
than one that traces the same as they move across artistic genres if for no

other reason than the fact that there is another variable to consider (i.e., not just the changing context inherent in all re-accentuations, but also the introduction of a new mode of transmission). Directed by Jean-Pierre Jeunet, *Le fabuleux destin d'Amélie Poulain* recalls the images and discourse of many different Cervantine works, although *Don Quixote* figures most prominently therein.[6] Curiously, the movie's title in English is *Amélie* or *Amélie from Montmartre* and not *The Fabulous Destiny of Amélie Poulain*. The latter of the two English options evokes the carefully constructed name by which we remember Cervantes's character—Don Quixote de la Mancha—itself a parody of the chivalric naming tradition. Both the novel and the film, however, are best known by their abbreviated titles, *Don Quixote* and *Amélie*.

The title alone does not necessarily draw the viewer into the world of Cervantes, but in the context of the film as a whole, there is definitely a point to be made about it. The full French title highlights one of the primary themes of the entire work: destiny. It shows up in ways both simple and profound. The two scenes involving the newsstand, for example, prominently display the issue of *Paris Match* dedicated to the death of Princess Diana. On the cover, below her picture, read the words "Un Destin." The deep structure of the film reveals a character paralyzed by anxiety and self-doubt. While Amélie's challenge is not to distinguish between windmills and giants, like Don Quixote she is tilting at fate. Her destiny is not fixed; it is hers to change if she can take inspiration from her dreams rather than retreating into them. At various times throughout the movie she finds herself confronted by two choices. As one character admonishes, Amélie will not have forever to decide which path to pursue. "Luck," he states, "is like the Tour de France. You wait, and it flashes past you. You have to catch it while you can."[7]

Destiny is also a mainstay within the writings of Cervantes. In his entry on "Destiny," Howard Mancing specifically names *La ilustre fregona*, *La Galatea*, and *Pedro de Urdemalas* as works typifying this theme, to which we might also add *Numancia*, *La española inglesa*, *La fuerza de la sangre*, *La gitanilla*, and *Don Quixote* among other possibilities.[8] In his article "Don Quijote's Windmill and Fortune's Wheel," Eric Ziolkowski argues that the iconic windmills of Part I, chapter 8, are a symbol of the fates; Don Quixote charges them in an attempt to take control of his own destiny, to persuade Fortune to turn in his favor. Whether one agrees with Ziolkowski's assertion or not, the central role of destiny within the novel cannot be denied. Indeed, a page hardly turns without a reference to fate, fortune, heaven, luck, vocation, or some other term associated with destiny. Sebastián de Covarrubias's entries on *destinar*, *fortuna*, *fortunado*, *hado*, *suerte*, and *ventura* all shed light on the way that these terms at times converge in the novel.[9]

Within the vast iconography of *Don Quixote* there is hardly anything more ubiquitous than the windmill. As long as there have been artists re-creating Don Quixote, there have been windmills. In a film, therefore, that frequently intersects with the writings of Cervantes, it would not be surprising to find a windmill. In fact, the *locus* around which the film revolves is Amélie's workplace, *Café des 2 Moulins* (or the Two Windmills). The windmills in this case refer to the Moulin de la Galette, which consists of both the Moulin de Blute-fin and Moulin du Radet—the former dates from the early seventeenth century and the latter from the early eighteenth. These are the only two left standing from the dozens of windmills that once populated Montmartre. They have been the subject of many paintings, including works by Renoir, Van Gogh, and Picasso. While it is more straightforward to see in Jeunet's choice of Les Deux Moulins a re-purposing of Montmartre's windmill tradition (and the artistic, social, and historical implications thereof), there may also be in this choice a reference to art's most famous windmills: those found in *Don Quixote* and four hundred years of related iconography.

Les Deux Moulins is a space not unlike the inn from Part I of *Don Quixote* nor is it lacking characters who recall aspects of Cervantes's life and writings. One of the regulars at the Two Windmills, Hipolito, for example, self-identifies as a "failed writer" who writes "crap that nobody publishes."[10] Those familiar with Cervantes's biography will know that the same could be said of the author for the better part of his life. The name Hipolito may actually refer to the secondary character, Ippolit Terentyev, of Fyodor Dostoevsky's *The Idiot*, a work with no shortage of connections to *Don Quixote*. Much has been written about Cervantes and Dostoevsky, and in particular Don Quixote and Prince Myshkin.[11] Were I to fully trace Amélie's literary pedigree, the novelistic image cut by Myshkin would surely appear. Although the subtlest of references, Jeunet's potential nod to *The Idiot* through a character name only emboldens the broader claims I am exploring related to *Amélie*, *Don Quixote*, and Bakhtin's concept of re-accentuation.

Overall, the film introduces a number of quirky characters of dubious mental fortitude that remind viewers familiar with Cervantes of the cast of crazies found within his literary corpus. There's the obsessive man who stalks two of Amélie's co-workers by narrating their every action into his tape recorder while assigning the worst possible intentions to their conduct. One of them, a hypochondriac, who's a bit unstable by her own right, claims that he is driving her nuts before storming off while calling him a psycho.[12] The other admits at one point in the film that the men she likes are "mentally unsound."[13] Such measures of madness are not limited to the café either. Nino, Amélie's love interest, for instance, is characterized at one point as an oddball, which seems fair considering that his primary interest in the film is filling photo albums with the damaged and discarded pictures he finds in and around metro station photo booths. Additional vignettes of madness include the following: the suicidal goldfish that Amélie had as a child that destroys her mother's nerves; her anti-social father whose obsessive-compulsive behaviors find their greatest expression in a gnome he takes care of better than his own daughter; the grocer, Mr. Colignon, whose mental state fractures as he faces a series of well-engineered pranks perpetrated by Amélie, who seeks retribution for the treatment of his developmentally and physically disabled employee, Lucien. Of interest is the fact that Jamel Debbouze, the actor who plays Lucien, does not have the use of his right arm, having injured it in a train accident during his adolescence. In a film replete with Cervantine echoes, it is difficult not to see in this apparent happenstance the *Manco de Lepanto* himself (having permanently disabled his left arm in the 1571 Battle of Lepanto).

A character important both to the development of the film and this essay is Raymond Dufayel, one of the tenants who lives in the same building as Amélie. Most know him as *l'homme de verre*, or the glass man. The narrator explains the reason for the nickname: "He was born with bones as brittle as crystal. All his furniture is padded. A handshake could crush his fingers."[14] This condition, known as osteogenesis imperfecta (or brittle bone disease), is the same genetic disorder that afflicts Samuel L. Jackson's character in *Unbreakable* (2000). In the director's commentary on the film, in fact, Jeunet affirms that it was only by coincidence that two films included such a character. The glass man in *Amélie* has stayed indoors for twenty years, during which time he has repeatedly painted Renoir's 1881 *Luncheon of the Boating Party*. For those familiar with Cervantes's writings, the reference to a glass character cannot go unnoticed. *El licenciado Vidriera*, or *The Glass Licentiate*, was published in 1613 as one of twelve novellas written over the course of two decades. Cervantes was not the first to make use of this idea in imaginative literature.[15] As Gill Speak explains, "the sheer volume of sixteenth-century accounts suggests that interest in the glass delusion had taken on epidemic proportions."[16] Although the character did not begin with Cervantes, his remains the most popular and an important precursor to the glass characters in both films.

The glass men of *Amélie* and *El licenciado Vidriera* are essentially the same, with at least one important distinction. Whereas Tomás Rodaja's condition is mental, Dufayel's is primarily physical; the one curable, the other not. Which is not to say that mental and physical health are mutually exclusive categories. After all, right before the closing credits of *Unbreakable* we learn that Jackson's character, Elijah Rice, "is now in an institution for the criminally insane."[17] Hence, as much as Dufayel suffers from a debilitating physical condition, there are signs of mental instability in his character as well (if nothing else, the result of profound isolation). In Dale Shuger's description of Cervantes's glass character it is not difficult to locate Dufayel as well: "Two years and twenty-four pages pass without any discussion of Vidriera's life, feelings, changes or relationships. He is not a 'rounded' character but a wise talking head, a rhetorical trope."[18] Dufayel is just as flat as Tomás Rodaja, although his interactions with Amélie add depth to her character and advance the film. Elizabeth Ezra explains: "the Glass Man functions as a kind of medium, a transparent window or 'index' directing attention to things beyond himself."[19] Thus, while neither character can claim any real depth of individual characterization, both are transcendent in the way they speak to the human condition:

> The motif of the man who thought himself made of glass and its related images seem then to mirror a number of characteristic aspects of the human situation, in a richly poetic representation of human fears and human violence and human longing. The fragile image of glass symbolizes what men and women value most and most fear to lose—their innocence and purity, their beauty, their health, their reputations, their happiness, and brittle life itself.[20]

Raymond Dufayel's portrayal, therefore, is relevant as it applies to both his character and as it connects to the broader theme of human fragility, which underscores the entire film.

No character intersects with Cervantes, however, more than Amélie herself. The persistent tension between reality and fiction that punctuates the entire film begins in her troubled childhood: "Deprived of playmates, slung between a neurotic and an iceberg [her parents], Amélie retreats into her imagination."[21] Unlike Don Quixote, she seems to know where her dreams end and her reality begins. While this saves her from the bodily harm and ridicule Don Quixote endures on a regular basis, it does not free her from the personal anguish and hurt that results from wanting to be more than she is. The life of meaning and fulfillment they both pursue is framed with a similar purpose. For Don Quixote the aim is more grandiose, more literary, more baroque; in essence, more quixotic. But even if she is not trying to right "all manner of wrongs,"[22] Amélie wants to do good; at least that is the quest she undertakes upon making a wonderful, chance discovery in her bathroom. A tin box full of treasures from some child's distant past lie hidden behind a tile in her bathroom until fortune had her way and Amélie discovered the box, and with it, her purpose. That night she determines to seek out the owner of the box and return it to him as an experiment: "If he was touched, she would become a regular do-gooder. If not, too bad."[23] Don Quixote's mission, on the other hand, finds him by way of the books of chivalry that he devours night and day until "his fantasy filled with everything he had read . . . enchantments as well as combats, battles, challenges, wounds, courtings, loves, torments, and other impossible foolishness."[24]

If at the core we accept a degree of likeness between the purposes driving each character, it would follow that an evaluation of their respective successes is possible. Well-chronicled are the feats and defeats of Don Quixote. Over the course of the entire novel he experiences a little bit of everything. In his *Lectures on Don Quixote*, Vladimir Nabokov famously scored the knight-errant's performance as one would a tennis match, with the overall score at two sets apiece before the match is suspended due to the protagonist's death.[25] Reuniting the grown man with his box of treasures proves transformative for Amélie: "a surge of love, an urge to help mankind comes over her."[26] It would be the first of a series of successes for her. Almost immediately she seeks out a blind man she had come across earlier in the film, guiding him joyfully through the streets while telling him all about the visible world in affecting detail. As her do-gooding gains momentum so does her ambition. She plays matchmaker at the Two Windmills; fabricates a letter in order to console a neighbor who had long before lost her lover in a plane wreck; avenges Lucien's mistreatment by turning the grocer, Mr. Colignon's life upside down; inspires her dad to finally see the world; and solves the mystery of the unknown man in Nino's photo album, which she also returns to him.

It would appear that Amélie only knows success, yet the good she does for others masks the fact that she herself is paralyzed with self-doubt. By focusing on do-gooding she is able to ignore the messiness of her own life. This is the point that the Glass Man drives home in one of their conversations about the mysterious woman with the glass in Renoir's painting:

Amelie: The girl with the glass . . . Maybe her thoughts are with somebody else.

Raymond: Somebody in the picture?

Amelie: More likely a boy she saw somewhere and felt an affinity with.

Raymond: You mean she'd rather imagine herself relating to an absent person than build relationships with those around her?

Amelie: Maybe she tried hard to fix other people's messy lives.

Raymond: What about her? Her own messy life? Who will fix that?[27]

It is actually through art (whether painting or video montages) that these two characters communicate throughout the film. Just as an actual love interest is absent from the canvas of Don Quixote's life, Dufayel would have Amélie realize that her life is as insulated as the girl's in Renoir's painting. She is willing to wear out her life in service to others but is afraid to take on her own personal giants. This is typified in a scene early on in the film in which we find Amélie alone in her apartment watching television when her imagination suddenly kicks in: "Amélie Poulain, Godmother of outcasts, Madonna of the Unloved, finally succumbed to exhaustion. . . . What a strange destiny for one who gave her all yet took such joy in life's simple pleasures. Like Don Quixote, she pitted herself against the grinding windmills of all life's miseries. It was a losing battle that claimed her life too soon."[28] At the same time that this scene draws a parallel between Don Quixote and Amélie, it also makes an important distinction. To exhaust her life as Don Quixote did would be "a strange destiny," and as spectators we know that she is destined for something fabulous.

In addition to its memorable characters, another defining feature of *Don Quixote* is the way in which Cervantes tells the story. He is so central to the work, in fact, that stage adaptations of the novel often make a character out of Cervantes. This is true of Dale Wasserman's *Man of La Mancha* as well as in more recent dramatic works such as Edward Friedman's *Crossing the Line: A Quixotic Adventure in Two Acts*. Cervantes's narrative structure is highly self-conscious. In the same way that Diego Velásquez's *Las meninas* is a painting about paintings, *Don Quixote* is very much a book about books. Both works manipulate and multiply frames to such an extent that the reader cannot miss the fact that each work is as much about the framing as it is the framed. These same observations extend to *Amélie*. There are two different narrators for example: one for the movie and another for Amélie's imagination. There are numerous examples of self-referentiality as well. Most consist of a character looking at and/ or communicating directly with the camera. This occurs with Amélie's parents, the neighbor's comatose wife, and numerous times in Amélie's life. Many of these exchanges happen in response to something the narrator has said, which has the dual effect of making the narrator part of the story rather than something external to it, and also calls attention to the fact that this is a film that knows it is a film. One such moment occurs at the movie theater where Amélie tells us how she likes to look back at people's faces in the dark. She also tells viewers that she enjoys noticing details that others miss, like the bug on the window from a scene in the 1961 French film, *Jules et Jim*. This metafictional breaking of the fourth wall repeats throughout the film. Also, consistent throughout *Amélie* are "heritage elements and stock characters, [which] suggest that the past is one of the film's principal subjects."[29] As Dayna Oscherwitz argues, however, nostalgia is clearly not Jeunet's objective: "*Amélie* . . . sets about reinventing the past by appropriating and reworking existing images [and characters]."[30] This is true as it pertains to France's cinematic heritage as well as some of Cervantes's writings.

When asked about how the plot of the movie came together, Jean-Pierre Jeunet offered a description that echoes what literary critics and historians have long said about the composition of *Don Quixote*: "I had worked on this collection of stories for maybe 25 years that I wanted to make into a film. In fact it was very hard to find a (unifying) concept. It was just one little story in the middle of the other stories, the story of the woman helping other people. And then everything was easy to write, easy to shoot, easy to edit."[31] The parallelism between Jeunet and Cervantes in this passage is uncanny; not that we have record of Cervantes ever saying these exact words, but there is general critical consensus on the topic. That is, *Don Quixote* is widely regarded as a "collection of stories" compiled over many years, built around an original story that grew out of the unifying concept of madness. In his novel Cervantes created a story about stories and storytelling; so much of it is grounded in texts. There are the books of chivalry that consume Don Quixote to the point of madness and the subsequent burning thereof; the text that the narrator runs out of at the end of chapter 8 and the translated text that allows for the story to continue; the various intercalated texts; the textualization of Don Quixote and Sancho and its transformative effect on the whole of Part II; and an imposter text, Avellaneda's sequel, without which we may have never seen Cervantes complete Part II. Overall, the novel offers a beautiful constellation of intertextualities.

Just as the written word plays a fundamental part in *Don Quixote*, the visual arts are central to *Amélie*. They hold everything together. Remove film, television, painting, and photography, and the movie would fall apart. It is the girl in the Renoir painting that allows the glass man and Amélie to indirectly talk about Amélie's struggles, for instance. These conversations lead to the exchange of a few video montages that Amélie makes for the glass man. She longs to be known but does not know how to make herself known except through metaphor. The first video shows a horse running with cyclists during a race. In order to do so it jumps a fence, leaving familiar pastures to blaze a new trail. This is symbolic of Amélie's desire to break out of life as she knows it. She is good at doing this for others but is unsure of how to do it for herself. Instead she retreats into isolation rather than risking failure.

The second montage communicates much of the same, although the centerpiece this time is a clip of Arthur "Peg Leg Sam" Jackson, who conveys an attitude toward hardship that Amélie will need to replicate if she is to succeed. This clip evokes the theme of destiny and fortune as well: "You look at me . . . You look at a man that was born for hard luck. I was born on the 13th day, an odd day, and on a Friday, on a bad luck day."[32] Amélie also had it difficult from birth. Peg Leg Sam, however, is not making excuses. You see him dancing despite the missing limb. You hear his positive disposition. This is who Amélie wants to be and there are no external obstacles keeping her from getting there. Just as Don Quixote repeatedly takes inspiration from chivalric romances, Amélie finds in painting, television, and video the catalyst she needs to realize her fabulous destiny. Unlike Don Quixote, whose freedom diminishes over the course of the novel, Amélie's agency expands throughout the film.

In her own thinking about Bakhtin's concepts, Julia Kristeva explains that "any text is constructed as a mosaic of quotations; any text is the absorption and transformation of another."[33] Jeunet states it even more bluntly: "That's the story of art. Everybody steals everybody."[34] Among the myriad texts of which *Le fabuleux destin d'Amélie Poulain* is composed, it is not difficult to locate Cervantes. He is there in ways both definitive and dubious. In some cases (e.g., Don Quixote and Vidriera) we can even describe the intertextuality through the more specific process of re-accentuation, although Bakhtin's concept does not capture all of the ways that the film and the novel converge and diverge. A series of re-imaginings across time and space make it possible for *Amélie* to reflect something of Cervantes. On the whole, however, Amélie is more quixotic than she is actually like Cervantes's knight-errant, exemplifying the former without expanding our understanding of the latter. Seventeenth-century views of Don Quixote would never have yielded a character such as Amélie, but as Bakhtin observes, great novelistic images cannot be contained: "they are capable of being creatively transformed in different eras, far distant from the day and hour of their original birth."[35] And while there is no way of knowing what will become of *Amélie* in the future, it seems pretty evident that Cervantes will be inspiring artists for at least another four centuries.

NOTES

1. M. M. Bakhtin, *The Dialogic Imagination*, ed. Michael Holquist, trans. Caryl Emerson and Micahel Holquist (Austin: University of Texas Press, 1981, e-book), 420.

2. Ibid., 420.

3. Ibid., 410.

4. Ibid., 422.

5. Ibid., 421.

6. Jeunet wrote the screenplay together with script writer Guillame Laurant.

7. *Le fabuleux destin d'Amélie Poulain*, dir. Jean-Pierre Jeunet, 2001 (Burbank, CA: Miramax Home Entertainment, 2002), DVD. 1:15:30.

8. Howard Mancing, *Cervantes Encyclopedia*, vol. 1, A–K (Westport, CT: Greenwood Press, 2004), 188.

9. Sebastián de Covarrubias, *Tesoro de la lengua castellana o española* (Barcelona: S. A. Horta, 1943).

10. *Le fabuleux*, 52:42.

11. Among recent publications on the subject, Slav Gratchev's "Prince Myshkin as a Tragic Interpretation of Don Quixote" and Karen Stepanian's "Don Quixote and Prince Myshkin in Search of Reality" stand out.

12. *Le fabuleux*, 1:54:02.

13. Ibid., 1:55:36.

14. Ibid., 13:30.

15. Alfred Garvin Engstrom, "The Man Who Thought Himself Made of Glass, and Certain Related Images," *Studies in Philology* 67.3 (1970): 391.

16. Gill Speak, "*El licenciado Vidriera* and the Glass Men of Early Modern Europe," *The Modern Language Review* 854 (1990): 852.

17. *Unbreakable*, dir. M. Night Shyamalan, 2000 (Burbank, CA: Touchstone Pictures, 2001), DVD. 1:42:23.

18. Dale Shuger, *Don Quixote in the Archives: Madness and Literature in Early Modern Spain* (Edinburgh: Edinburgh University Press, 2012), 155.

19. Elizabeth Ezra, *Jean-Pierre Jeunet* (Chicago: University of Illinois Press, 2008), 106.

20. Engstrom, "The Man Who," 404–5.

21. *Le fabuleux*, 5:42.

22. Miguel de Cervantes, *Don Quixote*, trans. Edith Grossman (New Yorker: Harper Collins, 2003), 1.1.21.

23. *Le fabuleux*, 15:45.

24. Cervantes, *Don Quixote*, 1.1.21.

25. Vladimir Nabokov, *Lectures on Don Quixote* (New York: Harcourt Brace, 1983), 110.

26. *Le fabuleux*, 34:57.

27. Ibid., 48:50.

28. Ibid., 37:32.

29. Dayna Oscherwitz, "Once Upon a Time That Never Was: Jean-Pierre Jeunet's *Le Fabuleux Destin d'Amélie Poulain*," *The French Review* 84.3 (2011): 508.

30. Ibid., 510.

31. Jean-Pierre Jeunet, "Eye on the Oscars—The Nominees: Best Original Screenplay—Guillaume Laurant, Jean-Pierre Jeunet," *Variety* (February 25, 2002), Proquest Central.

32. *Le fabuleux*, 1:39:27.

33. Julia Kristeva, *The Kristeva Reader* (New York: Columbia University Press, 1986), 37.

34. Jean-Pierre Jeunet, "An Intimate Chat with Director Jean-Pierre Jeunet," *Le fabuleux destin d'Amélie Poulain*, dir. Jean-Pierre Jeunet, 2002 (Burbank, CA: Miramax Home Entertainment, 2002), DVD.

35. Bakhtin, *Dialogic*, 422.

14

Extracting the Essence of
Don Quixote for a Puppet Film

Steven Ritz-Barr

Quixote by Cervantes is the second film of a series called Classics in Miniature. Filmed in 2011, the goal was to develop a story that would allow for the use of string puppets as the characters in a live-action animated film. Transforming this voluminous book into a thirty-minute film while retaining the integrity of the story was a challenge. I began by choosing parts that resonated personally with me, but I also chose scenes that best appealed to the limitations and advantages of puppet-film making. Our goal was to create a living, moving Don Quixote in the minds of the viewers, through a film to be watched and enjoyed by young viewers and adults, by educated and not-so-highly-educated people alike. Our version had to be an entity in itself, meaning it must contain story background, generate some dynamic buildup, and have a conclusive finale in order for the film to stand on its own.

At the time this project began, I had just finished a two-year affair with Faust I by Goethe, which resulted in a twenty-minute film with puppets without dialogue, the first puppet film of my own invention. The dark content of Faust made it difficult to continue with Faust II as previously planned. I needed a new direction. After reading Don Quixote, I knew that I would enjoy basking in Cervantes's fictional world for the time it took to make a good film, specifically two years. But coming up with a script tailored to a thirty-minute marionette film was no small task. Should I adapt it to make it more contemporary? Which scenes should I choose to focus upon? How much should I rely on verbal rather than non-verbal communication? Other questions revolved around the success of the book and the fact that so many film versions (including some animated versions) had already been made previously. Why do another?

I read the book again, slowly. I also discovered that a multitude of books had been written about this one book. I read a few of them, but the two books most inspiring to my work were Gustave Doré's *Illustrations*

Figure 14.1. QUIXOTE film poster by Luis Lopez
Courtesy of Steven Barr.

of Don Quixote and Howard Mancing's *The Cervantes Encyclopedia*. I never want to be overly influenced by the opinion of others, including experts, regarding a project, so I usually take their commentary lightly. I am not an academic. I did have some reservations concerning my film adaptation. My main thought was that there were simply too many words. This novel was written at a time (in 1608) when a new culture of street performance for commoners developed in 1570 in Italy had become known as the Commedia del Arte. This theatrical form relied primarily on gesture rather than dialogue. However, contrary to this verbal minimalism, books written at that time contained an abundance of words, often in the form of numerous tangential elements that blurred the plot. *Don Quixote* by Cervantes was no exception. To acquire the mood and the emotion of a scene, an abundance of words was used to convey the multi-level concepts within this work. Yet in order for a puppet story to work, the fewer the words, the better. Too many words in the mouth of a puppet character can kill the puppet. In order for the puppet to "work," it must convince the spectator to not only believe the words but also the actions of the performance. This concept is called the suspension of disbelief; it is like a spell. That spell is easily broken by too many words in the puppet's mouth. If the spell is perceived by the spectator, or more exactly, if the techniques used to create the spell are discerned by the audience, then the puppet loses the ability to communicate the story's emotional core. Needless to say, I did not want this to happen.

WHAT IS PUPPETRY?

At the heart of puppetry is Believing, or more rightly, suspending one's disbelief for long enough to listen and believe. It is difficult enough to believe a flesh-and-blood actor, because we know he is pretending, but, paradoxically, it can be easier to believe a puppet due to its lack of pretention and the neutrality of the character.

A puppet is materially an object. The job of the Puppeteer is to allow the viewer to see a "living" character. When we look at an actual human face, we use a part of our brain called the fusiform gyrus. It is an oddly sophisticated piece of brain software that allows humans to distinguish among literally thousands of faces that we know. (Picture in your mind the face of Abe Lincoln. You just used your fusiform gyrus.) When we look at an object, however, we use a different and less powerful part of the brain, the inferior temporal gyrus, usually reserved only for object recognition.

It takes a talented artist to trick people into seeing a human face when they know it is an object. When this trick is achieved, the emotional impact of the message can be very potent. The human actor is recognized as a real human being and, as such, benefits from the empathy of the audience. The puppet designers, makers, and operators must work very hard to achieve the same empathy usually reserved for humans and animals. When they achieve it and evoke real emotions in the audience member, the message can be more powerful than if it was conveyed by human actors because of the energy the audience has invested in making the characters come alive. Puppets "live" only in the imagination of the viewer.

Human actors often add affectation to their interpretations. This can be called over-acting. It can hurt the integrity of the character the author created. Affectation is defined as non-authentic or unnecessary movements added by the actor to his character that display attributes of his own personality rather than the character he is portraying. It is noted that "For affectation is seen, as you know, when the soul, or moving force, appears at some point other than the center of gravity of the movement. Because the operator controls with his wire or thread only this center, the attached limbs are just what they should be . . . lifeless, pure pendulums, governed only by the law of gravity."[1]

The puppet's movements start at the center of the puppet and not in its limbs. It is not the foot moving forward or the hand reaching that drags the body behind it, but rather the movement starts from the center and thereby the limb movement follows the center and creates the illusion of unity in movement. It makes the puppet come alive with one force that moves it and not separate limbs going off in different directions. It is what gives a string puppet the uncanny feeling that it is indeed "alive."

The main advantage with string puppets is a superb elegance of their movement. I chose realistic marionettes, proportioned and dressed like humans as my puppets. Since they resemble real people, they also had to move like real people to accomplish the illusion of life, unlike stylistic puppets such as Jim Henson's Muppets or glove puppets like Mr. Punch. These marionettes' main limitations are that they cannot easily grab, run, touch, or fight with their wooden, articulated arms and legs. In addition, it is almost impossible to change their clothes because the strings are sewn to their limbs through their clothes.

Heinrich Von Kleist tells a story in 1801 about an encounter he had with a friend concerning a string marionette performance he saw: "these marionettes, like fairies, use the earth only as a point of departure; they return to it only to renew the flight of their limbs with a momentary pause. We, on the other hand, need the earth: for rest, for repose from the effort of the dance; but this rest of ours is, in itself, obviously not dance; and we can do no better than disguise our moments of rest as much as possible."[2] In order to preserve the elegance of the movement of Don Quixote's characters, I had to find scenes devoid of movements that are difficult for these puppets.

Figure 14.2.   Don Quixote and Sancho Panza observing the windmills
Courtesy of Steven Barr.

The Quixote puppets were made by Eugene Seregin, who learned his craft while working for twenty years for the legendary Russian puppeteer Sergei Obrasov in Moscow, Russia, before moving to Los Angeles. He became a master builder of marionettes over the years because he not only knows how to carve a character's face, but he can also expertly engineer the controls to facilitate their operation. Don Quixote alone took four months to create. Mr. Seregin is one of few master marionette builders alive today with both the creative and technical vision to create elegant marionettes.

LIMITATIONS INHERENT WITH MARIONETTES

Marionettes cannot easily come in close intimate proximity of each other because the controls for their strings above them collide, and the strings become entangled. One can change the visual perspective by putting one puppet ahead of the other, but this throws off the center of gravity. So in the chapters I chose to adapt for my film I needed to avoid scenes that required tight close contact of characters. Furthermore, given their wooden and non-movable fingers, the need for them to grab things or carry items had to be kept at a minimum. For example, the simple act of Don Quixote riding his horse required his hands to be holding the reins. They had to be glued to his hands and unglued when he talked or when he was not on

Figure 14.3.   Don Quixote finding Lorenza or his "Dulcinea"
Courtesy of Steven Barr.

his horse. The patience required for these small movements is phenomenal, and the actions must be prioritized in order to keep the momentum of a scene going while one is shooting it.

WRITING MY SHOOTING SCRIPT

After envisioning some of the scenes in my mind, I made a short list of about twenty episodes possible to film. I analyzed each of these scenes and listed all of the actions the puppets would have to engage in. This list became the first blueprint of my screenplay. I needed the audience to understand the background of Don Quixote. I decided to develop the entire first scene to include the introduction of the main character, his living situation, his relationship with his other household members (including his horse), his hopes, and his dreams. I wanted the transformation from Alonso into Don Quixote to be clearly understood. I intended to show how his obsessive reading contributed directly to his subsequent adventures. It was important to plant his dream-vision (in the film) so the audience could see how he is motivated. In the film, when he falls asleep and dreams, he sees himself as a knight fighting off a dragon and protecting a young maiden. Of course this dragon is only a shadow figure, but he attacks it in spite of it only being an illusion, and the dragon just disappears. The audience is aware that the vision of the dragon was only in his head. A young maiden is grateful for his brave deeds. She is a foreshadowing of Dulcinea, although only in his own mind.

Figure 14.4.   Alonzo's Dream
Courtesy of Steven Barr.

I had originally wanted to locate the second scene of the film at the bar of the inn where he complimented the ladies. However, I dropped this scene due to complications related to non-movable hands (glued hands on beer glasses) and the close proximity of the characters to each other. I deduced it wasn't essential for my short version. I felt the power of the story lies in the relationship of Quixote with Sancho Panza; thus, I needed him to meet Sancho as soon as possible, after he became a knight. As he rode out of his village on that first adventure, he also had to meet his lady. I inserted a pleasant peasant woman in the field who could fill that role. Then I went directly to setting up the scene with Andrés, the beaten boy, who would appear as a key messenger figure in my story later on, and the Merchant scene in which two Merchants had to defend themselves from being attacked by Quixote for not obeying his silly command to bow down to the name of Dulcinea. All in all this proved to be enough content to set up the background story of the hapless knight Don Quixote before he met his trusted squire, his neighbor, Sancho Panza.

MY POINT OF VIEW

Throughout the book, Don Quixote blames his shortcomings, his mental lapses, on the "Enchanter." However, I wasn't sure whether Cervantes wanted his reading public to believe in this character as a real entity or not, i.e., to realize that it was a fiction of Don Quixote's imagination.

When I re-read the book, this diffusion of responsibility for all of his acts leading to pain and destruction in the name of knightly pursuits of the good began to gnaw at me. I understood that Cervantes's character is a comedic invention, a Clown character of the highest order, a contrarian of human behavior, but did he always have to divert responsibility to this supernatural power of the Enchanter, in such an obvious manner? Yet this lack of self-awareness seemed to remain a consistent element of his thinking throughout the book. He was simply not able to find fault in himself or flaws in his acts as a knightly savior.

For my film I needed a satisfying ending. Because of the short length of the film, I needed an ending other than his death. In order to allow for a story conclusion to exist, I decided to set up an emotional moment with the right character to deliver it. I figured that this story device, the messenger, had to be Sancho, who was closest to Quixote and suffered with him through all adventures. He not only had become close to Quixote, but he accepted the kind of flights of fancy Quixote displayed without mocking him. Yet it so happened that my messenger figure became Andrés, the beaten boy. He was the one character that could elicit sympathy because he personally suffered due to the delusions of Don Quixote. And he was almost a child.

But it meant I had to bring Andrés back to the inn to see the puppet show of Maese Pedro. And of course this was a huge jump cut in my interpretation. (A jump cut is a film editor's term for an abrupt passage of time.) After Quixote ransacked the puppet theater, he and Sancho were ousted from the performance. However, Andrés recognizes and follows Don Quixote and Sancho out of the inn at night. The confrontation between Andrés and Don Quixote is described in the book, but I added my own particular point of view to this interchange. Don Quixote is confronted for having not only added to but also caused Andrés's long-term physical distress. Sancho and Don Quixote remember the boy and remember the details of their last meeting especially since Andrés is now wounded badly (in my film). Quixote makes no comment to Andrés, now a hapless wonderer who appears crippled, as he barks, "you are the Enchanter, Don Quixote." The voice of Andrés in the film had become my own voice. In fact, I did the voice-over of this character myself in the final version of the film.

In my re-interpretation, after this scene in the dark forest, Quixote reassesses his quest for righteousness and decides to go home. Andrés's remark is able to startle Quixote out of his madness and cause him to recognize the voice of the enchanter as possibly his own. Then I finally allow him to connect with reality rather than to live only in his imagination. I decided to end my film by making Quixote aware of his surroundings. This conclusion allowed us to recap the film locations we used. It is dawn; he passes the sheep and sees them as sheep. He sees where he insisted that the merchants bow to the name of Dulcinea, and he sees the windmills as windmills. I freeze-frame the final shot by twisting the cliché scene of the hero riding off into the sunset by having them ride off into a sunrise.

I decided that it was not necessary that the viewer witness the death of Don Quixote in this short film. The abbreviated length of the film would have made it too powerful a scene and too sad. It would not have been the relief that death grants the character in the book. When he finally dies, there is a certain relief because the reader recognizes not only that he is old and his wanderings are over but also that he is now free to move into a fully imaginary world. Death is a satisfying ending to the book.

THE SETTING AND SCENE DESIGN

I saw the story as "an exploration of the place where our inner and outer worlds meet. Indeed, Cervantes' narrative moves in two dimensions at once: within the hearts and minds of Don Quixote and Sancho and through the physical world they actually traverse. They are equally important."[3] Cervantes is meticulous in his realistic depictions of scenery. He describes inns, palaces, forests, trails and paths, rivers, and mountains. The knight and his squire interact with many people throughout the novel, and it is in these interactions that their bond is forged.[4]

The scene design we used for the backgrounds of sets had to communicate the illusion of vastness. We originally experimented with craft materials to make artful handmade backgrounds but settled on photos of real landscapes. Thus, our backgrounds were mostly photos from La Mancha landscapes projected onto a screen from behind the set. My wife had taken the photos while we were visiting Spain. We then only had to arrange the foreground elements to fit these rear-screen projections to give us these vast expanses of countryside. In fact, we discovered that we did not have all the necessary images for all the scenes, so some of the projected photos were taken later where I live in Topanga, California, near the ocean of Southern California. The chaparral looks surprising similar to that of La Mancha. Again, this was part of how I made this story and this film personal.

THE MIDDLE OF THE FILM SCRIPT

I really wanted the book-burning scene in the film. After many attempts to do this, I inserted the event where Don Quixote hires Sancho Panza as

Figure 14.5.   Don Quixote attacks a Giant
Courtesy of Steven Barr.

his squire. I set up the book burning as a distraction for the two to escape the caring gaze of his aunt and his housekeeper. I wrote two montage sequences where both realities happen simultaneously. (A montage is a series of abbreviated sequences edited together.) The ambiguous reason Sancho had to hang around the house after he had delivered an injured Don Quixote was so that he would receive some reward for the services of bringing his neighbor home. So I had Quixote directly reward him with the outlandish promise of adventure and the Island as is in the book. I took great care to portray Alonzo's maid and his niece as responsible family members who were trying to do their best to take care of him. But alas, Don Quixote and Sancho Panza escaped out the back door while the others were busy clearing out his library and causing it to go up in smoke. This represented the second part of the film.

Finally, Don Quixote and Sancho were on the road. Here, I had hoped to be able to portray five or six important scenes with our two heroes but could only portray three events, due to my time constraints. The Windmill scene had to be there, because this iconic scene represents the most known episode in the novel to anyone who has ever heard of it. Second, the scene of the puppet theater of Maese Pedro had to be there as an homage to puppet theater in general. I have performed live puppet shows for many years before I made this film. Don Quixote as the heckler who believed the scene so much he was willing to help the main puppet character was a scene too precious for any puppeteer to pass up. The physical "double entendre" of puppets performing a puppet play was certainly one of the highlights of the film. We just had to create Maese Pedro's

Figure 14.6.   Maese Pedro's puppet show
Courtesy of Steven Barr.

puppets in a simpler style than what we were using with Don Quixote. While I adapted Maese Pedro's scene I imagined Cervantes laughing; it certainly had me laughing. Originally I had the Gaiferos and Melisanda story blocked to shoot with the mini-puppets just like Cervantes wrote it. But just before we began to shoot the film, I had the idea to include Cervantes's own Saavedra story in Algeria, one of the episodic stories Cervantes includes in his novel. I could grossly simplify it and switch out the characters, which worked.

So I had one last scene left to portray of the adventures of our heroes together. I chose to include the sheep scene, where he thinks he attacks an oncoming army but he is really only attacking sheep. I wanted to show how the collateral damage done by the deeds of Don Quixote could amount in death. However, the absurdity of an armored hero attacking sheep had me laughing so hard when I read it that it made it into the film.

My logic was as follows: (1) Quixote hurts only himself in his mistaking the windmill for giants; (2) he hurts only animals in the sheep scene; (3) but he committed the greatest of sacrilege in the Maese Pedro scene. By mistaking the puppet play as reality he breaks the imaginative spell that theater and art cast upon their audience. The spell ceases to exist when his physical blows destroy the illusion and flights of imagination that the play offers the audience members for a short while and hence the reprieve from their day-to-day lives.

I now had the blueprint for my interpretation of Don Quixote. However, there remained a rhythm problem; it didn't flow correctly. All of the episodes were high action, which is good for puppets, but there lacked a

Figure 14.7.   Don Quixote riding home with renewed wisdom
Courtesy of Steven Barr.

scene of retrospection. So I included a short scene with Don Quixote and
Sancho camping. I took several interchanges from the original book and
dropped them into one campfire conversation. I wanted to show Sancho
drinking and slowly becoming drunk while Don Quixote kept on talking
in his own world. Yet time constraints forced me to cut what I had written substantially. So in the final version of the film, Sancho appears to be
sleeping through the whole Quixote monologue. It worked.

The reality of time (real time) affects every part of the filmmaking
process, especially with a film that relies on puppets. The puppets broke
down a lot, repairs were made daily, and scenes had to be altered because
a prop was not ready when we had to shoot the scene. Almost every scene
was written to be longer than it ended up in the film. I had to make many
of those decisions while shooting, when literary judgment is working in a
very intuitive mode. Thus, many decisions to cut the script were made in
the hope that the visual world we created would be sufficient to convey
the messages.

THE ENDING OF THE FILM SCRIPT

For the conclusion of our film script, I decided to just put Don Quixote
going back through his three episodes after his confrontation with An-

drés, the beaten boy, and riding off with Sancho into the sunrise of a new day (hopefully toward a sequel). After Andrés declares, "It is you, the Enchanter, Don Quixote," we simply allowed this information to sink into Don Quixote's mind. His gesture of recognition came because he turned around to head home. He didn't need to say anything, but by turning around a response was clear. Andrés's comment jolted him enough to see "Spain" and the beauty of the world around himself.

Many of the decisions after we began to shoot the film were made collectively. Our co-director, Hoku Uchiyama, kept wanting "one more take"; our art designer, Seb Chardon, wanted "more time" to finish everything he made (windmills included); and our editors could have used a few more passes to clarify parts they felt could be tighter. We did no re-shoots of any sequence or inserts because the project was out of time and out of money, and I was out of energy.

After the filming was complete and a rough version of the editing was done, we gave the footage to some actors, asking whether they would be interested in lending their voices to a puppet, Don Quixote. I approached several Hispanic actors, with no success. Through a friend I heard that Michael York, the English actor, might be interested. I emailed Mr. York the script and the filmed images that contained a vocal "scratch track" (meaning that the voices were voiced by myself and Hoku only as markers for the puppet's mouth manipulation, never to be used as the final voices). Mr. York agreed to do it if I would consider changing a few words. The requested changes referred to the Maese Pedro scene, when the mini-white knight escapes the black knight. In the script I had written, "the tsunami of love," having taken complete modern liberty with Cervantes's text. Mr. York pointed out that a tsunami would be a bit of a stretch for anyone to know about at that time in Spain, and he asked me to change it to "tornado." I agreed to this, but during our recording session I had him say both lines. As it turned out, the tsunami line was much funnier in the mouths of those little puppets, and Mr. York thought so too; thus, historically correct or not, it stayed in the film.

In conclusion, my re-accentuating of this major literary work boils down to Don Quixote accepting his responsibility in the making of his madness. By producing a film with puppets, I was aware of the multitude of constraints that dictate how a story can be told. But most importantly, I picked scenes and moments that moved me the most in the novel. I made this work personal. I had to adapt and make changes to the story while creating visuals that could transport the spectator toward what I thought was essential in the spirit of the book. We may have altered many parts from the original, but we hope we kept faithful to the essential core.

NOTES

1. Heinrich von Kleist, translated by Idris Parry, *On the Marionette Theatre*, http://ada.evergreen.edu/~arunc/texts/literature/kleist/kleist.pdf, 4.

2. Heinrich von Kleist, translated by Idris Parry, *On the Marionette Theatre*, http://ada.evergreen.edu/~arunc/texts/literature/kleist/kleist.pdf, 5.

3. Ilan Stavans, *Quixote*, W.W. Norton and Company, 2015, 42.

4. Ilan Stavans, *Quixote*, W.W. Norton and Company, 2015, 31.

V

THEATER AND TELEVISION

15

The Spanish Knight Among the Soviet People: Dramatic Re-accentuations of Don Quixote as a Doomed Performer

Margarita Marinova and Scott Pollard

DON QUIXOTE IN RUSSIA AND THE SOVIET UNION

During the summer and fall of 2015, visitors to the Tsaritsyno Museum in Moscow had the opportunity to view a unique exhibit, "Don Quixote in Russia and the Don Quixotes on the Russian Throne," mounted as a part of the worldwide celebration of the four hundredth anniversary of the publication of Cervantes's masterpiece. On display were rare editions of the Spanish novel, paintings, various artifacts, suits of armor, dueling pistols, personal correspondence of Russian royalty, and other materials that showcased Russia's obsession with the famous hidalgo, and the tremendous influence that his adventures and personal traits have exerted over Russia's intellectuals and leaders (a good portion of the show focused on the self-identification of a number of Russian Tsars with Don Quixote, and their attempts to re-create the chivalric ideals of "noble" living, complete with jousting and troubadour entertainment[1]) over the last two and a half centuries. The exhibit drew a record number of viewers and received significant coverage in various national media outlets. From June to September of that year, the Spanish knight became the talk of not just the town but the country as a whole.

This should come as no surprise, considering the long history of Russia's fascination with the eponymous novel. Although Russian readers encountered Cervantes's hero much later than their European counterparts, once they did they immediately recognized the greatness of the work and the importance of the ideas presented in it. The first record of Quixote's presence in Russian culture goes back to 1716, when Peter I brought from Paris one of Coypel's marvelous illustrations used to create the famous "Don Quixote tapestries," which was to inspire similar works at home. *Don Quixote* as a text found its way first into the private libraries of the best-educated Russians during the early eighteenth cen-

221

tury. For example, we know that M. V. Lomonosov owned a copy of the novel. V. K. Trediakovskii and A. P. Sumarokov referenced *Don Quixote* in their discussions of the present and future of Russian literature. A. N. Radishchev mentioned Cervantes's character in his own *Journey from St. Petersburg to Moscow*. I. A. Krylov, the famous fabulist, was also familiar with the Spanish madman (though his opinion of the character was much more negative than that of most of his contemporaries). Many of the Russian intellectuals read (and preferred) French translations of the novel even when, finally, there emerged Russian versions of the original during the reign of Catherine II.[2]

The first known Russian rendition of *Don Quixote* appeared in 1769. The translation, done by I. A. Teil, a German teacher, was incomplete and of rather poor quality. The next Russian version (from the French), accomplished by Nikolai Ossipov, came out in 1791. It took some liberties with the original, especially the ending, but at least it strove to present the novel in its totality. There were more than thirty new translations to appear in Russia over the next two hundred years: a true testament to the popularity of the work among Russian readers.

The Knight of the Doleful Countenance and his faithful squire received attention through other artistic interpretations as well. For example, there were thirty-nine children's editions of *Don Quixote* in the period between the mid-nineteenth century and the beginning of the Second World War. The Soviet Revolution did nothing to curb the enthusiasm of the native audiences for Cervantes's hero in various guises. Ballets based upon the novel were very popular (Petipa's version being the one to stand out). Operas and operettas, such as Jules Massenet's *Don Quixote* or the 1926 A. Brushtein musical comedy, drew adoring crowds to every performance. Cinematic adaptations of the novel (the 1933 movie, starring the famous Chaliapin, being the first sound film version of the Spanish classic) were a welcome addition to the circulation of the archetypal hero in the Russian context. The citizens of the Soviet Union, just like previous generations of Russians, loved and identified with Don Quixote's iconic struggle to remain true to himself at all costs.[3] Yet the critical reception of the novel in the first two decades following the victory of the Bolsheviks in 1917 was anything but uniformly positive. In fact, *Don Quixote*, as the most often quoted example of a Western classic, suddenly found itself at the center of a larger debate about what role Art, and literature in particular, should play in the life of the Soviet people.

Many leading literary scholars and writers believed that engaging anew with classical texts was essential for the process of raising the consciousness of the people, which Marxism viewed as the ultimate goal in society. Maxim Gorky, for example, urged his contemporaries to read Cervantes, Balzac, Dickens, Tolstoy, Stendhal, Dostoevsky, Uspenskii, and Chekhov and familiarize themselves with such works as *Prometheus*, *Hamlet*, *Faust*, and especially *Don Quixote*, which he considered to be a "wonderful, intelligent book" (prekrasnaia, umnaia kniga).[4] Other critics were less enthusiastic about the value of world literature in the brave new order the Soviet state sought to construct. Convinced that "our socialist soil will begin to give birth to artistic giants"[5] soon enough, literary ideologues such as Anatoly Lunacharskii, the first Soviet People's Commissar of Education, proclaimed that foreign classics were destined to become outdated relics of the past and as such had no place in Soviet modernity. Even when members of the Soviet intelligentsia did not see older texts as completely irrelevant to the new cultural realities of their present or future, they still insisted upon the need to transform them in ways that best matched the needs of the time. For instance, the literary critic P. I. Novitskii argued that each new epoch "created its own image of Shakespeare, Pushkin and Cervantes. The artistic and ideological generosity of any work of genius empowers every new age and generation with the gift of those of its elements that are most needed."[6] Similarly, M. A. Chekhov, the famous actor, thought that classical texts have to be updated according to the expectations of contemporary audiences, and hoped that a modern-day author would write a Russian *Don Quixote*, capable of inspiring new feelings and ideas in the public.[7]

When scholars turned their attention to the formal and thematic features of Cervantes's work as a separate subject of study, they found topics for discussion that clearly resonated with the larger conversation about the usefulness of Western literary models of expression.[8] Out of the cacophony of critical voices there emerged two main opposing camps: those who celebrated the eponymous hero as an example of great courage and the timeless pursuit of freedom of the creative spirit and those who saw him as a "socio-historical lunatic,"[9] who had outlived his purpose, and could therefore offer nothing productive to the new generation of Soviet citizens. In that context, any artistic engagement with the source text amounted to a public announcement on the value of art (understood as both classical archetypes and the Artist as an individual) in socialist society.

DRAMATIC ADAPTATIONS OF
DON QUIXOTE IN THE 1920S AND 1930S

It is against that critical and cultural background that we must interpret the various dramatic actualizations of the original in the 1920s and 1930s. There are three theatrical reconfigurations of the novel from that period that deserve special note: Anatoly Lunacharskii's *Osvobozhionnyi Don*

Kikhot (The Liberated Don Quixote), published in 1922; Georgii Chulkov's *Don Kikhot, Tragikomedia v 4 aktakh* (Don Quixote, a Tragicomedy in Four Acts), completed in 1935; and Mikhail Bulgakov's 1939 *Don Kikhot*. Of those, Bulgakov's play offers the most interesting, original re-accentuation of the Spanish source text during the early Soviet era.

By the time Bulgakov began working on his play during the summer of 1938, he was already seriously ill[10] and a political *persona non grata*. Following the early success of his novel *The White Guard* (1925), and especially of its dramatic adaptation, *The Days of the Turbins* (1926), which was rumored to be Stalin's favorite play for a while, his original works had started running into censorship problems, and were prohibited from production by any of the available publishing houses or theater companies. Unwilling to compromise his artistic integrity yet desperate to find other venues for his creative efforts, he turned to reinterpreting classical authors for the stage. Yet even his plays about or based upon works by Gogol, Pushkin, and Molière were either banned during production or after only a handful of performances. When V. V. Kuza, the artistic director of the Vakhtangov Theater, approached him in the summer of 1937 with the proposition to try his hand at adapting Cervantes's masterpiece, he was eager to accept not just because he could hardly turn down any paying job at the time[11] but, more importantly, because he felt great affinity with the novel's main hero. The result was a deeply personal, philosophical play about the fate of the Artist in a society determined to use all available means to "normalize" and control the imagination of all of its constituents. The perfect companion to his own novelistic magnum opus, *The Master and Margarita*, which he was revising concurrently with the full knowledge that it would never see print during his own lifetime, if ever,[12] Bulgakov's *Don Quixote* finalized the hero's image in a way that made the original text reverberate with meaning for the Soviet audiences. Sadly, he did not see his play performed on the stage: by the time it premièred, after overcoming various censorship and production-related hurdles, at the Pushkin Dramatic Theater in Leningrad in the fall of 1940, Bulgakov was already dead.[13]

At the same time as Mikhail Bulgakov was struggling to find venues for sharing with the public his uncompromising views on the importance of freedom of artistic expression, another out-of-favor Russian scholar, Mikhail Bakhtin, was putting the finishing touches to his essays on the art of novelistic discourse and its genre-specific multi-voicedness, which he saw as liberating both Author and Hero from the monologic confines of an all-encompassing world-view. In texts such as "Epic and the Novel," "Forms of Time and the Chronotope in the Novel," or "Discourse in the Novel," the literary critic not only proposes a new way of reading and understanding the development of the novel as a genre, but also decisively intervenes in his contemporary polemics about the place and use of world classics in any historical era. Not surprisingly, Bakhtin's original ideas about the need for newly activating embedded potentialities in classical works in any meaningful subsequent engagements with their form and contents—an important process in the circulation of texts as world literature, which he calls "re-accentuation"—surpass the critical ideas already in circulation at the time.

Following closely Bakhtin's recommendation to take the practice of re-accentuation "continually into consideration" and to "rigorously coordinate the style under consideration with the background of heteroglossia, appropriate to the era that dialogizes it,"[14] our reading of Bulgakov's adaptation of Cervantes's novel begins with an exploration of different authorial choices in terms of both generic and inter-cultural translations of Don Quixote's character during the 1920s and 1930s. We then focus on the "Bulgakovization" of the original through the formally heightened theatrical nature of the narrated events, which allows us to draw conclusions about (1) the symbiotic, and thus doomed in the Soviet context, relationship between the Artist and his community; (2) the character-building but also self-destructive consequences of the merging of theater and life; and (3) the creative Artist, his pupils, and the pursuit of self-expression in a highly restrictive society.

RE-ACCENTUATIONS OF DON QUIXOTE'S CHARACTER IN EARLY SOVIET DRAMA

As other critics have already noted,[15] Turgenev should be credited with giving symbolic birth to the Russian Don Quixote in his 1860 essay, "Hamlet and Don Quixote." In it he erases the previously dominant Russian vision of the Knight as a comic buffoon in order to replace it with that of a new, idealized hero, ready to defend his ideas whatever the cost may be[16]:

> All men live (consciously or otherwise) by virtue of certain principles, certain ideals, in a word, by virtue of what they deem true, beautiful, good, and so on. Many take their ideals intact from specific, historically sanctioned institutions. They thrive by conforming their lives to the vision it offers. Sometimes, driven by passion or contingency, such a man may stray, but he neither ponders nor doubts.[17]

Each subsequent generation of Russian literati continued the tradition of admiring Don Quixote as the self-sacrificing defender of all the disenfranchised and added to his character more and more traits that brought them closer together. Eager to see itself better reflected in the image of the beloved hidalgo, the Russian intelligentsia endowed him with a formidable intellect and indefatigable desire to pursue the Truth that he first discovered in books. "Don Quixote is first of all the child of the intelligentsia," Merezhkovsky wrote in 1889, "and for him there's nothing higher in this world than the bookish truth [knizhnaia istina]."[18] The linkage between the two was so successful that Lunacharskii often referred to the revolutionary intelligentsia simply as "the Don Quixotes" in his critical articles and public speeches.

It is precisely that meaning of the character that Lunacharskii deployed in his own dramatic treatment of the adventures of the Knight of the Doleful Countenance.[19] According to the author's own reminiscences, he began writing *The Liberated Don Quixote* already in 1916, and spent the next six years working on it. The published 1922 version reflected Lunacharskii's approach to the role that the Russian intelligentsia played (or, rather, failed to) in the revolutionary movement. His ideas on this topic are clearly spelled out in the afterword to the 1924 edition of Cervantes's *Don Quixote*:

> The proletariat often encounters both Don Quixotes and Sanchos on the front. The cafes of all major cities are overflowing with quixotic intelligentsia, who, gesturing and screaming, opine about great ideals.
>
> Unfortunately, many of these Don Quixotes are really Hamlets, as described by Turgenev, who prefer to stay away from the real action. But there are those that are willing to fight for change, though under false, fantastic banners. [. . .] Among such Don Quixotes there are many who might, and probably will be, saved by the victorious onward march of the proletariat.[20]

Despite its obvious didactic goals and glaring character omissions (for example, Dulcinea was not deemed important enough to participate in the revolutionary plotline), Lunacharskii's play still retains "the idealistic, critical aspect of the knight, his name, a few of the episodes of the novel and the outer shell of Sancho and the ducal company."[21] *The Liberated Don Quixote* begins with a meeting between Don Quixote and three captives, thinly veiled representatives of the Russian revolutionaries, whom he frees but is then arrested himself and taken to the Duke's palace. There he is ridiculed and turned into a plaything for the amusement of the "hellish"[22] nobility. Don Quixote suffers at the hands of professional soldiers who pretend to be knights so he can be beaten viciously in a fight, but then recovers enough to emerge victorious in a duel with the Duke himself. Enraged, the Duke sends both the knight and his squire to prison, from which they are liberated once the rebellion that takes place in "Spain" succeeds in overturning the status quo. Here Lunacharskii clearly allows himself to rework his own experiences during the Civil War and pass judgment on the classes involved in the struggle for political dominance. When Don Quixote, a representative of the idealistic intelligentsia, does not approve of the cruel methods of his liberators (they are no better than the Duke and his retinue as far as he is concerned), he has to be punished for his ideological shortsightedness. At the end of the play, Quixote and Sancho must leave this new world, and wait to be called back after the class war is over and the true heroes of the revolution are finally able to take off their "bloody armor." Only then would Quixote feel truly free and be able to help others "do good." Still, as the revolutionary character Baltassar, expressing the author's own ideas on this matter, proclaims in a speech that brings the play to a close, even then the Knight would always "look back, at the abysses and horrors" carried out by others, and remain ignorant of the true demands of history: "Ah, you don't understand that we are ready to pay the price, without which it's impossible to forge a state where the liberated Don Quixote can find harmony and light."[23]

Lunacharskii's ideas about how the intellectual elite should be treated by the Soviets became the blueprint for the earliest purges in the Soviet Union: in 1922 many leading scientists, scholars, and philosophers unwilling to acknowledge the victory of the Bolsheviks, were forced to leave their country for good. In this case life imitated art with disastrous results. Wouldn't it be better to keep reality and the imagination separate for the good of society? Georgii Chulkov's 1934 play in verse, *Don Quixote, a Tragicomedy in Four Acts*, tackles that question through its focus on the struggle between "mystical anarchism" and crude rationalism.[24] The clash between the two is best captured in a scene at the Duke's estate that re-accentuates the famous Master Pedro puppet show episode from chapter 25 of volume 2 of Cervantes's novel. Similarly to the Spanish original, Chulkov has the Duke arrange for a theatrical reenactment (with live actors rather than puppets) of Quixote's own adventures in an attempt to convince him of their ridiculousness and, more importantly, their failure to bring about positive change. However, Don Quixote resists the "Renaissance" logic presented to him through the performance and rushes to the stage in order to punish the evil peasant who is beating the actor performing Quixote's role. The hidalgo's unwillingness to remain a passive consumer of the artistic spectacle jettisons him straight back into the fictional world his adversaries are trying to separate him from. Chulkov treats his character much more kindly in this scene than his Spanish predecessor did. Rather than being seen as stubborn and ruinously delusional, Don Quixote appears empowered to counteract those who treat him dishonestly, even if briefly and in the context of a fleeting artistic performance. When told directly that it is all just fiction, a lie, he responds that he can't "bear such shameless plays" and continues: "Honorable Señores! For those who have pondered the mysteries of life, it is hard to distinguish between Truth and lies."[25]

Sansón Carrasco's attempts to return Don Quixote to reality are similarly futile and as such constitute a veiled critique of the Soviet worldview.
In a society heavily promoting scientific rationalism, it is Carrasco's brand
of pure reason, rather than Hamlet's indecisiveness, that stands in direct
opposition to the Knight's idealistic anarchism. As in the novel, here too
Carrasco overcomes Quixote in a duel, but when the suffering hidalgo
tries to leave the Duke's estate he is forced to return in order to provide
further entertainment for the nobility. This time, however, Don Quixote
is able to see through the performance directed by the Duke himself, and
refuses to participate. He has finally found the Truth, and it lies beyond
either option previously presented to him as a solution to living a good
life. Neither pure reason nor limitless imagination can perceive reality for
what it truly is. Only the "divinely beautiful" (bozhestvenno prekrasnaia)
Earth can be viewed as real, and the hero dies a happy (if completely un-
motivated[26]) death, elated by his revelation. This Earth has nothing to do
with the materialist understanding of human existence espoused by the
communists. Instead, it is imbued with a Christian meaning. In a diary
entry from January 27, 1935, Chulkov left us a direct commentary on the
significance of his play's striking ending:

> In Cervantes's novel Don Quixote dies like a pious Christian. In my *Don
> Quixote*, the dying hero talks about Earth, the Truth of our Earth. It would
> be wrong for readers to see a contradiction here. Only the true Christian can
> love our Earth truly, to the end. Loving the earthly passions does not mean
> loving the Earth. On the other hand, abstract dreaminess is anti-Christian as
> well.[27]

Even if Don Quixote is defeated by Carrasco, then, he is not overcome
by Carrasco's ideology. Neither life (understood as material existence)
nor pure art can provide a true solution to the predicament Chulkov's
thinking and feeling man finds himself in. The only hope for salvation
lies in a mystical, religious awareness of one's place in this world. Although heartbreaking, his Don Quixote's end is also more optimistic, and
thus justifies the generic affiliation suggested by the title: *Don Quixote, A
Tragicomedy*.

Bulgakov's treatment of theater's powers (or lack thereof) to expose
problems in or govern social interactions differs greatly from those of his
two Soviet predecessors. Like Lunacharskii, he returns Don Quixote to
the community, in order to gauge the value of his singular voice against
the heteroglossia of the times. However, rather than banishing the Artist
from the socialist Republic because of his inability to speak the language
of the era, Bulgakov's conclusion insists upon the need for the inclusion
of Quixote's voice and a proper dialogue between all the involved parties.
Similarly to Chulkov's decision to highlight the symbolic significance of

theater in his own drama (but with different goals in mind), Bulgakov's treatment of the Knight's interactions with others as highly performative (especially in the second part of his adaptation) draws attention to the critical possibilities embedded in the very nature of the genre of his re-accentuation. This idea is most visible in Bulgakov's only openly original addition to the source text: the "play-within-the-play" in act 2, scene 4.

In that particular scene, the villagers quickly improvise a theatrical per-formance (complete with assigned roles and frequent costume changes) as a way to re-inscribe Quixote into his home space for good. Put differ-ently, art is called upon here to influence life in a definitive, practical way. This play has no corollary in Cervantes's novel, yet Bulgakov concocts it out of a variety of pieces of the novel. What precedes the villagers' theat-rical endeavor compresses Don Quixote's imitation of Amadis of Gaul in the Sierra Morena mountains and his return home in the "enchanted" cart at the end of volume 1. The play-within-the-play itself depends primarily on the Princess Micomicona narrative, but also uses elements of the Lady Dolorida hoax, and the "magical" disappearance of Don Quixote's library after the book burning scene in volume 1, chapter 6. Bulgakov's own *brico-lage* is reflected by the niece, priest, barber, and housekeeper's attempt to improvise on the fly an imaginary landscape for Don Quixote that would attract him home, although they have no idea how they will keep him once they get him. Their chivalric narrative successfully engages Quixote, allowing him to act out their fantasy in his own house with willing partic-ipants (rather than out in the world with unwilling, potentially dangerous participants or in his library alone, captive of his imagination). It is a chal-lenging scene to stage. The niece, barber, and priest double in the roles of the Princess Micomicona, her dueña (Dolorida), and the Princess's uncle, brother to the king, who was murdered by the monster Pandofilando. The three of them have retrieved Don Quixote from the Sierra Morena in the enchanted cart, and Quixote has been informed off-stage of the Princess's request for his services to rescue the kingdom. The scene begins in *medias res* as Don Quixote attempts to introduce his new friends to the niece, barber, priest, and housekeeper. In the ensuing quick costume changes and cross-dressings, the attempt to maintain the illusion falters, and the three avoid being found out by invoking Frestón the magician, now as kidnapper, who "disappears" with the Princess and her entourage. The disappearance frustrates and disappoints Quixote, producing in him a sudden debilitating weakness and causing his wounds (received in an earlier scene at the hands of the Yanguesans) to reopen, necessitating that he be put to bed to rest. The improvised chivalric ruse fails, and with it literally fails Quixote. The symbolism is clear. Entrapped by the villagers, Don Quixote has surrendered agency of his chivalric imagination. As in volume 2 of the novel, Don Quixote no longer produces the chivalric narrative in which he acts. And because the priest, barber, niece, and housekeeper's improvisational skills are so much weaker than Quixote's, the imaginary landscape in which they have embedded Quixote fragments, and he fails, literally and figuratively. The village cannot save Quixote but only damage or destroy him. The artist's existence is not preserved by the community. Just as it did in the Spanish novel, here, too, drama fails to achieve its goals. But whereas for Cervantes the failure is bound up with Quixote's (and the reader's) inability to keep his distance from the performed events, for Bulgakov the final catastrophe is the outcome of the inability of art and reality to co-exist in meaningful ways.

If Cervantes questioned the ability of dramatic discourse to bring about change, it may have been because he himself failed as a dramatist. After his captivity in Algiers and return to Spain, in the 1580s Cervantes began his literary career as a playwright in the vital Madrid theater scene, only to be bested by the younger, extraordinarily prolific playwright, Lope de Vega. Still, despite the fact that his successes were few—most notably *El trato de Argel* (*Life in Algiers*) and *La numancia* (The Siege of Numancia)—drama remained at the center of Cervantes's literary production for the rest of his life. *Don Quixote* has plenty of dramatic elements in Book 1 (Alonso Quejano's creation of the Quixote costume; the priest and the barber disguising themselves in their initial plot to bring Quixote home; Dorotea performing as the Princess Micomicona), but Book 2 is full to bursting with them (The Parliament of Death, The Knight of the Woods/ Mirrors, Camacho's wedding, the Duke and Duchess scenes, Sancho on the "island" of Barataria, Don Quixote in Barcelona, the Knight of the White Moon).[28] Among all the scenes that engage with theatrical expression in the novel, Master Pedro's puppet show has received the most critical attention—and deservedly so. As George Haley has noted in his canonical "The Narrator in *Don Quijote:* Maese Pedro's Puppet Show," the *retablo* should be viewed as the paradigmatic example of how Cervantes structures the metafictional elements of the novel, reinforcing Cervantes's intention that the episode is meant as "an analogue to the novel as a whole,"[29] and is thus designed to teach the reader to distrust the chivalric form and maintain a critical distance between history, fiction, and reality. Similarly, Bruce Burningham[30] highlights the importance of the theatrical tradition of the medieval *jongleur* and the overall relevance of theater in the public square[31] to *Don Quixote*'s main project, while Mary Malcolm Gaylord adds history and historiographical considerations at work in the culture at the time as forces that shape the narratological and theatrical elements of the scene.[32] Clearly, the novel presents fertile ground for a theatrical re-accentuation of the Quixote story, which Bulgakov intuits and makes the most of in his own adaptation.

As the most fully realized theatrical piece in the novel, Master Pedro's performance stands as the clearest antecedent to Bulgakov's play-within-a-play, but Bulgakov uses the villagers' improvised drama to pursue a significance that reverses the lesson of the Master Pedro scene while reflecting Stalinist Russia: the particular heteroglossia within which the villagers' actions play out. In short, while Cervantes uses the Master Pedro scene to reinforce the readers' ability to distinguish between the real and the fictive and, thus, isolate Don Quixote in his madness, Bulgakov uses the play-within-a-play to forge ineluctable bonds between Don Quixote and the villagers. And while Cervantes develops the remainder of the novel to reinforce Don Quixote's alienation and draw ever sharper distinctions between fantasy and reality, Bulgakov uses the remainder of the play to reinforce the linked fates of Don Quixote and the villagers. If Cervantes wanted to engineer a break between seventeenth-century Spain and its obsession with its heroic, *reconquista* past, Bulgakov presents to his audience the unavoidability of Stalinist Russia and the dangers it constitutes for everyone, artist and non-artist alike.

The village players are like Master Pedro's puppets; although not made of paste and string, they are buffeted by forces outside of their control. While Master Pedro works with a popular *reconquista* story—the Liberation of Melisendra—a set of props, and the usual expectations of an evening's entertainment at a roadside inn, he cannot control Don Quixote (although he tries), and the play ends in chaos. Throughout the novel this pattern repeats. Introduced into an otherwise orderly social context, Don Quixote is the unpredictable wild element, which others cannot control. A community cannot manage a madman without courting chaos; thus, the only option is for the community to divorce itself from that madman, which is what Cervantes achieves at the end of the novel. In the play, in an act of mimicry, Nicolás and Pérez concoct the outline of a chivalric plot, over which, as the scene progresses, they lose control. They and the other villagers do not have the ability to manage the improvisation, particularly in the face of Don Quixote's involvement and in the need to keep up the chivalric illusion for his sake. When they invoke Frestón the magician, who kidnaps and flies away with the characters they were playing, it is Don Quixote who is injured as he attempts to act heroically:

> *Don Quixote:* "The princess was under my protection! Let me go! You may all be frightened, but not me. I will catch him though he flies as fleet as the wind. Let me go! (*Drops his spear and falls back into his chair.*)
>
> *Antonia:* Uncle! What's wrong?
>
> *Don Quixote:* My wounds have opened up. I suddenly feel weak. He's put a spell on me . . .[33]

Unlike in the puppet theater scene when Don Quixote damages the players and once again makes himself *persona non grata*, here the players from their lack of skill as artists and improvisers bring on Don Quixote's injury but successfully keep him home, for the moment. If Cervantes alienates and neutralizes Quixote, Bulgakov works to tie him ever more firmly to community, which is more and more responsible for his well-being (or lack thereof). Moreover, the villagers and Quixote's household-ers feel that responsibility, and Bulgakov gives them no escape from it. As a proxy for the Soviet state, the village cannot save Quixote—cannot save the artist—but only damage or destroy him.

At the end of both works, these divergent signifying chains repeat. In the novel, Alonso Quijana gives over his madness, dictates his will using the responsible legal language of a landowning *hidalgo*, and then dies. After an appropriate period of mourning, his family and neighbors move on with their lives, which is Cervantes's point:

> Andaba la casa alborotada; pero, con todo, comía la sobrina, brindaba el ama, y se regocijaba Sancho Panza; que esto del heredar algo borra o templa en el heredero la memoria de la pena que es razón que deje el muerto.[34]

> (The house was in a perpetual uproar—but, all the same, the niece ate, and the housekeeper drank, and Sancho was joyful, because for the man who inherits, the business of inheriting softens and moderates the memory he rightly retains of the pain and suffering which gave rise to his inheritance.[35])

And if George Haley is to be believed, readers have had their final lesson in maintaining critical distance. After Sansón Carrasco defeats Don Quixote in Barcelona, in Book 2, chapter 65, Don Antonio Moreno notes the problem of taking Don Quixote out of the world—impoverished meaning, impoverished heteroglossia—but his criticism is forgotten as Cervantes ends the novel with a safer, more manageable heteroglossia. In contrast, at the end of the play Bulgakov does not signal the return of ordinary life. Although Carrasco defeats Don Quixote in the joust, Quixote also wounds Carrasco, who feels that his injury ties him to Quixote like a ghostly *döppelganger*. Carrasco understands Quixote's loss, and Bulgakov ensures the inescapable tie between them. As Quixote dies, the niece, Antonia, rushes in with a lamp, exclaiming, "What can we do, Sansón? What can we do?" To which Sansón, recognizing that he too has failed, replies, "I can do nothing more. He is dead."[36] The village is bereft without Quixote, without the artist, and, unlike Cervantes, Bulgakov offers no glimpse of life for the village beyond Quixote's death: there is no future. In Stalinist Russia, life without the artist is unimaginable. For Bulgakov, the Soviets successfully corral everyone's inner madman/artist. If Cervantes ends the novel with a slightly reduced, more manageable heteroglossia,

Bulgakov ends the play with a severe monological discourse (as signifier of the oppressive power of the Soviet state).

Bulgakov's dramatic re-accentuation of Cervantes's novel is about the limits and the powers of adaptation in both society and art. Novels like *Don Quixote*, Bakhtin wrote, force "all exhausted and used up, all socially and ideologically alien and distant worlds to speak about themselves in their own language and in their own style—but the author builds a superstructure over these languages made up of his own intentions and accents, which then become dialogically linked with them."[37] Correlatively, for Bakhtin the author has great powers in polemical encounters, for his is the overarching frame, the "superstructure," that contains all other speech acts. In their dramatic adaptations of *Don Quixote*, Lunacharskii, Chulkov, and Bulgakov accent Quixote's story to produce distinct linguistic and ideological interactions within Soviet heteroglossia. Lunacharskii privileges Bolshevik ideology and punishes Quixote as a retrograde intellectual, while Chulkov views the knight and his imagination as worthy of pity. In both cases, the Soviet signifying regime thoroughly disempowers Quixote's creative and affective potential. Exploring the existence of the creative Artist in a society otherwise dominated by constraining political ideas, Bulgakov paradoxically pursues the subjugation of multivoicedness to the imperative of an authorial "accent." To that end, he flips expectations, allowing the collective to be superseded by the voice of the Artist. Don Quixote's "accent" infects all around him. Bulgakov's play dramatizes the power of the hero's voice—like a gift, bestowed from without (by the playwright but also the other characters in the work)—yet with that power comes an attached price which, in Stalin's Russia, all involved must pay.

NOTES

1. The Gothic architecture of the Tsaritsyno residence itself (built by Queen Catherine II in 1776) was inspired by European medieval castles, and was thus the perfect backdrop to an exhibit dedicated to the theme of Don Quixote's enduring presence in Russian culture.

2. For a discussion of the early history of Cervantes's novel in Russia, see Yurii Aikhenval'd, *Don Kikhot na russkoi pochve* (Moskva: Gendal'f, 1996), esp. 19–23, and V. E. Bagno, *"Don Kikhot" v Rossii i russkoe donkikhotstvo* (Saint Petersburg: Nauka, 2009), esp. 14–20.

3. That Cervantes's novel was among the most beloved by Soviet readers during the 1920s and 1930s can be gleaned through the sheer number of available editions at the time: no less than fifteen by the end of 1930.

4. Maxim Gorky, *Sobranie sochinenii v 30 T.* (Collected works in 30 volumes), vol. 5: *Povesti, razkasy, ocherki, stikhi, 1900-1906* (Novellas, short stories, essays, poems, 1900–1906) (Moskva: Hud. Lit., 1950), 215.

5. Lunacharskii, quoted in Nailya Safiullina, "The Canonization of Western Writers in the Soviet Union in the 1930s," *The Modern Language Review*, 107.2 (April 2012), 562.

6. P. I. Novitskii, "Don Kikhot Servantesa: vvedenie" (Cervantes's Don Quixote: Introduction) *Khitroumnyi Idalgo Don Kikhot Lamanchskii*, M. de Cervantes Saavedra. (Leningrad, 1929), 20.

7. Mikhail Chekhov, "Dnevnik o Kikhote." (Diary about Quixote) *Literaturnoe nasledie* v 2 t. (Moskva, 1986), 1: 336. Chekhov attempted writing his own version of the legendary adventures of the Spanish hidalgo, but unfortunately his efforts did not lead to the desired results: his work was never completed and certainly never staged.

8. Some prominent examples of the trend include Dz. Kelly's "Ispanskaia literature" (Spanish literature) (1923), A. G. Gornfeld's "Boevye otkliki na mirnyie temy" (Military responses to peaceful themes) (1924), A. B. V. Lunacharsky's "Posleslovie" (Afterward) (1924), V. V. Shklovsky's "Teoria Prozy" (Theory of prose) (1925), P. N. Medvedev's "Fromalnyi metod v litarurovedenii" (The Formal method in the study of literature) (1928), B. A. Krzhevskii's "*Don Khihot* na fone ispanskoi literature XVI-XVII c." (*Don Quixote* in the context of Spanish literature of the XVI-XVII c.), K. S. Derzhavin's "Cervantes i Don Kikhot" (Cervantes and Don Quixote) (1933), B. M. Engelhard's "Cervantes i ego roman" (Cervantes and his novel), 1938.

9. I. M. Nusinov, "Don Kikhot," *Literaturnaia entsikopedia* (Literary encyclopedia) (Moskva, 1930), 3: 386.

10. The kidney disorder that M. Bulgakov had inherited from his father got progressively worse as he grew older, and eventually brought about his early death.

11. He actually turned down three earlier propositions by Kuza to write stage adaptations of Zola's *Nana*, Maupassant's *Bel-Ami*, and Balzac's *Eugenie Grandet*. Although hard-pressed for money, he needed the right material, which did not present itself until the suggestion to work on Cervantes's *Don Quixote* came along.

12. An abridged version of the novel, kept safe through the years by Bulgakov's third wife, Yelena Sergeevna, the prototype for Margarita, was published first in the literary journal *Moskva* in 1966. The full text came to light seven years later, in 1973.

13. For a fuller account of Bulgakov's life and work, see our introduction to *Don Quixote. A Dramatic Adaptation* by Mikhail Bulgakov, trans. Margarita Marinova (New York: MLA, 2014), especially ix–xxii.

14. Bakhtin, *The Dialogic Imagination*, 422.

15. O. Essipova, "Russkii Don Kikhot i M. Bulgakov" (The Russian Don Quixote and Bulgakov) *Bulgakovskii sbornik, III: Meterialy po istorii russkoi literatury XX veka* (Tallin, 1998), 23.

16. Manuel Durán and Fay R. Rogg, *Fighting Windmills. Encounters with Don Quixote* (New Haven, CT: Yale University Press, 2006), 180.

17. Ivan Turgenev, "Hamlet and Don Quixote," trans. Moshe Spiegel, *Chicago Review* 17.4 (1965), 93.

18. Quoted in Essipova, 24. Unless otherwise noted, all translations from Russian are by Margarita Marinova.

19. He based his version of Don Quixote on one of Russia's leading intellectuals at the time, the writer and populist Vladimir Korolenko. See Bagno 178 and Yurii Aikhenval'd, *Don Kikhot na russkoi pochve* (Moskva: Gendal'f, 1996), 95–99, 111.

20. Quoted in Bagno, 177.

21. Turkevich, 196.

22. Aikhenval'd, 65.

23. A. B. Lunacharskii, *Osvobozhdennyi Don Kihkot* (Moskva, 1922), 144.

24. Bagno, 179.

25. Quoted in Aikhenval'd, 195.

26. Unlike Cervantes's Alonso Quixano, who has to die because he doesn't like the reality he is now able to see for what it is, Chulkov's Don Quixote is actually enamored by the beauty of what he is awakened to. Thus, his sudden demise is much more tragic because his revelation brings him the true happiness he has always pursued in life.

27. Quoted in Aikhenval'd, 200.

28. Many scholars have commented on the radical theatricality of Cervantes's novel. See, for example, Verónica Azcue Castillón, "La disputa del baceyelmo y 'El retablo de las maravillas': sobre el carácter dramático de los capítulos 44 y 45 de la primera parte de *Don Quijote*," *Cervantes* 22.1 (2002), 71–81; Jay Farness, "Festive Theater, Restive Narrative in Don Quixote, Part 1," *PMLA* 107.1 (1992), 105–19; Karen Marie Kraft, "Arte es vida: El uso de figura en el retablo de Maese Pedro," *Gaceta Hispánica de Madrid* 1, 2003, 1–11; Jill Syverson-Stork, *Theatrical Aspects of the Novel: A Study of Don Quixote* (Valencia: Albatros Ediciones, 1986); Francisco Vivar, "Las bodas de Camacho y la sociedad del espectáculo," *Cervantes* 22.1 (2002), 83–109.

29. George Haley, "The Narrator in Don Quijote: Maese Pedro's Puppet Show," *MLN* 80.2 (1965), 163.

30. Bruce R. Burningham, "Jongleuresque Dialogue, Radical Theatricality, and Maese Pedro's Puppet Show," *Cervantes: Bulletin of the Cervantes Society of America* 23.1 (2003), 165–96.

31. Burningham rightfully notes that none of the theatrical events in *Don Quixote* take place in formal theaters, which require patronage, finance, infrastructure, and civil government. Informal, quotidian theatrical events, like the puppet show at the inn, come about because of a short-lived contract between entertainer and audience that leads to an event outside of socially sanctioned theatrical spaces.

32. Mary Malcolm Gaylord, "Pulling Strings with Master Peter's Puppets: Fiction and History in *Don Quijote*," *Cervantes: Bulletin of the Cervantes Society of America* 18.2 (1998), 117–47.

33. Bulgakov, *Don Quixote: A Dramatic Adaptation*, 69.

34. Miguel de Cervantes, *Don Quijote de la Mancha* (Barcelona: Editorial Planeta, S.A., 2004), 617–18.

35. Miguel de Cervantes, Burton Raffel, and Diana A. Wilson, *Don Quijote: A New Translation Backgrounds and Contexts, Criticism* (New York: W.W. Norton, 1999), 745.

36. Bulgakov, 115.

37. M. M. Bakhtin, *The Dialogic Imagination: Four Essays*, ed. Michael Holquist, trans. Caryl Emerson and Michael Holquist (Austin: University of Texas Press, 1981), 409.

16

A Russian Lancelot and His Don Quixote

Victor Fet

Evgeny Shwartz (Евгений Шварц, 1896–1958) has never seen the arid plains of Spain, but his last work was a Russian *Don Quixote*—a screenplay for Grigori Kozintsev's 1956 film, written and filmed at the brief time of hope in the tragic recurrent Russian history.

The choice of this writer for *Don Quixote* to be reincarnated and reaccentuated on screen with a Russian accent was fortunate: Shwartz was one of our best Russian re-accentuators. A survivor of the Western civilization, Shwartz conveyed its moral values, too fundamental to be called myths or archetypes.

For his play *The Shadow* (1940), loosely based on Adelbert von Chamisso and Hans Christian Andersen stories, Shwarts took an epigraph from Andersen: "Someone else's story has become so much a part of my own flesh and blood that I remade it and only then released it to go its own way in the world."

Shwarts's *Don Quixote* screenplay is discussed in this volume by Slav Gratchev.[1] Here, I will talk in detail about another, earlier Shwartz's reaccentuation of European legends that provides a bridge to his *Don Quixote* and to the European tradition.

It is *The Dragon* (1944), an original play, central in Shwarts's work.[2]

Its protagonist is called simply "Lancelot, a knight-errant."

The Dragon was written under the most severe circumstances.

In June 1941, Hitler attacked his ally, and the Soviet Army drew back, leaving millions of war prisoners. Huge areas, including all of Ukraine, fell under the advancing Nazis, and the tragic nine-hundred-day siege of Leningrad began.

Shwartz volunteered to be drafted into the Army but was dismissed (he was fifty), and his hands shook so uncontrollably that he could not hold a gun! He could still hold his pen, and he joined an anti-Nazi propaganda team on the Leningrad radio, which kept broadcasting heroically through the siege.

We will never know how many Leningrad citizens died during the siege from hunger and cold; estimates are over one million. Shwartz and his family were slowly dying, too. Reluctantly, he agreed to escape from the dying city using a narrow window open to a few.

Shwartz and his family were evacuated from Leningrad's siege to faraway Tajikistan in Central Asia. There, in the darkest hour of human history, would Shwartz write his play *The Dragon*.

The Dragon is not a direct retelling of a literary prototype—but a completely original, intentionally European story by a Russian author.

This light, sad, deep, and witty play was written in 1942–1944 in Stalinabad; "abad" means "city" in Arabic, combining the ancient toponymy with a new tyrant's name. The city is now Dushanbe, the capital of an "independent," post-Communist Tajikistan, the high Pamir Mountains looming around it.

Shwartz carefully described for us tyranny's inner workings, obviously thinking of Hitler as his Dragon. It seems incredible for us today that he most likely did not realize that he also described Stalin.

Shwartz's Lancelot is not an Arthurian knight, not even a *Connecticut Yankee* version; there is no king to serve or queen to love or Grail to find. The *Don Quixote* story, however, shines through the canvas of this play, which becomes a re-accentuation of a quintessential myth about a fearless deliverer who single-handedly will slay the Dragon.

Lancelot comes to a Western European, Germanic town where a Dragon rules for four hundred years. The town citizens are content to pay the tribute (a maiden per year plus food supplies) and are used to having their own Dragon who protects them.

In a characteristic dialogue, the newcomer is told that "when our town was threatened by cholera, the municipal physician asked him [the Dragon] to breathe fire on the lake and set it a-boiling. The whole town drank boiled water and was saved from the epidemics" (translated here and below by Laurence Senelick).

"Believe me," says Charlemagne, the Keeper of the Public Records, "the only way to be free and clear of dragons is to have one of your own."

We are shown the monster who likes to don a human guise (he has three different personae, by the number of his heads). One definitely recognizes one of these images described in author's notes as a middle-aged, rough military type with blonde, close-cropped hair; rather Teutonic in nature, although not a portrait of Hitler.

As Lancelot challenges the Dragon, their dialogue is very clear:

Dragon: Your name is Lancelot?

Lancelot: Yes.

Dragon: Any descendant of the famous knight errant named Lancelot?

Lancelot: We're distantly related.

Dragon: I accept your challenge. Knights errant count as gypsies. You all have to be exterminated.

The Dragon has long ago exterminated all gypsies (read also Jews), who—as the citizens are taught at school—are "vagrants by nature, it's in their blood. They're enemies of the law and order . . . Their songs are unmanly and their ideas seditious. . . . They worm their way in everywhere. Nowadays we're quite purified of them, but no more than a hundred years ago anyone with dark hair had to prove he had no gypsy blood."

In a series of well-crafted episodes preparing him for the fight, Lancelot faces unexpected assistance from his helpers and an expected betrayal by the servile town authorities. The corrupt Mayor and his son Henry (in the Russian original Shwartz uses Germanic Burgmeister and Heinrich) sabotage the knight's efforts. At the same time, a submissive Elsa, an intended Dragon victim, who is given a poisoned dagger by the Dragon, cannot bring herself to kill the knight.

Shwartz, unlike Cervantes, writes a true legend, so he can and will employ magic. Thus, in a folkloric fashion, Lancelot gets help from local craftsmen who clandestinely equip him with a magic sword and shield, a cap of invisibility, and a flying carpet to fight the Dragon in the air.

And thus Lancelot defeats the Dragon. This, however, does not immediately win him the hearts of the townsfolk, which are corrupted by the generations of life under the Dragon and his protection.

The dying Dragon tells Lancelot about the legacy he leaves behind—the "charred" human souls. "Human souls, dear boy, are very resilient. Chop the body in half—a man kicks the bucket. But chop up the soul—he just knuckles under . . . Bed-wetting souls, money-grubbing souls, charred souls, dead souls." The last term, of course, comes directly from the immortal work by Nikolai Gogol, a century earlier.

Wounded in the battle, Lancelot leaves the city. When in a year he returns, healed, he finds the former Mayor in charge, having taken credit for slaying the Dragon—and Elsa, the girl who was delivered from the Dragon, preparing to wed the new dictator.

The Mayor is deposed but there is no folkloric happy ending. The play is open-ended: Lancelot and Elsa depart, and the townfolk are left to their own designs.

In a touching, very Shwartzian detail, one of Lancelot's helpers provides him with an unnamed musical instrument, an embodiment of poetry. It has no magic it plays by itself, and helps the knight to endure the loneliness in his battle. When Lancelot falls wounded, he talks to this instrument and, the playwright remarks, "the instrument replies."

Other playful and reverent markers are deployed that take us directly to the Don Quixote story. One of such markers is the unmistakable *barber's basin* (Russ., *tazik tsiryul'nika*), which the City Council "issues" for Lancelot in lieu of a helmet.

This "Mambrino's helmet" image of Cervantes (Part I, chapter XXI) is easily recognizable to a Russian reader. However, in a recent English translation, I think, the reference to that famous image was lost:

> *The First Servant gives Lancelot a brass cuspidor with a leather chinstrap attached.*
>
> *Lancelot:* This is a spittoon.
>
> *Mayor:* True, but it's been commissioned to serve as your helmet. And this metal ashtray has been conscripted as your shield. . . .

There is no arm-bearer, and not even a horse; this Lancelot travels alone and on foot. But there are two talking animal helpers right from the Grimm Brothers: a wise Cat and a stubborn Donkey in whom we gladly recognize a cousin of Sancho's mount. This Donkey will carry the wounded Lancelot away to the Black Mountains where the knight will recover to come back.

The most important Quixotic feature of *The Dragon* is Lancelot's unending quest: not just to kill the Dragon but to help the town citizens to eradicate the monster's legacy. This proves not to be easy. Evgeny Shwartz's unmistakable dialogue, sparse, careful, and humorous, has matured by that time. We will recognize his cadence a decade later in his *Don Quixote* screenplay, which should be compared to *The Dragon* in any analysis.

The play's protagonist is described as a "professional knight-errant." He is only known by his first name that comes from the chivalry tradition. Sir Lancelot du Lac of the Arthurian cycle, so dear to Don Quixote, first appeared in the late twelfth-century poem by Chrétien de Troyes, *Lancelot, the Knight of the Cart.*

That Lancelot is mentioned already in chapter 2 of Cervantes's novel; in chapter 13, in reply to señor Vivaldo, who "asked him what he meant by 'knights errant'," Don Quixote recites a poem:

> Oh, never surely was there a knight
> So served by hand of dame,
> As served was he, Sir Lancelot
> When from Britain he came.

Then, Don Quixote comments, famously, "The same things that these knights of old that I've mentioned professed, I also profess. Thus, I travel about this wilderness and these unpopulated areas seeking adventures, and I'm committed to offering my arm and my person in any perilous adventure that comes my way to help the weak and needy."

Very reminiscent of these words, Lancelot in Shwarts's play explains:

> Me and few others. We are observant, buoyant people. . . . We interfere in other people's business. We help those who must be helped. And we exterminate those who must be exterminated. . . . Thrice have I been mortally wounded, and each time by those whom I helped against their will. Therefore, even if you don't ask it, I shall challenge the Dragon to combat!

Sir Lancelot du Lac was never a dragon-slayer. Shwartz keeps two of his Lancelot's other names to the end of the play: only in act 3 we learn that Lancelot is "alias Saint George, alias Perseus the Barefoot—he's got a different moniker for every country." Both Perseus and Saint George are famous monster-slayers connected with a sacrificial virgin. Andromeda in Perseus's pagan myth was delivered from a sea monster.

On seeing an image of Saint George, Don Quixote explains to Sancho: "*Este caballero fue uno de los mejores andantes que tuvo la milicia divina: llamóse don San Jorge, y fue además defendedor de doncellas.* ("That knight was one of the best knights-errant the army of heaven ever owned; he was called Don Saint George, and he was moreover a defender of maidens.") (*DQ*, Part II, chapter 58).

Therefore, Shwartz's Lancelot is equated in the play with the most iconic dragon-slayer of Western civilization, Saint George. The myth of Saint George and the dragon is Eastern Orthodox in origin, known in icons from tenth- and eleventh-century Cappadocia and Georgia, and from Russian miniatures in the ninth century. Based on a Christian martyr (according to hagiography, killed in 303 CE under Emperor Diocletian in Cappadocia), as Saint George the Victorious (Russ., *Sviatoi Georgy Pobedonosets*), he has been also a patron saint of Moscow Princedom (and later the whole of Russia) since the fourteenth and fifteenth centuries. The serpent he slays is traditionally depicted with a single head, not three as in Shwartz's play.

The Order of Saint George was the highest purely military decoration in Russia. Today, as the post-Soviet Russia picks and chooses its hybrid heraldry, Saint George again is seen (although sans his halo) on its coat of arms, military decorations, and even coins. He looks exactly as Cervantes described him, "*puesto a caballo, con una serpiente enroscada a los pies y la lanza atravesada por la boca, con la fiereza que suele pintarse*" (on horseback with a serpent writhing at his feet and the lance thrust down its throat with all that fierceness that is usually depicted). The sacrificial virgin is traditionally omitted on this imagery.

It is not immediately obvious for a modern reader that the dragon-slaying episode in the Christian tradition usually refers to a *posthumous* miracle by Saint George, who comes down from heaven as a warrior of *la milicia divina*. In Don Quixote's image series, Saint George is followed by Saint Martin, Saint James (San Diego), and Saint Paul.

However, there are other versions of an ancient dragon-slayer story, where a young Saint George performs the delivery in his lifetime before becoming a martyr. Such is a Russian popular hagiography *Chudo Georgiya o zmie* [*Saint George and the Dragon Miracle*] translated in the eleventh century from the Greek, and further folklore and art based on it.[3] There, Saint George appears as a son of Saint Sophia, and the maiden he delivers has the name Elizaveta or Elisava—very close to Shwartz's Elsa! Of course, Elsa is a common name in European fairy tales, including Andersen (*The Wild Swans*); it is also name of a princess in Shwarts's *The Snow Queen* (1938).

In Russian folklore, Saint George was fused with pagan dragon-slayers. Russian epic legends (*byliny*) feature Dobrynya Nikitich, a knight (*bogatyr'*) who slays the dragon named Zmei Gorynych (a three-headed, fire-breathing species, exactly as in Shwartz's play). These epics, similar to the Arthurian cycle, date to medieval time and their events are placed at the court of the historical Prince Vladimir the Great (980–1015), who baptized Russia.

It should have taken some courage to mention Saint George in Stalin's atheist Russia in 1943—but let us not forget that as Stalin began to overcome Hitler at that time at Stalingrad, he sought patriotic help from the long-prosecuted Russian Orthodox Church.

The Dragon was written and immediately accepted for the Leningrad Comedy Theatre headed by Shwartz's friend, the famous director Nikolai Akimov, who successfully staged his pre-war play *The Shadow*. The play was rehearsed already over 1943 in Stalinabad, where the troupe was evacuated. It was performed once in Moscow, August 4, 1944—and immediately banned for performance by the central Moscow censorship. "Someone saw something in it," mysteriously said Akimov. Did the censors see more in it that a satire directed at the Nazi regime—as Shwartz himself, *quite sincerely and openly*, proclaimed? Was it another case, similar to that of Cervantes, when conscious intentions of the author are overcome by the inner force of the story?

Avril Pyman commented on *The Dragon* that "the very diversity of interpretations, all of which can be quite convincingly argued, discourages the interpretation of this play as an anti-fascist (or anti-Stalinist) 'pamphlet'. It is a parable of high seriousness, courageous spirit and great freshness of vision, written by a man, who, together with his whole nation, had just escaped destruction by a hair's breadth."[4]

I do not entirely agree: Shwartz, who just escaped with his family from the Leningrad siege, clearly intended and wrote an anti-Nazi satire, but under his marvelous pen it indeed became a parable for all ages. Also, if the play were written after the war, say, in 1945, it would be quite different, but Shwartz wrote it when the tides of war were just turning, and its outcome was not at all clear.

The most recent English translation of *The Dragon* is by Laurence Senelick (Tufts University), who also translated Gogol's *Inspector General* and a stage version of *Dead Souls*. Professor Senelick writes, "Shwartz uses the eternal conflict of good and evil to unmask the disguises power dons to perpetuate itself. The play's ending is far from the rosy optimism prescribed by Socialist Realism. One critic even viewed the townspeople as reincarnations of Gogol's dead souls. Certainly, the play suggests that human beings get the leaders they deserve." It certainly does that, but without cynicism; Shwartz was wise enough to supply us with tormenting hope. It shines at times, mostly through his magic animal helpers and unmistakable sad humor.

Akimov renewed the play in 1962 after the dramatist's death, but its stage life again was brief. Also in 1962 it was staged by Mark Zakharov in the Student Theatre of Moscow State University; it was banned, but the theater ran seventeen performances. *The Dragon* was not commonly played on the Soviet stage in the 1960s–1970s.

Recently, Seth Wilson addressed *The Dragon* as "Anti-Stalinist Theatre for the youth."[5] It is hard to agree with this labeling. "Through the fairytale form," writes Wilson, "Shwartz is able to cloak criticisms he made of a regime and also to create a play that will entertain a young audience." First, *The Dragon*, as well as *The Naked King* and *The Shadow*, is not a children's play: far from that. It might be seen as such today, but Shwartz, early on, created his own genre, aimed primarily at the adults! Second, yes, the play is political—but it was definitely written as an anti-Nazi pamphlet.

"Cloaking criticisms of a regime" would fit the 1960s–1970s semi-dissident legal theater (such as Grigory Gorin's, who in 1988 co-authored a screenplay for a film version of *The Dragon*)—but this is not applicable to the murderous 1930s–1940s. Wilson writes further, "Shwarts employs . . . convention of a fairy-tale form to criticize a totalitarian government." In 1944?! No; this is a very naïve interpretation. It was unimaginable for Shwartz, even in a veiled form, as Wilson optimistically assumes, to "criticize Stalin's regime" consciously, especially in a play intended for stage. Hundreds perished from Shwartz's closest circle. His friend Oleinikov was killed for no offense. His friend Zabolotsky at that very time suffered in the Gulag. Shwartz was not suicidal.

Wilson also overestimates the return of *The Dragon* on stage in post-Stalin years. It hardly can be said that the play "enjoyed a successful life in production all over the country"—definitely not until the late 1980s. Although it was several times published in Shwartz's books along with other plays, the play's performance was not welcomed by the multi-layered Soviet censorship; the allusions ran too close.

In 1965, a posthumous "open letter" to Shwartz, his friend Veniamin Kaverin wrote: "Your expressions have passed into our language and, repeating after Lancelot, 'Do you think it is so easy to love people?', we are sometimes forced to agree that it is difficult indeed. . . . It was no time for you to die when there was so much left to do, and if, most unjustly, this 'greatest of madnesses' has nevertheless come to pass, it means that you knew or guessed that your fairy-tales would help us to live, to live on, untiring in the struggle, until the Golden Age."[6]

We find an interesting page in Grigori Kozintsev's 1964 diaries[7] where the famous director imagined how he would film *The Dragon*—soon after his *Don Quixote* fame. His Dragon rules and flies over the entire humankind, choosing his victims, at the verge of the Great War.

Kozintsev jotted in a vertiginous shorthand:

> *The Dragon.*
> To shoot from a diving plane.
> To add the claws. A scaly tail. [. . .]
> The Dragon flies over the minarets of Samarkand and over the skyscrapers. Maternity wards. Cemeteries. An insane asylum.
> He flies over a desert; camels are running. Flies over a theatre which plays *Three Sisters* or *Swan Lake*. Over the Eiffel Tower and Westminster Abbey, over the Kizhi [the famous wooden church in Northern Russia.—VF]. A shadow of the Dragon in flight.
> Time: the early twentieth century, before automobiles. People walking dachshunds. A tandem bicycle. [. . .] An idyll under the Dragon's rule.
> Shwartz's lyric philosophy, which I have not yet seen in his plays performed onstage. (transl. V. Fet)

The *perestroika* reform years in Russia immediately yielded a popular, uneven film version, *To Kill a Dragon* (1988) by Mark Zakharov (screenplay by Grigory Gorin and Mark Zakharov), with a great Oleg Yankovsky as the Dragon and, in my opinion, less convincing Alexander Abdulov as Lancelot. The treacherous Mayor was played by Evgeny Leonov, one of the best Russian film and stage actors. The inner energy and inherent kindness of Shwartz's work was not fully realized in Zakharov's grim cinematic version. Especially Elsa in this version is not Shwartz's pensive but strong heroine but a vulgar type for whom betrayal appears natural. The film's open finale is very different from that of the play—the Dragon comes back, possibly reincarnated, to play with a new generation of local children.

I would like now to connect a few dots across important episodes of Evgeny Shwartz's life—to track the pursuits of this Russian knight-errant that shed light on the origin of his late writings. This information is gleaned from numerous sources, memoirs, and diaries. Shwartz 's extremely detailed diaries as well as brilliant memoirs of his childhood and youth were published in 1999 as a part of his most complete four-volume works.[8] Virtually none of this biographic information exists in English.

His friends recalled that Shwartz's hands were always shaking: he suffered from an uncontrollable tremor. The writer himself mentions it half-jokingly in his memoirs. This nervous tremor is reflected in his uneven, large handwriting. Everyone was told that the tremor was due to a concussion he suffered as a young man during the Civil War.

This was true, but there was a deadly secret in Shwartz's life: in this bloodiest conflagration of the Russian history, he fought on the side that lost. Only recently the truth came out that Shwartz served in the Volunteer (White) Army against the Communists. In 1918, Shwartz was one of those who went with General Kornilov on his famous Ice March ("Ledovyi pokhod") from Rostov to Kuban, which signified the birth of the White Army. He suffered his heavy concussion during the battle for Yekaterinodar in early April 1918, the first large battle of the Russian Civil War.

This means that for the rest of his life Shwartz lived under a Damocles's sword, as he had to hide his military past. In Stalin's era, as late as in the early 1950s, such a discovery would mean an immediate arrest and a possible death in the labor camp. People died for a much lesser blemish in their biographies, or without any. How does one exist with such a load, knowing that they can be discovered and denounced at any moment? It is hard to imagine; but maybe we can feel this constant, daily risk and defiance in the light, fearless tone of Evgeny Shwartz for the next forty years of his life in the Soviet Russia—his "senseless joy of being," as he put it in one of his poems.

In 1921, immediately after the Russian Civil War, another very important episode in young Shwartz's life defined his future and transferred him from the provinces, where he grew up, to Petrograd—earlier, the Imperial capital of Saint Petersburg, soon to be renamed Leningrad.

With his wife and other young friends, Shwartz was part of a small theater troupe. The young actors performed *Gondla*, a play by Nikolai Gumilev (1886–1921), one of the best Russian poets of the so-called Silver Age, a fearless explorer of Africa, and a volunteer fighter in World War I. It is fitting to mention here that Gumilev was twice awarded the Cross of Saint George that was given for "undaunted courage" to the soldiers and NCOs:

Но Святой Георгий тронул дважды
Пулею нетронутую грудь

(But St. George touched twice
the chest touched by no bullet).
(Gumliev, The Memory," 1921)

The poet survived the war, but was shot by the Communist government in August 1921, at the age of only thirty-five.

Gumilev was a mentor to many younger poets who maintained professional literary standards through the most miserable years of Communist terror and hunger in Petrograd of 1918–1920. In spring 1921, Gumilev traveled through the provincial Rostov-on-Don and saw his *Gondla* performed—the first time this play was ever staged. The grateful poet invited the young actors to move to the northern capital. They arrived in fall 1921 to learn that their benefactor Gumilev was dead. The young troupe still managed to perform *Gondla* in Petrograd.

In this play, in cold Iceland, a gentle Irish prince of the ninth century faced the wild, pagan Norsemen, armed only by his spirit against the sword. Prince Gondla's trace is easily seen in Shwarts's later wonderful stage retellings of Hans Christian Andersen.

The lessons of Gumilev, another veritable Don Quixote of Russian poetry, were well learned by Evgeny Shwartz, and the 1921 appearance of the older poet in Rostov was nothing short of a blessing and an initiation into the order of knights-errant by that *uno de los mejores andantes*.

We fast-forward through twenty years of the Soviet regime—Stalin's era. As many young people of his time, Shwartz apparently was a sincere supporter of the Communist idea. He slowly evolves as a writer; his first, still very uneven children's plays appear on the Leningrad stage in the early 1930s. Only later he acquired his inimitable voice and found his true niche as a poetic re-accentuator of European literature, and especially fairy tales.

A humorous, jovial young Shwartz was among a brilliant group of children's writers of the 1920s, the time of New Economic Policy and a liomitede, short-lived freedom for the intellectuals. His closest friends, poets Daniil Kharms, Nikolai Oleinikov, and Alexander Vvedensky, of the Real Art Group (Oberiu), all would be killed by the Stalin regime as the "enemies of the people."

Shwartz watched helplessly as Stalin's tectonic meat-grinder consumed his friends, the most talented and outspoken, often politically quite harmless. At the same time, we know that Shwartz did not denounce Oleinikov in public and protested when asked to do so. He did not hide or evade; very few had this bravery and survived. One cannot call Shwartz mad, but his carelessness was truly Quixotic. His younger friend Nikolai Zabolotsky (1903–1958), one of the deepest philosopher poets of the twentieth century, would survive after years in labor camps—where wardens would watch specifically so Zabolotsky would not *write* any poetry. Gone were the years of Dostoevsky, who could write in his Siberian exile! Shwartz and his second wife would help Zabolotsky's family and raise his daughter. Zabolotsky would not write much after he was released, along with thousands of other survivors when Khrushchev denounced Stalin.

Miraculously, this is where Shwartz's literary talent came to its fullest fruition, as if a fearless hidalgo channeled evil forces of a Freston into his creative energy. Shwartz, who survived unharmed, created a series of plays that are brilliant philosophical satires. He re-accentuated life with joy in a dead vacuum that was Soviet Russia of the late 1930s, in *The Shadow* (1940) and then *The Dragon*.

In addition to a rich supply of Russian folklore, there had been a steady influx of literary tales coming from the West. In the nineteenth century, most of E. T. A. Hoffmann's and H. C. Andersen's works were translated into Russian and reaccentuated into the Russian literary tradition, and even famous ballets such as *The Nutcracker*.

When we as children in 1960s Russia watched or read his plays, it was Evgeny Shwartz who reestablished a moral universe anew. His reaccentuations were the life-sustaining stories of my childhood. Shwartz provided simple, written moral rules not easily found in the fallout ashes of the civilization left over under the Communist dictatorship.

His stage characters in *The Naked King* (1934), *The Snow Queen* (1939), *The Shadow* (1940), *The Dragon* (1944), and *The Ordinary Miracle* (1956), told us that in the end, goodness and poetry will prevail and evil will be defeated. In Shwartz's version of *The Snow Queen*, his Snow Queen was my quintessential image of soulless tyranny and corrupting power; his brave Gerda was my image of love and loyalty, and his young, Quixotic Storyteller—the author's alter ego—was my ideal of friendship and wisdom.

The Dragon has been translated to some foreign languages and won audiences across the world. A new English translation by Laurence Senelick appeared in 2012.

The back cover of Senelick's translation quotes Nikolai Akimov, who said in 1961, on rehearsing his first, short-lived production of *The Dragon*:

> I propose to stage *The Dragon* about human dignity. The kingdom of the Dragon left behind corrupt souls, wherein dragonets dwell. To kill the dragon dwelling inside us is Shwarts's concept. One must extirpate the evil the dragon leaves behind him. . . . We will not allude to the past, because

that's cheap and dissipates the theme, which is important and meant for "tomorrow." The Dragon will not have a Georgian accent.

Then, eight years after Stalin's death, it seemed that the dead dictator would not affect "tomorrow" if his accent would be forgotten.

One of the most famous quotes from the play is applicable to all dictatorships of all times:

Henry: I am free of any personal responsibility. I was instructed to do it.

Lancelot: Everyone was instructed, but why did you have to go to the head of the class, you swine?

In one of his few poems, written in the darkest years of the Dragon's rule (1946–1947), Evgeny Shwarts says:

> The Lord blessed me to go,
> To walk on without thinking about the goal,
> He blessed me to sing in my way
> To make my companions happier.
> I go, I walk on, I do not look around
> So I won't violate God's will,
> So I won't howl as a wolf instead of singing,
> So my heart won't stop beating from fear.
> I am a man. And even a nightingale,
> Its eyes tightly shut, sings in its wilderness. (transl. V. Fet)

In the play finale, the Gardener tells Lancelot: "You know, when you think about it, people really and truly, maybe, when all's said and done, require very careful tending."

The Dragon was written more than seventy years ago. Today, as dragons and dragonets of all kinds and accents breed free, human dignity and its careful tending are increasingly elusive concepts—but, hopefully, Don Quixote's heavenly warriors, *la milicia divina*, still fight for tomorrow.

NOTES

1. Slav N. Gratchev, "The art of re-accentuation: *Don Quixote* by Grigori Kozintsev," chapter 10, this book.

2. Evgeny Shwarts, *The Dragon*, trans. Laurence Senelick (New York: Broadway Play Publishing, Inc.), 2012.

3. Vladimir Ya Propp, "Zmeeborstvo Georgiya v svete fol'klora (Saint George's dragon-slaying in the light of folklore)," in *Fol'klor i etnografiya Russkogo Severa* (Folklore and Ethnography of the Russian North), 190–208 (Leningrad: Nauka, 1973) (in Russian).

4. Avril Pyman, Introduction and notes to *Three plays*, by Yevgeniy Shvarts (Oxford: Pergamon Press, 1972).

5. Seth Wilson, "Fairy Tale of Subversion? Evgeny Shvarts's 'The Dragon' as Anti-Stalinist Theatre for the Youth," *Theatre Symposium, Vol. 23: Theatre and youth*, ed. David S. Thompson and Becky K. Becker, 55–66 (Tuscaloosa: University of Alabama, 2015).

6. Veniamin B. Kaverin, "Yevgeniyu Shvartsu," Sobranie Sochineniy (The Collected Works), Moscow: Izdatel'stvo Khudozhestvennoi Literatury, 1966, vol. 6, 604–6 (in Russian). English translation after Pyman, "Introduction."

7. Grigori M. Kozintsev, "Iz knigi 'Glubokii ekran'" (From the book *The Deep Screen*), in Zhitie skazochnika (A Life of a Storyteller), ed. Lyudmila V. Polikovskaya and Evgeny M. Binevich, 286–90 (Moscow: Knizhnaya palata, 1991) (in Russian).

8. Evgeny Shwarts, Bessmyslennaya radost' bytiya (A senseless joy of being, Moscow: Korona-print, 1999 (in Russian). Evgeny Shwarts, Pozvonki proshedshikh dnei (The vertebrae of the days past), Moscow: Korona-print, 1999 (in Russian). Evgeny Shwarts, Predchuvstvie schastya (A foreboding of happiness), Moscow: Korona-print, 1999 (in Russian). Evgeny Shwarts, ". . . ya budu pisatelem" (". . . I will be a writer"), Moscow: Korona-print, 1999 (in Russian).

VI

DON QUIXOTE
IN THE NEW WORLD

17

The Visionary's Quixote: What Does Quixote Mean for Businesspeople?

Roy H. Williams

I am an ad writer, mostly for radio and television, and I am enchanted with Don Quixote. Peter O'Toole introduced me to him in 1972.[1] But the Quixote I met wasn't the Quixote of Cervantes's book. It was the Quixote of *Man of La Mancha*.

A story will adapt itself not only to a generation but to a narrow cohort within that generation as well. In the words of John Steinbeck, "[A] story has as many versions as it has readers. Everyone takes what he wants or can from it and thus changes it to his measure."[2] Perhaps no story has ever been changed to fit the measure of its readers as much as *Don Quixote* has been changed to fit twenty-first-century businesspeople and entrepreneurs.

I took three approaches to determine how—and how strongly—the Quixote story resonates with both businesspeople and entrepreneurs; I invited comments from a large group of entrepreneurial people, I had my publisher and mentor survey over one thousand other people engaged in sales or general business, and I asked some business associates whose judgment I value. These results may not be statistically robust, yet they reveal the firm, multi-faceted hold that Quixote still exerts over the modern businessperson's mind. I unpack their responses below.

GETTING THE VIEWS OF QUIXOTIC "ACAD GRADS"

At the dawn of this millennium, I opened the Wizard Academy, a school[3] for imaginative, courageous, ambitious people. Our classroom tower rises, like a windmill without vanes, from a plateau nine hundred feet above Austin, Texas. From its rooftop "Star Deck," you can just about see the edge of the world. At dusk, shadowy words have been known to appear on the horizon in the Uncial script of ancient maps: "Here There Be Monsters."

Business owners, entrepreneurs, and artists journey to the Academy from all points of the compass to learn communication skills alongside scientists, scholars, and advertising professionals in intensive, multi-day classes. We refer to these people as "our brand of crazy." They are the Quixotes of our time.

On June 13, 2016, I issued this appeal[4] to all Wizard Academy graduates:

> When I was a boy, I wanted an older brother. Not just a year or two older, but six or eight or ten years older. I wanted to be able to ask him things and trust the motives behind his answers.
>
> Over the years, I've been lucky enough to accumulate seven older brothers who speak wisdom into my life. These brothers give me the benefit of all their experiences—their successes and their mistakes—and help me remember who I am.
>
> I've never told you this, but I like to think of myself as your older brother. I try to give you the benefit of my experiences, if indeed there is any benefit to be found.
>
> Today your brother needs a favor. Will you indulge me?
>
> I've always been proud and ashamed that I never went to college. So when a group of scholars—department heads of major universities, mostly—asked me to contribute a chapter to their book about what Don Quixote means to the average person in the 21st century, well, I jumped at the chance.
>
> And then I put off getting started. And now I need to get it done. That's where you come in. Will you write me a sentence or two or twenty about what Don Quixote represents to you?
>
> Every generation for the past 400 years has seen Don Quixote differently. How do you see him today? What do you take from the story? Who is Sancho Panza, and why does he matter? Who is Dulcinea, and what does she mean to you? And if you are familiar with any of the other characters and elements of the story, I'd love to hear your thoughts and interpretations of those as well.
>
> Your response can be as brief or as in-depth as you choose.
>
> Twenty different Cervantes scholars will each contribute a chapter to the book. I was the nineteenth person to receive an invitation, but at least I got invited. It means a lot to me.
>
> My chapter is supposed to be 5,000 words, so I need to hear from a lot of you. . . .
>
> Two of my older brothers, Ray Bard and Don Kuhl, have already contributed their thoughts and will definitely be represented in my chapter. I'd love to see your name alongside theirs.

Don Kuhl is the CEO of The Change Companies®, publishers of behavior modification curricula for several thousand rehab centers and the majority of our municipal jails and state and federal prisons. When a person lost in addiction or detained behind bars needs to change and see the world differently, our court system often seeks guidance from The Change Companies. This is what Don Kuhl had to say about Don Quixote:

> Around 6th grade, I read the first grown-up book of my life: *Don Quixote*. Blessed with naïveté and a limited vocabulary, I gave myself entirely to the adventure side of the novel, sidestepping all of the nuances and social commentary.
>
> It was as if I were another Sancho Panza, the plump and loyal laborer, buying into Quixote's chivalric ideals. In school, I would close my eyes and immediately become lost in a great quest. It beat Sister Mary Catherine's history class every time.
>
> It may have been the hangover from this book that has caused me to chase after so many windmills in my life. I uncovered all kinds of mischief in my early years before finally getting rescued. As I recall, Don Quixote was brought home on an ox cart by an empathetic priest and a barber. I was saved by a brilliant, gay English professor and a loving family.
>
> What is it about dreaming the impossible dream that continues to stay with me? Why, after a full night's rest, do I still awaken some mornings thinking my duty and destiny is to "defend the hopeless and destroy the wicked"? There may be something in common between my aging, robin's-egg-blue Chevy and Rocinante, the old barn nag Quixote rode into battle. And, even at my age, I keep trying to impress the Dulcineas of my world whenever they show up at a grocery store or crosswalk.
>
> I hope there will always be quixotic moments in my life. I hope I continue to gravitate toward people who follow their dreams and ideals and those who make positive differences in people's lives that could never have been imagined at the outset of their journey.
>
> Whenever I wake up a little sore or feel like I'm out of energy, I try to remember these words from *Don Quixote*: "he who's down one day can be up the next, unless he really wants to stay in bed . . ."
>
> Let's all continue to chase those impossible dreams.
> —Don Kuhl, CEO, The Change Companies

Below are some of the other replies I received in response to my appeal.

> I left my perfectly solid, stellar, successful career at IBM in 1988 after a decade of leading the world in New Account Sales for Big Blue . . . because of my "Impossible Dream." Of course I'm grateful to Joe Darion for the lyrics from *Man of La Mancha*. Don Quixote reminded me that my present Quest was dull and uninspiring and that I needed to revisit it. When I took Don's words to heart ("I will act as if the world were what I would have it to be, as if the ideal were real"), I was reminded that No Dream Is Impossible—including my own. I then wrote my first of three books, polished my speaking skills, and quit my job to become the person I am today.

Quixote reminded me that the opposite of courage is not cowardice. It's conformity. So I started zigging when everyone else was zagging. I haven't quite reached my unreachable star. In fact, I may never reach it. But along the way, Mr. Quixote has transformed my life with his philosophy. That's my story and I'm gonna stick with it.
—Jack Warkenthien, CEO, www.nextstep-solutions.com

At the core of *Don Quixote* is something that has been central to every generation of people since the day that book was written: . . . the drive to have a purpose and a meaning in our everyday lives. To strike out on a mission, a goal, a quest to accomplish, love, or put [things] right. It can come in ordinary circumstances. It can come in extraordinary circumstances. How we find happiness and accomplishment in our lives is captured in the story of Don Quixote. The windmills are scary but simple, and if we do not give up, quit, and hang our heads in shame but keep moving forward no matter how impossible it may seem, we will come to understand fullness in life and what it means to really embrace it.
—Bryan Nangle, technological innovator

I like the idea that Cervantes wrote the first novel and opened up the human imagination through the written word to the oral storytelling tradition that marks our species and has organized the structure of our brains. As a result, stories continue to inspire, captivate, and transform our lives long after the tellers have passed away. Stories are essential to a meaningful life.
  Don Quixote is a story about a man with a vision, inspired by a woman, supported by a loving companion, who sets out on a quest and refuses to give up his vision no matter what. It's a hero's journey of the highest order.
  Don Quixote may be called "crazy, delusional, and downright nuts," but thank God for this kind of crazy passion existing in the world. Without it, we would be a dull and lifeless species.
—Curtis Knecht, MFT, CPCC, forty years licensed by the state of California as a Marriage and Family Therapist, sixteen years certified as a professional CoActive Coach, and sixty-eight years as a soul-searching, truth-seeking son-of-a-bitch

Our current economic, social, and political situation teaches us a harsh lesson about the American Dream.
  The rising economic divide makes it difficult to find social mobility. According to Wikipedia, the US and UK have the lowest social mobility among comparable nations. Meanwhile, wealth and income disparity continue to widen. In spite of this, we continue to Dream the American Dream.
  This is who we are in America. We fight for what we believe in. We dare to expect—no, DEMAND—to be heard and be given a chance to succeed in life. Whether success is being who we want to be, having wealth, or building a great country to live in, we fight for our cause. In defiance of the status quo and in spite of pressure to sit down and behave, we rise up together and incite a new revolution—a new and greater country and way of life.

The American Dream is becoming Don Quixote's Impossible Dream. Yet we Americans keep leveling our lances at the dragons before us as we charge on defiantly. For we really believe in the dream and know deep in our hearts that although we may be charging a windmill, we can make a difference.
—Aaron Bono, Aranya Software Technologies, Inc.

Here's what Don Quixote means in my life:

- The conviction to tackle the impossible comes from within. The goals or dreams aren't always rational, but they're ours and they're critical to our well-being.
- Having a companion on the journey is essential, even when they don't always agree with you.
- Dreaming about your princess (or prince) along the way adds beauty, charm, and a spring to your step on the difficult path.
- When we lose the will or are too discouraged to continue tilting at windmills, we perish.

Long live Don Quixote!
—Joyce Eisenbraun, writer and marketer

I believe the centuries-old appeal Alonso Quijano holds in our hearts is that he speaks to a secret desire: that we too can be fearless enough to set out on an adventure of our own making.

Maybe it's a wish to be somebody other than who we've become. To have a do-over of sorts. To change our names and take on new personalities the way superheroes do.

Maybe it's to recapture our youth, when we embraced imagination. Knights are easily created when discarded materials become armor, cardboard boxes become castles, stick horses become steeds, girls become damsels in distress, and large objects become giants to overcome.

Maybe it's to impress that ever-elusive soulmate. To see only the very best and beautiful in those we love. To embrace a romance where love conquers all, even if it remains one-sided.

Maybe it's to pursue a noble cause and find a purpose for living. To prove that chivalry is not dead. To be the one who provides aid to the abandoned, sets the prisoner free, and protects the innocent.

Maybe it's to right wrongs. To recognize when it's time to turn the other cheek and when it's time to boldly speak. To recover what's been stolen. To ignore the ridiculers. To be the only sheriff in town: to make the laws, punish the offenders, and be the hero riding triumphantly off into the sunset.

Maybe it's a sense of comradeship with trusted friends who love us in spite of our many obvious faults and eccentricities. Who provide us balance. Who go along with our wacky schemes and dreams, even if it takes bribery to do so. Eventually they may even share the vision.

Maybe it's the bit of lunacy in each of us that says it's okay to live in a world we create. That life is what we make it, whether that's cynical, sappy, spontaneous, or superlative.

Maybe we're drawn so deeply to Don Quixote because we believe we too can dream the impossible, pursue the unpredictable, and love the unlovable.
—Cynthia Williamson, editor extraordinaire

I feel a connection to Don Quixote in that:
   I see the world from a different, brighter perspective than most all of those around me.
   I believe I am a hero.
   I have a mission.
   I am special.
   I will not be vanquished.
   I need a Sancho close by, for I need my story to be heard.
   I may be a little crazy—but to survive, you must be a little crazy.
—Rob "Robo" Hendrickson, creative director

You've probably noticed that, for the above quoted businesspeople, Quixote tends to symbolize the irrational optimism essential to every visionary entrepreneur. However, not everyone interprets Quixote this way, as we will see.

I have never identified strongly with the motif of the impossible dream. I am too reserved for that, I guess. (Although I am currently launching out into some uncharted waters!)
   For me, the defining metaphor in Don Quixote is Aldonza—and the Don's view of her. Every Aldonza is Dulcinea, whether they know it or not . . . and we are all Aldonza.
   Years ago I had the opportunity to visit Robert Schuller's Institute for Successful Church Leadership, a venue that at one time set the trajectory for many of the nation's most innovative church leaders. One of the images he used was that of Dulcinea. Schuller never met a person in whom he did not see Dulcinea, the image of God, planted deeply within each of us.
   I regret that Aldonza never encountered Don Quixote in the book. Sophia Loren had it much better.
—Carolyn B. Smith, communications director, University Carillon United Methodist Church (Orlando, Florida) and author of *Grown-Up Parenting: Conversations about Life with Adult Children*

Don Quixote represents both the importance and hazards of idealism. Tilting at windmills may mean fighting imaginary enemies. Or maybe it's fighting something that you can't defeat. But if an idealist, a Don Quixote, leads the charge, well, perhaps practical people get a little closer to their dream[s] than they otherwise would have.
   Don Quixote was idealistic but delusional. He did some good but he hurt others and himself needlessly. He was convinced he was right and so was determined to do whatever it took to achieve his goals. But his goals could not be achieved. Eventually he returned to his senses and gave up the cause.

Yesterday [June 12, 2016], an idealistic and delusional young man killed about 50 people and wounded another 50 or so [in Orlando]. Some of them probably will die in the coming days and months. Their families and friends and communities are devastated. That delusional young man was convinced he was right and so he was determined to do whatever it took to achieve his goals. He killed himself and many others in his quest. His goals will not be achieved.

—Laura Gordos, accounting and finance consultant

SURVEYING QUIXOTIC BUSINESSPEOPLE

My publisher, Ray Bard, helped me research how businesspeople see Quixote by surveying just over a thousand businesspeople[5] serving as "quote judges" for an upcoming book of quotes.[6] Below I have catalogued his questions and provided a tally of the responses.

Which of these is known as the first modern novel?

- *Hamlet*   4%
- *The Odyssey*   15%
- *Don Quixote*   50%
- *The Count of Monte Cristo*   7%
- *Moby Dick*   23%

Have you read *Don Quixote* from cover to cover?

- No   84%
- Yes   16%

I found this result fascinating. Less than one in six respondents had actually read the second-most-read book in history all the way through; yet most respondents knew its content and had strong views on its influence.

Who was Don Quixote's sidekick?

- I don't know Don Quixote   12%
- Pancho   23%
- Tonto   1%
- Sancho   58%
- El Cid   4%

About the lyrics to the song, "To dream the impossible dream, To fight the unbeatable foe, To bear with unbearable sorrow, And to run where the brave dare not go . . ." (Check as many as apply)

- I don't know the song   15%
- From the Broadway play, *Man of La Mancha*   65%
- Drawn from the book, Don Quixote   27%
- It's a wonderful, inspirational song   48%
- It's my favorite inspirational song   5%

Miguel de Cervantes died 400 years ago. Which other famous person died the same year?

- Christopher Columbus   9%
- William Shakespeare   73%
- Joan of Arc   5%
- Saint Augustine   4%
- Voltaire   8%

Do the lyrics and the Don Quixote story have any meaning for sales and business?

- No   27%
- Yes   73%

If Yes, please explain.

Most of the explanations offered in response to Bard's last question referred to the themes discussed above: pursing your dream, believing, perseverance, resilience, commitment, never giving up, positive attitude, vision, hope, and principle. However, the following answer sums up all the others:

> The story and song embody the American Dream. The hopes of every immigrant who steps off the boat with a few dollars in their pocket. The dream in the head—the courage in their heart—the will to keep moving toward their goal. It embodies the Entrepreneur's Dream much for the same reasons. And many salespersons are entrepreneurs and know it's their dream that really counts.

MORE VIEWS FROM PEOPLE WHO HAVE TILTED AT WINDMILLS

I asked other businesspeople—and business partners—whose perspective I value how Quixote remains relevant in the twenty-first century. Their responses are outlined below.

For me personally, Quixote represents seeing the world differently. Not as it is, not as we think it should be, not as we want it to be, but just seeing it differently. Kind of like being colorblind to certain hues. It's just the way we see it. No need to explain or define. This is not by choice, but simply because that's the way we see it, and reacting accordingly to our personal desires and drives. "The world according to me."
—Mike Jenkins, director of marketing, Rick Ball Ford-Lincoln

Don Quixote to me is someone without a full view of the forest, but who courageously charges ahead to battle the trees.
—Dan Terrien, Woodward Radio account executive

To me, Don Quixote represents the spirit of adventure in all of us. He is our right brain, our wanderlust, and the childlike guru that lives inside seeing what is possible, and what is ideal. Sancho Panza is our left brain, our logical-rational fool, who "knows" too much to see what could be. And Dulcinea is our dream, our fantasy, the object of our deepest desire, the drive behind our adventure, and the one we want to share the adventure with.
—Vi Wickam, Fiddle Tune a Day, www.vithefiddler.com

My furtive imagination was fostered and encouraged by my paternal grandmother. But somewhere, somehow, I became so left-brain-dominant that I became intolerant, rule-oriented, and incapable of seeing others in the light of the unique gifts that God had bestowed upon them. Thankfully, this time was relatively short and not catastrophic. The Dark Age, they called it.

Fast forward to age 19. Through a wonderful set of circumstances I met my Sancho, who initially appeared as my Dulcinea. Strange, huh? Initially unattainable and with no similar interests but a value set and dedication to her family above all else, I knew I had found my love and the mother of my children. She was a nurturer to many as she ran a day home out of our house for 15 years.

She has remained my faithful Sancho for over 30 years and accompanies me on dreams with the occasional "slap upside the head" when I'm not making sense.

We currently find ourselves working at an establishment nestled in Kananaskis Country in the Canadian Rockies, working together to be in service of others while they enjoy one of many wonders Mother Nature created.

The mission? Be a smile that can be reflected millions of times over. Like Don Quixote, we have no time for BS and naysayers. Let's get on with it!
—Hugh A. Benham

What *Don Quixote* has always meant to me is this: we exist for the quest, all the quests that are the adventure that is life. If there were no windmills, we would invent them, if only to tilt at them. Every quest seeks honor and defends beauty. And every quest is successful, because it fills that void that is no quest. In writing this, I have mounted my steed, armed my psyche, and attacked the demons. Who's next?

—Michael Zaplitny, investment attraction specialist at the Regina Regional Opportunities Commission, Regina, Saskatchewan, Canada

Optimism. Encouragement. Audacity. Determination. Freedom. Non-conformity. These are the resounding themes heard in *Don Quixote* by the North American businesspeople I questioned.

Don Quixote means a perspective on life that is defined by something greater than I am, not the culture that surrounds me. Quixote is best summarized by his statement to Sancho Panza, "It is easy to see that you are not used to this business of adventures." Quixote chose to see a common village girl, Aldonza, as a woman who had beauty beyond compare, his Dulcinea and his motivation. Even in his encounter with the evil shepherds, Quixote chose to see men who would change after simply being told.

I choose to live that life, and to see Don Quixote's world. My perspective, not my circumstances, dictates who I am.
—Shane Richardson, an account manager for a staffing company in Holden, Missouri

The Don Quixote I see most readily is the one at the end of *Man of La Mancha*, lying on his deathbed, surrounded by those four other characters. Each person sees him as noble and ridiculous . . . and he has affected each of them profoundly. "Quixotic" describes someone that is simultaneously noble of cause and ridiculous. Who dreams bigger than he can possibly achieve, and then sets out to make that dream real. Someone we both root for and ridicule. And that's what makes his story so magical.
—Tobias Beckwith, www.tobiasbeckwith.com

Maybe there never was a knight errant of the kind we read in Romances or want to see depicted in movies and that poor Mr. Alonso Quijano read in his chivalric romances. Perhaps there's simply no reality to those tales of the virtues of the knight errant at all. It's possible to believe that knights were nothing more than armored mercenaries, or rich-kid braggadocios jocks, who behaved as others of their kind generally do. Doesn't matter. Because Don Quixote was able to dream a reality capable of licking hollow the cynical and degenerate "real world" of Spain's late, declining empire.

Maybe he was mad, but he was also a giant among ants, because he believed in things worth believing in. And his mad antics put the "sanity" of the Spanish court to shame. What wouldn't we give to have a Don Quixote running amok among our plutocrat rulers here in this cynical, late declining empire of ours? And that, for me, is the essence of Don Quixote.
—Jeff Sexton, partner, Wizard of Ads Group

THE QUIXOTIC "REALITY FRAME"

Like all brilliant marketers, Jeff Sexton (quoted directly above) understands the difference between objective reality—which is beyond any of our abilities to alter—and subjective reality, perceptual reality, which depends entirely upon a customer's frame of mind and point of view. Changing that frame of mind and point of view is the goal of anyone who would persuade. Monumental events explode with energetic words, and great leaders are remembered for the things they say. A grand idea may carry within it the seed of change, but it takes powerful words to launch that idea skyward—words strong enough to carry the full weight of vision.

Likewise, the best ad campaigns and speeches begin with grand ideas and come alive with vivid words. This is the business I am in. Perhaps it is Machiavellian. Perhaps it is simply Quixotic. Oddly enough, most businesspeople have fabulous ideas; they simply don't have the words. Their wonderful ideas are sadly short-circuited when they cannot find the words to carry them skyward.

Most of us have seen Rodin's signature sculpture, *The Thinker*, and were intrigued, but how our interest increases when we hear Rodin speak of it: "What makes my Thinker think is that he thinks not only with the brain, with his knitted brow, his distended nostrils, and compressed lips, but with every muscle of his arms, back, and legs; with his clenched fist and gripping toes."[7] Seeing it now with our ears, we find Rodin's *Thinker* far more interesting than when we saw it with only our eyes.

Cervantes knew that words should be chosen for the emotional voltage they carry. Weak, predictable words cause grand ideas to appear so dull that they fade into the darkness of oblivion. But powerful words in unusual combinations illuminate the mind brightly.

Yes, words can be electric. If a sentence does not shock a little, it carries no emotional voltage. And unjolted hearers are unmoved hearers. Small plans have no power to inflame the heart. Words start wars and end them, create love and choke it, bring us to laughter and leave us in tears. Words cause men and women to willingly risk their lives, their fortunes, and their sacred honor. Our world, as we know it, revolves on the power of words. This is what Cervantes taught us in *Don Quixote*.

DREAMS WITH TANGIBLE RESULTS

In the truest spirit of Quixote, Wizard Academy revels in symbolic ritual. The thunderous music we play when students graduate[8] is known among alumni as the "Something Very Important Is About to Happen" music.

But just before it starts, we replay Honda's 2005 television commercial,[9] which shows a modern-day Quixote—clad in a racing jacket and crash helmet—setting out proudly from his travel trailer on a puny mini-bike. As he lip-synchs Andy Williams singing *The Impossible Dream*, he changes to a series of faster, stronger vintage Honda vehicles, finally ending up in a speedboat that leaps into the mist off the edge of Niagara Falls. After a shocked pause, we see "Quixote"—still singing—as he rises through that mist in the gondola of a hot-air balloon. The ad ends with our hero's arms outstretched expansively as he sings the climax, "to reach the unreachable stars!" So every "Acad Grad" gets a heroic, quixotic jolt before heading back into the world.

But what does Quixote mean to me? I composed my best answer to that question back in March 2005, when I sent the following e-mail to alumni announcing Chapel Dulcinea, the free wedding chapel that juts out over the cliff of our plateau:

She is Tom Sawyer's Becky Thatcher. She is the Little Red-Haired Girl of Charlie Brown. She is the sacred muse of Alonso Quijano, who in 1605 stepped into some rusty armor to become the immortal *Don Quixote de la Mancha*. In Cervantes' book we never meet Dulcinea. She exists only in Alonso's mind.

Believing himself to be a knight, and a peasant girl of his village to be the magnificent Princess Dulcinea, every deed, every journey, and every quest is made in her name. But the girl, Aldonza Lorenzo by name, is utterly unaware of these events, as Alonso never speaks to her and loves her only from afar. But his "Lady Dulcinea" plays a vital role in Alonso's life and her presence is felt throughout the book.

Outwardly, we laugh at the absurdity of a man jousting with windmills, thinking them to be giants. But inwardly, we crave his sense of mission and purpose, his dedication to a cause, his willingness to pay any price to achieve the honor of his beloved.

So who is the silly one? He, for seeing beyond what is, to serve a beauty that could be, should be, ought to be? Or me, for remaining trapped in a black-and-white world where little men hide behind technicalities?

The most celebrated writer in Spanish literature, Miguel de Cervantes, laid down his pen on April 23, 1616, and quietly passed away simultaneously with William Shakespeare, the most celebrated writer in English literature. In a single sunset, these two great voices were silenced.

Neither will ever be forgotten.

Shakespeare gave us *Romeo and Juliet*, a love story with a tragic ending, but Cervantes gave us *Don Quixote*, with its shimmering image of the feminine ideal. Others might look at Aldonza Lorenzo and see only an average woman of the village—strong, funny, and down-to-earth, but Don Quixote sees her differently: "Her name is Dulcinea, her kingdom, Toboso, which is in La Mancha, her condition must be that of princess, at the very least, for she is my queen and lady, and her beauty is supernatural, for in it one finds the reality of all the impossible." Don Quixote sees himself as her knight and champion, and Dulcinea as the most perfect woman on earth. Every groom is Don Quixote. And every bride, his Dulcinea.

Wizard Academy is proud to offer—as our gift to lovers worldwide—Chapel Dulcinea, a romantic open-air wedding chapel in Austin, Texas. Just as it doesn't cost money to fall in love, it doesn't cost money to be married at Chapel Dulcinea. And just like God, Chapel Dulcinea is always wide awake and ready for visitors.

Chapel Dulcinea provided a free, panoramic marriage venue for 984 couples in 2014. In 2015, it was 999. Perhaps this year we will unite a thousand happy couples in a chapel inspired by the chaste, rose-colored idealism of a knight-errant.

At the risk of stating the obvious, my entire avocation as the shepherd of Wizard Academy has been informed and inspired by the Quixote epic. To read Don Quixote is to look into a mirror. We see in him what we see in ourselves. So it only makes sense that the starry-eyed entrepreneurs and visionary businesspeople of our century see an excited adventurer who dreams, takes action, and embraces the consequences. Long live Don Quixote!

NOTES

1. *Man of La Mancha,* MGM (1972).

2. *The Winter of Our Discontent,* John Steinbeck (1961).

3. Wizard Academy is a 501(c)(3) educational organization at 16221 Crystal Hills Drive, Austin, Texas, 78737. Details regarding the school can be found at http://www.WizardAcademy.org.

4. *The Monday Morning Memo;* "Encouragement," entry by Roy H. Williams, June 13, 2016; http://www.mondaymorningmemo.com/newsletters/encouragement.

5. Ray Bard sent his e-mail on July 9, 2016, to 1,005 "quote judges" winnowing the quotes to be published in *Fired UP! Selling*™. 209 judges responded.

6. *Fired UP! SellingTM: Great Success Quotes to Inspire, Energize, Win,* Bard Press, to be published in 2016.

7. Jacques de Caso and Patricia B. Sanders, *Rodin's Sculpture: A Critical Study of the Spreckels Collection, California Palace of the Legion of Honor* (The Fine Arts Museum of San Francisco. Rutland, Vermont, 1977), 133.

8. "Conquest of Paradise," composed by Vangelis and recorded in 1992 as part of the soundtrack for the film *1492: Conquest of Paradise.* The composition topped music charts in five European countries in the early 1990s.

9. Honda launched its cinematic two-minute "Impossible Dream" commercial in the United Kingdom in December 2005 as part of its "Power of Dreams" campaign.

Bibliography

Abril Sánchez, Jorge. "Ah Gan's Don Quixote (魔俠傳之唐吉可德, 2010): Sun Tzu, Sun Bin, and the Warrior Spirit of the Chinese Knight of La Mancha." *Don Quixote: Interdisciplinary Connections.* Newark, DE: Juan de la Cuesta, 2013. 107–35.

Acker, Kathy. *Don Quixote: Which Was a Dream.* London: Paladin, 1968.

Aguilar, Jesús. "Can Pierre Menard Be the Author of *Don Quixote*?" *Variaciones Borges* 8 (1999): 166–67.

Aikhenval'd, Yurii. *Don Kikhot na russkoi pochve.* Moskva: Gendal'f, 1996.

Anderson, Poul. "Quixote and the Windmill." In *Strangers from Earth.* New York: Ballantine Books, 1961 (1950): 26–35.

Annacondia López, José Manuel. *From Don Quixote to The Tick: The Reflection of Sancho Panza in the Comic Book Sidekick.* Diss. University of Oviedo, 2012. http://digibuo.uniovi.es/dspace/bitstream/10651/28577/6/TFG%20JMAnnacondia.pdf. Web. July 11, 2016.

Álvarez de Miranda, Pedro. *Palabras e ideas: el léxico de la Ilustración temprana en España (1680-1760).* Madrid: Real Academia Española, 1992.

Andrew, Dudley. "*Amélie*, or Le Fabuleux Destin du Cinéma Français." *Film Quarterly* 57.3 (2004): 34–46. http://fq.ucpress.edu/content/57/3/34.

Arancibia, Adrian. "Postmodernity and the Latin American City: Mexico City and *The Savage Detectives.*" *Black Renaissance* 2.3 (Winter 2009): 204–19.

Ashbee, Henry Spencer. *An Iconography of Don Quixote, 1605-1895.* London: Printed for the author by the University Press, Aberdeen, and issued by the Bibliographical Society, 1895.

Ashby, Hal, dir. *Midnight Cowboy.* Screenplay by Waldo Salt and Robert C. Jones, story by Nancy Dowd. Featuring Jon Voight, Jane Fonda, and Bruce Dern. United Artists, 1978.

Austen, Jane. *Northanger Abbey.* New York: Bigelow, 1943.

Auster, Paul. *City of Glass.* Los Angeles: Sun and Moon Press, 1985.

Azcue Castillón, Verónica. "La disputa del baceyelmo y "El retablo de las maravillas": sobre el carácter dramático de los capítulos 44 y 45 de la primera parte de *Don Quijote.*" *Cervantes: Bulletin of the Cervantes Society of America.* 22.1 (2002): 71–81.

Bagno, V. E. *"Don Kikhot" v Rossii i russkoe donkikhotstvo*. Saint Petersburg: Nauka, 2009.

Bakhtin, M. M. "Author and Hero in Aesthetic Activity." In *Art and Answerability. Early Philosophical Essays by M.M. Bakhtin*. Edited by Michael Holquist and Vadim Liapunov. Translated by Vadim Liapunov. Austin: University of Texas Press, 1990. 4–256.

Bakhtin, M. M. *Speech Genres and Other Late Essays*. Edited by Caryl Emerson and Michael Holquist. Translated by Vern W. McGee. Austin: University of Texas Press, 1986.

Bakhtin, M. M. *The Dialogic Imagination*. Edited by Michael Holquist. Translated by Caryl Emerson and Michael Holquist. Austin: University of Texas Press, 1981. E-book.

Bakhtin, M. M. *The Dialogic Imagination: Four Essays*. Edited by Michael Holquist. Translated by Caryl Emerson and Michael Holquist. Austin: University of Texas Press, 1982.

Bakhtin, M. M. "The Problem of Speech Genres." In *Speech Genres and Other Late Essays*. Translated by Vern W. McGee. Austin: University of Texas Press, 1986. 60–102.

Bakhtin, M. M. "The Problem of the Text in Linguistics, Philology, and the Human Sciences: An Experiment in Philosophical Analysis." In *Speech Genres and Other Late Essays*. Translated by Vern W. McGee. Austin: University of Texas Press, 1986. 102–31.

Bakhtin, Mikhail. *The Dialogic Imagination: Four Essays*. Edited by Michael Holquist. Translated by Caryl Emerson and Michael Holquist. Austin: University of Texas Press, 1981.

Barrett, Eaton Stannard. *The Heroine, or Adventures of Cherubina*. Second ed., 3 vols. London: Henry Colburn, 1814 (1809).

Berger et al. *Ways of Seeing*. London: British Broadcasting Corporation, 1973.

Berra, John, and Liu Yang. "Cheap Laughs: The Mass-Production of Low-Budget Chinese Comedies from *Feng Kuang De Shi Tou/Crazy Stone* (Ning Hao, 2006) To *Gao Xing* (Agan, 2009)." *Asian Cinema* 23.1 (2012): 45–58.

Biskind, Peter. "Midnight Revolution." *Vanity Fair* (April 8, 2010).

Black, Georgina Dopico. "Pierre Menard, traductor del *Quijote*; or Echo's Echoes," *Cervantes: Bulletin of the Cervantes Society of America* 31.1 (2001): 27–49.

Bolaño, Roberto. *The Savage Detectives*. Translated by Natasha Wimmer. New York: Farrar, Straus and Giroux, 2007.

Bonnaud, Frédéric. "The *Amélie* Effect." *Film Comment*. November/December 2001. http://www.filmcomment.com/article/the-amelie-effect/.

Borges, Jorge Luis. *Collected Fictions*. Translated by Andrew Hurley. New York: Viking, 1998.

Borges, Jorge Luis. "Pierre Menard, Author of the *Quixote*." *Labyrinths* New York: New Directions, 2007. 36–44.

Borges, Jorge Luis. "Pierre Menard, autor del *Quijote*." In *Ficciones*. Madrid: Debolsillo, 2012. 39–53.

Borges, Jorge Luis. "Pierre Menard, autor del Quijote." In *Ficciones*. Caracas: Ayacucho, 1993. 17–22.

Breslin, Catherine. "The Artful Dodges of a Very Hot Screenwriter." *New York* (April 26, 1971): 48–52, 57–58.

Buhle, Paul, and Dave Wagner. *Blacklisted: The Film Lover's Guide to the Hollywood Blacklist*. New York: Palgrave, 2003.

Bulgakov, Mikhail. *Don Quixote. A Dramatic Adaptation*. Edited by Margarita Marinova and Scott Pollard. Translated by Margarita Marinova. New York: Modern Language Association, 2014.

Burling, William J. "Periodizing the Postmodern: China Miéville's *Perdido Street Station* and The Dynamics of Radical Fantasy." *Extrapolation: A Journal of Science Fiction and Fantasy* 50.2 (2009): 326–44.

Burningham, Bruce R. "Don Quixote in The American Imaginary." *Approaches to Teaching Cervantes's* Don Quixote. New York: Modern Language Association of America, 2015. 153–58.

Burningham, Bruce R. "Jongleuresque Dialogue, Radical Theatricality, and Maese Pedro's Puppet Show." *Cervantes: Bulletin of the Cervantes Society of America* 23.1 (2003): 165–96.

Burningham, Bruce R. *Tilting Cervantes: Baroque Reflections on Postmodern Culture*. Nashville: Vanderbilt University Press, 2008.

Burton, Richard. *The Richard Burton Diaries*. Edited by Chris Williams. New Haven, CT: Yale University Press, 2012.

Calvin College. "Jerry Siegel Attacks!" http://research.calvin.edu/german-propaganda-archive/superman.htm. Web. June 25, 2016.

Campbell, Joseph. *The Hero with a Thousand Faces*. Princeton, NJ: Princeton University Press, 1972.

Canavaggio, Jean. *Don Quijote del libro al mito*. Madrid: Espasa-Calpe, 2006.

Casillas, Jorge S. "Adiós al Cervantes héroe." *ABC*. Accessed June 6, 2016. http://www.abc.es/cultura/abci-adios-cervantes-heroe-201602111931_noticia.html.

Castillo, David R. *(A)wry Views: Anamorphosis, Cervantes, and the Early Picaresque*. West Lafayette, IN: Purdue University Press, 2001.

Ceplair, Larry, and Steven Englund. *The Inquisition in Hollywood: Politics in the Film Community, 1930-60*. Urbana and Chicago: University of Illinois Press, 2003.

Cervantes, Miguel de. *Don Quixote*. Translated by Edith Grossman. New York: Ecco, 2003.

Cervantes, Miguel de. *Don Quixote*. Translated by Edith Grossman. Introduction by Harold Bloom. New York: Harper Collins, 2003.

Cervantes, Miguel de. *Don Quixote*. Story adaptation by Samuel H. Abramson. Illustrations by [Louis] Zansky. New York: Classic Comics, 1943.

Cervantes, Miguel de. *Don Quijote de la Mancha*. Barcelona: Editorial Planeta, S.A., 2004.

Cervantes, Miguel de. *Don Quijote de la Mancha*. Vol. II. Edited by John Jay Allen. Madrid: Cátedra, 2009.

Cervantes, Miguel de. *Don Quijote de la Mancha*. Edited by E. C. Riley. Translated by Charles Jarvis. Oxford: Oxford University Press, 1992.

Cervantes, Miguel de. *El licenciado Vidriera. Novelas ejemplares*. Edited by Jorge García López. Madrid: Real Academia Española, 2013. 265–301.

Cervantes, Miguel de. *Novelas ejemplares*. Edited by Jorge García López. Madrid: Real Academia Española, 2013.

Cervantes, Miguel de. *Obras completas*. Edited by Florencio Sevilla Arroyo. Madrid: Editorial Castalia, 1999.

Cervantes, Miguel de. *Persiles y Segismunda*. Edited by Carlos Romero. Madrid: Cátedra, 2002.

Cervantes, Miguel de. *The Trials of Persiles and Sigismunda: A Northern Story*. Translated by Celia Richmond Weller and Clark A. Colahan. Indianapolis: Hackett Publishing Co., Inc., 2009.

Cervantes, Miguel de, Burton Raffel, and Diana A. Wilson. *Don Quijote: A New Translation, Backgrounds and Contexts, Criticism*. New York: W.W. Norton, 1999.

Chan, Annie Hau-Nung. "Fashioning Change: Nationalism, Colonialism, and Modernity in Hong Kong." *Postcolonial Studies* 3.3 (2000): 293–309.

Chekhov, Mikhail. "Dnevnik o Kikhote." *Literaturnoe nasledie* v 2 t. Moskva, 1986.

Chen, Xiaoming. "The Mysterious Other: Postpolitics in Chinese Film." *Boundary 2: An International Journal of Literature and Culture* 24.3 (1997): 123–41.

Cherchi, Paolo. *Capitoli di critica cervantina (1605-1789)*. Roma: Bulzoni, 1977.

Chu, Karen. "Filmko on a Quest to Make 3D 'Quixote'." *Hollywood Reporter*. Online March 22, 2010. Available August 15, 2016.

Close, Anthony. *The Romantic Approach to "Don Quixote."* Cambridge: Cambridge University Press, 1978.

Cole, Lester. *Hollywood Red. The Autobiography of Lester Cole*. Berkeley, CA: Ramparts, 1981.

Collins, Marsha S. "Going Global: Cervantes' *Don Quixote* Rides into the Future." *Expositions* 6.2 (2012): 33–40.

Corr, Eugene, and Robert Hillmann, directors. *Waldo Salt: A Screenwriter's Journey*. [For PBS series *American Masters*] New York: Eagle Rock/WNET, 1992.

Covarrubias, Sebastián de. *Tesoro de la lengua castellana o española*. Barcelona: S.A. Horta, 1943.

Crouching Tiger, Hidden Dragon. Directed by Ang Lee. Performed by Yun-Fat Chow and Michelle Yeoh. Sony, 2000.

Cui, Shuqin. "Stanley Kwan's *Center Stage*: The (Im)Possible Engagement Between Feminism and Postmodernism." *Cinema Journal* 39.4 (2000): 60–80.

Darius, Julius. "On 'How Superman Would Win the War.'" *Sequart Magazine* (June 10, 2013). http://sequart.org/magazine/23691/on-how-superman-would-win-the-war. Web. April 17, 2016.

Davin, Eric Leif. *Partners in Wonder: Women and the Birth of Science Fiction*. Lanham, MD: Lexington Books, 2005.

de Caso, Jacques, and Patricia B. Sanders. *Rodin's Sculpture: A Critical Study of the Spreckels Collection, California Palace of the Legion of Honor*. Rutland, VT: The Fine Arts Museum of San Francisco, 1977. 133.

DiPiero, Thomas. *Dangerous Truths and Criminal Passions: The Evolution of the French Novel, 1569-1791*. Stanford, CA: Stanford University Press, 1992.

Dirlik, Arif, and Xudong Zhang. "Introduction: Postmodernism and China." *Boundary 2: A Journal of Postmodern Literature and Culture* 24.3 (1997): 1–18.

Django Unchained. Directed by Quentin Tarantino. Culver City: Sony Pictures, 2012. DVD.

Don Kikhot. Directed by Grigori Kozintsev. Performed by Nikolay Cherkasov and Yuriy Tolubeev. Lenfilm, 1957.

Don Quixote Rides Again. Directed by Roberto Gavaldón. Performed by Cantinflas [Mario Moreno] and Fernando Fernán Gómez. Rioma, 1973.

Don Quixote [Tang Ji Ke De]. Directed by Ah Gan. Performed by Tao Guo, Gang Wang, and Kar Yan Lam. Filmko, 2010.

Donnelly, Marcos. "The Resurrection of Alonso Quijana." *The Magazine of Fantasy and Science Fiction* (March 1992): 31–46.

Duran, Manuel, and Fay R. Rogg. *Fighting Windmills. Encounters with Don Quixote*. New Haven: Yale University Press, 2006.

Eckhart, Gabriele, and Meg H. Brown. *Shifting Viewpoints: Cervantes in Twentieth-Century and Early Twenty-First-Century Literature Written in German*. Newcastle upon Tyne: Cambridge Scholars, 2013.

Eco, Umberto. *The Name of the Rose*. Translated by William Weaver. San Diego: Harcourt Brace, 1994.

Efron, Arthur. "Perspectivism and the Nature of Fiction: Don Quixote and Borges," *Thought* 50 (1975): 148–75.

Egginton, William. *The Man Who Invented Fiction. How Cervantes Ushered in the Modern World*. New York: Bloomsbury, 2016.

Emerson, Caryl. "Bakhtin and the Intergeneric Shift: The Case of Boris Godunov." *Studies in 20th Century Literature* 9.1 (1984): 145–67.

Emerson, Ralph Waldo. *The Letters of Ralph Waldo Emerson*. Edited by Ralph L. Rusk. Vol. 1. New York: Columbia University Press, 1939.

Engstrom, Alfred Garvin. "The Man Who Thought Himself Made of Glass, and Certain Related Images." *Studies in Philology* 67.3 (1970): 390–405.

Essipova, O. "Russkii Don Kikhot i M. Bulgakov' [The Russian Don Quixote and Bulgakov] *Bulgakovskii sbornik, III: Meterialy po istorii russkoi literatury XX veka*. Tallin, 1998. 21–37.

Estrella Cervantes. http://estrellacervantes.es.

Ezra, Elizabeth. *Jean-Pierre Jeunet*. Chicago: University of Illinois Press, 2008. E-book.

Farness, Jay. "Festive Theater, Restive Narrative in *Don Quixote*, Part 1." *PMLA* 107.1 (1992), 105–19.

Fernández de Navarrete, Martín. *Don Álvaro de Bazán, primer marqués de Santa Cruz* (1830). In *Marinos y descubridores*. Madrid: Atlas, 1944.

Fielding, Henry. *Amelia* (1751). Edited by M. Battestin. Middletown, CT: Wesleyan University Press, 1984.

Fielding, Henry. *Joseph Andrews*. Edited by Martin C. Battestin. Middletown, CT: Wesleyan University Press, 1967.

Fielding, Henry. *The Criticism of Henry Fielding*. Edited by Ioan Williams. London: Routledge and Kegan Paul, 1970.

Fitzgerald, F. Scott. *The Great Gatsby*. Preface and notes by Matthew J. Bruccoli. New York: Scribner, 2003.

Fitzpatrick, Tony. *Max & Gaby's Alphabet*. Chicago: Museum of Contemporary Art, 2001.

Flaubert, Gustave. *Madame Bovary*. Translated by Margaret Mauldon. Introduction by Malcolm Bowie. Notes by Mark Overstall. Oxford: Oxford University Press, 2004.

For a Few Dollars More. Directed by Sergio Leone. Beverly Hills, CA: United Artists, 1965. DVD.

Freire, Paulo. *The Pedagogy of the Oppressed*. Translated by Myra Bergman. New York: Continuum, 1997.

Frost, Jennifer. *Hedda Hopper's Hollywood: Celebrity Gossip and American Conservatism*. New York: New York University Press, 2011.

Fuentes, Carlos. *Cervantes o la crítica de la lectura*. Alcalá de Henares: Centro de Estudios Cervantinos, 1997.

Game of Thrones. Directed by Alan Taylor et al. Written by David Benioff and D. B. Weiss, HBO, 2011–2018.

Garrido Ardila, J. A. *Cervantes en inglaterra: El* Quijote *y la novela inglesa del siglo XVIII*. Alcalá de Henares: Centro de estudios cervantinos, 2014.

Garrido Ardila, J. A. "Cervantes y la novela moderna: literatura experimental y realismo en el Quijote." *Cervantes: Bulletin of the Cervantes Society of America* 33.2 (2013): 145–72.

Garrido Ardila, J. A. "El *Quijote* hoy." *Bulletin of Hispanic Studies* 92.8 (2015): 855–60.

Garrido Ardila, J. A. "Itinerario de la novela modernista española." *Revista de Literatura* 75.150 (2013): 547–71.

Garrido Ardila, J. A. "Las rutas del *Quijote* por la novela inglesa del siglo XVIII." *Cuadernos de Estudios del Siglo XVIII* (2016).

Garrido Ardila, J. A., ed. *The Cervantean Heritage: Reception and Influence of Cervantes in Britain*. London: Legenda, 2009.

Garrido Ardila, J. A. "The Influence and Reception of Cervantes in Britain, 1607-2005." In *The Cervantean Heritage. Reception and Influence of Cervantes in Britain*. Edited by J. A. Garrido Ardila. London: Legenda, 2009. 2–30.

Gasta, Chad. 2011. "Cervantes's Theory of Relativity in *Don Quixote*." *Cervantes* 31.1 (2011): 51–82.

Gibu Shimabukuru, Ricardo. "En torno a la esencia del poder. Un estudio comparativo entre Max Scheler y José Ortega y Gasset." *Franciscanum* 163.57 (2015): 125–53.

Gilliland, Alexis A. *Long Shot for Rosinante*. New York: Ballantine Books, 1981.

Gilliland, Alexis A. *The Pirates of Rosinante*. New York: Ballantine Books, 1982.

Gilliland, Alexis A. *The Revolution from Rosinante*. New York: Ballantine Books, 1981.

Ginés, Montserrat. *The Southern Inheritors of Don Quixote*. Baton Rouge: Louisiana State University Press, 2000.

Giskin, Howard. "Borges' Revisioning of Reading in 'Pierre Menard, Author of the Quixote'." *Variaciones Borges* 19 (2005): 103–23.

Givanel y Mas, Juan, and "Gaziel." *Historia gráfica de Cervantes y del Quijote*. Madrid: Plus Ultra, 1946.

González Echevarría, Roberto. "The Novel after Cervantes: Borges and Carpentier,." In *Love and the Law in Cervantes*. New Haven, CT: Yale University Press, 2005.

González Moreno, Fernando. "Aproximación a una teoría del arte de ilustrar libros: Quijotes del siglo XVIII." In *Teoría y literatura artística en España: revisión historiográfica y estudios contemporáneos*. Edited by Nuria Rodríguez Ortega and

Miguel Taín Guzmán. Madrid: Real Academia de Bellas Artes de San Fernando, 2015. 679–704.

González Moreno, Fernando. "Don Quijote en los albores del Romanticismo o el prodigio ilustrado de Tony Johannot." In *Don Quijote, cosmopolita. Nuevos estudios sobre la recepción internacional de la novela cervantina*, coordinated by Hans Christian Hagedorn, 343–68. Cuenca: Empresa Pública Sociedad Don Quijote de Conmemoraciones Culturales de Castilla-La Mancha/Ediciones de la Universidad de Castilla-La Mancha, 2009.

González Moreno, Fernando, and Beatriz González Moreno. *Andanzas tras los pasos de don Quijote por H. D. Inglis*. Vigo: Editorial Academia del Hispanismo, 2012.

González Moreno, Fernando, and Eduardo Urbina. "*Don Quichotte Conduit Par La Folie*: la herencia de Charles-Antoine Coypel en las ediciones ilustradas del *Quijote*." *Anuario de Estudios Cervantinos* 4 (2008): 1–50.

González Moreno, Fernando et al. "La colección de Quijotes ilustrados del Proyecto Cervantes: catálogo de ediciones y archivo digital de imágenes." *Cervantes. Bulletin of the Cervantes Society of America*, XXV.1 (2005): 79–104.

Gorky, Maxim. *Sobranie sochinenii 30 T*. Vol. 5: *Povesti, razkasy, ocherki, stikhi,1900-1906*. Moskva: Hudozhestvenaia Literatura, 1950.

Gracia, Jorge J. E. "Borges's Pierre Menard: Philosophy or Literature?" *The Journal of Aesthetics and Art Criticism* 59.1 (2001): 45–57.

Graham, John T. *The Social Thought of Ortega y Gasset: A Systematic Synthesis in Postmodernism and Interdisciplinarity*. Columbia: University of Missouri Press, 2001.

Gratchev, Slav N. "Prince Myshkin as a Tragic Interpretation of Don Quixote." *Cervantes* 35.1 (2015): 137–51.

Gratchev, Slav N. "The art of *re-accentuation*: 'Don Quixote' by Grigori Kozintsev." Chapter 10, this book.

Greene, Graham. *Monsignor Quixote*. New York: Simon and Schuster, 1982.

Gyulamiryan, Tatevik. "Homecoming Festivals: The Re-accentuated Image of Don Quixote in Western Novels." PhD diss., Purdue University, 2015. ProQuest (AAI 3735173).

Hage, Volker. "Mit '*Don Quijote*' nach Amerika. Über Thomas Manns 'Seitensprung' im Jahre 1934." *Thomas Mann Jahrbuch* 10 (1997): 53–65.

Haley, George. "The Narrator in Don Quijote: Maese Pedro's Puppet Show." *MLN* 80.2 (1965): 145–65.

Harris, Mark. *Five Came Back*. New York: Penguin Press, 2014.

Heer, David. "The Caped Crusader: Frederic Wertham and the Campaign Against Comic Books." *Slate* (April 4, 2008). http://www.slate.com/articles/arts/culturebox/ 2008/04/the_caped_crusader.html. Web. January 17, 2016.

Hochschild, Adam. *Spain in Our Hearts: Americans in the Spanish Civil War, 1936-1939*. New York: Houghton Mifflin Harcourt, 2016.

Hoffman, Lee. *Always the Black Knight*. New York: Avon Books, 1970.

Holcombe, Daniel. "Salvador Dalí as Surrealist Illustrator of Don Quixote." *News and Events* (blog), ACMRS, n.d., https://acmrs.org/news/salvador-dal %C3%AD-surrealist-illustrator-don-quixote.

Homer. *The Odyssey.* Translated by Robert Fagles. Introduction and notes by Bernard Knox. New York: Viking, 1996.

Hsu, Carmen. "Dos cartas de Felipe II al emperador de China." *eHumanista: Journal of Medieval and Early Modern Iberian Studies* 4 (2004): 194–209.

Hsu, Carmen Y. "La imagen humanística del gran reino chino de Juan González de Mendoza." *Bulletin of Hispanic Studies* 87.2 (2010): 187–201.

Hsu, Carmen Y. "Writing on Behalf of a Christian Empire: Gifts, Dissimulation, and Politics in the Letters of Philip II of Spain to Wanli of China." *Hispanic Review* 78.3 (2010): 323–44.

Hughes, Rhys. "The Quixote Candidate." *In Orpheus on the Underground and Other Stories.* North Yorkshire, UK: Tararus Press, 2014. 113–27.

Hutcheon, Linda. *A Theory of Adaptation.* New York: Routledge, 2006.

Hutcheon, Linda. *A Theory of Parody. The Teachings of Twentieth-Century Art Forms.* New York: Methuen, 1985.

International Speculative Fiction Database: http://www.isfdb.org.

Ivens, Joris. *The Spanish Earth.* Documentary film. Madrid, 1937.

Jaksić, Iván. "Don Quijote's Encounter with Technology." *Cervantes* 14.1 (1994): 75–95.

Jameson, Frederic. *Postmodernism; or, The Cultural Logic of Late Capitalism.* Durham, NC: Duke University Press, 1991.

Jamieson, Ian. *Charles-Antoine Coypel. Premier Peintre de Louis XV et Auteur Dramatique (1649-1752).* Paris: Librairie Hachette, 1930.

Jerrold, Blanchard. *The Life of George Cruikshank: in Two Epochs.* London: Chatto and Windus, 1882.

Jeunet, Jean-Pierre. "An Intimate Chat with Director Jean-Pierre Jeunet." *Le fabuleux destin d'Amélie Poulain.* Directed by Jean-Pierre Jeunet. 2002. Burbank, CA: Miramax Home Entertainment, 2002. DVD.

Jeunet, Jean-Pierre. "Eye on the Oscars—The nominees: Best Original Screenplay—Guillaume Laurant, Jean-Pierre Jeunet." *Variety* (February 25, 2002). Proquest Central.

Jian, Guo. "Resisting Modernity in Contemporary China: The Cultural Revolution and Postmodernism." *Modern China* 25.3 (1999): 343–76.

Johnson, A. E. *The Book of W. Heath Robinson. Brush, Pen, and Pencil.* London: Adam and Charles Black, 1913.

Johnson, Samuel. *Lives of the English Poets.* Edited by L. Archer-Hind. London: Dent; New York: Dutton, 1968.

Jones, William B. *Classics Illustrated: A Cultural History.* Jefferson, NC: McFarland and Company, 2011. Kindle edition.

Jurado Santos, Agapita. *Recorridos del Quijote por Europa (siglos XVII y XVIII).* Kassel: Reichenberger, 2015.

Kang, Liu. "Popular Culture and the Culture of the Masses in Contemporary China." *Boundary 2: An International Journal of Literature and Culture* 24.3 (1997): 99–122.

Kaverin, Veniamin B. "Yevgeniyu Shvartsu." *Sobranie Sochineniy* [The Collected Works]. Moscow: Izdatel'stvo Khudozhestvennoi Literatury, 1966, vol. 6, 604–6 (in Russian). English translation after Pyman, "Introduction."

Kennedy, Maev. "Salvador Dalí Diary Up for Sale in Auction of Surrealist Artifects." *The Guardian* (April 19, 2016) https://www.theguardian.com/artanddesign/2016/apr/19/salvador-dali-diary-auction-surrealist-dada-artists-artefacts.

King-Collector. "Classic Comic Books Identifying Reprints." http://www.ebay.com/gds/ CLASSICS-ILLUSTRATED-comic-books-IDENTIFYING-RE-PRINTS-/10000000000084872/g.html. Web. October 18, 2015.

Kozintsev, G. *Sobranie sochinenij.* 5 vols. Leningrad: Iskusstvo, 1982.

Kozintsev, Grigory M. "Iz knigi 'Glubokii ekran'" [From the book *The Deep Screen*], in *Zhitie skazochnika* [*A Life of a Storyteller*]. Edited by Lyudmila V. Polikovskaya and Evgeny M. Binevich. Moscow: Knizhnaya palata, 1991 (in Russian). 286–90.

Kozo. Review of *Don Quixote* [Ah Gan]. LoveHKFilm.com. Available August 15, 2016.

Kraft, Karen Marie. "Arte es vida: El uso de figura en el retablo de Maese Pedro." *Gaceta Hispánica de Madrid* 1 (2003): 1–11.

Kristeva, Julia. *The Kristeva Reader.* New York: Columbia University Press, 1986.

Kurzke, Hermann. *Thomas Mann.* Translated by Leslie Wilson. Princeton, NJ: Princeton University Press, 1999.

Lambiek Comiclopedia. "Louis Zansky." https://www.lambiek.net/artists/z/zansky_louis.htm. Web. July 4, 2016.

Larson, Wendy. "Women and the Discourse of Desire in Postrevolutionary China: The Awkward Postmodernism of Chen Ran." *Boundary 2: An International Journal of Literature and Culture* 24.3 (1997): 201–23.

Le fabuleux destin d'Amélie Poulain. Directed by Jean-Pierre Jeunet. 2001. Burbank, CA: Miramax Home Entertainment, 2002. DVD.

Lee, Christina, ed. *Western Visions of the Far East in a Transpacific Age, 1522-1657.* Aldershot, UK: Ashgate, 2012.

Lefrançois, Thierry. *Charles Coypel. Peintre du Roi (1694-1752).* Paris: Arthena, 1994.

Lekesizalin, Ferma. "Art, Desire, and Death in Orhan Pamuk's *My Name Is Red.*" *English Studies in Africa* 52:2 (2009): 90–103.

Lennox, Charlotte. *The Female Quixote, or, The Adventures of Arabella.* London: Oxford University Press, 1970.

Levin, Harry. "The Quixotic Principle: Cervantes and Other Novelist." In *The Interpretation of Narrative: Theory and Practice.* Edited by Morton W. Bloomfield. Cambridge, MA: Harvard University Press, 1970. 45–66.

Lie, Nadia. "Who Is the Reader of Pierre Menard? Borges on Cervantes Revisited." In *International Don Quixote*, eds. Theo D'haen and Reindert Dhont. Amsterdam: Rodopi, 2009. 89–108.

Lin, James J. *The Chinese Knight-Errant.* London: Routledge and Kegan Paul, 1967.

Lo Ré, A. G. "A Possible Source for Picasso's Drawing of Don Quixote." *Cervantes:Bulletin of the Cervantes Society of America* 12.1 (1992):105–10.

López Alemany, Ignacio. "A Portrait of a Lady: Representations of Sigismunda/Auristela in Cervantes's *Persiles.*" *Ekphrasis in the Age of Cervantes.* Edited by Frederick A. de Armas. Lewisburg, PA: Bucknell University Press, 2005.

Lu, Sheldon Hsiao-peng. "Global Postmodernization: The Intellectual, the Artist, and China's Condition." *Boundary 2: An International Journal of Literature and Culture* 24.3 (1997): 65–97.

Lu, Sheldon Hsiao-peng. "Postmodernity, Popular Culture, and the Intellectual: A Report on Post-Tiananmen China." *Boundary 2: An International Journal of Literature and Culture* 23.2 (1996): 139–69.

Luce, Henry R. "The American Century." *Life* (February 17, 1941): 61–65.

Lucía Megías, José. *La juventud de Cervantes: Una vida en construcción (1547-1580).* Madrid: Edaf, 2016.

Lukács, Georg. *Die Theorie des Romans.* Darmstadt and Neuwied: Hermann Luchterhand, 1982.

Lukács, Georg. *The Theory of the Novel.* Translated by Anna Bostock. Cambridge, MA: MIT Press, 1989.

Lukács, Gyorgy. *Teoría de la novela* (1920). Barcelona: Edasa, 1971.

Malcolm Gaylord, Mary. "Pulling Strings with Master Peter's Puppets: Fiction and History." *Cervantes: Bulletin of the Cervantes Society of America.* 18.2 (1998): 117–47.

Mancing, Howard. *Cervantes Encyclopedia.* Vol. 1. A-K. Westport, CT: Greenwood Press, 2004.

Mancing, Howard. "Don Quixote Miscellany." In *The Cervantes Encyclopedia.* 2 vols. Westport, CT: Greenwood Press, 2004. I, 241–42.

Mancing, Howard. "Dulcinea del Toboso: On the Occasion of her Four-Hundredth Birthday." *Hispania* 88.1 (2005): 53–63.

Mancing, Howard. "Embodied Cognition and Autopoiesis in Don Quixote." In *Cognitive Approaches to Early Modern Spanish Literature.* Edited by Isabel Jaen and Julien Jacques Simon. New York: Oxford University Press, 2016. 37–52.

Mancing, Howard. "Jorge Luis Borges (1899-1986)." In *The Cervantes Encyclopedia.* Westport and London: Greenwood Press, 2004. I, 81–82.

Mann, Charles. *1493: Uncovering the New World Columbus Created.* New York: Vintage, 2012.

Mann, Thomas. *Meerfahrt mit Don Quijote.* Wiesbaden: Im Insel Verlag, 1956.

Mann, Thomas. "Voyage with Don Quixote." In *Essays.* Translated by H. T. Lowe-Porter. New York: Vintage, 1957. 325–67.

Mare, Walter de la. *Henry Brocken: His Travels and Adventures in the Rich, Strange, Scarce-Imaginable Regions of Romance.* London: Faber and Faber, 1942 (1904).

Márquez Villanueva, Francisco. *Personajes y temas del Quijote.* Madrid: Taurus, 1975.

Martínez Illán, Antonio. "Don Quijote en el cine soviético: Kozintsev y Kurchevski." *El telón rasgado: El Quijote como puente cultural con el mundo soviético y postsoviético.* Edited by Jorge Latorre, Antonio Martínez y Oleksandr Pronkévich. Pamplona: Eunsa, 2015. 317–41.

Martínez Mata, Emilio. "El *Quijote,* sátira antiespañola." *Voz y Letra* 16.1–2 (2005): 95–104.

Martínez Mata, Emilio. "La caracterización de los personajes en el *Quijote.*" In *Cervantes y los cauces de la novela.* Edited by Emilio Martínez Mata. Madrid: Visor, 2014. 157–77.

Matilda. Directed by Danny DeVito. Culver City, CA: TriStar, 1996. DVD.

Matthews, Steven. "Jorge Luis Borges: Fiction and Reading." *Ariel* 6 (1989): 62–67.

McConkey, James. *Kayo, The Authentic and Annotated Autobiographical Novel from Outer Space.* New York: Dutton, 1987.

Melville, Herman. *Moby Dick or, The Whale.* Introduction by Leon Howard. New York: Modern Library, 1950.

Miguel, Armando de. *Don Quijote en la España de la reina Letizia.* Barcelona: Stella Maris, 2016.

Miller, Lori. "In the Tradition of Cervantes, Sort Of." *New York Review of Books* (November 30, 1986): 10.

Mingxian, Wang [translated by Zhang Xudong]. "Notes on Architecture and Postmodernism in China." *Boundary 2: An International Journal of Literature and Culture* 24.3 (1997): 163–75.

Mitchell, Ken. *The Heroic Adventures of Donny Coyote.* Ontario: Fitzhenry, 2003.

Montalvo, Garci Rodríguez de. *Amadis of Gaul, Books I and II.* Translated by Edwin B. Place, Herbert C. Behm, and John E Keller. Lexington: University Press of Kentucky, 2003.

Moréri, Louis. *Le grand dictionnaire historique, ou le melange courieux de l'histoire sacree et profane.* 7ª ed. Amsterdam: Utrech and La Haya, 1694.

Morris, Kenneth. "The Last Adventure of Don Quixote." In *The Dragon Path: Collected Tales of Kenneth Morris.* New York: Tor Books, 1995 (1917). 165–72.

Morrissey, Jim. "Paris and Voyages of Self-Discovery in *Cléo de 5 à 7* and *Le fabuleux destin d'Amélie Poulain.*" *Studies in French Cinema* 8.2 (2008): 99–110. doi: 10.1386/sfc.8.2.99/1.

Mr. Smith Goes to Washington. Directed by Frank Capra. Performed by James Stewart. Columbia, 1939. B/W.

Myers, John Myers. *Silverlock.* New York: Ace Books, 1966 (1949).

Nabakov, Vladimir. *Lectures on Don Quixote.* New York: Harcourt Brace, 1983.

Nabokov, Vladimir. *The Annotated Lolita.* Introduction and notes by Alfred Appel, Jr. New York: Vintage, 1991.

Navasky, Victor S. *Naming Names.* London: John Calder, 1982.

Nelson, Cary. *Revolutionary Memory. Recovering the Poetry of the American Left.* New York and London: Routledge, 2001.

Novitskii, P. I. "Don Kikhot Servantesa: vvedenie." *Khitroumnyi Idalgo Don Kikhot Lamanchskii,* M. de Cervantes Saaveda. Leningrad, 1929.

Nusinov, I. M. "Don Kikhot." *Literaturnaia entsiklopedia.* Moskva, 1930.

Odom, Glenn A. "Socialist Realism and New Subjectivities: Modern Acting in Gao Xingjian's *Cold Theatre.*" *Asian Theatre Journal* 31.1 (2014): 153–78.

Olea Franco, Rafael. "La lección de Cervantes en Borges." *Inti* 45 (1997): 99–103.

Ortega y Gasset, José. "El Genio de la guerra y la Guerra alemana (*Der Genius des Krieges und der deutsche Krieg,* por Max Scheler. 1915)." In *Obras completas,* vol. 2, 192–223. Madrid: Revista de Occidente 1963.

Ortega y Gasset, José. *Meditaciones del Quijote.* Madrid: El Arquero, 1975.

Ortega y Gasset, José. *Meditaciones del Quijote / Ideas sobre la novela.* Madrid: Espasa-Calpe, Austral, 1969.

Oscherwitz, Dayna. "Once Upon a Time that Never Was: Jean-Pierre Jeunet's *Le Fabuleux Destin d'Amélie Poulain.*" *The French Review* 84.3 (2011): 504–15.

Pabst, G. W., dir. *Adventures of Don Quixote.* Paris: Vandor, 1933.

Pamuk, Orhan. *My Name Is Red.* Translated by Erdağ M. Göknar. New York: Alfred A. Knopf, 2001.

Pardo García, Pedro Javier. "La tradición cervantina en la novela inglesa: De Henry Fielding a William Thackeray." In *Entre Cervantes y Shakespeare: Sendas del Renacimiento*. Edited by Zenón Luis-Martínez and Luis Gómez Canseco. Newark: Juan de la Cuesta, 2006. 73–112.

Paulson, Ronald. *Don Quixote in England. The Aesthetics of Laughter*. Baltimore and London: Johns Hopkins University Press, 1988.

Pendleton, Gene R., and Linda L. Williams. "Themes of Exile in Thomas Mann's 'Voyage with Don Quixote.'" *Cervantes: Bulletin of the Cervantes Society of America* 21.2 (Fall 2001): 73–85.

Petaja, Emil. *The Nets of Space*. New York: Berkeley Medallion Books, 1969.

Peyron, Jean-François. *Nouveau voyage en Espagne fait en 1777 et 1778 . . .*, t. II. London: P. Elmsly, 1782.

Plank, Robert. "Quixote's Mills: The Man-Machine Encounter in SF." *Science Fiction Studies* 1.2 (1973): 68–78.

Propp, Vladimir Ya. "Zmeeborstvo Georgiya v svete fol'klora [Saint George's dragon-slaying in the light of folklore]." In *Fol'klor i etnografiya Russkogo Severa* [*Folklore and Ethnography of the Russsian North*], 190–208. Leningrad: Nauka, 1973 (in Russian).

Pyman, Avril. Introduction and notes to *Three plays*, by Yevgeniy Shvarts. Oxford: Pergamon Press: 1972.

Quixote. Directed by Steven Ritz-Barr and Hoku Uchiyama. Topanga: Classics in Miniature, 2010. DVD.

Radcliffe, Ann. *The Mysteries of Udolpho*. Introduction by Jacqueline Howard. London: Penguin Classics, 2001.

Rango. Directed by Gore Verbinski. Hollywood: Paramount Pictures, 2011. DVD.

Rapin, René. *Les reflexions sur la poètique d'Aristote et sur les ouvrages des poètes anciens et modernes* (1674-1675). Edited by E. T. Dubois. Paris: Muget, 1970.

Ray, Robert B. *A Certain Tendency of the Hollywood Cinema, 1930-1980*. Princeton, NJ: Princeton University Press, 1985.

Red Channels: The Report of Communist Influence in Radio and Television. New York: Counterattack, 1950.

Reulecke, Anne-Kathrin. "Voyage with Don Quixote: Thomas Mann between European Culture and American Politics." In *Escape to Life: German Intellectuals in New York: a Compendium on Exile after 1933*, eds. Eckhart Goebel and Sigrid Weigel, 371–90. Berlin and Boston: Walter De Gruyter, 2012.

Richardson, Donna. "Classics Illustrated." *American Heritage Magazine*44.3 (May/ June 1993). http://www.americanheritage.com/content/classics-illustrated. Web. February 15, 2016.

Rigney, Todd. "Windmills Enter the Third Dimension in Agan's *Don Quixote* 3-D." BeyondHollywood.com. Available August 15, 2016.

Riley, E. C. "*Don Quixote*: From Text to Icon." *Cervantes* special issue (winter 1988): 103–15.

Río y Rico, Gabriel-Martín del. *Catálogo bibliográfico de la sección de Cervantes de la Biblioteca Nacional*. Madrid: Tipografía de la Revista de Archivos, Bibliotecas y Museos, 1930.

Rivero Iglesias, Carmen. *La recepción e interpretación del Quijote en la Alemania del siglo XVIII*. Argamasilla de Alba: City Council of Argamasilla de Alba, 2011.

Robinett, Stephen. "The Linguist." In *The Year's Best Science Fiction* No. 9. Edited by Harry Harrison and Brian Aldiss. London: Futura Publications, 1976. 98–111.

Robinson, Elisabeth. *The True and Outstanding Adventures of the Hunt Sisters*. New York: Little, Brown, 2004.

Robinson, Heath William. *My Line of Line*. London and Glasgow: Blackie and Son Limited, 1938.

Rodríguez Luis, Julio. "El *Quijote* según Borges," *Nueva Revista de Filología Hispánica* 36 (1988): 477–500.

Roosbroeck, Gustave Leopold van. *Grotesques*. New York: Living Art, 1929.

Rowell, Rainbow. *Carry On: The Rise and Fall of Simon Snow*. New York: St. Martin's Press, 2015.

Sacerio-Garí, Enrique. "Towards Pierre Menard," *MLN* 95.2 (1980): 460–71.

Safiullina, Nailya. "The Canonization of Western Writers in the Soviet Union in the 1930s." *The Modern Language Review* 107.2 (April 2012): 559–84.

Salt, Waldo, and Earl Robinson. *Sandhog*. Musical drama. Howard da Silva, dir. New York: Phoenix Theatre, 1954.

Sawyer, Michael. "Albert Lewis Kanter and the Classics: The Man Behind the Gilbert Company." *The Journal of Popular Culture* 20.4 (1987): 1–18.

Scatton-Tessier, Michelle. "*Le Petisme*: Flirting with the Sordid in *Le fabuleux destin d'Amélie Poulain*." *Studies in French Cinema* 4.3 (2004): 197–207. doi: 10.1386/sfci.4.3.197/0.

Scham, Michael. "*Don Quijote* and *Lolita* Revisited." *Cervantes: Bulletin of the Cervantes Society of America* 26.1 (Spring-Fall 2006): 79–101.

Scheler, Max. *Der Genius des Krieges und der deutsche Krieg*. Leipzig: Verlag der Weißen Bücher, 1915.

Schepisi, Fred. Interview with Cynthia Fuchs. *Pop Matters* (December 7, 2001). http://www.popmatters.com/feature/schepisi-fred/.

Schlesinger, John, dir. *Midnight Cowboy*. Screenplay by Waldo Salt. Featuring Jon Voight and Dustin Hoffman. MGM, 1968.

Schlesinger, John, and Jerome Hellman. Audio commentary. *Midnight Cowboy* (1969). Laserdisc. Criterion Collection, 146. Irvington, NY: Voyager, 1991.

Schmidt, Rachel. *Forms of Modernity*. Don Quixote *and Modern Theories of the Novel*. Toronto: University of Toronto Press, 2011.

Schmidt, Rachel. *The Canonization of Don Quixote through Illustrated Editions of the Eighteenth Century*. Québec: McGill-Queen's University Press, 1999.

Schwartz, E. *Pozvonki minuvshih dnej. Proizvedeniya 40-50 godov*. Moscow: Korona-print, 1999.

Serrano-Plaja, Arturo. "*Magic" Realism in Cervantes:* Don Quixote *as Seen Through* Tom Sawyer *and* The Idiot. Translated by Robert S. Rudder. Berkeley: University of California Press, 1970.

Shaftesbury, Lord (Anthony, Earl of Shaftesbury). *The Moralists, A Philosophical Rhapsody*. In *Characteristics of Men, Manners, Opinions, Times*. Edited by John M. Robertson. Indianapolis: The Bobbs-Merrill Company, 1964.

Sheckley, Robert. "The Quixote Robot." *The Magazine of Fantasy and Science Fiction* (December 2001): 136–60.

Sheckley, Robert. *Uncanny Tales*. Waterville, ME: Five Star, 2003.

Shilliday, Susan. *Don Quixote.* Screenplay by Waldo Salt, revised by Susan Shilliday. 1994.

Shwarts, Evgeny. *Bessmyslennaya radost' bytiya.* [*A senseless joy of being*]. Moscow: Korona-print, 1999 (in Russian).

Shwarts, Evgeny. *Pozvonki proshedshikh dnei* [*The vertebrae of the days past*]. Moscow: Korona-print, 1999 (in Russian).

Shwarts, Evgeny. *Predchuvstvie schastya* [*A foreboding of happiness*]. Moscow: Korona-print, 1999 (in Russian).

Shwarts, Evgeny. *The Dragon.* Translated by Laurence Senelick. New York: Broadway Play Publishing, Inc., 2012.

Shwarts, Evgeny. ". . . *ya budu pisatelem*" [". . . *I will be a writer*"]. Moscow: Korona-print, 1999 (in Russian).

Shuger, Dale. *Don Quixote in the Archives: Madness and Literature in Early Modern Spain.* Edinburgh: Edinburgh University Press, 2012.

Sigüenza y Góngora, Carlos de, and Alonso Ramírez. *Infortunios de Alonso Ramírez.* Edited by Estelle Irizarry. San Juan, PR: Editorial cultural, 1990.

Silverberg, Robert. "Enter a Soldier. Later: Enter Another." In *Time Gate.* Edited by Robert Silverberg, with Bill Fawcett. New York: Baen Books, 1989. 1–61.

Simak, Clifford D. *Out of Their Minds.* New York: DAW Books, 1983 (1970).

Smith, Michael Allen. "Thomas Mann's 'Meerfahrt mit *Don Quijote*': The Case against a Formalist Approach to Essay Criticism." *The German Quarterly* 49.3 (May 1976): 318–29.

Sorin, Gerald. *Howard Fast. Life and Literature in the Left Lane.* Bloomington: Indiana University Press, 2012.

Speak, Gill. "*El licenciado Vidriera* and the Glass Men of Early Modern Europe." *The Modern Language Review* 85.4 (1990): 850–65. http://www.jstor.org/stable/3732644.

Stavans, Ilan. *Quixote: The Novel and the World.* New York: W. W. Norton & Co., 2015.

Steinbeck, John. *The Winter of Our Discontent.* New York: Viking Press, 1961.

Stepanian, Karen. "Don Quixote and Prince Myshkin in Search of Reality." *Russian Studies in Literature* 47.3 (2011): 25–72. doi: 10.2753/RSL1061-1975470302.

SuperHeroMultiverse. "World War II and the Superhero." http://www.superheromultiverse.com/world-war-ii-and-superhero. Web. June 12, 2016.

Syverson-Stork, Jill. *Theatrical Aspects of the Novel: A Study of Don Quixote.* Valencia: Albatros Ediciones, 1986.

Temple, William. "An Essay upon Ancient and Modern Learning." In *Critical Essays of the Seventeenth Century.* Edited by J. E. Spingarn. Bloomington: Indiana University, 1957. 3: 32–72.

Temple, William. "Of Poetry." In *Critical Essays of the Seventeenth Century.* Edited by J. E. Spingarn. Bloomington: Indiana University, 1957. 3: 73–109.

Thompson, J. Lee, dir. *Taras Bulba.* Hollywood: Harold Hecht Productions, 1962.

Tolstoy, Leo. *Anna Karenina.* Translated by Richard Pevear and Larissa Volokhonsky. Introduction by Richard Pevear. New York: Penguin Books, 2002.

Turello, Dan. "War and Superheroes: How the Writer's Board Used Comics to Spread Its Message in WWII." *Library of Congress Insights*, November 3, 2015.

https://blogs.loc.gov/kluge/2015/11/war-and-superheroes-how-the-writers-war-board-used-comics-to-spread-its-message-in-wwii. Web. July 5, 2015.

Turgenev, Ivan. "Hamlet and Don Quixote." Translated by Moshe Spiegel. *Chicago Review* 17.4 (1965): 92–109.

Turkevich, Ludmilla. *Cervantes in Russia.* Princeton, NJ: Princeton University Press, 1950.

Turkevich, Ludmilla Buketoff. *Cervantes in Russia.* New York: Gordian, 1975.

Twain, Mark. *Adventures of Huckleberry Finn.* New York: Oxford University Press, 1996.

Twain, Mark. *The Adventures of Tom Sawyer.* Illustrations by Paul Geiger. Afterword by Bernard DeVoto. Pleasantville, NY: Reader's Digest, 1985.

Unbreakable. Directed by M. Night Shyamalan. 2000. Burbank, CA: Touchstone Pictures, 2001. DVD.

Urbina, Eduardo et al. "Visual Knowledge: Textual Iconography of the Quixote." In *Don Quixote Illustrated: Textual Images and Visual Readings.* Edited by Eduardo Urbina and Jesús G. Maestro. Pontevedra: Mirabel Editorial/Cátedra Cervantes, 2005. 15–38.

Valbuena, Padre. *La resurrección de Don Quijote.* Barcelona: Antonio López, 1905.

Vampires in Havana. Directed by Juan Padrón. Screenplay by Ernesto Padrón and Juan Padrón. Performed by Frank González, Manuel Marín, and Irela Bravo. Instituto Cubano del Arte e Industrias Cinematográficos (ICAIC) and Radio Televisión Española (RTVE), 1985.

Vargas Llosa, Mario. *The Bad Girl.* Translated by Edith Grossman. New York: Farrar, 2007.

Vaughan, Carrie. "Don Quixote." In *Armored.* Edited by John Joseph Adams. New York: Baen Books, 2012.

Vauthier, Bénédicte. "Ejercicio(s) de estilo(s) en *Amor y pedagogía* de Miguel de Unamuno: el *Ars magna combinatoria* del gran mixtificador unamuniano," in *Miguel de Unamuno estudio sobre su obra I: actas de las IV Jornadas unamunianas, Salamanca, Casa-Museo Unamuno, 18-20 de octubre de 2001.* Edited by Ana Chaguaceda Toledano. Salamanca: Universidad de Salamanca, 2003. 113–22.

Verhey, Jeffrey. *The Spirit of 1914: Militarism, Myth, and Mobilization in Germany.* Cambridge: Cambridge University Press, 2000.

Vivar, Francisco. "Las bodas de Camacho y la sociedad del espectáculo." *Cervantes: Bulletin of the Cervantes Society of America* 22.1 (2002): 83–109.

Voight, Jon. Interview by Roger Moore. *Orlando Sentinel* (March 30, 2009).

Wang, Ning. "A Reflection on Postmodernist Fiction in China: Avant-Garde Narrative Experimentation." *Narrative* 21.3 (2013): 296–308.

Wasserman, Dale. *Man of La Mancha.* Directed by Arthur Hiller. Beverly Hills, CA: MGM Home Video, 2004. DVD.

Welky, David. *The Moguls and the Dictators.* Baltimore: Johns Hopkins University Press, 2008.

West, Goeff. "The Early Illustrated Editions of *Don Quixote.*" *European Studies Blog,* British Museum (March 29, 2016). http://blogs.bl.uk/european/2016/03/the-early-illustrated-editions-of-don-quixote-the-low-countries-tradition.html.

Wertham, Frederic, MD. *The Seduction of the Innocent: The Influence of Comic Books on Today's Youth.* Waltham, NY: Rinehart and Company, 1954.

Williams, Roy H. *The Monday Morning Memo*; "Encouragement," June 13, 2016; http://www.mondaymorningmemo.com/newsletters/encouragement.

Williams, Roy W. "Wedding Chapel Dulcinea." *The Monday Morning Memo* (March 1, 2005). http://www.mondaymorningmemo.com/newsletters/wedding-chapel-dulcinea/

Williams, Walter Jon. "Daddy's World." In *Not of Woman Born*. Edited by Constance Ash. New York: Roc Books, 1999. 240–72.

Williamson, Chet. "Rosinante." *The Magazine of Fantasy and Science Fiction* (April 1984): 43–58.

Wilson, Seth. "Fairy Tale of Subversion? Evgeny Shvarts's "The Dragon" as anti-Stalinist Theatre for the Youth." In *Theatre Symposium. Vol. 23: Theatre and youth*. Edited by David S. Thompson and Becky K. Becker. Tuscaloosa: University of Alabama, 2015. 55–66.

Wood, Sarah F. *Quixotic Fictions of the USA, 1792-1815*. New York: Oxford University Press, 2005.

Wright, Bradford W. *Comic Book Nation: The Transformation of Youth Culture in America*. Baltimore: Johns Hopkins University Press, 2001.

Yenne, Bill. *Tommy Gun: How General Thompson's Submachine Gun Wrote History*. New York: St. Martin's Press, 2009.

Ziolkowski, Eric J. "Don Quijote's Windmill and Fortune's Wheel." *The Modern Language Review* 86.4 (1991): 885–97. https://ldr.lafayette.edu/bitstream/handle/10385/940/Ziolkowski-ModernLanguageReview-vol86-1991.pdf?sequence=1.

Index

Page references for illustrations are italicized.

Kamins, Ken, 168
Kanter, Albert Lewis, 53–55
Kaplan, Meyer, 54–55
Kar Yan Lam, 183
Kaverin, Veniamin, 244
Kerouac, Jack, 169
KGB, 141
Kharms, Daniil, 246
Khrushchev, Nikita, 8, 142, 247
King Arthur, 125–26
Kirby, Jack, 57
Kleist, Heinrich von, 208
Knecht, Curtis, 256
knight-errant, 6, 15–19, 55, 74, 78, 111, 114, 123, 125, 130, 184, 202, 237, 240, 265
knight-errantry, 19, 134, 167, 184, 188
knighting ceremony. *See* scenes and places in *Don Quijote*
Knight of the Lake. *See* characters from *Don Quijote*
Knight of the Mirrors. *See* characters from *Don Quijote*
Knight of the White Moon. *See* characters from *Don Quijote*
Kornilov, General Lavr, 245
Kozintsev, Grigori, 6, 151n2, 189; *Don Quijote*, 7, 141–51, 237, 244; *Hamlet*, 141; *King Lear*, 141
Kuhl, Don, 254–55
Kuza, V. V., 224

Lacan, Jacques, 79, 85–86
Lady of the Lake, 125
Lancaster, Burt, 153
Lanier, Sidney, *The Boy's King Arthur*, 53
Lardner, Jr., Ring, 167
Lascaux, cave paintings, 70
Lazarillo castigado, 83
Lazarillo de Tormes, 83, 284
Lekesizalin, Ferma, 85–86
LenFilm (Leningrad Film Studio), 141
Leningrad, 224, 237–38, 242–43, 245–46
Leonela. *See* characters from *Don Quixote*
Leonov, Evgeny, 244

Lepanto, 89, 100, 197
Lépicié, Bernard, 26
Lennox, Charlotte, *The Female Quixote*, 16, 20, 44
Le Sage, René, *The Adventures of Gil Blas of Santillane*, 28
Les Lettres Françaises, 72
Levin, Jon, 168, 177n1, 179n17
El licenciado Vidriera. See Cervantes's works
Lie, Nadia, 95
Lincoln, Abraham, 207
Lisbon, 182
Litto, George, 157
Lomonosov, M. V., 222
Look magazine, 57
López Alemany, Ignacio, 80
López de Úbeda, Francisco, *La pícara Justina*, 83
Lotario. *See* characters from *Don Quixote*
Lubin A. Ronald, 154, 174
Luce, Henry, 183
Lucía Megías, José, 89
Lucian, 42
Lukács, Georg (Gyorgy), 5, 40, 107–8, 110, 116–17; *Theory of the Novel*, 111–13
Lunacharskii, Anatoly, 28; *The Liberated Don Quixote*, 223, 226–28
Lurie, Jerome B., 156–57
Lu, Sheldon, 189

M*A*S*H, dir. Robert Altman, 167
Madrid, 89, 135, 159, 182, 220
Maese Pedro. *See* characters from *Don Quijote* Maritornes, 31, 59; Maese Pedro's puppet show. *See* scenes and places in *Don Quijote*
Maeztu, Ramiro de, 5; *Don Quijote, Don Juan y La Celestina*, 102
Malory, Thomas, 53
La Mancha, 17, 35, 59, 143, 165, 184–85, 213. *See also* scenes and places in *Don Quixote*
Mancing, Howard, 5, 100, 195, 207
Manco and Mortimer. *See* pairings

About the Editors

Dr. Slav N. Gratchev is associate professor of Spanish at Marshall University. His profound interest in Miguel de Cervantes, Mikhail Bakhtin, and Fyodor Dostoevsky originated during his studies at Saint Petersburg State University, Russia, back in the time of the Soviet Union. He continued developing his ideas in doctoral dissertation at Purdue University, as well as in his recent publications:

- "Prince Myshkin as a Tragic Interpretation of Don Quixote" in *Cervantes: Bulletin of the Cervantes Society of America*;
- "Duvakin's Oral History and Bakhtin in His Own Voice" (co-authored with Dr. Gyulamiryan) in *CLCWeb: Comparative Literature and Culture*;
- "Bakhtin in His Voice: Interview by Victor Duvakin" (*College Literature: A Journal of Critical Literary Studies*);
- "Another Adelaida: Dostoevsky's *The Idiot* in Nabokov's *Ada*" (co-authored with Prof. Victor Fet) in *The Nabokovian*;
- "*Don Quixote* in Russia in the Eighteenth and Nineteenth Centuries: The Problem of Perception and Interpretation" (*The South Atlantic Review*).

Dr. Howard Mancing is professor of Spanish at Purdue University. He is the author of

- *The Chivalric World of Don Quijote: Style, Structure, and Narrative Technique* (1982);
- *Text, Theory, and Performance: Golden Age Comedia Studies*, co-edited with Charles Ganelin (1994);
- *Miguel de Cervantes' "Don Quixote": A Reference Guide* (2006);

- *The Cervantes Encyclopedia*, 2 vols. (2004); *Miguel de Cervantes' "Don Quixote": A Reference Guide* (2006);
- *Theory of Mind and Literature* (2011), co-edited with Paula Leverage, Jennifer Marston William, and Richard Schweickert.

In addition, he has published over sixty articles and essays on Cervantes, Unamuno, *Lazarillo de Tormes* and the picaresque novel, narrative theory, comparative literature, the canon, the teaching of literature, academic administration, cognitive approaches to the study of literature, and other subjects, in a variety of books and in journals such as *Anales Cervantinos*, *Cervantes*, *Estudios Públicos*, *Europe*, *Forum for Modern Language Studies*, *Hispania*, *Hispanic Review*, *MLN*, *Modern Fiction Studies*, *PMLA*, and *Semiotica*.

At the present time he is working on two books: one on cognitive science and literary theory and one on the theory and history of the novel 1475–1700.